MW01174918

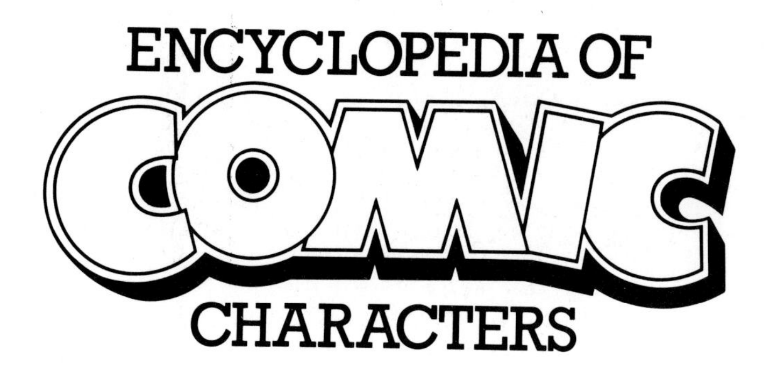
ENCYCLOPEDIA OF
COMIC
CHARACTERS

ENCYCLOPEDIA OF

CHARACTERS

Over 1200 characters

Denis Gifford

Longman

Longman Group UK Limited,
Longman House, Burnt Mill, Harlow,
Essex CM20 2JE, England
and Associated Companies throughout the world.

First published 1987

British Library Cataloguing in Publication Data

Gifford, Denis
Encyclopedia of comic characters.
1. Comic books, strips, etc. — Dictionaries
2. Cartoon characters — Dictionaries
I. Title
741.5'03'21 PN6710

ISBN 0-582-89294-5

Edited and designed by Curtis Garratt Limited,
The Old Vicarage, Horton cum Studley, Oxford OX9 1BT.

Set in Linotron Rockwell series.

Printed in Great Britain by The Bath Press Ltd,
Bath, England.

Acknowledgments
We are grateful to the following for permission to reproduce copyright material: the copyright in all D. C. Thomson characters belongs to D. C. Thomson and Co. Ltd; the copyright in all illustrations of IPC Magazines Limited characters belongs to IPC Magazines Limited (arranged with Syndication International Limited and including characters originally published by Amalgamated Press, Fleetway Publications, Odhams Comics and Newnes); Marvel comics Group; Walt Disney Productions. Special acknowledgments are made to DC Comics/National Periodicals; ITV Publications; King Features Syndicate; Polystyle Publications. And of course, to the hundreds of artists without whom this illustrated encyclopedia would have been impossible. Though every effort has been made to trace the owners of copyright material, in a few cases this has proved impossible and we take this opportunity to offer our apologies to any copyright holders whose rights may have been unwittingly infringed. The author wishes to thank Ray Moore of the Association of Comic Enthusiasts, whose specialised interest in the D. C. Thomson comics enabled many early artists to be identified by name for the first time.

Dedication
This book is for the thousands of comic characters for whom there was no room – from Ambrose the Autocrat to Zombi the Cave Man.

Also by Denis Gifford
The Best of Eagle (with Marcus Morris)
The British Comic Catalogue 1874-1974
The Complete Catalogue of British Comics and Price Guide
Discovering Comics
Happy Days! 100 Years of Comics
The International Book of Comics
Stap Me! The British Newspaper Strip
Victorian Comics

THE WHO'S WHO OF HO! HO! THE WHAT'S WHAT OF SPLAT!

No introduction needed!

Comics, those weekly journals of pictorial mirth and mayhem, have been part of Britain's leisure reading for so many years – some 150 by a conservative count – that there can be no person in the land, and perhaps far beyond, that needs a description of them here. Say *Beano* to a British child, and the eyes light up with anticipation: what is Dennis the Menace up to today? Say *Beano* to an adult, and the eyes go misty with nostalgia: what was Dennis the Menace up to yesterday? And no doubt, in ten years' time, a newborn child of today will be asking what Dennis the Menace is up to then. For the best comics and the best characters seem immortal, the former often outliving their publishers, the latter regularly outliving their creators. Dennis the Menace, a stripe-shirted scruffbag looking all of eight years old, celebrated his thirty-sixth birthday on 17 March 1987, while his creator, David Law, died in 1971, and never saw his hairy hero achieve promotion to the front page in 1974.

The history of comic art is fraught with such tragedies. Tom Browne, the father of the form (*see* later), died in 1910: the characters he created, Weary Willie and Tired Tim, tramped on for another forty-three years, finally turning up their toes as permanent guests of Millionaire Murgatroyd Mump in the last, and 2997th, edition of *Chips* on 12 September 1953. A double depression here: the cartoonist who took over Tom's two tramps and painstakingly pictured them for most of those years was never once allowed to sign his work. So let's give a cheer here for Percy Cocking, and all those other anonymous inkslingers who laboured so lovingly and long over the thousands of characters and millions of strips that have entertained so many generations of us for so many years.

Although today's more enlightened publishers now permit their artists to sign their work, there are others who remain staunch to their feudal edicts of anonymity. D. C. Thomson of Dundee stands steadfastly on its creed that it is the characters that count, not who draws them, and, because most of their characters, from Desperate Dan and Korky the Cat of their *Dandy* to Lord Snooty and his Pals and the above-mentioned Menace of their *Beano*, have all survived far beyond the mere mortality of their original pen people, they would seem to have a point. But who of the Thomson clan is the one most admired, most celebrated cartoonist? Dudley D. Watkins, the only one they ever allowed to sign!

A long engagement

While comics and their characters are now so seemingly inseparable (save when one of those mysterious mergers occurs, as when Dan Dare of *Eagle* suddenly found himself inside his old enemy, *Lion*), the two took quite some time to come together. The early comics, developed from the nineteenth-century caricature prints, were essentially topical satires. The first regular weekly comic, *Funny Folks*, ran from 1874 to 1894, twenty years, without ever establishing a regular character (unless you count a couple of appearances of a fat little chap called Tympkins). Even Alfred Harmsworth, the young blood of Victorian popular publishing who started the boom in comics with his half-price, halfpenny *Comic Cuts* in 1890, saw no need for regular characters as a way to bring back the reader and his ha'penny, week after week. It would be four years before the brilliant stylist, Jack Butler Yeats (yes, *the* Jack Butler Yeats), tried a tentatively satirical stab at Conan Doyle's *Strand Magazine* detective with his cigar-puffing Chubblock Homes in 1894. And even then, regular placing in the pages (the strip drifted about across the centre spread and back page), regularity of form (it varied from three panels to six or more, sometimes across, sometimes running downwards), and even regularity of comic (it suddenly switched from *Comic Cuts* to *Funny Wonder* without explanation), seem so alien in editorial thinking as to make Chubblock Homes the original Baker Street Irregular.

The concept of the regularly appearing character had been established well before the concept of the regularly appearing comic, however. The lesson of Ally Sloper was there for the learning. Ally Sloper (the name is a Victorian pun: he sloped down the alley when the rent collector came acalling), the first true comic-strip hero of them all, made his debut in a full-page strip entitled 'Some of the Mysteries of Loan and Discount', in the weekly humorous magazine, *Judy*, on 14 August 1867. Sloper's artist was Charles Henry Ross, a regular cartoon contributor to *Judy* who soon became its editor. Instead of striving to create a new, different strip page every week, Ross decided there was more mileage in Ally than met the eye. So he brought him back in another page, then another, and another, until soon there were enough pages to be gathered into a book. *Ally Sloper: A Moral Lesson*, 220 pages of reprinted strips for a shilling, was published in November 1873 and became the first comic-book. The next step was an original Sloper publication: *Ally Sloper's Comic Kalendar* No. 1 came out for Christmas in 1875, and *Ally Sloper's Summer Number* started in 1880. It was obvious that the public could stand for more Sloper than twice a year, and so, on 3 May 1884, No. 1 of *Ally Sloper's Half-Holiday*, the eminent's own weekly comic, was published. It was destined to run for forty years.

While *Ally Sloper's Half-Holiday* was clearly bought for Ally Sloper, therefore, it would be a long time before the dozens of comics that followed in its wake would be bought for their own particular heroes, and an even longer time before a hero and the comic would be linked again through the title. Sloper had little influence on other comics, apart from perhaps the lowlife nature of his exploits. Chokee Bill and Area Sneaker, a couple of cracksmen, broke into *Comic Cuts* in 1897 and started something that is still with us today: no self-respecting comic-strip burglar would go on the job without his official kit of cloth cap, mask, striped jersey, and bag clearly marked 'SWAG'. Weary Willie and Tired Tim made their debut in *Illustrated Chips* in 1896, and so many other tramp double acts followed in their well-worn footsteps that a roll-call would overflow the Embankment. Tom Browne's classic fat-and-thin double act, inspired by his personal admiration for Don Quixote and Sancho Panza, became, for a decade, the dominant image of British comics. Editors strove to fill their front pages with tramps, while artists strove to imitate Tom's style, a combination of clean linework, well-spotted blacks, and slapstick action. And thus did Tom B. (as he was forced to reduce his signature) father the form.

Kids' comics

The combination of comics and characters gradually grew, with imitation setting in quite early in the saga. But it was not until the century was well and truly turned that comics and children became inextricably entwined. The appeal to children was there at the start, of course, although children were in no way considered buying targets for comics. In those days of the Saturday ha'penny, few children would have thought it worthwhile blueing the lot on just one comic. So James Henderson fashioned his *Funny Folks* for adults, observing in his editorial that 'Children will also grow merry with it, and even baby will laugh and crow over the picture pages'. Some of those picture pages were reprints from the old German picture sheets, the *Münchener Bilderbogen* for which Wilhelm Büsch had first drawn his occasional adventures of Max and Moritz in 1865. These twin brothers-in-lawlessness showed no discrimination: they played their pranks on man and beast alike. Of course, they got their come-uppance in the end, a spanking in the final panel, and thus Büsch won parental approval for his moral tales. But the approval he won from his young readers was far greater: when Max and Maurice (or Tootle and Bootle as Harmsworth called them when he reprinted them in *Comic Cuts* in 1896) stuffed gunpowder down their teacher's pipe, it was, vicariously, their readers' own teacher who got blown to bits! A hundred years later the Bash Street Kids play the same explosive jokes, and their readers smile the same smiles. In half-a-million minds' eyes a week, half-a-million teachers are battered, shattered, and splattered. Revenge is wreaked, and aggressive instincts siphoned off into laughter. The comic is salted away for future swaps, and it's time to get on with the homework.

Feminists will note one improvement over the century: from no girls at all to a minority one or two. Before the development of the girls' comic in the 'Fifties, the fair sex was reduced to token appearances as a sop to the second sex. Sometimes there were true heroines, such as Peggy the Pride of the Force in *Larks* (1931) but, more usually, they were just good friends of the hero, as with Don and Doris in *Puck* (1937). More often still they were objects of derision: the classic Keyhole Kate in *Dandy* (1937).

Animal crackers

Funny animals evolved early on, outside the mainstream, inside women's magazines. *Home Chat* started a pull-out supplement for children called *The Playbox*, and Aunt Molly (Alfred Harmsworth's brother Leicester) introduced 'Jungle Jinks' in 1898. This strip about a school for anthropomorphic animals proved so popular that the *Daily Mirror* (run by Leicester Harmsworth's brother Alfred) commissioned one Julius Stafford Baker to devise a similar strip for their young readers. Thus was born 'Mrs Hippo's Kindergarten' and with it, Tiger Tim. The *Mirror* dropped the strip, but it continued in another Harmsworth magazine, *The World and His Wife*, and was soon so popular that Tiger Tim and the Bruin Boys were the obvious choice to be the front-page stars of the first full-colour comic designed for nursery readership: *The Rainbow* (1914). When *Jack and Jill* was finally combined with *Playhour* in 1985, Tiger Tim and Co were pensioned off at the grand old age of eighty-one, the longest-running strip heroes in the business. Shorter lived were their twin sisters, Tiger Tilly and the Hippo Girls, who were born for a companion comic, *Playbox*, in 1925.

Comic courageous

The adventure-strip heroes or picture-story people arrived in comics in 1920, and the first of them was Rob the Rover. Walter Booth, previously a comic-strip man, turned his meticulous pen to depicting the worldwide wanderings of this homeless youngster. Pathos, an early ingredient of so many picture serials (Little Snowdrop of *Tiny Tots*; Motherless Mary of *Sunbeam*), was soon washed overboard as Rob roved land, sea, and air, and often all three at once, thanks to that all-purpose vehicle, The Flying Fish. Rob the Rover was clearly the father of Dan Dare, Pilot of the Future, invented for *Eagle* by Frank Hampson, the artist who brought a new realism to science-fiction strips. *Eagle* is a perfect example of the intertwining of comic and character: when a new publisher took over and demoted Dan to an inside page and stripped him of his colour, *Eagle* declined and fell. And, although one might wince to express the thought, just as Rob the Rover of the 'Twenties linked to Dan Dare of the 'Fifties, so Dan in turn links to Judge Dredd of the 'Eighties.

A choice of characters

Finally, a word on this selection, for, even with over 1200 entries, this 'who's who in comics' can only be a representation of the many characters who have come and gone over the last 150 years. I have tried hard to include all the important ones, the influential ones, the once famous and now forgotten ones, and ones which seemed worthwhile either because they were original in concept (or even derivative in concept) or for their artist's sake. Some artists, such as Wally Robertson, spent most of their working lives drawing other artists' creations, so that their representation here may be unfair. This is a lot that befell me personally, back in the 'Fifties, and affects many a good artist today: Ken Harrison, for instance, who for some years has been continuing, and splendidly, the late Dudley Watkins' characters. So I offer my apologies if your own personal favourite is not to be found herein. Although my original plan was to include only British comic heroes, it was thought worthwhile to include those famous superchaps from the United States, and other foreigners, who have been reprinted in British comics over the years. Again, my apologies if your favourite is missing: perhaps the character didn't have a very good run of reprints and is more at home in his or her own imported comicbooks.

How the book works

The arrangement of this book and the layout of each entry within it are simple. The characters are arranged in alphabetical order of their names but please note that when you wish to find a character you should look for, say, Ally Sloper and not Sloper, Ally. This rule also applies to real-life characters, such as Dan Leno rather than Leno, Dan, although I have not included many of these because I have preferred to concentrate on characters created for comics rather than on those taken from other media. The first heading of each entry is the name of the character followed by the name of the original illustrator or creator. Where I have been unable to discover the name of this person, it reads 'Illustrator unknown'. The final heading includes the title of the comic(s) in which the character appeared with the dates of run, and the publisher(s) of the comic(s) given in brackets. Where the character was still running in December 1986, a space has been left following the year of its first appearance.

Any corrections, amendments, or additional information would be welcomed by the author in the care of The Association of Comics Enthusiasts, 80 Silverdale, Sydenham, London SE26 4SJ.

Abra and Cadabra
Joe Hardman
Puck 1926-35 (Amalgamated Press)
'Abra and Cadabra and their Magic Carpet' was a small strip but an ingenious one. For ten years these two little pantomime Persians blew their twin flutes and turned their magic carpet into something surprising. The real magic was artist Joe Hardman's genius, of course, but *Puck* readers did not know that. The carpet's tricks included turning into a giant shrimp, a propeller for a becalmed boat, folding up into a frog, and rolling up into a giant Christmas cracker.

Ace Hart
C. Purvis
Superthriller 1948-50 (Foldes)
'Ace Hart, a young scientist, has been able to harness atomic energy to his own body, which gives him the strength of twenty men and enables him to fly faster than a jet.' Small wonder, then, that he should be billed as 'Ace Hart the Atom Man'. Unusual for a British superhero, Ace's evil opponent was the lovely Zonda, known as 'Satan's Daughter', assisted by the giant Kinga: 'Kinga! Kill him!' Zonda intends to become the ruler of Britain with the aid of her 'evil eye', a long-range beam that hypnotizes her victims into blind obedience.

Ace Eagle
Reg Perrott
Golden 1937-40 (Amalgamated Press)
'The Golden Eagle' was the title of the serial in which readers of *Golden* No. 1 (23 October 1937) were bidden to 'Come flying round the world with Vic Vernon and Mr Eagle, the famous airman, in their Wonder Plane'. It was six months or more before 'Eagle the Flying Ace' dropped his formal 'Mr' to become Ace Eagle to his young chum Vic. With the coming of World War 2 in 1939, the Wonder Plane was pressed into service, and the strip changed title to 'Kings of the Air'. Before Ace could win the war, *Golden* folded (18 May 1940).

Ace Malloy
Mick Anglo
Ace Malloy 1951-54 (Arnold)
'Ace Malloy of the Special Squadron' was Squadron Leader Malloy, a Canadian-born Englishman and hero of World War 2. He was also the title star of his own comicbook series, written and drawn by Mick Anglo under the pen-name of Kirk Logan, and published by the Arnold (Miller) Book Company. Ace's first adventures were set in Korea where he uncovered Colonel Kagusi and his Japanese soldiers behind a series of supply truck ambushes in a mad plan to restore the glories of the Nipponese Empire.

Ace Rogers
Alf Farningham
Comic Adventures 1943-49 (Soloway)
Originally billed as 'Ace Rogers of the Submarine Salvo', Lieutenant Rogers signed on in the black-and-green pages of *Comic Adventures* Vol. 3, No. 2. After a couple of successful operations against the Nazis, Ace took on the Japanese, changing his subtitle to '. . . of the Submarine Service'. His peacetime adventures began in Vol. 5, No. 2 when he set out to locate 'Lost Gold of the Incas' in Professor Marton's amphibious submarine, *The Platypus*. Ace was last seen heading for the Moon in Vol. 7, No. 2: a full-colour finale.

Adam Eterno
Eric Bradbury
Thunder 1970-71; *Lion* 1971-74; *Valiant* 1974-76 (IPC)
'Doomed never to die, he wandered the Earth for centuries on end!' This was the fate of Adam, impatient assistant to an old alchemist in the sixteenth century. Quaffing the newly blended Elixir of Life before the chemicals had sufficiently simmered, his master cursed him thus: 'I vow, by the seven roses of Ranas, you are doomed to wander the world through the labyrinths of time! Only one thing will restore you to your normal self. A mortal blow delivered with a weapon of solid gold!' The laboratory goes up in flames, but Adam remains unsinged: 'I am invincible! *Hah-hah-heeee!*'

Ace Trucking Co
Belardinelli
2000 AD 1981-85 (IPC)
The Ace Trucking Company (motto: 'Any Space, Any Time') rocketed into *2000 AD* No. 232 (3 October 1981) as a future parallel to the 'Eighties' obsession with trucking movies. Sole proprietor of ATC was alien, Ace Garp, his second-in-command, the hirsute GBH, outcast of the Shaika'kan tribe of space nomads. Their main rival was Earth-born Jago Kain, boss of the Yellow Line Fleet; their main pain the Creepy Jeepies, trucker slang for the Galactic Police Patrol. A Truckers Dictionary was provided to translate the dialogue: 'Got Speedo Ghost lugging five-five dadispads of phisphate on line for B-hive-K! Ten ten till we do it again!'

Addie and Hermy
Sam Fair
Dandy 1939-41 (D. C. Thomson)
Billed as 'The Nasty Nazis', this was the *Dandy* version of Der Führer, Adolf Hitler, and Field Marshal Hermann Goering. They were depicted, not as evil warmongers, but as a couple of ever-hungry buddies always up to dodges to win free food. Suspecting the worst when their Chinese cook bakes them a pie and their pet pup goes missing, their tummy-aches double when the dog turns up: the cook is using it as a rat-catcher. The cook's tonic doesn't help: it is wagon grease! 'Ach, mine dodboggled goodness!'

Action Force
Kenner Parker Toys
Battle Action Force 1983-86 (IPC)
Based on the Action Man/Action Force toys for boys, a number of strips was introduced into *Battle Action*, adding *Force* to its title from 8 October 1983. These were pulled together to form a separate centre section in 1984. Z-Force, commanded by Captain Campbell, fought the fanatical Gibli in the African desert (artist: Vanyo). SAS-Force, under Captain Buckingham, fought Baron Ironblood's Red Shadows in the Andes, (artist: Geoff Campion). Q-Force featured Jean-Paul Rives, code-name Shark, underwater expert (artist: Jim Watson). Space Force commander Chuck Conners outmanoeuvred evil Karl Vagan (artist: Ron Turner; illustrated).

Addy and Squibs
Harry Banger
Rocket 1935-38 (Target)
'The Admiral's Log' was the original title of this strip which sailed on to the back page of *Rocket* No. 1 (26 October 1935). Apoplectic Admiral Applecart was boss of the flagship *Popcorn*, and his crew consisted of cabin boy Squibs, although the odd matelot could be glimpsed jigging in the rigging. Addy and Squibs frequently had fun in foreign parts. Once they landed on Idiotic Island seeking buried treasure, but a local lad looking black in the face saw them off. 'Walla-walla-golliwog!' he cried. Artist Banger revamped the strip as 'All at Sea' for *New Funnies* (1940).

Ad Lad
Trevor Metcalfe
Whoopee 1974-75 (IPC)
'He'll do anything to get on TV – As you will all soon see!' The headline in *Whoopee* No. 1 (9 March 1974) described Ad Lad to a T (or a TV!). The announcer was presenting a packet of Krispy Nosh, the super cereal that goes 'Snap! Crackle! Burp!' The unexpected last noise came from Ad Lad, who had sneaked into the studio and was tucking into a bowlful of breakfast. Booted forth, he returned as the surprise gift in the jumbo-sized pack: 'Yoo-hoo, folks!' Ad Lad finally made it into the commercial at the receiving end of the announcer's slipper. 'Krispy Nosh gives you lots of energy!' 'Yaaagh! Howl! Mercy!'

Airy Alf and Bouncing Billy
Tom Browne
Big Budget 1897-1907 (Pearson)
'The Adventures and Misadventures of Airy Alf and Bouncing Billy' began at Queen Victoria's Jubilee Procession, and ended in jail. These two keen bicyclists rode on to page one, number one of *Big Budget* which was published 19 June 1897, created by Tom Browne, himself a devoted cyclist. Their ten-year tenure outlasted both Browne and the bicycle fad for, under another excellent artist, 'Yorick' (Ralph Hodgson), Alf and Billy sank socially to the more popular footpad fraternity. This did not stop them getting patriotically involved in whatever war might rage.

Ah Wong
Jock McCail
New Funnies 1940-49 (Swan)
Ah Wong was an oriental detective who, unlike his inspiration, Charlie Chan, of the popular films, wore oriental costume and pigtail. Like Chan, however, Ah Wong (billed as 'The Wily Chinese') was given to quotable phrases: 'Hully along, Terry, he who is on spot first sees most!' Terry was Wong's young assistant, well able to understand his master's voice. 'Maybe murdeller has followed victim velly quickly!' was fairly intelligible, but what of 'The Cobla has stluck again! Hollible!' The Cobla was not a shoe repairer running amok, but the Cobra, a crook who dressed as a snake to terrorize London.

Aladdin and his Wonderful Lamp
Joe Hardman
Sunbeam 1928-40 (Amalgamated Press)
Based upon the long-popular pantomime character, Aladdin was a Chinese conjurer who wore the pigtail proudly, rubbing his magic lamp whenever a good deed was in the offing. Most of his tricks were reserved for Mabel and Eric, a couple of children who accompanied him on his wanderings. When they had no castle for their toy soldiers, a rub on the lamp created one out of their mother's cruet. And, at Christmas, he turned some Chinese lanterns into little men to carry in the pudding.

Al Change
Tom Bannister
Topper 1980-86 (D. C. Thomson)
Al Change's bill-matter gave long-term readers of Thomson comics pause for thought: 'He's His Own Granny!' Back in *Beano* No. 1 (30 July 1938), there was a story called 'The Wangles of Granny Green', and here in *Topper* No. 1440 (6 September 1980) was the same idea in pictures. Only instead of Jimmy Green, here was young Al Change disguising himself as his own grandmother while his actor father was away in Australia. Never let a good idea go bad seems to be the Thomson motto. Currently Al has expanded into a schoolboy Master of Disguise.

Alf Tupper
Pete Sutherland
Victor 1963- (D. C. Thomson)
'The Tough of the Track' began his running career in a serial story in *Rover* (1949). He was a welder's apprentice at Greystone. In 1962 his story was told in strip form in *Victor*. By 1964, Alf had become helper to Bill Moggs, scrap-metal dealer. Living in a disused workshop under a railway viaduct and buying oddly matched running shoes for 4/6d at Sol Nathan's second-hand shop, would hardly seem conducive to winning races, but he soon won the mile for Greyshire in the Inter-Counties contest at the White City. Many wins followed.

Ali Barber
Frank Minnitt
Knockout 1939-40: *Sun* 1951 (Amalgamated Press)
'The Whisker Wizard of Bagdad' he called himself. His high-powered opponent, the Caliph, was less particular: 'Thou maggot-faced mongrel!' and 'O worm!' were more his line, as he threatened to throw the saucy snipper to his barber-biting lions. Later Ali went 'In Search of the Magic Winkle Pin', a silly serial involving the kidnapping of the Caliph by Tubad the Terrible, a pet rat called Rube, and a serpent known as the Wriggling Rock-sucker.

Alfie the Air Tramp
Albert Pease
Joker 1930-40; *Chips* 1940-52 (Amalgamated Press)
'If you don't roar with laughter at the comical capers of Alfie the Air Tramp and his Sky Terrier in their extraordinary aeroplane, I should advise you to see a doctor!' was the warning of Arthur A. Wagg (Richard Chance), editor of *The Joker*, introducing the new front-page character on 22 November 1930. Alfie's one-man 'plane was inspired by the Flying Flea, although the propeller was peculiarly his own: a hambone tied to a cricket bat! His sky terrier, Wagger, served as a rudder: he had a fan tied to his tail! When *Joker* was absorbed by *Chips*, Alfie flew across to that comic's two-colour back page for another twelve years' skylarking. Best of his several artists was John Jukes (illustrated).

Ali and his Baba
Malcolm Judge
Sparky 1970-77; *Topper* 1977- (D. C. Thomson)
'The Babe with the Flying Bodyguard' arrived in *Sparky* No. 261 (17 January 1970). Fortunately, their page was printed in red and black, otherwise half the fun would have been missing. For Ali, a buttoned-up baby in his one-piece romper suit, was printed in black, while his Baba, his protective spirit floating on a flying cloud, was printed in red. The same colour scheme applied to their respective speech balloons, making their page decidedly uneasy on the eyes.

Ali Ha-Ha
Ken Reid
Dandy 1960-63; *Hotspur* 1971 (D. C. Thomson)
Ali Ha-Ha was the son of the Police Chief of old Baghdad, and Dad was forever trying to bag the Forty Thieves. This gang of desert rats was led by Mustapha Phag but, despite their daring robberies, they invariably left a clue: forty clues, in fact. Thus, young Ali would soon find himself following their trail, which might be forty banana skins, or forty ice lolly sticks. But little good it did the lad or his dad for, even when they led to their secret cave, ('Open, sez me!'), Ali would end up with forty bumps from forty thumps.

Ali Oop

John L. Jukes

Jester 1940; *Crackers* 1940-41 (Amalgamated Press)

'Ali Oop and his Merry Magic' arrived on page one of *Jester* in time to celebrate its two-thousandth edition (9 March 1940). Described as the son of Sultana Bunn and a relative of Rajah Ricecake, the boy wizard worked wonders with his wand. When the starving Coffdrop Kids wished for food to come their way, Ali did the trick: a cooked chicken strolled up on its drumsticks! Ali's magic words varied: 'Oojahkapiv!' and 'Flatfootfloogy!' Later chants were more elaborate: 'Oojah! Oojah! Jack-a-Jones! Flowers change to old fish bones!' For the result, look at the cartoon.

The Amazing Peet

Paddy Brennan

Topper 1973-75 (D. C. Thomson)

'Great purple planets!' gasped Klutonian Ordinary Class Peet when he was banished to Earth for raiding King Klute's royal fruitorium. Sentenced to obey all orders given to him by Earthlings, Peet was unceremoniously booted out of a flying saucer at the feet of young Stan Stenson of Rodford. Young Stan was given to similarly outraged, if Earthbound, oaths. 'Great tanks of tadpoles!' he cried on sighting the saucer, and 'Sizzling sausages!' on encountering Peet. A jab from Peet's forefinger sent Stan reeling: 'Great gobstoppers!'

Ally Sloper

Charles H. Ross

Judy 1867-; *Ally Sloper's Half-Holiday* 1884-1923 (Dalziel)

Alexander Sloper Esq F.O.M. (Friend of Man) was born as half of a double-act, Sloper and Moses, in a one-off strip cartoon entitled 'Some of the Mysteries of Loan and Discount', in the magazine *Judy* on 14 August 1867. He made such a hit that he returned to become Britain's first continuing comic-strip hero, graduating to his own comic weekly, *Ally Sloper's Half-Holiday* (3 May 1884) and a series of annual *Comic Kalendars* and paperbacks. His creator was Charles Henry Ross assisted by Marie Duval (Mrs Ross), but it would be the brilliant W. G. Baxter (illustrated) who developed Sloper into the boozy, battered character all England adored for half a century.

The Amazing Three

Trevor Metcalfe

Jackpot 1979-80 (IPC)

England's answer to America's 'Fantastic Four', the Amazing Three were, in reality, Sue and her brother Craig, and Sam Pacey. When the three teenagers used the magic words, 'Rings of Zorr', they changed with a 'Chung!' into three superheroes, Tanya, Blue Wizard, and Oakman the wooden one. Tanya had lasers at her fingertips – 'Zap!'; Blue Wizard had a magic cane, and bullets bounced off Oakman's bark. Their exploits took place in Newton City where their arch enemy was Vogler the villain, whose pink cloud could turn people into outsize frogs: 'Croak! Croak!'

The Amazing Mr X

Jack Glass

Dandy 1944 (D. C. Thomson)

Len Manners, a private enquiry agent, was tall and loosely built but, behind his hornrimmed glasses, his eyes sparkled keen and bright. Len Manners had a secret: hidden in his bookcase was a strange costume – black skin-tights, white woollen jersey emblazoned with a black X, a black cloak, and a mask to match. Yes, Len Manners was also The Amazing Mr X, the first all-British superhero! But the secret of his superstrength was less supernatural than his Transatlantic predecessors: 'For some time Len had been building up his strength and faculties. Now he would show the world what he could do!'

Andy Pandy

Mary Adams

Robin 1953-69 (Hulton); *Pippin* 1971-73 (Polystyle)

Andy Pandy, a puppet, was the first star of *Watch With Mother*, the BBC television series for nursery-age children which started on 11 July 1950. Andy became the front-page star of the new coloured comic for young readers, *Robin*, which started on 28 March 1953: transferred without strings. Just as Andy holds a record for his television series (twenty-six shows repeated regularly for twenty-one years), so he holds a record in *Robin* (on the front page of 836 issues). Andy and his playmates, Teddy and Looby Loo, were drawn by anonymous artists working for the Grestock & Marsh Agency.

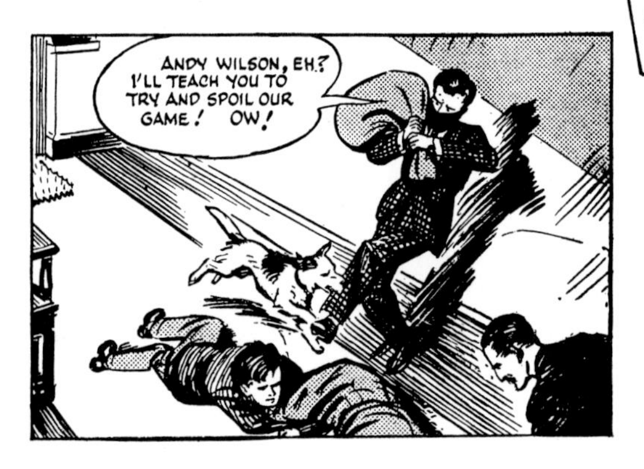

Andy and Sandy
John Woods

Radio Fun 1956-61; *Buster* 1961 (Amalgamated Press)
'A Delightful Story of a Boy and his Dog' was the subtitle that set the scene for this five-year, two-page serial strip. Andy Wilson, aged fifteen, chums up with a scruffy terrier he names Sandy but, when his bullying stepmother, Mrs Slade, refuses to let the dog in the house, Andy runs away to Sunnydale in search of his aunt. He is befriended by Sally Henshaw who lives on a barge, and then gets a job at Mr Clifford's stables and, with the help of his ventriloquial powers, exposes a sinister butler called Blood.

Angel and Her Merry Playmates
Bertie Brown

Puck 1914-36 (Amalgamated Press)
'The Amusing Adventures of Angel and Her Merry Playmates' was the awful fate that befell Jolly Joe Jinks, an old clown who had once held the coloured cover of *Puck*. Given a gang of Pocket Pierrots in 1911, in 1914, he was made butler to the household of Angel and Bertie. Soon the boy disappeared, leaving the blue-eyed blonde in charge, but worse was to come. The little clowns reduced to three (Claude, Charlie, and Clarence) and in 1920 a new artist, Walter Booth (illustrated), introduced Bertie Bear, Ollie Ostrich, and Peter and Popsie Penguin!

Andy's Ants/Adam and his Ants
Terry Bave

Cor 1970-74; *Wow* 1982-83 (IPC)
One day (8 June 1970: No. 1 of *Cor*) Andy was walking across the common on his way home from school, whistling. But Andy has no ordinary whistle. It was so high pitched that it was picked up by tiny ears nearby. In a flash he was surrounded by hundreds of ants! 'You are the first human to make contact with us!' cried the ants. By the next picture, Andy was home. 'Mum, can I bring my new friends in to tea?' Of course you can, dear, said Andy's Mum. The next thing she said was 'Eek!' as the ant army marched in. The strip was revamped as Adam and his Ants in *Wow* from 6 June 1982.

Angel's Proper Charlies
Trevor Metcalfe

Jackpot 1979-82 (IPC)
Love came into kids' comics when Angel moved into No. 6 on page three of No. 1 of *Jackpot* (5 May 1979). With a cry of 'Wow!' and a great show of beating hearts, two to a boy, three neighbouring lads promptly fell for the curly headed blonde. Inspired by the television series, *Charlie's Angels*, Angel called the trio her Proper Charlies. Their constant cry was 'We'll do anything for you, Angel!', and they did, including dressing up as her favourite pop group, the Swinging Three, to lure away the queue so Angel could get a seat at a pop concert.

Animalad
Roy Mitchell
Whoopee 1984-85; *Whizzer & Chips* 1985-86 (IPC)
Andy had an amazing ability: he had only to think of an animal to change into it! This came in handy for Andy, such as the time when he saved a small girl's kite from a treetop by turning into a squirrel. When a bully tried to stop him he turned into a bulldog. One night the Briggs brothers played at spooks to scare him, so Andy changed into a vampire bat and saw them off with fangs. Another time, his vampire bat wings made an instant umbrella on a rainy day and, by changing into an octopus, he caught a clutch of thrown eggs.

Aqua Lad
Terry Bave
Whizzer & Chips 1969-70 (IPC)
Hans and Lotte Hass, who explored the wonders of the underwater world for television, were the undoubted spiritual parents of this crop-topped young scuba diver. 'Makes me shiver!', cried a jellyfish in alarm as Aqua Lad came skimming through the sea in his frogboy's suit. The calm and placid waters of Neptune's domain would never be the same again now that man, and worse, boy, had penetrated its mysterious depths. Fortunately for fish lovers, the finny folk struck back: 'Eeouch!'

Artie the Autograph Hunter
Albert Pease
Tip Top 1950-54 (Amalgamated Press)
Artie arrived on the full-colour cover of *Tip Top* on 20 May 1950, accompanied by his faithful pup, Inky. Both were autograph hounds, and their first quarry was Sam Skidd the Demon of the Dirt Track. It took fifteen pictures, but Artie got the autograph in the end. Other celebrities' signatures soon included Signor Sago, singing star of 'Song of the Bullfrog', a 125-year old truant who upset the teacher when asked his name ('Hugh R. A. Chumpe'), and Esther Billyums, the Hollywood swimming star.

Antchester United
John Geering
Plug 1977-79; *Beezer* 1979 (D. C. Thomson)
The insect football team with all the talent and all the legs. Manager Mat Bugsy introduced them from Antfield Stadium in No. 1 of *Plug* (24 September 1977): Stirling Moth the winger, David Larvae, Brian Greenfly, Gnat Lofthouse, Mantis Buchan, Crawlin' Todd, Francis Flea, Spider Webb, George Beastie, Kevin Beetle, Anty Gray, Mike Summerbee, and referee Samuel Peeps. The official programme was called *The Fly Paper*, and Bugsy told readers about the team of flies that were beaten 36-nil. Their manager committed insecticide!

Argo
Nat Brand
All Star 1942-45; *Comic Adventures* 1947 (Soloway)
'Argo Under the Ocean' was the full title of the serial concerning this aquatic adventurer's exploits in the undersea city of Tremuda, somewhere beneath the North Pole. Clad in an electrically heated, rubberized suit, and 'aided by electrical propulsion, Argo cleaves his way through the ocean depths' in response to an SOS message engraved on a golden tablet, borne by a fish. Saving a water-breathing boy from a giant crawfish, Argo soon finds himself in conflict with Svang the Regent, who plans to leave the sea and conquer the land.

Asterix/Beric the Bold
Albert Uderzo
Ranger 1965-66 (Fleetway)
The popular French strip *Asterix le Gaulois* ('Asterix the Gaul') began in No. 1 of *Pilote* (29 October 1959) and rapidly became one of the most popular strips of all time. But, although his albums have been reprinted in English, Asterix has not had much success in British comics. The strip was given the title 'Britons Never, Never, Never Shall Be Slaves!' on its first appearance in England, in No. 1 of *Ranger* (18 September 1965), while Asterix himself was given the name of Beric the Bold, henchman to Chief Caradoc.

The Astro-Nuts
Alan Rogers
Cracker 1975-76 (D. C. Thomson)
This trio of astronauts took their inspiration from the crew of the star ship *Enterprise*, from the television series *Star Trek*. In charge was Captain Cork, who wore a top hat under his space helmet just to show that he was the boss. He was assisted by Malcolm and the long-eared Mister Spot; and the threesome explored a different planet every week in *Cracker*. For instance, they landed on Planet Isoar where King Irool and his people had eyes in the backs of their heads. They only escaped by virtue of making the monsters' eyes water – secret weapon: onion sandwiches!

The Avengers
Brian Clemens
TV Comic 1965-71 (ITV); *June* 1966 (Fleetway); *Diana* 1967 (D. C. Thomson)
The popular secret agent series, *The Avengers* began on ABC Television on 18 March 1961, with Patrick Macnee as the gallant, gentlemanly hero, John Steed. His partner varied from series to series: it was Mrs Emma Peel (Diana Rigg) when the first strip version appeared in *TV Comic* in 1965. Curiously 'The Avengers' also appeared in *Diana* (1967), published by a rival, D. C. Thomson, and in a sixty-eight-page comic book by the independent Thorpe & Porter. 'The Growing-up of Emma Peel' was serialized in *June* from 29 January 1966.

Aunt Tozer
Oliver Veal
Coloured Comic 1902-06 (Trapps Holmes)
The evolution of this overweight lady's affairs may be gauged by the changing title of her front-page adventures: 'Aunt Tozer in Lunnon Town', 'Aunt's Tozer's Courtship', and 'Aunt Tozer's Married Troubles'. The man responsible for her changing status was Captain William Doormat, who sported a top hat and a red nose to rival Ally Sloper's. Aunt Tozer's temper easily tipped over into violence. When the Captain admired what he took to be her portrait, she screeched: 'That me? That squint-eyed, bald-headed ugly old pusson? Why, you hinsulting old wagabone!' And 'she ups with her noo umbrelly and cuts him clean acrorst the dial! Wot-O!'

The Avengers
Jack Kirby
Terrific 1967-68; *Fantastic* 1968 (Odhams); *Avengers* 1973-76; *Mighty World of Marvel* 1976; *Titans* 1976; *Spiderman* 1976-79 (Marvel)
'The Invincible Iron Man, the Mighty Thor, Giant Man, and his companion the Wasp, Captain America – these are the Avengers, the mightiest fighting team of all time, united in their battle against evil wherever it may be found.' Thus, the introduction to British readers in No. 1 of *Terrific* (15 April 1967). The Mighty Avengers originally made their debut in the United States in *Avengers* No. 1 (September 1963). As created by Stan Lee, the team was slightly different, including The Hulk and Ant-Man.

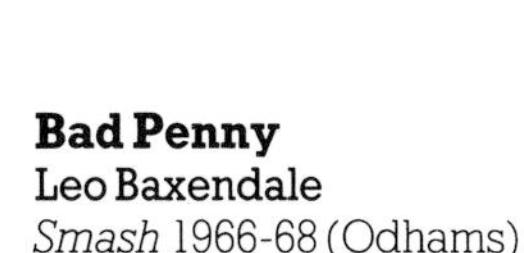

Baby Crockett
Bill Ritchie
Beezer 1956-; *Bimbo* 1961-72; *Little Star* 1972-76 (D. C. Thomson)
'Meet the Tiny Mite who's Dynamite!' was the headline introducing Baby Crockett into *Beezer* No. 34 (8 September 1956). That his inspiration was the Walt Disney film of *Davy Crockett* is proven by the parody of that hero's signature song:

Born in a bungalow and not yet three,
The wildest babe in the whole countree,
The terror of his ma and pa is he,
And his old Gran'pa feels safer up a tree!
Baby, Baby Crockett,
King of the Familee!

Baby was tamed a little for his run in the nursery comics, *Bimbo* and *Little Star*.

Bad Penny
Leo Baxendale
Smash 1966-68 (Odhams)
Abandoning his Minnie the Minx to other *Beano* artists, Leo Baxendale recreated her as Bad Penny for *Smash*. She made her devastating debut across two packed pages of *Smash* No. 1 (5 February 1966). In thirty-four pictures Penny's fun with a water pistol escalated from squirting the reader with pussy's milk, to building a super-size water weapon with a drainpipe and some bagpipes. In the end, the tables were turned when she chucked away a banana skin, upset an elephant, and got super-squirted for her pains.

Babyface Finlayson
Ron Spence
Beano 1972-(D. C. Thomson)
'The Cutest Bandit in the West' zoomed into *Beano* No. 1553, arriving in Vulture Gulch riding his trusty steed: a high-powered pram! For Babyface Finlayson was, literally, a baby, complete with bib (marked 'bib'!). Soon he and his gang (Goo-Goo McGoo, Sid the Kid, and Miss Jessie James) became the bane of Marshal (known as 'Marsh' for short) Mallow's life, raiding gobstopper stockists and firing arrows at Injuns with their musical instruments: 'robbery with violins', get it?

Ball Boy
Malcolm Judge
Beano 1975- (D. C. Thomson)
Ball Boy, a football-crazy kid, booted his way into *Beano* No. 1735, and has been scoring ever since. With his blond quiff and his uniform of striped shirt and shorts, Ball Boy is bent on practising his play at every opportunity – which is once a week in *Beano*. When Dad tries to get him to work in the garden, a cabbage makes a fine football! B.B., as he is known for short, turns out regularly for the school eleven, and it is nice to note that equal time is often given to his black buddy, Benjy.

The Badd Lads
Malcolm Judge
Beezer 1960- (D. C. Thomson)
'Kings of the Blunderworld' was the appropriate billing for this gang of no-goods. The littlest Lad was Boss, the largest Lad was Knuck, short for Knucklehead, and the last Lad was Fingers. Once a week in their full-colour page of *Beezer* the Badd Lads set out to do their baddest, blow a bank, perhaps, or bust a bullion van, and, once a week, they wound up in jail, or worse. Like all good comic-strip crooks, they never learned that Crime Does Not Pay.

The Ball's Pond Banditti
George Gordon Fraser
Larks 1893-94 (Dalziel)
'From 'enceforth I hemilate the doin's of the Robber Chiefs of hold!' observed Ticko Scuppins of the Ball's Pond Clothing Stores. 'Sussiety shall tremble at the name of Bloodwing.' 'Garn!' replied his admiring friends, Gorger Pain the doctor's youth, Piggy Waffles from the grocery establishment, Lurcher Geeson the butcher's boy, Sweppy Titmarsh from the rag shop, and, probably, Bocco the bold bloodhound. The historic date was 1 May 1893, the historic site the front page of *Larks* No. 1. For, with the establishment of this shop-boy banditti, the British juvenile delinquent took over the comics!

Bamboo Town
Chick Gordon
Dandy 1937-44 (D. C. Thomson)
Bongo and Pongo, a pair of snappily dressed chimps, return home to the jungle after a civilizing spell in the Big City Zoo. Bongo is the one sporting a bowler hat and cigar; Pongo prefers a trilby and a fag. They arrive on the back page of *Dandy* No. 1 (4 December 1937) to find Bamboo Town something of a slum: 'Darn my socks, what an awful mess!' They enlist the animals in a clean-up campaign, watering the streets with punctured melons while the giraffe sweeps chimneys, and the pelican's bill does for a dustbin.

Bananaman
John Geering
Nutty 1980-85; *Dandy* 1985- (D. C. Thomson); *Beeb* 1985 (Polystyle)
Little Eric Wimp may look like an ordinary schoolboy (stubble headed, spotty, clad in a scruffy dufflecoat), but he isn't. Oh, no! Eric comes from the moon which, we are told on the back page of *Nutty* No. 1 (16 February 1980), is really the biggest banana in the sky! Thus, when Eric scoffs one of his special bananas he becomes none other than Bananaman! Armed with his super bananarang, Bananaman soon has crime crushed in Weirdsville: 'Zabadoobydoo!'

Barnacle Ben
Bert Hill
Dazzler 1933-36 (Target)
'The Breezy Buccaneer' was the back-page star of *Dazzler*, a yellow comic first published in Bath on 19 August 1933. Described as 'a second-hand sailor', Ben sculled himself ashore intent on a bit of smugglery with a barrel of baccy. 'Sufferin' shrimps!' he cried, 'I'm spotted!' 'Twas the first appearance of Ben's mortal enemy, the Coastguard. 'Shiver my corncases!' swore Ben amid other 'naughty-cal' oaths, but draped in seaweed he soon scared the patrol person away. 'Trembling tiddlers, the beach is haunted!'

The Banana Bunch
Leo Baxendale
Beezer 1956- (D. C. Thomson)
The boys from Banana Crescent School originally cut their capers in one large picture which took up the whole back page of the tabloid comic, *Beezer*. The cartoon class was composed of Porky Simmons, Tiny Jenkins, Softy Simpkins, Joe Porter, Dick Mullins, and Dopey, to name but a few. Soon, however, the Bunch moved to a two-colour inside page where their adventures were depicted in a more orthodox strip. Here they emerged as a middle-class version of the notorious Bash Street Kids: same artist, of course.

Barbie
Mattel Toys
Tina 1967; *Princess Tina* 1967-73; *Barbie* 1985- (IPC)
Said to be the most successful toy in the world, Mattel Incorporated's Barbie Doll came to life 'in a story of laughter and surprise' in No. 1 of *Tina* (25 February 1967). This was the first attempt at an international comic for girls with simultaneous editions in Australia, New Zealand, South Africa, Italy, Germany, France, Austria, Switzerland, and Luxemburg. Barbie was depicted as a resentful teenage office girl with an urge to become a fashion model with the connivance of her kid sister, Skipper.

Barnacle Bill the Sailor
H. C. Milburn
Chips 1930-32 (Amalgamated Press)
Inspired by the popular song of the day ('It's only me from over the sea, says Barnacle Bill the Sailor'), this 'saucy sea-pup' signed on the complement of *Chips* on 22 November 1930: 'It's nicer to have a "loaf" on land than a "roll" on sea!' he tootled, half suspecting that his coming comic career would consist of collisions with crusty Captain Clump. Bosun Ben, the bully of the SS *Neversink*, caused his share of mutinous mayhem, too. Bill got permanent shore leave on 12 November 1932.

Barney Bulldog
Bill Ritchie
Sparky 1968-74 (D. C. Thomson)
Something unusual happened to this odd animal. When he made his debut on the back page of *Sparky*, he was called John Bull Dogg. Promoted to the front page early in 1969, his name was changed to Barney Bulldog. Later in the year, he was joined by a slightly smaller bulldog called Ben, who shared his strip until, in 1973, the multipicture approach was dropped in favour of a single large cartoon. After a year during which his buddy Ben disappeared, Barney, too, was pensioned off to the Old Dogs' Home.

Barney Boko
John Mason
Dandy 1937-44 (D. C. Thomson)
Barney Boko was the first physically deformed hero in a veritable freak show of funniosities that thronged the pages of the early D. C. Thomson comics. Barney was a tramp and, as his name suggested, the victim of an unusually prominent proboscis. This veritable wurlitzer of a nasal organ led him into all kinds of trouble, from No. 1 of *Dandy*, where he poked it through a tent only to be bowled at as an Aunt Sally, to having it sharpened to a point on a grindstone and being gulped down by a sword-swallower!

Barney's Barmy Army
Ken Hunter
Beezer 1971-73 (D. C. Thomson)

Way back when Britain was at war,
Old Barney had his army,
Every time they went to fight,
They drove their own side barmy!

Inspired by BBC Television's popular wartime comedy series, *Dad's Army*, Captain Barney and his Barmy Army (all six of them) signed on for World War 2 in *Beezer* No. 788 (20 February 1971). Having shot down one of our own fighter 'planes, Barney & Co were promptly posted 600 miles away to guard the Scottish coastal town of Invertattie. This pleased Private McTavish, but soon the silly soldiers found themselves facing Colonel Schnozzelblick in France.

Barney's Bear
George Ramsbottom
Dandy 1950-54 (D. C. Thomson)
His name was Smarty, and he was billed on his debut in *Dandy* No. 440 (29 April 1950) as 'The Cheeky, Chirpy Little Chappy who will always keep you happy!' The previous week, Smarty was trailed as 'Twenty Pounds of Furry Fun', with the added editorial jingle: 'He's got mischievous eyes, and a cheeky nose – He's a bundle of fun from his head to his toes?' Smarty was also a cub hungry for honey. He ran away from his parents in search of a bees' nest and found instead the camp of Barney Brennan and Digger Merry, gold prospectors.

Baron von Reichs-pudding
Illustrator unknown
Sparky 1974-76 (D. C. Thomson)
'The Flying Hun from World War Wun!' buzzed on to the back page of *Sparky* and, in no time at all, zoomed into the full-colour centre spread. Here his batty battles with such Englander schweinhunds as Squadron Leader Roger Spiffing-Show were able to spread themselves into riots of sound effects: 'Budda-budda! Pring-prang! Chrung! Sploo-eerch!' But however der Baron tried to pring-prang der Englander dogs and impress der Kaiser, the Raff chaps always came out on top with merry cries of 'Cheery-ho and toodle-pip, old chappies!'

The Bash Street Kids
Leo Baxendale
Beano 1954- (D. C. Thomson)
'With a roar, Out they pour, Every afternoon at four!' They were the Bash Street Kids, although they didn't attain that title officially until 1 December 1956. Originally, their strip was called 'When the Bell Rings': one large panel of frenzied activity depicted what the boys and girls of Bash Street School got up to after the caretaker let them free at four o'clock. Their first epic, skating on the frozen mill pond, exploded in *Beano* No. 604 (13 February 1954). The kids: Wilfred, Sidney, Herbert, Smiffy, Toots, Danny, Plug, Fatty, Jimmy, Ella, and Teddy.

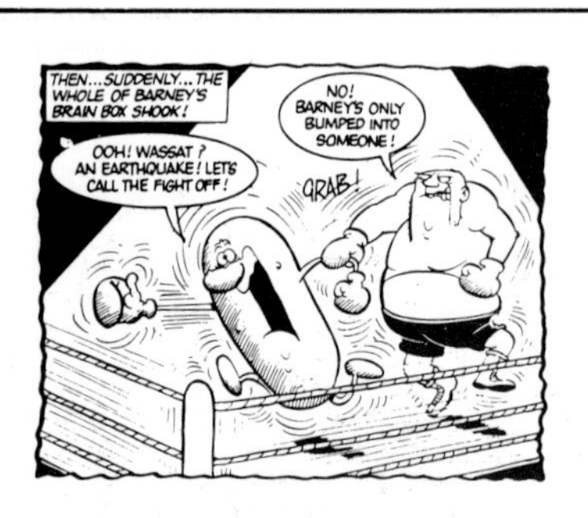

Barney's Brainbox
Mike Lacey
Cor 1970-71 (IPC)
'Here's something well worth looking into!' advised the editor of *Cor* No. 1 (6 June 1970). It was Barney Biggs' bonce for, while he was the doziest boy in his class, the scene inside his head was hyperactive. Busy little brainwaves busted out of their brain cells echoing whatever filtered into Barney's ears. When Teacher Scraggs talked about the Roman Conquest, Caesar and the Ancient Brits got mixed up with Barney's daydreams of football. And, when Barney's pal whispered in his ear, the wind blew right through and scored a goal!

Barracuda
Illustrator unknown
Lion 1966-69 (Fleetway)
'Code Name Barracuda' was the original serial starring this extremely special agent. Barracuda liked to exercise his fantastic brain against a computer: 'The answer is nine hundred million, seven thousand, five hundred and seven, point two six three.' 'Correct. The electronic brain gives exactly the same answer, two seconds after you!' His partner was Frollo, bald and muscular, who pulled up palm trees for exercise. Having rid the world of its arch-criminal, King Cobra, they buy an island in the West Indies with their reward, little knowing that, in Hong Kong, the most dangerous man to stalk the earth is stealing a special face mask.

Basil and Bert
Don Newhouse and Roy Wilson
Jester 1923-40 (Amalgamated Press)
'The World Wide Wanderings of Basil and Bert' lasted eighteen years, a goofy globetrot that wound up in the unlikely land of Boompsadaisy. Basil, the toff in the topper, and ex-batman Bert, were a team created by a team: Newhouse and Wilson who worked as one. They sent their stars to Spain to save Signorita Margerina from Rudolf Givembeno, and to Africa to thwart Chief Chewemup. But B & B's great days came after George Parlett took over in 1932. As 'Our Very Private Detectives' they tripped to Taterland, dictated over by Dick Tater and his Stormtaters. From 1939, DT was revealed as 'Ateful Adolf 'imself,' boss of the Doublecross Party (Gobbles, Snoring, and Von Drippintop).'

The Bat
William Ward
Thrill Comics 1940; *Extra Fun* 1940 (Swan)
'Ten lives for a life! Twenty groans for a groan! Such is the Bat's vengeance!' Inspired by the success of the American comicbook hero, Batman, William A. Ward created 'The Bat' for *Thrill Comics* No. 1 (April 1940), but added a twist of his own taste for the macabre. Ward's Bat owed as much to Bram Stoker's Dracula as to Bob Kane's Batman, although he was definitely on the side of right over might. Using his 'wonderful buoyance-ray diffuser', the Bat flies to free Stahl from the Black Guards.

Battler Britton
Geoff Campion
Sun 1956-59; *Knockout* 1960-61 (Amalgamated Press)
Billed as 'The Fighting Ace of Land, Sea and Air', Battler Britton became the front-page hero of *Sun* from No. 490 (28 June 1958). 'During the Second World War, many brave men became famous for their daring exploits, but the most renowned name of all was that of the amazing fighting-ace, Wing Commander Robert Britton, RAF, known to all as Battler Britton!' Leading his Spitfire wing in a screaming dive in picture one, Battler yells: 'Tally-ho! That's one more Jerry who'll have to swim home!' In 1959 *Sun* became *Battler Britton's Own Weekly* and, by 1960, he was on the coloured cover of *Knockout*.

Batman
Bob Kane
Smash 1966-69 (Odhams); *Super DC* 1969-70 (Top Sellers); *Batman Pocketbook* 1978-79; *Super Heroes* 1980 (Egmont)
Millionaire playboy of Gotham City, Bruce Wayne, made a vow when, as a boy, his parents were murdered. Now in the guise of Batman, the Caped Crusader, he wages war on all criminals, accompanied by his ward, a former circus performer named Dick Grayson, as Robin the Boy Wonder. Batman, then The Bat-Man, made his American debut in No. 27 of *Detective Comics* (May 1939), and, with the popularity of his television series, was featured on the full-colour front page of *Smash* from No. 20 (18 June 1966).

The Beans
Hugh McNeill
Bonnie 1974-75; *Playhour* 1975-83 (IPC)
'Meet the Beans – They will Make you Beam' introduced the Bean family of Beanland: Mummy Bean, Daddy Bean, Robbie Bean the schoolboy, French Bean in his beret, Runner Bean the jogger, Baby Bean in his pram, Butter Bean in her skirt, Baked Bean in his sunglasses, Broad Bean the fat one, Jumping Bean in his Mexican sombrero, Soya Bean in his Chinese pigtail, Koko Bean with his bongo drum, snooty Aunt Haricot Bean with her pince-nez, and old Uncle Haz Bean with his warped walking-stick. These packed pictures formed the last great pages by Hugh McNeill.

Bella
John Armstrong
Tammy 1974-84 (IPC)
'Bella at the Bar' was the title of the serial that introduced Bella Barlow to *Tammy* readers on 22 June 1974. Bella lived in the seedy, terraced home of Uncle Jed and Aunt Gertrude, doing the cooking and cleaning for Auntie and helping Uncle in his window cleaning. Between times, her every spare moment was spent balancing on her home-made bar in the garden. Despite her mercenary Uncle, Bella got the breaks and became a brilliant gymnast. Helped by the wealthy Courtney-Pikes and coached by enthusiastic Miss Davis, Bella made the World Championships at Texas.

Belle of the Ballet/Belle and Marie
John Worsley
Girl 1952-64; *Princess* 1964-67 (Hulton)
'The Enchanting Story of a Girl at a Dancing School' was scripted by George Beardmore and Terry Stanford, and strikingly illustrated in full colour by John Worsley. Belle was the poor orphaned daughter of the famous ballerina Marie Auburn, allowed to stay at Madame Arenska's dancing school. Monica, whose mother is financial backer of the school, is jealous of Belle and sees that she is made maid-of-all-work. David, the star pupil, befriends her, but Belle's confidences are saved for her beloved stuffed doll, Petrouchka. By 1962, the strip became 'Belle and Marie', telling of her professional life as one of 'The Telegang'.

Ben and Bert the Kid Cops
John L. Jukes
Funny Wonder 1932-40 (Amalgamated Press)
These 'brothers-in-law', Inspector Ben the boss and P. C. Bert, a short arm of the law, opened their shed as a 'Police Stashun' on 22 October 1932 in the centre spread of *Funny Wonder*. 'Bert the boss-cop was so worried that he couldn't look a stick of free toffee in the wrapper.' But soon they found a mum's lost Horatio and were rewarded with a bob in the poor box (for fireworks). It was the sucessful start to an eight-year career of crime crushery: on 16 March 1940, they rode off on a pair of wooden horses, promoted to the mounted constabulary.

Beric the Briton
John McCail
Sparkler 1935 (Amalgamated Press)
'From Freedom to Slavery' was the subtitle to this three-colour picture serial in *Sparkler*. 'Beric, a young Briton, is captured and taken as a slave to Rome by Mario, a Centurion. He fights in the arena with a leopard and rescues Mercia, a slave girl, from her brutal master.' And this was only the beginning. Mercia's runaway chariot plunges into a river; Beric dives to her rescue; hounds attack them in a forest; they are captured by Roman soldiers; they escape on horseback; they are captured by Moors; survive a sea battle; made captive by Egyptians; sold as slaves . . .

Beric the Cave-Boy
James Walker
Magic 1940 (D. C. Thomson)
Ten thousand years ago, 'long before civilisation had come to Britain', a family of ancient Britons lived in a cave. They were Beric, his father and mother, and two little sisters, all of whom wore animal skins, but none of whom seemed to have names – save Beric! Forced to move when an avalanche blocks the entrance to their home, they find their alternative accommodation occupied by a *Triceratops*. Chopping up a dead deer, Beric leads a dinosaur to the cave; it kills the *Triceratops* and the family moves in.

Bernard Briggs
Tony Harding
Hornet 1963-76; *Hotspur* 1976-80 (D. C. Thomson)
'The Goalie who is Good for a Laugh' first scored in No. 1 of *Hornet* (14 September 1963), in a serial strip entitled 'Bouncing Briggs'. He was a young rag and scrap-metal dealer who toured the country on his old motorcycle (number AEF 69) making a living buying and selling scrap. Instead of a standard sidecar, Bernard had fitted his bike with a battered old bathtub. He made his first call at the Blackton Rovers football club grounds to pick up some old iron railings, insisting on paying five bob in threepenny bits and coppers. His vocal criticism of the Rovers' goalkeeper was so loud that they gave him a go. Come the weekend, he was in action against Liverport.

Bertie Bounce
Louis Diamond
Rocket 1935-38; *Sunshine* 1939 (Target)
'Bertie Bounce the Bonny Bounder' strode into his first picture on page one, No. 1 of *Rocket* (26 October 1935), announcing his presence with a cheery 'Here we are, folks!' With his big bow tie and his little bowler hat. Bertie was one of those cheerful chappies whose sole purpose in life was to wander into and out of a pageful of pictures, once a week. Beaned by a brick, Bertie lands in wet cement. This clings to his chin like a beard, so a passer-by presents him with a fistful of quidlets, crying 'You're too old to be out! Go home and have a feed!' Life was full of surprises then.

Bessie Bunter
Hilda Richards
School Friend 1963; *June* 1964-74; *Tammy* 1974-81 (IPC)
Bessie Bunter, almost as immortal as her elder and even fatter brother, Billy Bunter, was created by Charles Hamilton writing as Hilda Richards for the girls' weekly, *School Friend* (17 May 1919). Billed as 'The Funniest Girl in the School', Bessie was later turned into a two-page comic strip by Cecil Orr. Cliff House School was still the setting, with its headmistress, Miss Stackpole. Bessie shared her study, but not her cream buns, with skinny Mary Moldsworth.

Betty Buttercup
Jim Lorimer
Twinkle 1972-74 (D. C. Thomson)
Little Betty Buttercup and the Funny Flower Folk first bloomed across the full-colour centre spread of Twinkle No. 224 on 6 May 1972. Everybody who lived in Garden City was named after flowers: even Betty's pet pussy was called Catmint! There was P. C. Periwinkle who rode a pennyfarthing bike; Lizzy Daisy; Heather MacThistle, whose daddy played the bagpipes; Mrs Candytuft who owned the sweet shop; Doctor Dock the doctor; Dandy Lion, Tiger Lily, and Snap Dragon who all lived in Willow Wood; Witch Hazel of Creepy Cottage; and they all came to Mayor Marigold's garden party.

Beryl the Peril
David Law
Topper 1953- (D. C. Thomson)
'She's nearly always in disgrace – This tomboy with the funny face!' The editorial couplet that introduced Beryl the Peril in No. 1 of *Topper* (7 February 1953) gave David Law's new comic character the perfect feminine counterpart of his Dennis the Menace, a superbly succinct description, but scarcely could anyone have predicted the years of success ahead. Law died in 1971, but Beryl lives perilously on, suffering spankings from Dad's slipper as depicted by Robert Nixon

Betty, Bimbo, and Bunny
Freddie Crompton
Chicks Own 1940-56 (Amalgamated Press)
They were actually billed as 'Bet-ty, Bim-bo and Bun-ny', being front-page serial stars of a hy-phen-a-ted com-ic for be-gin-ners. Their early adventures were even more helpful than hyphens: the trio (small girl, pony, and rabbit) found themselves in ABC Land, where K the King and Q the Queen sent them to W the Wizard, who lived in T the Tower, to help them get H for Home. The following year, 1941, was entirely taken up with visits to the Month Fairies, while Betty spent 1947 escaping from pixie pirates. Then it was off to Crossword Land!

Betty and Golly
Vera Bowyer
Chicks Own 1936-54 (Amalgamated Press)
'The Tale of Betty and Golly' was a back-page serial in *Chicks Own*, a hyphenated comic. The synopsis (sorry, syn-op-sis) ran: 'Betty and Golly are two jol-ly dol-lies who be-long to a lit-tle girl named Jenny. Jenny's mum-my is ver-y poor. She cuts up her own best frock to make a new one for Jenny.' But they reckon without the help of Betty and Golly, who come to life every night and help, getting elves to plant bulbs in Jenny's garden so that her flowers win first prize at school. Poor Golly fell victim to changing attitudes and, in 1955, the strip switched to 'Betty and Sailor Boy'!

B

Bewitched Belinda
Reg Parlett
Whizzer & Chips 1980-83 (IPC)
This wide-eyed witch used her wonderful powers to help, not hex. When a frightened fox crosses her path, she makes a quick pass at the huntsman: 'Frightened fox you will escape – nasty hunter take his shape!' Instantly, the hunter turned into a fox with howling hounds on his tail. Although Belinda always wore a pointed witch's hat, she was at great pains to hide her powers from her pals. 'Somefink weird always 'appens when Belinda's around! I fink she's a witch!' said fat Elsie, but Belinda turned the tables with a wave: 'Upsy Daisy, zap and zip – take her for a broomy trip!' And the broom flew Elsie into a lake!

Biffo the Bear
Dudley D. Watkins
Beano 1948- (D. C. Thomson)
'Hip Hurrah! Hip Hooray! Biffo Bear is Here Today!' Everybody echoed that headline on *Beano* No. 327 (24 January 1948) except Big Eggo: his ten-year tenure of the full-colour front page was over at last. Biffo, a black bear cub wearing red shorts and blue braces, was another member of the D. C. Thomson menagerie, animals who strolled casually among humans without causing comment. Biffo's early adventures were 'silent', but the ability to talk came to him on 10 September 1949. Biffo, too, felt the editorial elbow when Dennis the Menace bagged the front page from 14 September 1974.

Biff/Sam
Leo Baxendale
Wham 1964-68 (Odhams); *Thunder* 1970 (IPC)
'Biff – He'll Have a Bash at Anything!' had his first bash in No. 1 of *Wham* (20 June 1964). Biff's bash was at boxing, a fiver for two rounds with big Basher. Being but a boy, he bashed Basher's toes and soon cut him down to size. When the editor of *Wham* tried to decide which of his many characters should become the front-page hero, it was Biff who emerged victorious after a full-page scrimmage featuring a furious fight between all the comic's characters. Biff's reign ran from No. 5, but he was disloged by 'The Tiddlers'. Reprinted as 'Sam' in *Thunder*.

Big Ben and Little Len
Bertie Brown
Comic Cuts 1927-51 (Amalgamated Press)
'Twas exactly twenty-twelve minutes to ten last 'Twiceday', or Saturday 16 April 1927 to be even more exact, when a lanky lad, called Ben, and his little brother, Len, were introduced on the back page of *Comic Cuts*. They would remain stalwarts of that paper for twenty-five years, neither of them growing an inch older. Originally inspired by the American strip heroes, 'Moon Mullins and Kayo', their early adventures were hardly British Traditional: both were love rivals for the hand of fair Flossie! But most of their years were spent squeezing pictures money out of Pa.

B

Big Daddy
Mike Lacey
Buster 1982-84 (IPC)
This overgrown all-in wrestler proved surprisingly popular with young television viewers, and so was featured in a *Buster* strip. Sporting a spotty topper and cloak, he needed no comic costume to accentuate his good humour, although an added touch was the telephone – 'My daddyphone!' he called it – in his hat. Costarring in the strip was BD's trainer (called Trainer!), who spent most of his time trying to get the big man to exercise. Roadwork was something Daddy did his best to dodge, except when it was in a good cause, like a twenty-mile sponsored bed push!

Biggles
W. E. Johns
T. V. Express 1960-62 (TV Publications)
James Bigglesworth, 'Biggles' to his chums Bertie and Ginger, first appeared in a long-running series of stories and serials written by Captain W. E. Johns and published in the prewar boys' weekly, *Modern Boy*. Adapted as a television series, Biggles became the full-colour front-page hero of *T. V. Express*, drawn by Ron Embleton. Air Police Inspector Biggles was hot on the trail of a British diplomat's son, kidnapped by an international crook, Von Stahlein, on behalf of the San Felipian government. The exciting action continued on the back page.

Big Eggo
Reg Carter
Beano 1938-49 (D. C. Thomson)
Billed as 'The *Beano*'s Brainy Bird', Big Eggo was the full-colour front-page star of that comic for its first 326 issues – then he was shunted off to an inside page to make way for Biffo the Bear, a triumph of fur over feather. Eggo, an awkward ostrich, originally spent his six pictures protecting his egg from other desert-island animals, but soon settled down in that odd comic-paper world where outsize talking animals live side-by-side with unquestioning humans.

Big Head and Thick Head
Ken Reid
Dandy 1963-67 (D. C. Thomson)
Big Head and Thick Head were a couple of lads who operated as a team, or tried to, on the full-colour back page of *Dandy*. The small one as Big Head, a bespectacled brainbox who conceived their wheezes, while Thick Head was the bulgy boy who did his dim best to carry them out. Their respective IQs were illustrated when a baddie bumped their heads together: the result was a combined clunk, one labelled 'solid', the other 'hollow'. Their respect for each other is illuminated by this dialogue 'You stupid half-baked clot!' . . . 'You bossy little blighter!'

Big Fat Boko
Ken Hunter
Topper 1953-67 (D. C. Thomson)
'The Funniest Pair you've ever met – a Hungry Wizard and his Hungry Pet!' This was Big Fat Boko and his crafty crow, Koko, who began their tricks in *Topper* No. 1 (7 February 1953). They lived in the country of Bolonia, on the other side of Wonderland, where Boko's spellbook was famous. It contained only formulas for food! Having conjured up a light snack of chop and chips, Boko and Koko were interrupted in mid-munch by the King's herald. King Kole the Fourth had forbidden all magic, and Boko's wands, crystal balls, and even his chop and chips were confiscated!

Big-Hearted Arthur
Reg Parlett
Radio Fun 1938-50; *TV Fun* 1953-58 (Amalgamated Press)
Arthur Askey (catchphrase: 'Big-Hearted Arthur, that's me!') was the top comedy star on the radio with his BBC series, *Band Wagon*. Thus, he was a natural for No. 1 of *Radio Fun*, 15 October 1938, and soon moved from the two-colour back page to the full-colour front. His costar in the radio series, Richard 'Stinker' Murdoch, joined him from 18 November 1939, as did Arthur's succeeding radio partners, Kenneth Horne in 1946, and daughter Anthea in 1949. Arthur's television success, *Hello Playmates*, put him on the front page of *TV Fun* No. 1, 19 September 1953, where he was drawn by Arthur Martin.

B

Big-Hearted Martha
Cyril Price
Comic Cuts 1939-51 (Amalgamated Press)
Big-Hearted Martha (her name echoing the popularity of Big-hearted Arthur on the radio) clocked on in *Comic Cuts* No. 2555 (6 May 1939), billed as 'Our Clever Cleaner'. A cheerful, chubby old charlady, Martha's biggest problem was a pain in the housemaid's knee called Lena, the sort of rival who tipped sherbet into her clothes' boiler instead of Fizzo Washing Powder. Then came the war, and from No. 2578 (14 October 1939), Martha joined up to do her bit, changing her billing to 'Our A.R.P. Nut'. Lena enlisted, too, when she niffed lunch on the boil: 'Kippers, my favourite fruit', but Martha Kept Smiling.

Big Klanky
Jeff Bevan
Sparky 1966-74 (D. C. Thomson)
Big Klanky, a mechanical man from outer space, landed on Earth and was adopted by a couple of kids called Ernie and Sis Huggins. He addressed the children as 'young masters', and their mum, Mrs Huggins, as 'earth-mother'. When Big Klanky wasn't outwitting such odd enemies as the crafty Kraznovians ('We must smuggle him to our beloved country, Vladislov!') with cries of 'Unk-gluggle! Onk-yonk-glerg!', he was doing his best to help his adoptive family by moving their house single handedly to a nicer area.

Big Heep
Basil Blackaller
Beano 1940-42 (D. C. Thomson)
Not content with his headline rhyme, 'Big Heep, he Beats the Band – and shakes the whole of Redskin Land!', this oversized Injun was wont to roll around the reservation chanting, 'I beat the band, or so they say – I'm the fattest boy alive today!' Naturally, the other papooses put their feathers together to plot his downfall with a well-placed wangle. Just as naturally, they failed: 'See the Indian Kids' jape fail – 'Cos Big Heep's sneeze is like a gale!'

The Big Palooka
Pete Sutherland
Hornet 1965-67 (D. C. Thomson)
'When Sergeant Jim Ransom of Scotland Yard came to New York to study American police methods, his simple appearance gave the Yanks a big laugh. But once he sprang into action the laugh was on them!' So read the front-page introduction to 'The Big Palooka' in *Hornet* No. 75 (13 February 1965). Inside, the four-page serial showed Joe Rooney of Captain Mike Logan's detective squad meeting the big, bowler-hatted Britisher: 'Fancy being a nursemaid to a big palooka like that dopey limey!' But soon the Big Palooka was swinging into action against Waldo Weist and his machine-gun mob at the Farmers' Union Bank.

B

Big Uggy
George Drysdale
Topper 1958-62 (D. C. Thomson)
Quite why this comical caveman should have been christened Big Uggy is lost in the mists of time. He was a short sport, particularly when lined up with his best pal, a hulking sort of dinosaur known as Dopeydokus. Big Uggy was the bright brain of his tribe, always inventing things. His stone-age version of tiddleywinks came in handy for shooting an Abominable Blowlamporus back into his fiery volcano. The more traditional type of long-necked dinosaur was also put to good use. A ring of them made a great stone-age switchback!

Billy and Bunny
James Crichton
Fairyland Tales 1925-39 (Leng)
Billy and Bunny first appeared as a newspaper strip, the children's feature of the *Dundee Advertiser*, on 4 July 1919. Stories about them began to appear in *Fairyland Tales*, and finally a four-picture serial strip, printed in red and blue, was featured in that weekly's centre spread. It started in No. 194 (19 September 1925) and remained to the final issue, No 902 (25 November 1939). 'Let's try to liven things up a bit in Fairyland!' suggested Bunny to Billy, and between them they did.

Billy Binns
Illustrator unknown
Boys World 1963-64; *Eagle* 1964-65 (Odhams)
Beginning in *Boys World* No. 1 (26 January 1963) as a standard schoolboy adventure serial entitled 'The Boys of Castleford School', by the end of the year the title had changed to focus on 'Billy Binns and his Wonderful Specs'. Billy, the biggest duffer at sports, had been given a new pair of spectacles with strange powers: they changed the weedy lad into Castleford's sporting star! But the odd thing was that Billy knew nothing about the power of his special specs: 'I swot up sport like mad, but it's strange how I'm so skilful!' said his Indian chum Jumbi, 'great is Billy's skilfulness!'

Billy Brave
Tony Weare
Mickey Mouse Weekly 1950-57; *Zip* 1958-59 (Odhams)
'The Story of a Boy who Never Gave In' started as a full-page serial in the newly enlarged *Mickey Mouse Weekly*, No. 545 (21 October 1950). Said the editor: 'Not only is Billy thin and weak-looking, but he comes from a poor family. His struggles against poverty, the sneers of his fellows, plus his determination to shine at the sport he loves best, makes our picture story of his life one of the finest of the year.' In the end it lasted ten years, beginning with his war-wounded dad winning the football pools and sending Billy to Mannington College, soccer a specialty.

Billy Brock
Fred White
Playhouse 1955-64 (Fleetway)
Billy Brock the Badger bore a startling resemblance to Rupert Bear when he began 'Billy Brock's Schooldays' in No. 32 of *Playhour* (21 May 1955). There was Daddy puffing his pipe, and Mummy wiping her eye as young Billy set off in Farmer Fox's lorry to catch the train to Woodlee School. By Christmas, however, a cartoony quality had set in, with school chums Leonard Leverett and Hector Hedgehog and, by 1957, the strip had changed title to 'Billy Brock and his Funny Friends'. To celebrate, Leonard Leverett changed his name, too, to Leonard Longears.

Billy Bunter
Frank Richards
Knockout 1939-63; *Comet* 1952-53; *Valiant* 1963-76 (Amalgamated Press)
'The Fattest Schoolboy on Earth', as William George Bunter was billed in *Knockout*, began his grub-munching, pop-swigging life in *Magnet* No. 1, a storypaper published on 15 February 1908. 'The Owl of the Remove', as he was then known, was adapted as a strip in No. 1 of *Knockout*, 4 March 1939, by Charles Chapman. Frank Minnitt (illustrated) took over from No. 12, but did not live to see the Fat Owl take over the comic's title: *Billy Bunter's Knockout*, 10 June 1961. Minnitt's contribution to life at Greyfriars was the undersized egghead, Jones Minor.

Billy the Kid
Geoff Campion
Sun 1952-59 (Amalgamated Press)
'Yip! yip! yip! Hi-yo! was the cry of Billy the Kid as he raced into action astride his black horse, Satan. In an unusually long picture serial for the period, five pages, the story of young Will Bonney and how he shot down Bad Bill Thompson, the man who killed his father, appeared in No. 184 of *Sun* (16 August 1952). From No. 190 Billy moved to the full-colour cover, too, making six pages a week, seven by 1953, and ten by 1957! For a while, his popularity was so great that the comic's title became *The Cowboy Sun*, and a Billy the Kid Crackerjack Banger was given away on 28 June 1958.

Billy Muggins
Roy Wilson
Wonder 1944-46 (Amalgamated Press)
Private Billy Muggins enrolled on the red-and-black front page of *Wonder* as the tide of World War 2 was turning. Sharing his twelve pictures with his playful pet, Mousey, Billy battled his way to Berlin despite all the enemy, his Sergeant, could do! Others included General Newsance, Corporal Burnwater the cook, and the Colonel, who rewarded Billy and Mousey's capture of Kapitan Katzwisker by mentioning himself in despatches! On 4 August 1945, Billy was demobbed. He and Mousey joined Bodgit the Builder, but Foreman Alf was as tough as their old Sergy.

Billy the Cat
Sandy Calder
Beano 1967-74; *Buddy* 1981-82 (D. C. Thomson)
'The amazing adventures of a mysterious young crime-fighter, renowned for his courage and agility' began in *Beano* No. 1289. Billy the Cat, a black-clad lad in a crash-helmet made to resemble a cat's head was, in reality, William Grange, a bespectacled pupil of Burnham Academy. When danger threatened, however, such as a pickpocket at large on a seaside beach, William swiftly and secretly switched to his athletic alter ego, caught the criminal, and threw in a display of trampoline bouncing. Later joined by cousin Kathleen as 'Billy the Cat and Katie'.

Billy the Kid and Pongo
Gordon Bell
Cracker 1975-76 (D. C. Thomson)
'He's one of the best – at being a pest!' This tough young scruff and his four-legged friend forced their way into *Cracker* No. 1 (18 January 1975) via the slumbering editorial office. 'Hiyah, lucky people! We've come to join the comic!' An unusual entry, made all the more unusual by Billy firing a shooterful of peas at the editor's pants! 'Pongo's a very nice dog, but he's got a funny habit', explained Billy. 'He chews things – like chair legs! Hoo-har-har!' The editor found this out for himself, while Pongo simply said, 'Snigger!'

Billy's Boots
John Gillatt
Scorcher 1970-74; *Tiger* 1974-85; *Eagle* 1985-86; *Roy of the Rovers* 1986 (IPC)
Billy Dane was a junior at Bingley Road School where all the boys were football crazy. Billy was no exception – he just wasn't any good! 'You can't play football for toffee!' jeered the other lad. 'Your legs are like bloomin' matchsticks!' Cleaning out his grandmother's attic, Billy comes across a pair of old-fashioned football boots, souvenirs stored away by his dead granddad. He learns they belonged to Dead-shot Keen, once centre forward for England and, when he tries them on – 'Ftoom! Krack!' – Billy scores like a champion.

Billy Whizz
Malcolm Judge
Beano 1964- (D. C. Thomson)
Billy Whizz zoomed into *Beano* No. 1139, the fastest kid on two legs, and he has been rushing through its pages ever since; twenty-one years so far without a pause for breath. Luckily for Billy, his page is printed in two colours, so that useful words like 'Zoom!' and, of course, 'Whiz!', can appear in red among the clouds of dust and streak-marks that decorate his panels. Oddly, Billy's strip presents no wonderful scientific explanation for his superspeed.

Bing-Bang Benny
Ken Reid
Dandy 1956-60 (D. C. Thomson)
'Hi, folks! Bing-Bang Benny is my name, and I like bangs, I do!' And he did, setting out to prove it by loading his pop-gun with a mixture from his Whizzo Chemistry Set. The bing-bang that resulted soon wiped the sneers off those cowboys fool enough to scoff. Benny was a buckskinned young westerner who made his explosive entrance in *Dandy* No. 760 (16 June 1956). He did his weekly best to help the sheriff, but usually wound up on the wrong side of Big Chief Flappylugs.

Bimbo
Bob Dewar
Bimbo 1961-72 (D. C. Thomson)
Bimbo was the title star of *Bimbo*, a nursery comic first published by D. C. Thomson on 18 March 1961. A small boy in a big cap (he needed one to fit his big head), he moved to the front page of No. 3, but perhaps the deliberately simplistic style of drawing failed to catch young readers' eyes, for he was soon displaced by the detailed artwork of Dudley Watkins' Tom Thumb. Bimbo remained the comic's hero, however, running a Puzzle Page, a colouring contest, and starring in a strip which he shared with his pet puppy, 'Bimbo and Winkie'.

Birdie and Napoleon
Will Spurrier
World's Comic 1904-06 (Trapps Holmes)
Physically, Birdie and Napoleon were just another fat-and-thin double act, doing their lawless best to make enough ha'pence to last them to the next front page of the *World's Comic*. It was their clobber that made them odd men out. Birdie wore a pillbox hat and a whitewash-brush sporran dangling over his nobbly knees, while Nap sported a pirate's titfer complete with crossbones. Except, of course, for Christmas din, as per our engraving.

Birdman and Chicken
Trevor Metcalfe
Krazy 1977-78 (IPC)
With cries, or perhaps squawks, of 'Gabbling Geese!' and 'Hurtling Hawks!', Birdman (Dick Lane) and Chicken the Boy Blunder (Mick Mason) swooped down on nests of crooks in *Krazy*, a birdbrained burlesque of the American superheroes, Batman and Robin. They usually failed abysmally but, in the final issue (15 April 1978), the Caped Canaries netted the Giggler and his gang. 'Heroes at last!' chirped Chicken, only to be chased off by cops. 'Pestiferous Partridges!' peeped the Police, 'All that extra paperwork!'

Blackbow the Cheyenne
Geoff Campion
Swift 1961-63; *Eagle* 1963-69 (Hulton)
Grey Cloud, Chief of the Cheyenne, found a white child wandering alone: 'The Great Spirit in his wisdom sends this paleface papoose to fulfil the destiny of my own son, who is dead! He shall become a warrior chieftain second to none!' At sixteen, the youth was tattooed with a hawk, and named Blackbow. Dr Tad Barnaby nursed the wounded youth back to health and sent him to Boston University. He returned to Powder Creek as Dr Jim Barnaby, but no man knew his secret identity. As the last Cheyenne Chief he was a fighting figure of justice and righter of wrongs.

Bizzy Beaver
Basil Reynolds
Robin 1962-68 (Longacre)
'The Adventures of Bizzy Beaver' were illustrated in eight large pictures spread across two pages of *Robin*. Bizzy wore dungarees with a spotted patch just above his tail, and his little brother, Baby Beaver, was still in nappies, supported by a large safety pin. They lived with Mummy and Daddy Beaver in Lullaby Lodge, a house built in a river, and Bizzy's best pal was Ricky Raccoon. Other animal chums included Boo the bear cub, very fond of honey, of course. In 1966, Baby Beaver graduated to his own baby-sized strip.

Black Bun
Bill Hill
Beezer 1969-75 (D. C. Thomson)
'Get the habit! Have a laugh with this rabbit!' With that spot of editorial advice, Black Bun was introduced to readers of *Beezer* No. 683 (15 February 1969). Bun began as he was destined to continue for years to come: by raiding the local farmer's yard for carrots. Despite all the fat farmer could do with his loaded blunderbuss, not to mention his dog (known to Bun as Hairyface), Bun managed to get away with a bunch of crunchy lunch to munch: 'Hippety-ho! Here we go!'

Black Bob
Jack Prout
Dandy 1956- (D. C. Thomson)
'The Dandy Dog', originally billed as 'The wisest sheepdog in Scotland', started his long career as the hero of a serial story in *Dandy* No. 280 on 25 November 1944. Twelve years and countless adventures later he was turned into a picture strip (5 May 1956) and, as such, continues to this day. Black Bob, a border collie five years old, was owned by Andrew Glenn, shepherd of Selkirk. Kidnapped by rival farmer, Jake Lang, Bob found his way home from Liverpool in time to win the Championship Cup at Ettrick.

Black Hawk
Jeff Bevan
Hotspur 1966-68 (D. C. Thomson)
'The Robber whose Highway is the Skyway' flew into *Hotspur* No. 362 on 24 September 1966. He wore a black eye-mask, a black, skin-tight suit, and black batwings. His headquarters were an old hulk moored in a deserted part of the River Thames, where he was tended by his dumb oriental servant, Soyo. Calvin Crisp, private detective and richest man in the world, with his assistant Bill Budd, called on Scotland Yard. Inspector Tarrant showed them a letter: 'Today the Bank of England will be robbed. Don't say I did not give you warning'. It was signed 'The Black Hawk'.

Black-Hoof
Dudley Watkins
Dandy 1948-49 (D. C. Thomson)
'The Adventures of Brave Young Black-Hoof' started in *Dandy* No. 360 (4 January 1948). Black-Hoof, the youngest foal in a wild horse herd, stood beside his mother, Greysmoke, his black coat glistening and his neck proudly arched. 'In his veins ran the fiery blood of his forefathers, the warhorses brought to America by the Spanish conquerors centuries before.' His destiny was to be tamed by Hawkeye, young son of the Blackfeet Chief, who knew when he saw him that Black-Hoof was 'the great totem horse promised by the Gods'.

Black Sapper
Jack Glass
Beezer 1959; *Hotspur* 1971-73 (D. C. Thomson)
In the police records of Scotland Yard, no name occupies more space than the Black Sapper. Such was the title given to the crooked genius who invented the Earthworm, against whose diamond-hard drills no bank vault was safe. The Sapper, aided by mechanic Marot, first robbed the Bank of England in *Rover* No. 384 (24 August 1929), but Commander Breeze of the Yard found himself up against him again, in pictures, in *Beezer* No. 196 (17 October 1959). When he turned up again in *Hotspur*, Sapper and his burrowing machine were on the side of the law, fighting invaders from Khansu.

Black Max
Illustrator unknown
Thunder 1970-71; *Lion* 1971-72 (IPC)
'Death rode the skies in the bat-wing triplane!' In the late winter of 1917 (on 17 October 1970 in No. 1 of *Thunder*), a black-painted Fokker came wheeling across the skyline like a sinister, triumphant bird of prey. Morg had done his work well, and Baron Maximilien Von Klor screeched, his voice filled with hate: 'I go to kill the British dogs who gave me this scar. I shall repay them, not just with death, but also with fear!' And when Captain Howarde R.F.C. flew his Sopwith on dawn patrol, he was brought down, not by bullets, but by Black Max's beast, a giant vampire bat!

The Bleak Street Bunch
Peter Foster
Spike 1983-84; *Champ* 1984 (D. C. Thomson)
Virtually a 'straight strip' version of The Bash Street Kids, the Bleak Street Bunch were freckled Ray Taylor, chubby Tub Dutton, lanky Big Little, and bespectacled Hi-Fi Harris. With their old school burned down, new term began at a new school, Slagley Comprehensive, on 22 January 1983, somewhere in north-east England. Also arriving, but by bus, were the 'toffee-nosed twits' from Parkside, led by Jeremy Cranford: 'Oh, I say, chaps, don't Jeremy look smart with his natty little case, an' all?' Class war was declared.

Blunder Girl
J. Edward Oliver
Penny 1979-80 (IPC)
Although bespectacled schoolgirl, Diana Squints, looks ordinary, she has a mysterious secret power, as was quickly revealed in No. 1 of *Penny* (28 April 1979). As she enters Selfreezers Department Store intent on buying a new skateboard, she spots a robber. 'This looks like a job for Blunder Girl!' she cries, twirling in best Angela Redfern telly-style. In a literal flash, she turns into clumsy Blunder Girl, complete with chicken insignia. She slips on a skateboard and cops the robber in a bright burlesque of 'Wonder Woman'.

B

Bobbie and his Teddy Bears
Walter Bell
Sunbeam 1928-39 (Amalgamated Press)
Bobbie had four bears, one more than Goldilocks. Their names were Tony, Tommy, Timmy, and, of course, Teddy. They may not have been the first teddy bears in comics, but they had the longest lives: twelve years. Frankly, they were copies of a much earlier strip, 'Bobby and the Woolly Bears', which ran in *Butterfly* in 1908. And this, too, was a swipe: 'Little Johnny and the Teddy Bears' started in the American weekly *Judge* in 1907. There was a common denominator: each strip featured one bear in a striped jersey and knitted hat!

Bobby in Blue
Illustrator unknown
Little Star 1972-74 (D. C. Thomson)
'Bobby in Blue and his Sister Sue' went on their first pedal-car patrol in No. 1 of *Little Star* (29 January 1972). Their father was P. C. Walker, the only policeman in the village of Blairham, and the twins were determined to follow in their father's footsteps. They wore blue uniform jackets, and Bobby had a toy helmet on his head. They used their two-seater pedal car to patrol the village streets and, on their first day, they found a lost dolly in the park. Daddy was so pleased that he built them a wooden police box in the garden.

Bob and Betty Britten
Alexander Akerbladh
Crackers 1937-41 (Amalgamated Press)
'The Adventures of Bob and Betty Britten' formed an unusual front page on *Crackers*, the first full-colour picture serial in British comics. Adventures piled up at the rate of twelve panels a week, shared in everything but the title by Koko, the comic relief, who cried 'Golly! Look, sah! Dere am a shark attacking Missie Betty!', and other useful phrases like 'Dat am one for his knob!' and 'Gobblijinks!' Bob and Betty were stranded on a volcanic island inhabited by hillmen whose Big Chief had his eye on Missie Betty: 'We mak' yo' our White Queen! Yah!' But he reckoned without Koko and Massah Bob.

Bobby Blue
Freddie Adkins
Tiger Tim's Weekly 1931-37 (Amalgamated Press)
'Bobby Blue – He Knows What to Do,' – tap it with his magic truncheon! Bobby was a funny little policeman blessed with lengthy sidewhiskers and a magic wand in the form of a truncheon. Touch any object with it, and that object would enlarge. For instance, his whistle chain pulled pussy out of a well; an enlarged key made a fine substitute for Mr Longman's lost fishing rod; and oversized icicles made nice tubular bells for playing carols.

Bobby Dazzler
Giorgio Letteri
Judy 1965- (D. C. Thomson)
A feminist without knowing the meaning of the word was Roberta Dazzler. She was the only girl at a boys' school! Her mother was matron of the Westbury Boarding School for Boys, and young Bobby was allowed to attend the Third Form. This led to a constant feud between Bobby and Mike Norton, leader of the Third and chief claimant of the superiority of boys over girls. Bobby, however, more than held her own, invariably proving just the opposite. A neat role reversal occurred when Mike insisted on playing the lead in the school panto: Bobby played the Prince and Mike donned skirts as Cinderella!

Bobo Bunny

Illustrator unknown

Bobo Bunny 1969-73; *Hey Diddle Diddle* 1973 (IPC); *Rupert* 1984 (Marvel); *Robin* 1985 (IPC)

This bouncy bunny was the title star of his own comic, which started on 22 March 1969. Printed in full-colour photogravure on every page, Bobo and his Jolly Family made full use of this technique because each was a different colour. Bobo himself was bright blue, Mummy was brown, Daddy green, Grandma white, Baby mauve, sister Scribbler pink, Watch-the-Trains Bunny was light blue, Read-to-Me Bunny was pale pink, Auntie Justso Bunny was light green, and fat old Uncle Muncher was red! Bobo was translated from the Dutch.

Bob the Pet Navvy

George E. Studdy

Jester and Wonder 1903-06 (Amalgamated Press)

This prime example of the British working man joined the centre spread characters of *Jester* on 24 January 1903. He was pensioned off some four years later having done singularly little labour, hard or otherwise. His first adventure involved a 'balmy cove' intent on 'a slap-up skewercide'; next came a boxing bout with Smiff the Tailor, won by a lucky horseshoe; and, in the episode illustrated, Bob guinea-pigged for Professor Flynut. Unhappily, 'that machine could no more fly than a cockadoodle wot's got the pip!'

Bonehead

Reg Parlett

Jet 1971; *Buster* 1971-75 (IPC)

Billed as 'the Barmy Bulldog', Bonehead was a lolloping lump of hungry hound, ever in pursuit of his favourite fruit, bones. In his early days, he was a pet shop's permanent resident, the one unsold animal in an otherwise successful business. Folks bought him, all right, but quickly returned him when they discovered his permanent hunger pains. Taking to the road, Bonehead wandered from job to job. Trying out as a guard dog at a circus, a bite at the clown's rubber bone bounced him into the lions' cage.

Boney Prince Charlie

Harry Banger

Rocket 1935-38 (Target)

Boney Prince Charlie lived in ye good old bad old days when knights were knuts or nibs, as represented by *Rocket* No. 1 (26 October 1935). In his first picture, shown here, the skinny Prince is nabbed by a Roundhead, 'not to be confused with the more modern squarehead or blockhead!' Snaffled for clambering an oak tree, Charlie is yanked inside ye castle walls and invited to stay while they sharpen ye chopper. Not intending to lose his head, ye noble one nipped off by sandwiching ye guard with ye drawbridge: 'He felt like a stale saveloy between a couple of doorsteps!'

Bookworm

Sid Burgon

Whoopee 1978-85 (IPC)

This bespectacled boy bore a big 'B' on his tee-shirt. It stood for 'Bookworm' and his one delight was burying himself in a book. A true sport hater, he tried to get out of a paper chase by faking a stiff leg: he packed his trousers with paperbacks! But, to the sports master's surprise, Bookworm won the race – he picked up all the torn paper and shuffled it back into a book! He learned ballet just so he could carry an extra pile of books – on his head – and, when his bookshelves gave way, he built a new set – with a stack of encyclopedias.

Boomerang Burke

Jack Glass

Dandy 1941 (D. C. Thomson)

Not for nothing was Bill Burke of the Royal North West Canadian Mounted Police known as 'The No-Gun Mountie'. Instead of the usual service-issue revolver, Bill carried an Australian boomerang. One throw of his unusual weapon was enough to disarm the most notorious crooks in Canada, even eventually, the evil Scarface: 'wanted in a dozen countries for various crimes!' The pursuit of this scoundrel took the No-Gun Mountie into the strange terrain of the South American jungle for several suspenseful weeks.

The Bootneck Boy
Illustrator unknown
Battle 1975-77 (IPC)
In 1942, orphan Danny Budd of the tough northern town of Tynecastle volunteered for the Royal Marines. 'Come back when you've got muscles on your arms instead of pimples, son!' said the Sergeant. On his way home Danny digs old Pop Murphy out of air-raid rubble, but his Uncle Fred Bircher, furious at the lad's lateness for his coal round, flays him with his belt. The sergeant spots Danny beating up a gang of bullies and bends the rules, but the new recruit is soon in trouble. Swimming to warn a destroyer of a floating mine, he loses his new cap badge!

Bounderby Bounce
Charles Genge
Big Budget 1899-1900 (Pearson); *Funny Cuts* 1915-1918 (Trapps Holmes)
'The Extraordinary Adventures of Bounderby Bounce, the War Correspondent' began in *Big Budget* during the Boer War. In 1900, fortified by a flagon of Dewar's Cold Tea, he bested his rival reporter, Yarnslinger, by capturing General Joubert with a squirt of soap and water. 'Thunderweather and beeranskittles!' roared the old Boer. In 1916, he bested his rival Yarnsnatcher by capturing the Kaiser with his patent sausage machine. 'Schmittmusterbogen-hoftokajer!' gasped the old Hun. 'Kamerad!'

The Bouncers
Peter Maddocks
Swift 1959-60 (Hulton)
The Bouncers, a legless lot, came bouncing up from the centre of the Earth to make their way into fresh air and sunlight. Finding a tropical island, they help a pirate dig for treasure but get captured by Blackbeard. They escape by blowing themselves up and floating away like big balloons. Their next stop is among Arabs who have stolen the Golden Rainmaker of Kostobah: every time the bag is opened, it rains! Further bouncings take them to the moon.

Boxatricks
Brian Walker
Buster 1980-81 (IPC)
A simple little box, not much bigger than a gravy cube, but it bounced around the world whirring and clicking, looking for good deeds to do. When the cops wanted to know what a crook called Camouflage Ken looked like, Boxatricks popped out an X-ray camera and revealed the foul face behind the fungus. Then out popped a radar scanner and an electronic trail sniffer, tracking Ken to his underground lair. A quick drill downwards and Ken was caught, literally pinched by Boxatricks' patent grabbers.

Boy Biffo the Brave
Sam Fair
Magic 1939-40 (D. C. Thomson)
The familiar fairy tale of the Brave Little Tailor was adapted as a merry medieval strip which started in No. 1 of *Magic* (22 July 1939). This time the hero was a gardener's boy, Young Biffo, the butt of many a cruel jest by the knights in armour, who mocked his spindly legs. One day flies attack Biffo's bread and cheese. He swats them with his trowel and proudly commemorates the victory by emblazoning a dustbin lid as a shield: 'One Biff Slew Nine!' Naturally everyone assumes he killed nine men, not flies!

Boy Butler
Mike Lacey
Whizzer & Chips 1984-86 (IPC)
Young Georgie went to visit his aging granddad on 16 June 1984. Granddad was Jonkers, butler to Lord Loot of Much-Munny-in-the-Banks, and Lord Loot's fat son and heir, Egbert, had always wanted his own butler. So Georgie's holiday turned into a working holiday, forced to act as butler to greedy Egbert. Georgie, however, was a lad with spirit and, when Egbert ordered high tea, he got it: a lump of mouldy cheese! 'One up to the downstairs team!' tittered Elsie the maid, 'tea-hee!' When Egbert got locked in his room, Georgie served dinner – with a tennis racket. (It was meatballs!)

Braddock
'George Bourne'
Victor 1961-83; *Warlord* 1974 (D. C. Thomson)
'I Flew With Braddock,' the wartime narrative by Sergeant George Bourne, navigator, was first published as a serial story in *Rover* No. 1414 (2 August 1952). The picture strip version began in No. 1 of *Victor* (25 February 1961), illustrating the exploits of Sergeant Matt Braddock, 'Britain's greatest pilot of the Second World War'. His daring adventures won him the Victoria Cross and Bar, but Braddock was not interested in winning honours. All he wanted to do was to get on with the war, and win it. So he did.

Boy Boss
Frank MacDiarmid
Wow 1982-83; *Whoopee* 1983-85 (IPC)
Boy Boss had the letters TC on his tee-shirt. They stood for The Company, the company that he had inherited – much to the aggranoyance of Jasper the Accountant. 'Bah! Boy Boss runs The Company in far too casual a manner. I believe in work, work, work!' he snarled, scratching away with his quill. Boy Boss tended to treat Vital Papers in a cavalier manner: he made paper aeroplanes out of them! The Company was a vast conglomerate that made everything from bossburgers to pencil holders in the shape of Jasper.

The Boy with the Iron Hands
Fred Sturrock
Dandy 1939-40 (D. C. Thomson)
'Who are you, wretched boy?' demanded King Roderick the Red of the city of Albion, capital of the land of Caledon. The youth returned the King's ice-cold stare. 'I am the Boy David,' he said simply. The youth from the hills had already thrown the King's bodyguard off his horse by hurling the giant steed on to its back; in time, he would overthrow the tyrant king himself, allied to the mysterious Master and his Sword of Truth. A saga which started on 19 August 1939 in No. 90 of *Dandy*.

Brassneck
Bill Holroyd
Dandy 1964-68; 1982-84 (D. C. Thomson)
Chuckler Charley Brand's best friend was Brassneck, an amazing metal boy. Brassneck accompanied Charley everywhere: at home, he caused trouble for Dad Brand; at school, he caused trouble for their teacher, Fatso Snodgrass. Brassneck's limbs were totally telescopic: he could extend a leg to save a sure goal in football, or extend his neck to head off a goal kick. He could even unscrew his legs and use them as knitting needles! When Brassneck returned to the *Dandy* in 1982, it was as the star of the full-colour centre spread.

Brave Joe
T. Gilson
Playbox 1938-53 (Amalgamated Press)
Brave Joe and his equally brave chum, Effie, not to mention brave Topsy the dog, shared amazing adventures on land, sea, and in the air, thanks to Captain Scott and his wonderful invention, the *Flying Fish*. This astounding vehicle served them well, and, even when it was lost in 1949, Mr Grim helped the Captain build a new improved model that lasted them another five years. Another inventor they met was Jean's Daddy, who made a magic picture machine: 'This is what they call television,' he smiled, 'It is a long word but I expect you know what it means!'

Breezy Ben and Dismal Dutchy
Tom Wilkinson
Chuckles 1914-23 (Amalgamated Press)
'Hip-pip-pip-hoo-ray!' piped Breezy Ben the sailor, opening ten years of front-page fun on No. 1 of the ha'penny, coloured comic *Chuckles*, 10 January 1914, and 'gleefully inhaling the dear old ozone from the glue factories of Wapping'. Dismal Dutchy was less enthusiastic: 'I vant to inchoy mineself but I don't know how to start!' There was something prophetic about their pets, a chatty parrot and a tripehound named Snitzel for, in 1915, they shipped to Jungle Island where they opened a school for Teddie Bear, Tobias Tiger, and their Merry Playmates. Enough to make a matelot heave-ho!

Brenda's Brownies
Mike Brown
Sandie 1972-73 (IPC)
Brenda and her Brownies held their first meeting of the Tarantula Troop in their ricketty old Brownie Hut in No. 1 of *Sandie* (12 February 1972). There were five of them in all, if you include Brenda and the pet pup, Tiger, who also wore a regulation beret. The others were Grubby Glenda, Clever Doreen, and Nosey Nelly. Brenda decided her girls would try for their cookery badge, but Glenda made so much mixture that the cake grew bigger than the hut! So the troop went in for their hut-building badge instead!

Brave Scottie
Dorothy Heather
Playtime 1919-23 (Amalgamated Press)
'The Adventures of Brave Scottie' began on the full-colour back page of *Playtime* No. 1 (29 March 1919); a tam-o-shantered doll accompanied by large and small dogs named Tim and Binkie. The threesome set off to see the world with versified captions:

> There's pints of ocean, lumps of rock,
> And forests rich and green,
> And pounds and pounds of golden sand
> That I have never seen!

Brett Brand
Illustrator unknown
Zip 1958-59 (Odhams)
'Brett Brand of the British Railways' was a special investigator in the double-standard days of steam and electricity, when almost every boy still wanted to grow up to be an engine driver. Working with Colonel Raven of the Special Branch, Brett catches a gang of spies at the cost of derailing a freight train. However, the load of secret warheads turns out to be a load of rubbish, to decoy the spies from the real thing – which went by road. 'A double bluff that paid off!' smiled Brett, lighting his pipe.

Brett Marlowe
John Fordice
Lion 1952-55 (Amalgamated Press)
'The Case of the Tailor's Dummy' was the first one for Brett Marlowe, detective. He solved it on 23 February 1952 in No. 1 of *Lion*. Marlowe lived in a Chelsea flat and owned a Silver Lynx sports car which was driven for him by his daredevil, uniformed chauffeur and assistant, Rusty Race, who called Marlowe 'chief'. Marlowe quickly nabbed Muggsy Gill for the theft of the gold tiger of Sabadah: he spotted that Muggsy had his false arms on the wrong way round!

Brimstone Bobs and Billy Belgium
Illustrator unknown
Picture Fun 1914-15 (Trapps Holmes)
'Brimstone Bobs and That Brick Billy Belgium' were the patriotic page-one stars of *Picture Fun*, signing up for World War 1 on 21 November 1914. 'Ever since the war broke out they've been practising the goose step. "What's good for the goose is good for the gander!" sez Bobs, "and we're going to pay the Kaiser with his own coin!"' In no time, they were 'making 'em bustle in Berlin', fooling Kaiser Bill and his Little Willie at least once a week. 'Ve must get oud of dis in kvicksticks! Come vay home, Villie!'

The Brownie Boys
Bertie Brown
Rainbow 1914-56 (Amalgamated Press)
The Brownie Boys attended Dr Acorn's School. They all looked alike, and the only way you could tell Peter Pippin from the rest was that he was the one in the black. The rest wore red, as befitted those who sported on the two-colour centre spread of *Rainbow*. Their names were Dicky Dandelion, Billy Buttercup, and Artie Artichoke, and they had many adventures with such fairy-tale folk as Aladdin, the Babes in the Wood, and even the evil Bluebeard. Their last artist was Freddie Crompton (illustrated).

Brian's Brain
Barrie Mitchell
Smash 1966-68 (Odhams)
While world scientists struggled to invent a robot masterbrain, in England, Professor Kingsley, working in his small private laboratory, created a real brain, the most powerful brain the world had ever known. Meanwhile, the professor's son Brian was having his birthday alone, father having forgotten in the excitement of completing his experiment. Then, when his father was kidnapped by foreign spies, Brian heard the voice of the brain: 'Take me with you wherever you go!' So Brian packed it in a cardboard box and took it to school. Then the adventures began.

Brownie
Alan Gelli
Tip Top 1941-45 (Amalgamated Press)
'The Tale of a Moorland Pony' was not only an eventful one (it took five years to tell), it was told by Brownie the pony himself! Not in speech balloons, of course, but in the narrative printed underneath the pictures. His early adventures with gypsies and escaped convicts gave way to a more humorous approach once he was conscripted into the army. Even when he catches some escaped Germans ('Heil! We have away got!'), he does so by shaking a Colonel out of an apple tree on top of them!

Bruce the Circus Dog
Illustrator unknown
Girls Crystal 1953-55 (Amalgamated Press)
Bruce the Circus Dog was the back-page serial star of *Girls Crystal*, a story paper that converted to a comic with No. 909 (21 March 1953). He belonged to young Lena but, no sooner had she signed with the circus, than she was kidnapped by the strongman's daughter. Bruce broke his tether and was soon on the track of the kidnap car. It was but the start of Bruce's problems, for soon Lena was off to Canada, leaving him behind. But Bruce made the boat and then he was following the rascally Hubert Grange and Clem who were after Lena's mystery wigwam.

Bruno, Lionel, and Percy Piggins
Fred Robinson
Golden 1937-40 (Amalgamated Press)
'Kwaint and Komical Adventures' was the billing for this trio, Bruno the Bear, Lionel the Sea-lion, and Percy Piggins. The latter, a pompous young porker, was the only one of the animals to sport clothing, if a teacher's mortar board and Eton collar can so be termed. But then Percival was a posh pig, being the son of Lord Bacon and a chipolata off the old chopping block. They lived in a world of humanized animals, including L. E. Phant and Policeman Hippo.

Buck an' Nero
Albert Pease
Chips 1926-30 (Amalgamated Press)
'Our Saucy Smugglers' shipped aboard the *Jolly Roger* under Captain Dogsbody, sneaking around the shores of England and elsewhere, doing their best to dodge their sworn enemy, Cuthbert the Coastguard. They were of classic comic proportions, Nero being described as 'a lanky loob', and Buck his 'portly pal'. When their irascible cap'n set sail for Timbuctoo, they fooled him by anchoring a starfish to the bowsprit. Mistaking the critter for the North Star, Cappy steered backwards to Cocklesea Cove and the lads popped off to the pictures!

Bubbles the Boy Clown
Freddie Crompton
Bubbles 1921-41 (Amalgamated Press)
Bubbles the Boy Clown had a career as long as his comic: as this was also called *Bubbles*, the achievement may not be so surprising. His subtitle was 'And His Clever Pets', which were a quintet of dogs. Like their owner, they all dressed in clown costume. They could also speak, and called each other 'Boys!' Their names were Jock, the scottie terrier, Pinkie the pug, Pat, possibly an Irish hound, and the twin puppies, Tinkle and Tiny. They could write, too, taking it in turns to describe their weekly adventures. Clever Pets indeed!

Buck Jones
J. H. Valda
Film Fun 1933; *Comet* 1949; *Cowboy Comics* 1950; *Sun* 1951 (Amalgamated Press)
'The Ace of Cowboys' rode into *Film Fun* in 1933, the first adventure hero in that otherwise all-comic comic. Also unusual was the fact that his serial strips were all adaptations of his western films, produced by Universal Pictures. Buck's best artist of his prewar period was Joseph 'Jos' Walker (illustrated). After the war, Buck rode again in the weekly *Comet* and the monthly *Cowboy Comics*, drawn by Geoff Campion, but Buck never saw them: he died in 1942.

Buck Wilson
Jack Glass
Dandy 1937-38 (D. C. Thomson)
'Buck Wilson, the stalwart young rider from Texas, came down the prairie trail to Five Forks on Snowfire, his great white horse. Buck was a roving rider who carried all his belongings tied to his saddle.' Not quite all, for Buck was plucking a banjo. As his subtitle said, this was 'The story in pictures of a Singing Cowboy and his Wonder Horse'. But, being the first issue of *Dandy* (4 December 1937), by picture number two, Buck had tucked his banjo into his saddle and was galloping to the rescue of Little Benny, carried off by a grizzly bear!

Buffalo Bill
Ned Buntline
Butterfly 1936; *Knockout* 1940; *Comet* 1950-59 (Amalgamated Press); *Buffalo Bill* 1948-53 (Boardman); *Buffalo Bill Cody* 1955-56 (Miller)
Colonel William F. Cody, the famous scout of the old west, was a favourite story-paper hero long before comic strips. G. W. Backhouse drew his adventures on the back page of *Butterfly*, and Steve Chapman (illustrated) was one of many artists who drew Bill's six-page adventures in *Comet*. The T. V. Boardman two-tone comicbooks originally reprinted a foreign strip by Lennart, but this was soon made his own by Denis McLoughlin, beginning with 'Buffalo Bill Meets Yellowhand' (August 1949).

The Bumpty Boys
Freddie Crompton
Tiger Tim's Weekly 1920-40 (Amalgamated Press)
'The Funny Adventures of the Bumpty Boys' began on the front page of No. 1 of *Tiger Tim's Weekly*, 31 January 1920, moved inside in 1939, and stayed until the final issue on 18 May 1940. The Bumpty Boys, triplets named Humpty, Dumpty, and Bumpty, lived at Dr Parsley's School, where they shared an upstairs single with their inseparable pet, a flop-eared white rabbit called Billy Bunny. Their playmates were nursery-rhyme folk, like greedy Tommy Tucker and, rather confusingly, an egg called Humpty Dumpty!

Bully Beef and Chips
Jimmy Hughes
Dandy 1967- (D. C. Thomson)
Bully Beef is the musclebound lout in the black-and-yellow striped shirt and the pudding-basin haircut. Chips is the chap in the checked jacket and six little kiss-curls. For twenty years they have been battling it out on the back page of *Dandy*, and still no armistice seems in sight. This, despite the fact that, for all big Beef's bullying, little Chips invariably turns the tables in the last picture, after many a 'Yaroo!', 'Ooaah!', 'Ooyah!', 'Howl!', and 'Groan!', always neatly lettered in red ink.

Bunny Cuddles
Hugh McNeill
Playhour 1959-75 (IPC)
Bunny Cuddles was another of Hugh McNeill's delightful rabbits (see Harold Hare and Flopsy Flufftail), a short-eared bun who lived in Leafy Wood with his best friend, Tiny Mole. There were two things Bunny Cuddles liked best in the world: one was buying jam, the other was eating it! In fact, Bunny's diet consisted solely of jam, and his motto was, 'You can't eat too much of a good thing, especially jam!' Small wonder he was soon billed as Funny Bunny Cuddles.

Bumpkin Billionaires
Mike Lacey
Whoopee 1974-85; *Whizzer & Chips* 1985- (IPC)
Dawn broke over Bumpkin Farm on 9 March 1974 in No. 1 of *Whoopee*. 'There's nothing I loikes better than to greet the morn by breathin' the rich smell of the compost heap!!' said Pa as he tackled Ma's tasty toasted mangel-wurzel. Then came a knock, the first visitor for fifteen years come Michaelmas. Pa's treble chance pool had come up: 'Well, dang my old boots! Poile of money be bigger than my compost heap!' So Pa bought a mansion and moved in with the kids, Billy and Daisy. Champagne corks were soon popping – to scare the birds, while Pa mowed the Persian carpet to make it neat! By 1976 they had moved to the front page in colour.

The Bunsey Boys
Illustrator unknown
Wonder 1901-06 (Harmsworth)
Percy and Ferdie the Bunsey Boys were Britain's answer to Hans and Fritz the Katzenjammer Kids. Not only look-alikes, they were act-alikes, spending the front page of their *Wonder* (later *Jester*) plotting elaborate pranks upon Sister Mary's jolly Cholly – 'Pojozzoks!' – or their regular butt, Happy Ike the tramp in the tin-can titfer. (Yes, Ike was a swipe, too, from the American Happy Hooligan!) 'Before you could say obbywobbletintakwumparooster fourteen times sideways, there wos a large heep on the grownd, of which Ike formed harf!' And, like the Katz Kids, the Bunseys ended bum-uppards in a striking pose!

The Bunty Boys
Herbert Foxwell
Bubbles 1921-41 (Amalgamated Press)
'Mrs Bunty's Boarding School' was modelled on those similar establishments of education run by Mrs Bruin and Mrs Hippo, the only difference being that Mrs Bunty and her Bunty Boys were all humans (save for Wuffie their pet pup). The mischief they got up to was almost identical, as was the artwork: not surprising – same artist. Jackie was the British boy, the rest being boarders from around the world: Hans the jolly Dutchie, Redwing the Indian, Ching the Chinee, Snowball the Eskimo, and Pompey the Nig (*sic*).

Buster
Reg Smythe
Buster 1960- (Fleetway)
Buster was originally billed as 'Son of Andy Capp', the popular *Daily Mirror* strip character created by Reg Smythe. He is the titular star and front-page hero of *Buster*, the first major comic published by the Mirror Group after its takeover of the Amalgamated Press. Buster's family connections were quietly dropped in 1961, although his classic clobber has remained obstinately Andy-like, notably the outsize floppy cap. Many artists have drawn him, including the Spaniards Nadal and Rafart, Hugh McNeill and Reg Parlett, and his adventures have included 'Buster's Dream World' and 'Buster's Diary'.

The Buzzies and the Fuzzies
Gordon Bell
Buzz 1973-75 (D. C. Thomson)
Inspired by the Gonks, those fat little stuffed dolls of the 'Sixties, these equally fat little fellows came in two varieties: the Buzzies were as bald as boiled eggs, and the Fuzzies as hairy as coconuts. These rival tribes were forever at loggerheads, and every strip ended up in a battle royal, whether there were only two of them involved, or a hundred. They had funny ways of talking, too. Cried the Buzzies: 'Get offs! You is a lousy pop groups!' Replied the Fuzzies: 'But we is a smashin' bop groups!', bopping Buzzies with their guitars to prove it.

Burglar Bertie
George Davey
Comic Life 1911-17 (Henderson)
Burglar Bertie stole into *Comic Life*'s centre spread, following a career of comic crime blazed by the likes of Chokee Bill. Once a week for seven years, he cracked a crib, only to be nabbed by the narks and sentenced to another ninety-nine years in the nick. One of Bill's more notable escapades was in 1912, when he was captured by some shemale suffragettes and forced to blow up Winston Churchill. As the bomb contained nothing but fireworks and 'Votes for Women' leaflets, Bill was let off – with another ninety-nine years!

Buster, Linda and Pip
Roy Wilson
Sparkler 1937-39 (Amalgamated Press)
Buster, Linda and Pip were not the usual front-page family trio. Buster was a schoolboy whose bespectacled dad ran the village grocery store; Linda was his girl chum, and Pip was the pup that shared them both. Their adventures began to gravitate towards the schoolroom, especially when they moved to an inside page, and artist H. C. Milburn (illustrated) revolved his slapstick pranks around Miss Sophie Stodgers the teacher, and especially Mona Snoop the sneak. 'What fun to be sure!' sniggered Miss Stodgers.

B. Ware
Steve Bright
School Fun 1983-84; *Buster* 1984-85 (IPC)
The shiny sign said 'B. Ware – Caretaker', but somebody scribbled an 'e' after the 'B'. Mr Ware first polished his plaque in No. 1 of *School Fun* (15 October 1983) and soon showed his mettle. 'What a wonderful place school is,' he mused, 'Except when they're here!' The pupils began to arrive. 'Wipe your feet, you little pests!' he shouted at the kids, but it was a different B. Ware when the Head arrived. 'Allow me to gently wipe the dust from your shoes, headmaster, sir!' A maniac for cleanliness, the caretaker succeeded in smothering everyone with clay by the end of his first day.

Cadman
Mike Dorey
Victor 1973-83 (D. C. Thomson)
'The Coward of the Fighting 43rd' was the title of the strip that introduced a new kind of hero to comics. It was in *Victor* No. 625 (10 February 1973) that the editorial headline read: 'Starts today! A super tale about the biggest cad in the cavalry. He's a liar, a cheat, a coward, and an out-and-out rotter.' In the summer of 1914, Lieutenant Gerald Cadman returned from leave to rejoin his regiment, Prince Rupert's Horse. Up to his eyes in gambling debts with Benny the Bookie, Cadman shoots a blackmailer who turns out to be a German spy and thus becomes the first British soldier wounded in the war! Only batman Tom Smith knew the truth.

Calamity Kate
George Martin
Buzz 1973-75 (D. C. Thomson)
'When Kate comes along – All goes wrong!' Calamity Kate was a classic comic tomboy. Dressed in a red checked shirt, black jeans, sneakers, and with a mop of unruly yellow hair, readers of *Buzz* No. 1 (20 January 1973) might easily have mistaken her for a boy had it not been for her boldly lettered name. Her Dad, of course, was the regular victim of Kate's cut-ups, but these were mostly accidental (as when she upset a tin of black paint on a skating pond and everyone thought it was a hole in the ice), or well meaning (as when she made some paste in a bucket and dad flung it all over his car!)

Calamity Jane
Hugh Morren
Beezer 1956-60 (D. C. Thomson)
'All is quiet – till Jane starts a riot!' The riot was usually accidental, but it managed to fill a full page of *Beezer* every week from No. 1 (21 January 1956). All this curly topped angel child had to do was stroll along a street: one loose shoelace and the damage escalated frame by frame until all hell seemed to explode. Calamity Jane (her name inspired by the Doris Day musical about the wild western heroine) was regularly taken home to her parents in the final frame. (Mum and Dad, by the way, shared similar hairstyles.) The payoff was the cry of 'Oh! Calamity!', a catchphrase borrowed from comedian Robertson Hare.

Calculator Kid
Terry Bave
Cheeky 1978-80; *Whoopee* 1980-85 (IPC)
1 July 1978 was Charlie Counter's birthday, and his Mum and Dad gave him a calculator. Charlie switched it on and it spoke: 'I calculate that you should take two steps backwards!' Charlie followed its instructions and just missed being hit by a dropped brick. But when his calculator told him to take a step backwards again, Charlie ignored it – so another boy picked up the ten pence coin he was standing on! From that moment on, Charlie obeyed his calculator's orders to the letter! Sometimes they seemed odd, as when it told him to wear his mac and carry an umbrella on a sunny day – but he was the only one not to get soaked by a park sprinkler.

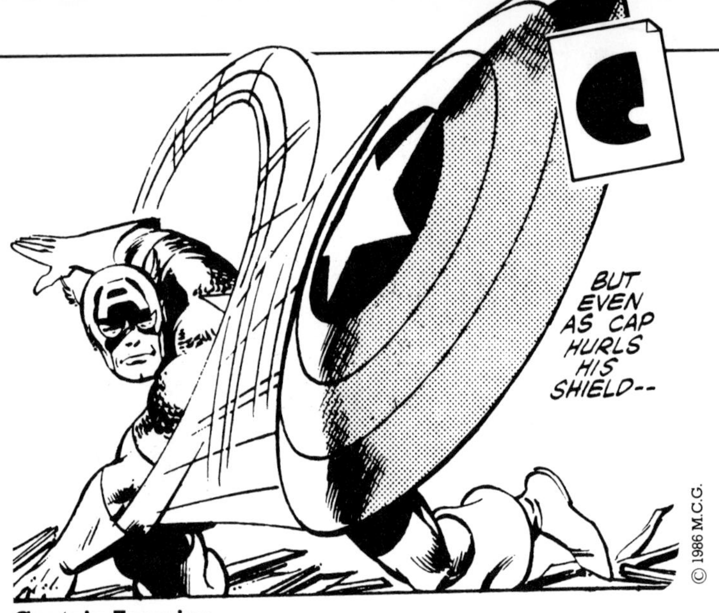

Captain America
Joe Simon, Jack Kirby
Captain America 1954 (Miller); *Titans* 1975-76; *Spiderman* 1977; *Captain America* 1981-82; *Big Ben* 1984 (Marvel)
'Back in the dawning days of World War Two, when Dr Erskine's super-soldier serum transformed frail Steve Rogers into the living dynamo known as Captain America, a life was changed for all time!' This was Stan Lee introducing his superhero in No. 1 of Marvel UK's *Captain America* (25 February 1981). Cap originally appeared in No. 1 of his own title in March 1941, and some of his American comicbooks were reprinted by L. Miller during the 'Fifties. Cap's youthful sidekick is Bucky.

Captain Bungle
George Martin
Topper 1953-60 (D. C. Thomson)
'Captain Bungle – He Lives in the Jungle' strode purposefully into No. 1 of *Topper* (7 February 1953). Your classic British big-game hunter, he wore the regulation gear: solar topee, baggy shorts, and white moustache at the bristle. Captain Bungle's first bag was a giraffe: he bagged it literally – his shorts fell down from above and trapped the long-necked animal to a tall tree! Bungle made the usual mistakes: a rhino for a rock, a croc for a log, but his man Sam was usually on hand to help.

Cap'n Hand
David Law
Beezer 1958-59; 1961-63; *Victor* 1972; 1982 (D. C. Thomson)
(D. C. Thomson)
'Cap'n Hand and his Mutinous Band' sailed into *Beezer* No. 103 on 4 January 1958, skull'n'crossbones a-flutter, cutlasses akimbo, and swashes unbuckled ready for affray. Unfortunately for Cap'n Hand, the affray was mostly between himself and his crew, who preferred the peaceful life rather than the piracy as required by their captain. When the pocket-sized pirate imported a pile of harpoons his crew threw them at him instead of the whale! This strip ran for less than a year but was frequently reprinted.

Captain Britain
Herb Trimpe
Captain Britain 1976-77; 1984-85 (Marvel)
The first superhero specifically designed for British comics by an American publisher, 'The Newest and Greatest Superhero of All' made his debut in *Captain Britain* No. 1 (13 October 1976). Created by the American Marvel Comics team of Chris Claremont (writer), Herb Trimpe, Fred Kida (artists), Marie Severin (colourist), Larry Lieber (editor), and I. Watanabe (letterer), not an Englishman among them, Brian Braddock of Darkmoor Nuclear Research Centre became 'Britain's greatest superhero, defender of the weak and oppressed, destroyer of evil and injustice, the mightiest, most mysterious man on Earth.'

Captain Condor
Ronald Forbes
Lion 1952-64 (Amalgamated Press)
The A.P.'s answer to Dan Dare blasted off on the front page of *Lion* No. 1 (23 February 1952), the A.P.'s answer to *Eagle*. 'Outlaw of Space' was the title of the original serial, scripted by Frank S. Pepper. Set in the year AD 3000 when the Earth was ruled by a dictator, Condor, once an ace pilot of Inter-planet Space Lines, was now exiled to Titan, a convict in a remote solar wilderness. He had refused to carry slaves from Venus to work on the dictator's palace. Now he and pal Pete were planning to escape from the Uranium Mines, guarded by Geeks armed with atomic paralyzers.

Captain Falcon
Frank Black
Rocket 1956 (*News of the World*)
Captain Falcon, Chief of the Moon Base Patrol, was the front-page star of *Rocket*, 'The First Space Age Weekly' which went into circulation on 21 April 1956. Commodore Fortescue-Fortescue, C.O. of Moon Base, was 'Forty-Forty' to Sparrow Smith and Crash Kale, two new fledglings from Earth Base Space Academy. The lads had scarcely landed on the Moon when Patrol Ship *Beta* reported an attack by unknown enemy craft off Phobos, one of the moons of Mars. By *Rocket* No. 2 Falcon and his crew were on their way in the new Space Ranger, the *Hawkins*.

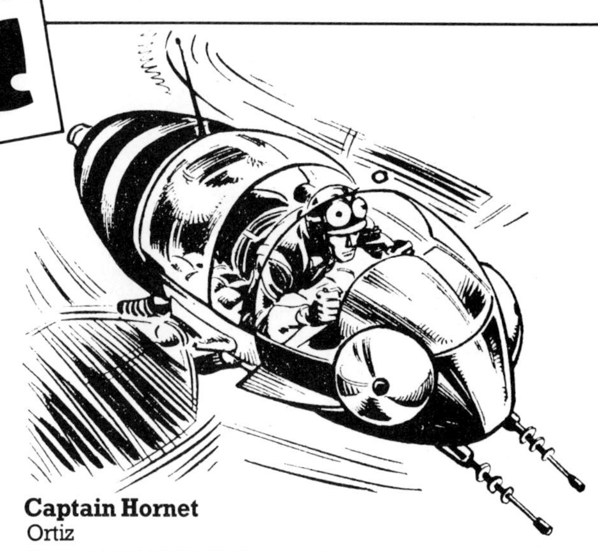

Captain Hornet
Ortiz
Hornet 1972-76 (D. C. Thomson)
'Bugman' was the contemptuous name crooks had for him, but soon they would be held paralyzed by the twin rays which arched down from his aircraft's antennae. Captain Hornet was a red-uniformed crimebuster who used superscience in his all-out, one-man war against crime. The Captain patrolled the darkened streets of London in his mobile headquarters, a fantastic laboratory disguised as a van, Hornet Removals. Spotting crime on his T. V. screen, locating bankrobbers with his seismograph, Hornet first flew into action in his amazing Hornet-Hoverer on 14 October 1972, in *Hornet* No. 475.

Captain Future
Norman Light
Spaceman 1953-54 (Gould-Light)
'In the year 1986 man at last broke the chains that bound him to the Earth! The first rocket made a successful landing on the moon, and interplanetary travel had begun! But even in the void of space, lawlessness, robbery and violence were not uncommon! The year of AD 2020 saw the formation of a Galactic Police Force known as the Star Rovers Patrol!' Of all the interplanetary pilots, none was so famous as Captain Future, who cried 'Holy space!' as his long-range telepath receiver buzzed with a mayday from the Krishna Republic: 'Zac su nerim! Zfft itz!'

Captain Hurricane
Illustrator unknown
Valiant 1962-76 (Fleetway)
'Thumbs up for No. 1!' said Captain Hurricane, giving the appropriate gesture on the cover of the first *Valiant* (6 October 1962). 'Storm into action with the toughest fighting man of World War II!' headlined the three-and-a-half-page strip that followed, introducing the Mighty Marine and warning readers to 'watch out for his raging furies!' Hurricane was cap'n of a rusty tramp steamer, S.S. *Sweetness*, when he and his mate, Maggot, were torpedoed by the U-484. Enlisting in the Royal Marine Commando, with Maggot as his batman, Hurricane swung into action – and sank the U-484.

The Captain, the Kid and the Cook
Roy Wilson
Jolly 1936-37 (Amalgamated Press)
Aboard the tramp steamer *Sea Rover*, Captain Tug Wilson, Cookie Kelly, and Tim Martin the cabin boy, were beset by a mutinous crew led by burly Black Jake. It happened on the back page of *Jolly* No. 94, on 24 October 1936, and it was not until No. 137 was published on 28 August 1937, that they sighted the good old white cliffs of Dover again. 'Now for a spot of easy!' cried the skipper. They deserved it, having meanwhile saved King Tumba from his wicked Witch Doctor, dealt with Omar the Outlaw, and thwarted Van Zeller and his Boring Machine.

Captain Marvel
Clarence Beck
Captain Marvel 1945-54; *Whiz Comics* 1945-54 (Miller/Fawcett)
Superman's greatest rival, Captain Marvel first appeared in No. 2 of *Whiz Comics* (February 1940) and the later *Captain Marvel Adventures*, two American comicbooks which were later reprinted in much truncated versions by the British publisher, L. Miller & Son. Marvel was in reality an orphaned boy named Billy Batson who was granted the power of turning into the World's Mightiest Mortal by shouting the name of an old wizard, Shazam: Solomon's wisdom, Hercules' strength, Atlas' stamina, Zeus' power, Achilles' courage, Mercury's speed. After a lawsuit, he continued in Britain as Marvelman.

Captain Klep
Kevin O'Neill
Tornado 1979; *2000 AD* 1979 (IPC)
'Faster than a micro-wave oven! Stronger than self-raising flour! Able to cut cleaning time to a quarter!' Such was Captain Klep, somewhat satirical superhero who filled the full-colour back page of *Tornado* (a comic which had as its mascot a 'real-life' superhero called Big E, posed by superhero artist Dave Gibbons!). Klep, anxious to be a full-time superchap, goes to Miniopolis, Mecca of the Mighty, and signs on at the D.H.S.S. (Department of Heroes and Social Security), where he is given the secret identity of Clark Clep, newspaper delivery boy.

Captain Marvel Jr
Mac Raboy
Master Comics 1945-54; *Captain Marvel Jr* 1945-54 (Miller/Fawcett)
Crippled newsboy Freddy Freeman was granted the power to change into a superhero whenever he shouted the name of his personal hero, Captain Marvel. This happened for the first time in *Master Comics* No. 23 (February 1942) and, by November, the character was so popular that he was given his own regular comicbook, *Captain Marvel Jr*. Both titles received reprints in Britain through L. Miller & Son, frequently in attractive two-tone photogravure which made up for the reduction of fifty-six-page comicbooks to a mere sixteen. After legal action, the character was revamped as Young Marvelman.

Captain Phantom
Illustrator unknown
Knockout 1952-54 (Amalgamated Press)
Billed as 'The Man of a Thousand Disguises', Captain Phantom, the Ace of Spies, was one of the first postwar heroes to refight World War 2. Swinging into appropriately red-tinted action across the centre spread, Captain Phantom's popularity grew so fast that a third page of pictures had to be added. Discovering that the Germans are building giant, aircraft-carrying U-Boats in bomb-proof pens in the French port of St Nazaire, Phantom is saved by the ubiquitous Chinese inventor, Hoo Sung and his Rolling Sphere, saviour of Sexton Blake!

Captain Valiant
Mick Anglo
Space Comics 1953-55 (Arnold)
'The Amazing Captain Valiant, Ace of the Interplanetary Police Patrol' starred in a series of sixpenny comicbooks which brought tomorrow into today. 'Sleek space freighters already streak the skies between Earth and the planets. Policing the skies are the superjets of Captain Vic Valiant's Interplanetary Police Patrol [an organization readers were invited to join!]. The exploits of Captain Valiant, tough veteran of space travel and hero of campaigns on Mars, Lurgo and Reus, are known throughout the galaxies. But now, at last, we are privileged to reveal them to you, our Earth readers!'

Captain Vigour
Philip Mendoza
Captain Vigour 1952-53; *Steve Samson* 1953-55 (Sports Cartoons)
'Strongman of Sport', Captain Vigour was an ex-Olympic champion and world-famed strongman, now a member of the Central Olympic Committee. His job was to search Britain and the Commonwealth for athletic talent and, in No. 1 of his comic, he flies off to Africa to investigate a story that a Labadi village boy can run 100 yards in 8.9 seconds: 'It sounds impossible!' He arrives to find the youth, Lahai, in a coma, paralyzed by a ju-ju spell cast by witch-doctor Levuma, but a hand-to-hand battle with giant lizards soon settles matters.

Captain Pugwash
John Ryan
Eagle 1950; *Swift* 1958-59 (Hulton); *Playland* 1974-75; *Pippin in Playland* 1975-76 (Polystyle)
'The story of a Bad Buccaneer & of the many Sticky Ends which nearly befell him' started in No. 1 of *Eagle* (14 April 1950). The Captain's piratical pranks aboard the good ship *Black Pig* with his slumbrous first mate, hideous wife, and cabin boy Tim, originally lasted only nineteen weeks, by which time Admiral Sir Splicemeigh-Maynebrace was thoroughly thwarted. However, artist John Ryan cleaned up the Cap'n for a popular television series, and he sailed again in full colour in several comics.

Carson's Cubs
Illustrator unknown
Lion 1966-70 (Fleetway)
Billed as 'The Most Amazing Football Team in the World', this was Newton Town, a team of teenagers formed by Joe Carson. The lineup read: Curly Mopp, a long-haired cockney ('Yer missed, flashy-pants!'); Rocky Stone; Sammy Fyre and his red-headed brother, Ginger; Pud Perry, whose bulk disguised his agility; Tiddler Smith ('Watch yer flippin' elbow, mate!'); Lord Algernon Davenport ('Con-bally-found it!'); Andy Streak; Twiggy Flint; and Swotty Brayne, who wore contact lenses underneath his spectacles. The club's rascally directors were Arthur Braggart and Herbert Snook.

C

Casey Court
Julius Stafford Baker
Chips 1902-53; *Puck* 1904-08 (Amalgamated Press)
'The Casey Court Rowing Season' opened on the back page of *Chips* on 24 May 1902, and 'The Casey Court Funny Face Contest' was held on 12 September 1953: fifty-two years during which time Billy Baggs and his Nibs neither grew one wrinkle, nor improved their spelling. Signs still read 'Boots Mendid' and 'Washin Dun Ere'! Their artists changed several times, the last being the best, Albert Pease (illustrated). The setting was always the same, a tenement courtyard, and only once did the format expand from one large picture into a strip: when H. O'Neill drew the Casey Kids for the full-colour front of *Puck*.

The Cat Girl
Illustrator unknown
Sally 1969-71; *Tammy* 1971 (IPC)
'Agile as an acrobat, quick as a lightning flash, this is the astonishing story of ordinary Cathy who was to become known as The Cat Girl!' With this peppy preamble, No. 1 of *Sally* (14 June 1969) launched its own superheroine. Cathy's mother was dead and her dad was a private detective, and, up in the attic, she chanced on a casket a grateful witch doctor had sent her dad from Africa. Inside was a cat suit which curious Cathy promptly tried on. 'Now I know what a cat feels like!' she meowed as she found herself leaping over the rooftops to rescue dad from thugs.

Cast-Iron Bill
Pollack
Wizard 1973-78 (D. C. Thomson)
Bill Steele, Britain's toughest goalkeeper, was originally the hero of a long-running series in the prewar story paper, *Rover*. His adventures were translated into picture serials in the revived *Wizard*, also the title of a prewar story paper. Cast-Iron Bill was a top-class goalie and, although he had been offered a place with First-Division team Newfort United, he had chosen to play for the Fourth-Division team, Barrowmere. His friendly butcher, Harry Dent, was chairman, and the team coach was Jack MacCallan, whom Bill called Mad Mac. Bill's inseparable trailhounds were Rikki and Lora.

Cecil the Stone-age Scrapper
Bagnall
Victor 1968-72 (D. C. Thomson)
Pete Pringle found a stone-age caveman preserved in a block of ice. Thawing him out, he named him Cecil and trained the caveman in boxing. He was soon heavyweight champion of the world! Cecil's conversation was fairly limited, as was his diet. 'Nana! Yaroosh! Me like!' he cried, tucking into bananas by the bunch. Everything else he dismissed as 'Punk!' Thus, it was easy for a crooked fight promoter to lure Cecil away in an attempt to secure a win by his man, Basher the Boston Bruiser. In a sequel series entitled 'Cecil: He's in the Army Now!', the caveman joined the Ben Nevis Highlanders.

Chalky
Arthur Martin
Cor 1971-74; *Buster* 1974- (IPC)
'I'm Quick on the Draw!' was the motto of Chalky, the boy artist, and he certainly was. He could rip off a drawing in seconds, so lifelike that it would fool anyone, especially bullies. Luckily for Chalky, his was a black-and-white page, or his sketches might have taken longer than a single panel to complete! When Bully Bates dirtied his mum's washing, Chalky drew a new lineful on the garden wall. Thus, when he went to grab them, the bad lad got a faceful of thud!' 'Ho-ho! Serves you right!', chuckled Chalky.

Chang the Yellow Pirate
Colin Merritt
Joker 1936-39 (Amalgamated Press)
Rare example of a picture serial named for its villain rather than its hero, 'Chang the Yellow Pirate' began on the back page of *Joker* on 18 January 1936. The real heroes were Lieutenant Jack Sanders, Bo'sun Tom Piper, and Midshipman Tony Keen, 'three seafaring chums'. Under orders to capture Chang and his Chinese bandits, and prevent them from blowing up the Wang-Se Dam, it took the three chums to 4 February 1939 to finish the job. Then they continued under a new title as 'The North Sea Patrol'.

Champ
Leo Baxendale
Whizzer & Chips 1969-75 (IPC)
'He's a Champ – or a Chump – as you'll soon see, pals!' was the editorial intro to this wonderkid in *Whizzer & Chips* No. 1 (18 October 1969). 'I'm the greatest!' claimed Champ, posing in front of his trophies: World Marbles Champ, World Sweet-eating Champ, and World Catty Champ (catapult, that is). Practising to be the sack-race champ, Champ bounced down a wet cement path (Spludge!) and got dumped into a coalbin by mistake ('Erk!' Thud!). Next week he tried to be Champion Chipper at football but wound up as Champ Chip Chomper ('Drool!').

Charley's War
Joe Colquhoun
Battle Action 1978- (IPC)
As written by Pat Mills and illustrated by Joe Colquhoun, the war as experienced by Charley Bourne lasted longer in comics (1978-84) than in real life (1914-18). Even longer, perhaps, for, in 1985, poor Charley Bourne went to war all over again, beginning in September 1939. Whether World War 2 will be as carefully and expertly translated into strip form as World War 1 remains to be seen. *Charley Bourne's A-Z of World War I* was a supplement to *Battle Action Force* (8 October 1983): it ran from H.M.S. *Argus* to Zeppelin.

Charlie Chaplin
Bertie Brown
Funny Wonder 1915-44
(Amalgamated Press)
'The Scream of the Earth' was the billing for film star Charlie Chaplin when he made his premier appearance on the front page of *Funny Wonder* No. 72 dated 7 August 1915. At the time, he was with Essanay Films but, from 1919, he was billed as 'The King of the Kinema'. From 1922 to 1932, Charlie was accompanied in his comic strip by 'The Kid' (Jackie Coogan) and a monkey called Mickey, but these companions were pensioned off after Charlie was relegated to an inside page from 22 October (No. 969). Charlie's final strip appearance was on 13 May 1944 (No. 1495), billed as 'The Great Dictator of Laughter'.

Charlie Chuckle
Bert Hill
Dazzler 1933-39 (Target)
Charlie Chuckle was the cheerful front-page star of *Dazzler* No. 1 (19 August 1933), the yellow penny comic published provincially in Bath. Supplying his own commentary under each picture, Charlie begins thus: 'Tother morn I thought I would sit myself upon a capstan and watch the sardines put themselves in cans, and listen to the kippers croon their love lyrics!' But Charlie's idle idyll is soon shattered by a well-placed wader from a salty seadog. Being seated on a capstan, Charlie revolves. 'Gur! Kick me in the neck behind me back, would yer?' and battle commenceth.

Charlie Peace
Jack Pamby
Buster 1964-75 (Fleetway)
'The Astounding Adventures of Charlie Peace' proved surprisingly popular when serialized in *Buster*. The introduction ran: 'Charlie Peace was the most daring and notorious criminal in Victorian London', and each week three pages were devoted to his latest crime. Charlie continually eluded his sworn enemy, Detective Inspector Tim Bannion, occasionally aided by his dog, his parrot, or his vicious goat, Hannibal. Several artists drew Charlie, but it was Jack Pamby (illustrated), who depicted the crook's tour of London 1968 via Professor Date's Time Machine.

Charlie the Chimp
George Ramsbottom
Dandy 1957-60 (D. C. Thomson)
'Charlie the Chimp is a lovable imp – You'll meet him each week in this paper – He plays pranks galore and you'll laugh till you're sore – at every crazy caper!' The editor did himself proud with his introduction to the double-page spreads of slapstick that started in *Dandy* No. 791 (19 January 1957). Charlie was a chimpanzee, brought back from Africa by an injured animal trainer, Mr Marsden. He acted as porter in the crippled man's boarding house, which meant bags of fun and trouble for the trainer's young son Jack.

Charlie Chutney
Allan Morley
Dandy 1944-47 (D. C. Thomson)
'Charlie Chutney the Comical Cook' was a cheerful chef who cooked up a merry mirth-filled menu for *Dandy* readers during the much-rationed 'Forties. From 28 October 1944 to 29 March 1947, he served up all the favourite funny-paper fodder, from plum duff to piping hot pies, cakes with one big cherry on top to puds like cannonballs covered with custard. Charlie's cooking was so good that, when he served up shoe leather in the guise of fried sole as 'own back' on his bad-tempered boss, the man mopped it up and asked for seconds!

Cheeky
Frank MacDiarmid
Krazy 1976-78; *Cheeky* 1977-80; *Whoopee* 1980-85 (IPC)
Cheeky, a toothy kid who will do anything for a laugh and frequently does, was officially a member of The Krazy Gang, the bunch that edited *Krazy*. But he also starred in his own strip, a free-wheeling four pager entitled 'Ello, It's Cheeky!' in which the bestriped boy bombarded everybody in sight with terrible gags. Among his regular victims: Posh Claude ('so posh he has jam on his bread and dripping!'), Young Sherlock, Bump-Bump Bernie, Six-Gun Sam, Gloomy Glad, Baby Burpo, Soppy Louise, Lily Pop the Cracking Crossing-lady, and, perhaps most remarkable of all, Walter Wurx, the only character in a British comic to suffer from a urinary problem!

The Children of the Forest
Vincent Daniel
Bubbles 1922-41 (Amalgamated Press)
The 'Splendid Picture Serial of the Adventures of Arthur and Joan in Robin Hood's Camp' survived for twenty years on a severe shortage of thrills. Arthur and Joan occasionally fell into a hole one week, to be rescued the next week by Strongbow the Dwarf, and once even went so far as to stop birds eating Friar Tuck's cherries with the aid of a roll of netting from Master Chandler's Shop. Otherwise life under the Greenwood Tree was fairly dull, except when Arthur was allowed to blow Robin's horn.

The Chimps
Ray Bailey
Sparkler 1937-39 (Amalgamated Press)
This animal family marks a moment in British comic history: the strip was the first to carry a byline for the artist, Ray Bailey. Chip and Clara were the twin terrors of the Chimp Family, Pa and Ma. Pa, like any non-animal parent in a comic, was invariably at the receiving end of any burst plumbing, exploding fireworks, and other hazards of everyday life, plus, on occasion, Ma's rolling-pin. Small wonder he retired behind a copy of the *Chimpville Times*, rubbing his bumps.

Chokee Bill
Frank Holland
Chips 1895-96; *Comic Home Journal* 1895; *Comic Cuts* 1897-1900; *Jester* 1905 (Amalgamated Press)
Chokee Bill the burglar, and his halfpint henchman, Area Sneaker (originally known as Snaggums the Skinny Kid), were the first comic strip antiheroes. True, they were preceded by tricksters and tramps but, for the first time, outright criminals got away with the loot week after week. From Chokee Bill on, the burglar and his bag became a familiar figure in comicdom. From 27 February 1897, Bill was promoted to the full front page of *Comic Cuts*, where he demonstrated his 'patent noomatic injyrubber booty-bag'.

Chimpo
Roy Wilson
Happy Days 1938-39 (Amalgamated Press)
Chimpo the chimpanzee was chief chuckle-champ of the comical cavalcade of cartoon mammals who cavorted on the cover of *Happy Days* No. 1 (8 October 1938). This was the first full-colour photogravure comic published by A.P. and, naturally, the front page was assigned to their finest artist, Royston Wilson. His strip, 'Happy Days at Chimpo's Circus', exploded all over the cover in a different design every week, and costarred Crackle the Porker, Jolly Jum and their butt, Lordy Leo the ringmaster.

Cholly and Gawge
Fitzpatrick
Jester 1902-03 (Harmsworth)
These merry mashers made their debut across the centre spread of *Jester*, and, even when they later moved to page one, they took with them their decorative panel borders. Plain outlines were clearly unsuitable confines for a pair of romantics like these. Although Cholly was lean and lanky while Gawge was rotund, as a double act, they could not have been less like Weary Willie and Tired Tim. For C & G were rivals for the fair hand of the elegant Miss Tootsie, a pursuit which often landed them in jug.

Chowgli
Frank Wilkinson
Chips 1899-1901 (Harmsworth)
With the inspiration for his name coming from Rudyard Kipling's character, Mowgli, in his *Jungle Book*, Chowgli, a happy little black boy, has the distinction of being the first black hero in British comic strips. Frank Wilkinson, an excellent illustrator, often permitted his characters to break through the borders of his panels, a rarity in those early days. Chowgli's inseparable companion in his six-picture adventures was Stripes, an ever-smiling tiger cub.

Chuckles the Clown
Joe Hardman
Comic Cuts 1912-26 (Amalgamated Press)
Chuckles the Clown was a cheerful circus and stage comedian, whose adventures were short but long. Seldom more than three or four pictures, they ran in *Comic Cuts* for fourteen years. Quickly exhausting gags with his pointed clown's hat (using it as a candle snuffer, a deaf aid, a 'tuppenny tube' to catch mice), artist Hardman gave his hero a rival called Sniggers as a butt for practical pranks. Note how the names tell all: Chuckles is cheerful while Sniggers is sneaky.

Chubblock Homes
Jack B. Yeats
Comic Cuts 1893; *Funny Wonder* 1894-97 (Harmsworth)
The first-ever cartoon burlesque of Sir Arthur Conan Doyle's *Strand Magazine* detective, Sherlock Holmes, appeared in No. 184 of *Comic Cuts* dated 18 November 1893. Only a three-picture strip at first, Jack Yeats developed his series into the first continuing serial strip, and then transferred it to the front page of a companion comic, *Funny Wonder*. The Great Detective, 'who hunted everything from gamps to lost hearts', was assisted in his cases by Shirk the Dog Detective, who was a parody of another fictional character, 'Dirk the Dog Detective' of the comic *Chips*.

Cinderella and the Ugly Sisters
Basil Blackaller
Beano 1940-41 (D. C. Thomson)
Beano's variation of the old fairy story cursed their Cinderella with three ugly sisters (Handie, Nosie, and Earie) instead of the usual two. Cinders, however, was blessed by the addition of a magic slipper which, when rubbed, conjured up a slant-eyed genie known as Goblin. For fairytale folk, their adventures were surprisingly up to date. When the sisters refused to wear their gas masks, Goblin worked a spell: 'O sister's gas masks hear me talking – Come to life, do as I say – When your owners go out walking – Follow them around all day!'

Chubb and Tubb
Harry Banger
Fresh Fun 1940-44; *Extra Fun* 1940; *Slick Fun* 1941-46; *Topical Funnies* 1942; *Thrill Comics* 1942; *War Comics* 1943; *New Funnies* 1943; *Cute Fun* 1948 (Swan)
Chubb and Tubb were a comical couple of cavemen with a family resemblance to Cliff and Clump, an earlier stone-age series by the same artist in *Rattler* (1938). Chubb and Tubb, unusual for a double act in that both were short and fat, made their double-page debut in No. 1 of *Fresh Fun* (April 1940). They went on to appear in almost every Swan comicbook during their ten-year run. Their first problem was with Tum-Tum, the Grub Cadger, but they were soon bedevilled by such prehistoric beasties as the Brontowotsit and the Long Necked Thingamajig.

Class Wars/Top of the Class
Nigel Edwards
Jackpot 1979-82; *Buster* 1982- (IPC)
At one end of town lived the posh kids: 'Children! Do come and have tea and muffins!' At the other end lived the scruffy kids: 'Erbert! if you're not home for tea in two minutes, your dad'll come and sort you out!' They went to different schools until the council decided to combine them into one. The result was class wars in the classroom – scruffy horrors versus toffee-nosed twits. Even the traditional goodwill time of Christmas was another excuse for battle. For presents, one lot gave the other socks, literally, on the nose! The title changed to 'Top of the Class' in 1980.

Claude and Cuthbert
Hugh McNeill
Comet 1951-53; *Buster* 1960 (Amalgamated Press)
'The Adventures of Claude and Cuthbert' started on the back page of *Comet* No. 152 on 16 June 1951. Two weeks later, they were filling the front page: promotion came fast at St Michael's School – although, oddly enough, the long and short schoolboys were still being billed as 'The Two New Boys' when they went on a long 'vac' two years later. Claude Ford and Cuthbert Bunn, a well-meaning but accident-prone pair, were the bane of Dr Driver, the benign headmaster, Mr Pettigrew, their irascible form master, and old Flowerdew the porter.

Claws
Leslie Harding
Whoopee 1977-80; *Katy* 1986 (IPC)
Known to readers of *Whoopee* as 'Our Furry Friend', Claws' tale was something of a shaggy cat story. This tatty moggy wandered from week to week looking for food and lodging in the traditional Felix-the-Cat manner. His first comic Christmas looked like being a cold one. Meowing at a likely door, Claws begged, 'Can you spare a bite for a poor, hungry stray?' 'Certainly!', barked a vast bulldog, snapping at Claws' tail! But for once, all ended well, as the poor puss found a Junior Father Christmas set and was welcomed into a kids' party as Santa Claws! His name, of course, was inspired by the hungry fish film, *Jaws*.

Claude Duval
Patrick Nicolle
Comet 1954-59 (Amalgamated Press)
Billed as 'The Laughing Cavalier', Claude Duval first flourished his sword in partnership with the fabled Three Musketeers in an adventure involving the young King Charles in France. Speedily promoted to *Comet*'s full-colour centre spread, Claude returned to Roundhead England to set up his own fighting trio with Nick Nevinson and the jolly giant, Jemmy Hind. As before, their main adversary was Major Midas Mould and his Roundhead Secret Police. 'Hola! Cavaliers for ever! Come and get us, you crophead oafs!'

Clever Dick
Leo Baxendale
Buster 1970-75 (IPC)
'The potty young inventor who always creates a sensation' created quite a few on his first appearance in *Buster*, 7 February 1970. Dick started the day with porridge, fed to him via spoons fixed to his clockwork helicopter: 'Blurp! Spludge!' But he was still late for school so, next morning, a complicated porridge feeder was strapped to his back. Unfortunately, it shot its load under teacher's feet: 'Skid! Aaagh! Crash!' Awarded 500 lines, Dick invented a line-writing machine: a fat boy fixed to a sweet-stoking device.

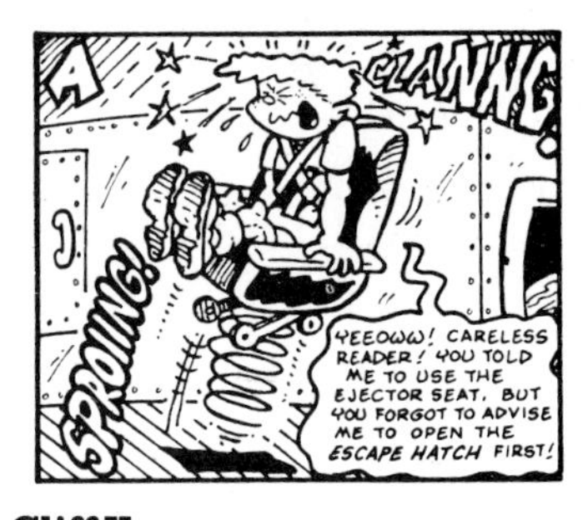

Cliff Hanger
J. Edward Oliver
Buster 1983- (IPC)
This is an ingenious series which gives readers of *Buster* a choice of endings. Cliff Hanger, a curly topped kid, is, for reasons best known to cartoonist, Jack Oliver, ever beset by the Mysterious Evil Spies Society (MESS for short), motto: Abolish Tuesdays. On orders from their Big Boss, they observe young Cliff's activities through their powerful telly, then use their Acme Ray Co ray to zap him into some perilous, cliff-hanging situation. The page ends with readers being given a choice: should Cliff go for A, B, or C? Turning hastily to the Letters Page, we see what would happen in each case.

Clip McCord, Special Agent
Reg Bunn
Sun 1950-52 (Amalgamated Press)
Clip McCord, ace reporter of the *Daily Bugle*, and his girl assistant, Mary Trent, were already in action when his serial started in *Sun* No. 68 (27 May 1950). Rounding up the Montelli gang single handed, Clip then received a note telling him to go to Barney's Barber Shop in Westminster and ask for a close shave. Clip got one: he was despatched to the cellar in best Sweeney Todd style! There he met Colonel Wye of Department 5, Military Intelligence: 'You're just the man to help us unmask a plot against Britain! Are you game?' Of course he was!

Cloris and Claire/Sue and Prue
Roy Wilson
June 1961-64; *Sally* 1969-70 (IPC)
'Here's a Cheery Twosome who have lots of Fun with Games!' was the headline that introduced Cloris and Claire the Sporting Pair to readers of *June* No. 1 (18 March 1961). Cloris was tall and thin, Claire was short and slim, and they were the schoolgirl counterparts of shorty Sporty and his pal, skinny Sidney, of *Knockout* fame. Indeed, many of Cloris and Claire's strips were reworked from Sporty's, with the odd sex change: for cricket read hockey! Reprinted in *Sally* as 'Sue and Prue the Clueless Two.'

The Cloak
Mike Higgs
Pow 1967-68; *Smash* 1968-69 (Odhams)
This rather odd-looking, slightly superhero was dressed all in black, had bulging eyeballs, and no nose. Assisted by the blank-eyed, bespectacled Mole and an oddity called Shortstuff, the Cloak was despatched on a series of strange missions by a very ordinary looking Chief. Most of his adventures touched on the supernatural, as when he unwittingly conjured up Warlock the Wizard, Master of the Mystic Arts. 'Skin and bones and clotted gravy, let a demon come to save me!' chanted the Cloak, and it did!

Clumsy Colin
David Mostyn
Buster 1984-85 (IPC)
Clumsy Colin is a character from the crisp packets who crashed into *Buster* as a comic-strip hero in his own right, although a small credit notes that Clumsy Colin is the copyright of K. P. Skips. Based on Hell's Angels bikers, Colin's clumsiness may be partly because he is always wearing black goggles. His attempt to emulate his pop idols, Marc Rizza and the Creepers, was so ear bending that he made more money by being bribed to shut up! Although not strictly an advertising strip, K. P. Skips produced a Clumsy Colin Broom-Broom Bike as a noise-making free gift in *Buster* (21 September 1985).

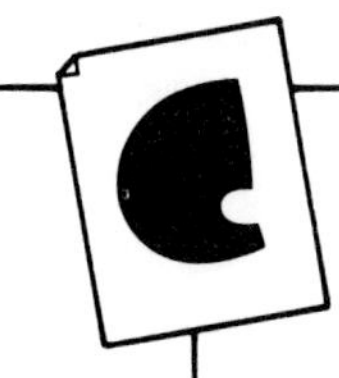

Coal Black Jones
Harry Banger
Topical Funnies 1940; *War Comics* 1941; *Thrill Comics* 1941; *Fresh Fun* 1941; *Slick Fun* 1941-46 (Swan)
Coal Black Jones, given the period in which he was popular, was the only black hero to be treated exactly as any similar white hero: he was a typical boy. Unusually in British comics, Jones cut his capers in a totally black environment: no 'white folks' interfered with his everyday life, and the only non-black was his mongrel dog, Hannibal. Artist Banger's concept of a Southern shanty town was inspired by Hollywood films, and his lingo by radio's *Kentucky Minstrels*: 'Dat book am drivin' dis coon crackers!'

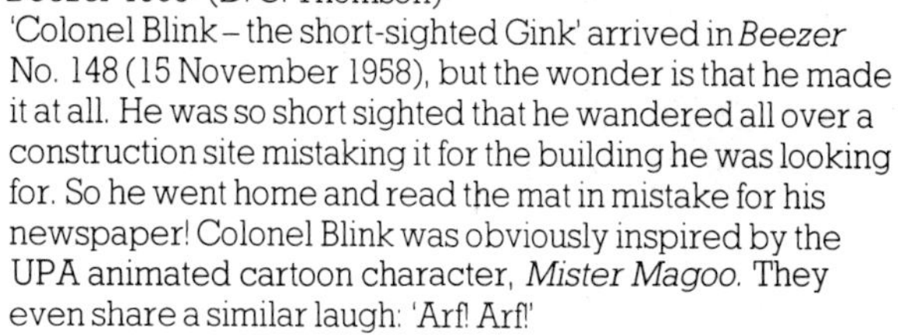

Colonel Blink
Carmichael
Beezer 1958- (D. C. Thomson)
'Colonel Blink – the short-sighted Gink' arrived in *Beezer* No. 148 (15 November 1958), but the wonder is that he made it at all. He was so short sighted that he wandered all over a construction site mistaking it for the building he was looking for. So he went home and read the mat in mistake for his newspaper! Colonel Blink was obviously inspired by the UPA animated cartoon character, *Mister Magoo*. They even share a similar laugh: 'Arf! Arf!'

Cocky Dick
Allan Morley
Beano 1940-47 (D. C. Thomson)
'Cocky Dick' – He's Smart and Slick!' flew into the wartime pages of *Beano*, wearing a red-and-blue striped pullover and a little black flat cap. Dick was the epitome of the chirpy cockney sparrow. He always came out on top despite the handicap of no hands, only wings (a problem he shared with that other *Beano* bird, Big Eggo). As a typical couplet claimed: 'Cocky will win your admiration – As the funniest birdie in the nation!'

Colorado Kid
John Wheeler
Colorado Kid 1954-59 (Miller)
'Howdy folks! Here's your new western comic, brim full of rootin' tootin' shootin' authentic stories of the Old West! Look inside for red-blooded action, thrills and excitement!' So spoke the Colorado Kid from the cover of his first comicbook (May 1954), produced in the American format by King-Ganteaume Productions for publishers L. Miller & Son. Originally intended to star the radio cowboy Cal McCord, star of *Riders of the Range*, last-minute changes left the hero with only his sidekick, Wyoming Joe, unchanged.

Code-name Warlord
Various Illustrators
Warlord 1974- (D. C. Thomson)
How Lord Peter Flint, Britain's ace racing driver, became Britain's top wartime secret agent was told in an unprecedented nine-page strip in No. 1 of *Warlord* (28 September 1974). On the day war broke out, Lady Bencham presented his lordship with a white feather; that same day he was off to Austria to recover a new alloy for aircraft manufacture under orders from the mysterious Kingpin. He was given the code-name Warlord and was soon running the Warlord Agents club from H.Q., 20 Cathcart Street, Kentish Town, NW5: entry fee 20 pence.

The Comical Kittens
L. Church
Tiny Tots 1927-55 (Amalgamated Press)
Their names were Tibby, Tabby, and Tinker (Tibby was the black one, Tabby had stripes, and Tinker, for no clear reason, wore a circus clown's costume) and they made their first appearance in No. 1 of *Tiny Tots*, a hyphenated comic for very young children, published 22 October 1927. Their artist, L. Church, was evidently obsessed by the nursery rhyme of 'The Three Little Kittens', for several of his (her?) strips followed this formula: 'Blackie, Tabby and Pops the Three Comical Kittens' in *Bubbles* (1921), 'Those Naughty Kittie Kats' in *Playtime* (1922), and 'Tibby, Tabby and Tubby' in *Comic Life* (1922).

The Comp
Ron Lumsden
Nikki 1985- (D. C. Thomson)
Samantha Greene, known as 'Sam', began her first term at Redvale Comprehensive School, known as 'the Comp', on 23 February 1985 in No. 1 of *Nikki*. The Greenes had been living in Germany for a few years, and Sam soon attracted the attention of the only German boy in the school, Klaus 'the class creep'. Sam's chums in class 3M are Julie, Lisa, and Megan, while her enemies are Lorraine Grover and her gang. Then there is the Deputy Head, 'Goggles' Graham, and the French teacher, Mr Russell, soon to receive a forged love letter.

Constable Cuddlecook
G. M. Payne
Jester 1909-40 (Amalgamated Press)
'The Comical Capers of Constable Cuddlecook', known in the 'Twenties as 'P.C. Cuddlecook, the Pride of the Force', filled the front page of the *Jester* for most of his thirty-two-year run. For part of his career, he was assisted by Percy the Pup Detective (1910) or Bobbie the Terrier Tec (1922): both sleuthhounds wore helmets, but Percy's flew the Union Flag! For a shameful while in 1920, Cuddy's name was dropped from the title of the strip in favour of his quarry: 'Slim Jim – They're After Him!' Cuddy's boss, fat Inspector Flipflap, was superseded by sawn-off Inspector Spadger.

Consternation Street
Reg Parlett
Buster 1965 (Fleetway); *Smash* 1970 (IPC)
Inspired by the long-running soap opera on Granada Television, *Coronation Street*, this unusual strip featured a cast which read from left to right: Cutprice the grocer who owned the corner store; Miss Primm the spinster and her pets, two pussies and a parrot; Colonel Curry and Caesar, his bully bulldog; the broke but cheerful Ardupp family; and the posh lot, the Snobs. The street was patrolled by Constable Clott. Involving this vast cast in a weekly plot was a tour-de-force by artist Reg Parlett.

Conan the Barbarian
Robert E. Howard
Savage Sword of Conan 1975-85; *Avengers* 1975-76; *Marvel* 1976-79; *Valour* 1980-81; *Future Tense* 1981 (Marvel)
'Come with us to the Hyborian Age! Come with us back to the dark centuries which sprawl between the sinking of Atlantis and the dawn of recorded time – to the days when the now forgotten land of Aquilona was the mightiest of nations – and a man's life was worth no more than the strength of his sword-arm! Come with us now to the raw, untamed world of Conan the Barbarian!' And so the saga began in No. 1 of the American comicbook in October 1970, illustrated by Barry Smith. British reprints began 8 March 1975.

Contrary Mary
Roland Davies
Beano 1938-40 (D. C. Thomson)
'Mary the Moke is Fond of a Joke!' is the best-remembered catchline for this character, although her original bill matter in *Beano* No. 1 (30 July 1938) was 'You can't play a joke – On Mary the Moke!' This lovable little donkey was different from the average comic animal: she had no voice, wore no clothes, and generally behaved much as a real-life donkey might, given the advantage of human intelligence. This was doubtless due to Mary's artist, Roland Davies, who was the creator of another four-legged friend, 'Come On Steve' of the *Sunday Express*.

Copycat
Graham Allen
Magic 1976-79 (D. C. Thomson)
'This cute little kitten likes to copy what he sees. That's why everyone calls him Copycat.' Thus, the editorial introduction to Copycat in No. 1 of *Magic* (31 January 1976). *Magic* was a new comic with new characters, yet there was much that was familiar about it. The title had been that of Thomson's 1939 comic for young children, which had been killed off by the wartime paper shortage; and Copycat looked familiar to anyone who had ever seen a copy of *Dandy*. If this kitten looked like a halfpint version of Korky the Cat, small wonder: as the editor explained, Korky was his uncle!

Coronation Street School
Colin Watson
School Fun 1983-84 (IPC)
The gang that gathered behind the bicycle sheds in *School Fun* No. 1 (15 October 1983) was a group that looked vaguely familiar. Their names had a familiar ring, too: Ken, Annie, Vera, Eddie, Fred, Mavis . . . These were the kids of Coronation Street School, a clever swipe both at and of the popular Granada Television soap opera. In the opening two-page episode, the junior versions of the familiar adult characters scheme to get a school tuckshop built. Named in honour of Mavis finding the builder's lost puppy, it is called 'Rover's Return'!

Cornelius Dimworthy
Sam Fair
Eagle 1964-66 (Odhams)
Cornelius Dimworthy, Corny to his chums, was the dreamiest, yet luckiest, fourth former in Moorlake School. He was always stumbling into something, such as his accidental discovery of a new, dynamic fuel for his model aeroplane. 'Dimworthy's Dart' is a soaring success, but not with form-master Flynn: it swipes off his mortarboard, much to the joy of Corny's bitter rivals, Smythe and Sweeting. As Corny would say, 'Great goosegogs!' Later, this expletive changed to 'Cosmic cauliflowers!' when he saw a Flying Saucer.

Corporal Clott
David Law
Dandy 1960-75 (D. C. Thomson)
Corporal Clott joined the Army by accident on 12 November 1960, in *Dandy* No. 990. Despite the luxury of the entire centre spread in full colour, Clott did not like the Army, and the Army did not like Clott. It was a war that was destined to continue well beyond the death of creative cartoonist David Law, whose scratchy heyday was the mid-'Sixties when he shipped Clott, Colonel Grumbly, and all out to the desert to do their short-trousered bit among Sheik Shadrar's awful Arabs.

Crackaway Jack
Paddy Brennan

Dandy 1955-60 (D. C. Thomson)
Modestly billed as 'The Greatest Western Picture-story of All Time', the adventures of Crackaway Jack, pioneer scout, began with a bang in *Dandy* No. 716, on 13 August 1955. He blew up the peak of Fire Mountain with gunpowder. 'The gods are angry!' cried Leaping Buffalo, chief of the Arapahos, enabling Jack to chop down and steal their sacred Eagle Totem. Jack was saved from certain death in the rapids by Red Mask, a mystery boy who cracked a snappy whip.

Crackers the Pup
Don Newhouse

Crackers 1932-41 (Amalgamated Press)
Billed variously as 'Our Merry Pup' and 'The Perky Pup', Crackers, cunningly christened after his comic, ambled on to the scene in No. 158 and stayed to No. 615. It was the last number of *Crackers*, and the last of Crackers, too. But he was always a homeless hound, wandering the wayside looking for any old bones that might get bunged his way. Then, with a doff of his battered old titfer, and what passed for a wag of his stumpy tail, he would sling his hammock with a satisfied sigh of 'F'lup!'

Crazy Kink
Bert Hill

Rattler 1933-36 (Target)
'The Goofy Gangster', front-page star from No. 1 of *Rattler*, 19 August 1933, reflected the current craze for Chicago-style crooks in Yankee talkies. Kink begins with a bang, exercising his pistol as it's flag day for the unemployed gangsters' association. 'Gee, I could shoot the whiskers off a goosegog with my eyes shut!', he boasts, banging away at an old iron man. 'I'm the big noise with a gun! I could shoot an elephant down to a greyhound!' But, despite regular jugging in jail, he was always at it again next week.

Cracker Jack
Jack Glass

Beano 1938-39 (D. C. Thomson)
Billed as 'The Wonder Whip Man', Cracker Jack Silver galloped into No. 1 of *Beano* (30 July 1938) where the headline described him as 'The Fighting Cowboy with the 30-Foot Lash'. Jack was the sensation of Sunset City Rodeo: 'Crack! Crack! Sounds like pistol shots rang out. It was the long lash of the great whip which was making the noise as Cracker Jack sent it flicking in all directions. The 30-foot rawhide lash was like a living thing. It seemed to flicker in and out like the tongue of a striking rattlesnake.' Having sliced an apple, Jack next used his whip to stop a bank-robber's car.

Crash Carew
Nat Brand

Comic Adventures 1942-49 (Soloway)
'Daredevil of the Stratosphere', Crash Carew rocketed into action as the front feature of *Comic Adventures*, a popular comicbook of the 'Forties. With Billy his boy assistant, Crash flew *The Marlin* into the snowy depths of an ice planet for an adventure among winged batmen. This two-page thriller was but the beginning: Crash was promptly promoted to five-page epics, space enough to deal with monster rhamphoryns, and – 'Great Scott! What now?' – a giant brachycan who mistakes the *Marlin* for a rival reptile and butts it over the cliff.

Creature Teacher
Tom Williams

Monster Fun 1975-76 (IPC)
The pitiful cries for mercy coming from Massacre Street School came, not from some unfortunate pupil suffering at the hand of a merciless master, but from a terrified teacher suffering from the little monsters of Form 3X. Mr Gimble was the ninety-seventh teacher to quit, a gibbering wreck, and the Head was at his wit's end. Then Mr Fume the Science Master came up with the solution. Deep in his underground laboratory something was coming to the boil. It was a monster master as monstrous as all his pupils put together: Creature Teacher – 'Sluurrsssh-Glooop!' – a one-eyed wonder who could wallop a whole class at once, thanks to his tentacles.

Creepy Comix
Reg Parlett
Wow 1982-83; *Whoopee* 1983-85; *Whizzer & Chips* 1986 (IPC)
June 6, 1983 was not Davey Doom's day. In No. 1 of *Wow*, he found himself lost in the fog while looking for the paper shop. The one he wandered into was much cobwebbed, with copies of the *Daily Wail* and *Woman and Groan* on the counter. The wheezing old shopman sold Davey a stack of *Creepy Comix* for a pound, and when a bully bagged them, they came to life: a giant hand slapped him down and a mummy bandaged him up! Later in the series, a page of *Creepy Comix* by Roy Mitchell was an added attraction, such as 'The Homeless Horrors' (No. 50).

Crowjak
Illustrator unknown
Buster 1976-77 (IPC)
'Crowjak the Crime-Busting Crow' flew into *Buster* on 27 March 1976, following the tremendous television success of the crime-and-cop series, *Kojak*. Like its star, Telly Savalas, Crowjak was bald, wore dark glasses, and liked lollipops. It was his well-known propensity for lolly licking that gave away Crowjak's disguise when he posed as a parrot to infiltrate Fatso's gang. His assistant's disguise as a tiger saved Crowjak from the feather pluckers, however, but the roaring required was tough on the tec's tonsils. Crowjak rewarded him with a eucalyptus lolly.

The Crew of the Ocean Wave
Percy Cocking
Sparkler 1937-39 (Amalgamated Press)
The crew of the S.S. *Ocean Wave* consisted of Chum the mate, Shrimp the cabin boy, and Sooty the cook, not to mention Nippy the parrot. In charge of them all was fat Captain Kipper, who navigated them around the seven seas or so on the full-colour front page of *Sparkler*, before shoving off for the interior. Among their escapades was the capture of Bad Bagdad the Bandit, doing ditto for Rattlesnake Rube, and finding the treasure of the Pasha of Pashaland.

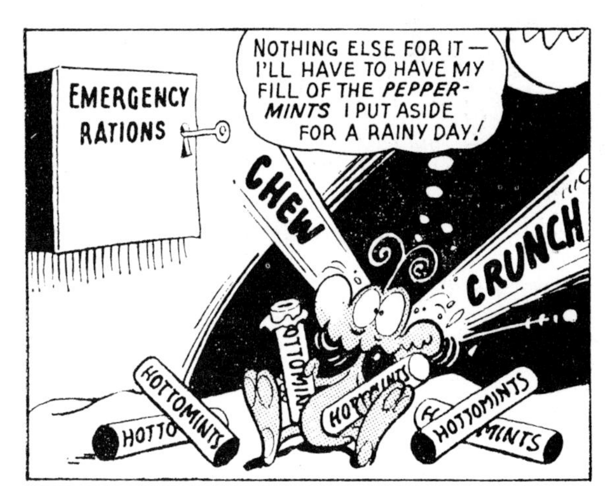

Cruncher
Frank McDiarmid
Giggle 1967; *Buster* 1968-70 (Fleetway)
'The Tiny Termite with the Big Appetite', Cruncher munched his way into *Giggle* on 30 December 1967. Waking bright and early in his home, Termite Towers, Cruncher announced that he was hungry enough to eat not a horse, but a house! And off he hopped to the nearest shack, residence of Farmer Hayseed and his folks. The battle of what passed for wits between this black-bearded hillbilly and the tiny but razor-jawed insect raged for some while, most of the rage roaring from Hayseed as Cruncher burped up yet another tummy-bulging victory.

C

Barrie Appleby
Nutty 1981-85; *Hoot* 1985; *Dandy* 1986 (D. C. Thomson)
"At's me!': the cry of Cuddles, a tough little nipper in the Baby Crockett tradition. With his one tooth, his three hairs, his safety-pinned nappy, and thick-soled wellies, Cuddles is the apple of his Mum's eye, the crab-apple of his Dad's! Starting as an inside page in red and black, Cuddles' career has been meteoric. Within a year, he was promoted to the full-colour back page of *Nutty* and, when that comic collapsed, Cuddles found himself the front-page star of the new comic, *Hoot*. Moving to *Dandy*, Cuddles teamed up with Dimples.

Curly's Commandos
Illustrator unknown
Cracker 1975 (D. C. Thomson)
'This Junior Army is Really Barmy!' Curly and his kids did their best to keep the peace, but the results were invariably vast explosions that fairly filled the second page of their weekly spread. The Commandos commenced operations in *Cracker* No. 1 (18 January 1975). There was Hamish in his tammy and kilt, Titch in the flying goggles, Podge in a pointed helmet, and little Herbert in his tin hat. The enemy was a rabble of rotters called Roger's Robbers, who muttered plots in their Gang Hut. A simple scrumping raid on Professor Potty's orchard resulted in the explosion of his patent Jupiter rocket.

Cuddly and Dudley
Illustrator unknown
Magic 1976-79 (D. C. Thomson)
'Bear cubs exactly alike. That's rare! One is called Cuddly, the other Dudley – their uncle is Biffo the Bear!' The D. C. Thomson editorial rhymester introduced these two black bear cubs in No. 1 of *Magic* (31 January 1976), although it is doubtful that any of the comic's nursery-school-age readers would have known about Biffo of the *Beano*. Dudley was the boy bear in the chequered dungarees, while his twin sister, Cuddly, also wore dungarees, but had a spotted bow in her hair as a mark of her femininity. In their first outing, the bears went camping, got blown away hanging on to the tent, and landed on top of an escaped circus lion.

Cursitor Doom
Illustrator unknown
Smash 1969-70 (IPC)
On a dark and stormy night (that of 15 March 1969) one Angus McCraggan entered the museum of the macabre that was the house of Cursitor Doom. He was answering an advertisement for an assistant, one whose physical strength would match the psychical powers of Doom. For this strange, bald-headed man was sworn to fight evil things, foes beyond the comprehension of ordinary men. Their first case was that of Kalak the Dwarf, an evil sorceror whose petrified corpse held a reporter named Sneed in his power.

Curly Kelly
G. M. Payne
Merry & Bright 1910-17 (Amalgamated Press)
'The Champion Laughter-Provider and Side-Splitter' was the front-page star of *Merry & Bright* for most of his 337-week career. The fair-haired fat one wrote his own comic commentary, opening each week with 'Dear Merry and Bright Ones' and closing with 'Yours joyfully'. Curly was something of an all-round comedian, and not just in the weight stakes: he was prone to raising the wind via one-man bands, or busking 'twiddley bits of "Wotcher me old brown son" on the banjoseph!' His venue varied: one week he was in Puddleton-in-the-Mud, the next in darkest Umgalooloo.

Custer
Geoff Campion
Jag 1968-69; *Tiger* 1969 (Fleetway)
'He was every inch a cavalryman. Tall, slim, yellow-haired, a born horseman possessing a lightning brain and a boyish sense of humour. Always splendidly dressed, his hat cocked at a rakish angle and golden spurs chiming at his heels, he would gallop at the head of his beloved 7th Cavalry.' So was Lieutenant General Custer introduced to readers of *Jag* No. 1 (4 May 1968), and to McLane the regimental bully of the newly formed 7th. 'Hogwash! If you're Custer you'll get down off that horse and prove it, man to man!' The Boy General proved it – in No. 2.

Dads as Lads
Bill Mevin
Whoopee 1977-80 (IPC)
A nice idea which started in the New Year's Day issue of *Whoopee*, 1977. Bob and Jerry are two old school pals who live next door to each other at No. 12 and No. 13. Their sons, Daniel and Jonathan, are junior mirror images of their dads: tubby with glasses and slim and fair. Watching their boys at play sets the dads to recalling their younger days, and the strip then depicts their childhood adventures, coming back to the present for the payoff. History repeated itself one Christmas: the Dads remembered how they gave their fathers a peashooter and waterpistol; then their lads gave them a popgun and a catapult!

D

Daffy the Cowboy Tec
Leonard Matthews
Knockout 1941-48; *Big One* 1964-65 (Fleetway)
'He's the Woolliest One in the West! was the subtitle for Daffy the depitty sheriff, a bespectacled simpleton who arrived in *Knockout* No. 127, 2 August 1941, in time to celebrate its wartime price rise to threepence. His first assignment was to capture the Sheriff Basher – 'Or I'll stop your Saturday penny!' threatened the Sheriff. Daffy built a cage and trapped the brute, but forgot that he was inside, too! The artist became the editor of *Knockout*.

Dan Dare
Frank Hampson
Eagle 1950-69 (Odhams); *Lion* 1969-70; *2000 AD* 1977-78; *Eagle* 1982- (IPC)
'Kingfisher's ready to go, Sir Hubert!' were the famous first words of Colonel Daniel MacGregor Dare of the Interplanet Space Fleet, better known to a million young readers as 'Dan Dare – Pilot of the Future'. Dan was the front-page star of the new full-colour photogravure tabloid, *Eagle*, which took off on 14 April 1950, launching British comics into the new Elizabethan Age, and the Space Age. Dan's chief was Sir Hubert Guest; his companion was Spaceman Class 1 Albert Digby, and his enemy the Mekon of Venus. Revival artists: Dave Gibbons (1977); Gerry Embleton (1982).

Dad Walker and Wally
Bertie Brown
Larks 1927-40 (Amalgamated Press)
'The Merry Adventures of Dad Walker and His Son Wally' filled the front page of *Larks* No. 1 (29 October 1927), retiring 656 weeks later when the comic was cancelled due to World War 2. Dad's final farewell was 'Yours till whelks wear woolly waistcoats!' The Walkers were a curious combination, a one-parent family of father and son with no fixed abode. Their 'Merry Adventures' consisted of their efforts to raise the dibs or win a tuck-in: 'Yum! I prefer my macaroni knitted!' In 1936, they went for a twenty-week tramp in the Sahara, and in 1937 won the Old Crocks Race in a tin lizzie called Thunderbolt: it took them twenty-one months!

Daisy Jones' Locket
Arthur Martin
Whoopee 1974-77 (IPC)
Mr Jones told his daughter Daisy that she couldn't go out to play until she had tidied up the attic. Starting on Granddad's old sea chest she found an oriental locket. Shining it up on her sleeve she gave a cry of 'Yikes!' as out floated the Genie of the Locket, motto: 'Your wish is my command!' His magic came in handy at school when Daisy's teacher, Grumpy Grabbit, got busy with her cane: the Head got walloped instead! Another day Daisy was playing hairdressers when a bully barged in demanding a wave. 'Kazam!' – and he was half-drowned when Genie summoned forth a wave from the sea!

Dandy McQueen
Nat Brand
All Star 1941-47 (Soloway)
Billed as 'Dude of the Royal Mounted', Dandy McQueen regularly got his man as the monocled member of the Royal Canadian Mounted Police who rode the leading feature of *All Star*, a popular wartime, two-colour comic. Among his men duly got were Joe Drage, bison poacher on behalf of a Nazi U-boat, Larsen the Mad Engineer ('Ha-ha! Another Mountie accounted for!'), Black Rogan, liquor seller to the Injuns ('A scar for every day you made me spend in prison, Mountie!'), and Menzel Hoffer, salmon poisoner. Dandy's horse was called Bruce.

D

Dane Jerrus
Crewe Davies
Super-Duper 1948-50 (Cartoon Art)
Dane Jerrus, Agent One of the Interplanetary Solar Force, and his partner Chummy Brown, were lying around the bar of the space landing cradles on the ultracold side of planet Mercury, when readers of *Super-Duper Comics* No 8 met him for the first time. Soon Dane is using his mighty strength to force entry into a newly arrived spaceship with no signs of life. 'Jeeze! Hep's Bells! Blind as a bat and ice cold!' Then the ship disappears ('Blimey!') and Dane is tracking space pirates and fighting the twelve-foot Horror ('Holy Mac!'), inventor of the F-Ray that freezes light.

Danger Mouse
Illustrator unknown
Smash 1966-67 (Odhams)
If the artistic engraving of a rodent in a black sweater marked 'D.M.' seems unfamiliar to Danger Mouse T.V. fans, that is because it is. This was the original Danger Mouse as he made his debut in *Smash* No. 3 (19 February 1966). A secret agent rather than a superhero, D.M. operated on behalf of his race against their mortal enemies, the cats. When a fat cat came luring the little mice – 'Come on, miceys, nice cheese bikky for you!' – D.M. was called in on the case. 'Squeak up, lad, what's the trouble?' D.M. soon put paid to pussy – with his catapult!

Danger Man/Danger Twins
Michael Darling
Beano 1959-62 (D. C. Thomson)
The Danger Man, brought to Earth by a flying saucer, had been taken to Mars at the age of five, kidnapped from his home on the Yorkshire Moors. Now, in *Beano* No. 885 (4 July 1959), he was home again. His mission: to foster interplanetary goodwill by helping anyone in danger. No sooner settled into his artificial island, than an S.O.S. call came from a submarine sunk off the coast of Ireland. Instantly Danger Man was roaring to the rescue in his Zoomar, a handy land/sea/air machine from Mars.

Daniel Dole and Oscar Outofwork
Charles Genge
Golden Penny 1922-28 (United)
'Dear Old Beans' was how this pair of penniless persons addressed their readers, purchasers of *The Golden Penny Comic* No. 1 (14 October 1922). While slightly up the social scale from such gentlemen of the road as Weary Willie and Tired Tim, they nevertheless kept the tramp tradition alive on the front pages of British comics, until they were shifted inside by a new strip 'High Jinks at the High School', from No. 100. The implication here is that young readers were more interested in characters of their own age group than adults with cash flow problems.

Dan Leno

Tom Browne

Dan Leno's Comic Journal 1898-99 (Pearson)

The first 'real-life' personality ever to appear as a comic-strip hero was Dan Leno, the uncrowned king of Music Hall comedians. With an entire comic weekly named after him, *Dan Leno's Comic Journal* (No. 1: 26 February 1898) might have been expected to run longer than its ninety-three editions. Perhaps there was insufficient Leno: he starred on the front page in one large cartoon, and inside in a six-picture strip. Dan was drawn by the top comic artist of his day, Tom Browne.

Danny Longlegs

Dudley Watkins

Dandy 1945-50 (D. C. Thomson)

'Old Dan Long and his wife Polly were very worried. Their young son Danny had grown so fast that he was ten feet tall, and had to curl himself up like a winkle at night!' Thus were readers of *Dandy* No. 286 (3 February 1945) introduced to their new and unusual hero: 'He's ten feet tall and up to the ears in trouble!' The setting was rural England in the Middle Ages, the village of Sleepy Valley to be precise, and trouble with Beardie the Schoolmaster soon led Danny's dad to call on Bombo the Wizard to bring his overgrown son down to size.

Dan the Merry Menagerie Man

F. McHutchon

Puck 1910-35 (Amalgamated Press)

Dan was originally something of a look-alike for the music-hall comedian Dan Leno, but this resemblance passed when artist J. MacWilson (illustrated) took over in the 'Twenties. MacWilson also added speech balloons, not only for Dan the Man but for his Merry Menagerie, too. In his early years, Dan did such things as looping snakes into hoops and ringing the gorilla when the ape snatched a visitor's ticker. The later lot included Harry Hippo, Frankie Fox, and the inevitable Jumbo.

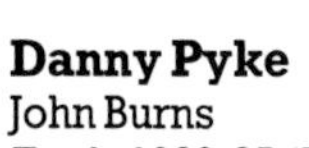

Danny Pyke

John Burns

Eagle 1983-85 (IPC)

'The Fists of Danny Pyke' fought their first round in *Eagle* on 24 September 1983. 'He had fought his way up from the back streets of Liverpool, a kid with nothing going for him but the dynamite in his hands and fire in his heart!' Now he was in Madison Square Garden, New York, in the blue corner, weighing in at two-hundred-and-eight-and-one-half pounds, the challenger, Dynamite Danny Pyke. In the red corner, weighing in at two-hundred-and-twenty-two pounds, from Akron, Ohio, the reigning Heavyweight Champion of the World, the Akron Assassin, Alvin Sharkie. Three pages later the champ was down.

Danny Dare

Leo Baxendale

Wham 1964-68 (Odhams)

Dan Dare's Number One Fan rocketed into *Wham* No. 1 (20 June 1964): 'Sorry I'm in a rush, but I'm off in Dan Dare's space-ship *Tempus Frangit* to help him stop the Mekon conquering the solar system!' Mekon spaceships attacked, but Danny managed to use his ejector seat just in time. But – 'Sufferin' satellites!' – his retro-rockets failed and Danny crashed to earth – straight out of bed! From dreams to daydreams was but one small step for Danny. He slid down the bannisters on a cushion, like Dan Dare on a launching pad, and he was through the street door in his oil-drum spaceship before his Dad (the Mekon) could swing a slipper.

Danny's Tranny

Ken Hunter

Topper 1972-86 (D. C. Thomson)

'Young Danny Wilson owns a super-marvellous transistor radio which, for short periods of time, can make objects larger, smaller, lighter than air, or even invisible!' Thus the regular editorial opening that heralded a page of pictorial pranks as Danny pressed buttons innocuously marked LW, MW, and VHF. Dinner at a posh restaurant with the stuck-up Braggs was soon sneezed away when Danny enlarged a pepper pot. The fun grew even greater when, in 1975, Danny and his Tranny were promoted to the full-colour front page.

D

Dare-a-Day Davy

Ken Reid

Pow 1967-68 (Odhams)

Back-page hero of the new comic *Pow* (21 January 1967), Davy was quickly established as a boy who would take any dare. His first is to ask sexy Mavis Font for a date. She gives him one – 1066 – plus a clobber with her handbag. From then on it was the comic's readers, *Pow*-pals as Davy called them, who supplied the dares, winning themselves a crisp quid for their trouble. Davy's good and bad selves, who lodged in his ear-wax, did their best to dissuade/persuade Davy but, after eighty-six weeks, he was rocketed into orbit in Sir Egbert's water tank.

Darrell King

Jock McCail

Thrill Comics 1940-48; *New Funnies* 1949; *Slick Fun* 1950 (Swan)

Darrell King of the Secret Service starred in six pages of whirlwind action in No. 1 of *Thrill Comics* (April 1940), during which he palled up with young Jim Dent who became to King what Tinker was to Sexton Blake. Also like Blake, King was a master of disguise: he begins his first case by posing as a sailor in a low riverside dive ('I'm just in from 'Frisco, guv'nor!'), then finds his chief dead, the safe ransacked of defence plans ('Great Scot! It's the crook from the East End!'). Soon they find a secret passage: 'Come on Englanders, if you dare!' They do, of course.

Daredevil

Bill Everett

Marvel 1973-79; *Spiderman* 1979; *Marvel Teamup* 1980-81; *Captain America* 1981; *Marvel Super Adventure* 1981 (Marvel)

'A brand new name in the world of superheroes! But one which is destined to reach the very heights of glory! For Daredevil has a special type of power such as no adventurer has ever had before!' Stan Lee introducing Daredevil in No. 1 of his own title (June 1964) and again in Britain in *The Mighty World of Marvel* No. 20 (17 February 1973). For Daredevil was blind, losing his eyesight when, as teenage athlete Matt Murdock, he was hit by a truckload of radioactive material. But his remaining senses became supersharp.

David and Alice at Sunshine Farm

D. Frances Wood

Chicks Own 1936-56 (Amalgamated Press)

Subtitled 'A Love-ly Tale of Your Old Friends David, Alice and Gaga', this serial strip for the young readers of *Chicks Own* centred around a brother and sister (white) and their girl chum (black). Gaga was better behaved than the black sheep in Daddy's flock: 'The black one is a lit-tle ras-cal, he keeps run-ning a-way!' laugh-ed Gaga. There was heartbreak among the sunshine, too: 'David has a dog-gie named Patch, but Dad-dy says Patch must go a-way, be-cause he chase-s the chick-ens.' But it was a naugh-ty fox aft-er all!

Davy Crockett
James Holdaway
Mickey Mouse Weekly 1955-57 (Odhams); *Knockout* 1955-60 (Amalgamated Press); *Davy Crockett* 1956-60 (Miller)
'Before Buffalo Bill, before Kit Carson, before Hawkeye the Hunter, there was one man in the Wild West whose courage and fearlessness spread his fame through the land. This man was Davy Crockett, King of the Wild Frontier.' Cheekily swiping the subtitle from the Walt Disney film, thus did *Knockout* introduce the coonskin-capped hero in No. 869 (22 October 1955). Meanwhile, the official film adaptation ran in *Mickey Mouse Weekly*, drawn by Jim Holdaway and, in unofficial Miller comicbooks, drawn by Don Lawrence.

Deadly Hedley
Martin Baxendale
Buster 1981-83 (IPC)
'Deadly Hedley the Vampire Detective' was the oddest employee of the Stinkerton Detective Agency. Quite why such a decided descendant of Dracula should take a stake in law enforcement was never very clear, although it was certainly a handy ability to be able to change into a bat from time to time. One of Hedley's cases is worth recording as historic. On page seven of *Buster*, dated 24 October 1981, he apprehended a burglar robbing Blogg's Jewellery Store. It was none other than Babyface Finlayson, whose patch is normally page two of a rival publisher's, *Beano*!

The Deathless Men
Philpott
Hornet 1966-75; *Hotspur* 1976-80 (D. C. Thomson)
'V for Vengeance' was the title of this wartime serial which first appeared in the 1942 *Wizard*, and it was the title again when it was adapted as a picture serial for the 1966 *Hornet*. The Deathless Men were a grey-clad, grey-masked secret army of men who escaped from Nazi concentration camps. Each was code-named Jack and a number, and their leader was Jack One. He was in reality Colonel Von Reich, second-in-command of the Gestapo, the dreaded secret police of Nazi Germany and, in true reality, Aylmer Gregson, a British secret agent planted in the Gestapo in 1936. The Deathless Men's signature was the letter 'V'.

D-Day Dawson
Geoff Campion
Battle 1975-77 (IPC)
Sergeant Steve Dawson, 'The British Soldier who has a Date With Death', led the thirty-two pages of pictorial warfare that was *Battle Picture Weekly* No. 1. For readers, it was 8 March 1975, but for Dawson it was D-Day, 6 June 1944 as he jumped ashore on the Normandy beaches: 'The big day at last, lads! Give it to 'em good 'n' hot!' Unfortunately for Dawson, the Jerries gave it to him: he was shot. The bullet lodged close to his heart and a medic gave him a year to live. Against orders Dawson went back into action: 'I'm living on borrowed time, anyway. As long as I stay alive, the Germans had better watch out – they're up against a man with nothing to lose!'

Death Wish
Vanyo
Speed 1980; *Tiger* 1980-85; *Eagle* 1985- (IPC)
The greatest speed race in history was held on 23 February 1980 in No. 1 of *Speed*, and the most eager of the many competitors was Blake Edmonds, 'a former world motor-racing champion, still a king of speed, and one of the great superstars of British sport'. He led in the hang-glide leap off a London skyscraper, was first in the no-limit road race across London, but, in the third lap crashed his aeroplane into a tree. Miraculously, Blake escaped with his life, but his badly burned face had to be hidden in a headpiece that made him known as the Man in the Mask.

Deed-a-day Danny/Gussie
Hugh McNeill
Knockout 1939-54; *Sun* 1949; *Comet* 1951; *Big One* 1964-65; *Giggle* 1967; *Pixie* 1972 (IPC)
'The Big-Hearted Scout' made his well-meaning debut in No. 1 of *Knockout*, 4 March 1939. In best Raleigh tradition, he covered a puddle with his mac: in best comic tradition, the fat lady stepped on and sank with a splosh! Danny's rise to popularity is recorded by his promotion to page one from No. 15, where his catchphrase became 'Another good deed gone bad!' Danny's final indignity was to suffer a sex change: from No. 1 of *Pixie* (24 June 1972) he was redrawn as Gussie the Girl Guide!

Dene Vernon
Jock McCail
Thrill Comics 1940-46 (Swan)
'Dene Vernon, Ghost Investigator', was the hero of the first truly supernatural strip series in British comics. Tall, lean, with a high forehead and thinning hair, none of his investigations was as horrific as his first, in *Thrill Comics* No. 1 (April 1940). Vernon spends the night in a haunted bedroom where a weary wanderer was found on the floor: 'A gasp of horror came as they gazed on the terror-distorted features of the dead traveller!' Vernon saves Dick from being throttled by a grinning black monster, chained by its neck since 1785. But he has to burn the house down to do it.

Derickson Dene
Nat Brand
Triumph 1939-40 (Amalgamated Press)
'Derickson Dene, Super-Inventor', appeared in *Triumph* on 8 July 1939 in a four-page serial strip that established him as the first British superhero in the American comicbook style. Dene 'a noted inventor, is working on a detector which will respond to the approach of the mechanism propelling the Bat-Men'. These are bank-robbers bossed by the hideous Vampire. The action suddenly shifts by Planet-Rocket to an unknown world where Dene deals with Rhamdhorns, Medusa Snakes, and Dryptosaurs, returning home on 17 February 1940.

Deep-Down Daddy Neptune
Basil Blackaller
Beano 1939-40 (D. C. Thomson)
'Moaning minnows!' cried Deep-Down Daddy Neptune, *Beano*'s variation on the classical God of the Sea, 'What a din!' It was Sammy and the Water Babies having a blow at some bagpipes they found in a sunken ship. Bursting them with his bow and arrow, Old Nep (as he was known) got a shock when he tried the same stunt later. This time they were not bagpipes but swordfish painted tartan by the boys! Wallace the whale and other deep-down denizens also helped with the fishy fun.

Dennis the Menace
David Law
Beano 1951- (D. C. Thomson)
The headline read: 'Look! Here's a new pal you'll enjoy – He's the world's wildest boy!' The comic was *Beano* No. 452, the page was five, and date was 17 March 1951. In No. 555 (7 March 1953) Dennis the Menace expanded from half-a-page to the whole of page two. In No. 604 (13 February 1954), he moved to the back page and appeared in full colour. On 14 September 1974, Dennis was promoted to both the front and back pages, ousting Biffo the Bear. The victory of boykind over funny animals was complete, although Dennis shares his strip with an equally scruffy hound called Gnasher.

Desperate Dan
Dudley D. Watkins
Dandy 1937- (D. C. Thomson)
Desperate Dan, the roughest, toughest cowpoke in comics, is the terror of Cactusville, a wild western township where lamp-posts lean on street corners and gasometers lower on the horizon. Dan's favourite fodder is cow pie baked with the horns in, lovingly prepared fresh daily by his Aunt Aggie, sometimes shared with his tough little nephew Desperate Danny (1949). Dan's original artist is said to have modelled Dan on his editor, Albert Barnes. After 2242 inside adventures Dan was promoted to the cover of his comic on 17 November 1984.

D

Desperate Dawg
George Martin
Dandy 1973-86 (D. C. Thomson)
Desperate Dawg, a two-gunned, two-legged, quick-draw canine variation on Desperate Dan, strode into that well-established hero's own comic, *Dandy*, on 29 September 1973. Dan had already demonstrated his desperateness 1661 times, but it seems *Dandy* readers still had room for another page of wild-west walloping. 'That's what they call me, Desperate Dawg!', announced this muscle-bound hound. 'One blow from this [his fist] and the biggest outlaw gets flattened!'

Dick Barton
Geoffrey Webb, Edward J. Mason
Comet 1953-54 (Amalgamated Press)
'Dick Barton – Special Agent', a daily radio serial highly popular with youngsters, was first broadcast on 7 October 1946. His first appearance as a comic strip was on the coloured cover of *Comet* No. 247 dated 11 April 1953. It was a little belated: the programme had been off the air since 30 March 1951! There were other differences: Dick was reduced to a single assistant, Snowy White, and he was reduced, too – in age. Also Dick's first case was unlike anything he ever tackled on radio. It was entitled 'The Flying Saucer Mystery' and Dick soon found himself to be the first man on the moon!

Diana's Diary
Illustrator unknown
June 1961-65 (Fleetway)
Diana opened her diary on Saturday 11 March 1961, one week before the date printed on No. 1 of *June*, which published it in pictorial form. It began: 'My name is Diana Todd. Yesterday was my eleventh birthday and I had lots of dreamy presents and a super party! But the best present was this diary.' Through Diana's diary we met Jimmy, her nine-year-old brother, and his bike ('Dad calls it the Bitza because it's made of bits and pieces'), Mum washing ink from her school tunic, Dad impersonating Harry Secombe while gardening, Punchie her boxer dog, her best friend Peggy Wilson, and Madame Anya, her ballet teacher. By 1965 we were reading 'Diana's Diary in Australia'.

Dick and Daisy
Frank Watkins
Merry Moments 1919-21 (Newnes)
Dick and Daisy were the back-page brother-and-sister stars of *Merry Moments* No. 1 (12 April 1919). They began in the usual red and black of the period, but burst into full colour from No. 67. Although it was never specified that their adventures occurred during their sleep, the fact that they always dressed in pyjamas and nightshirt suggested that their impossible escapades were dreams. After their first flight of fancy to Lollipop Land, they visited Baby Land, Red Land, Stickleback Land, and the Funnikings.

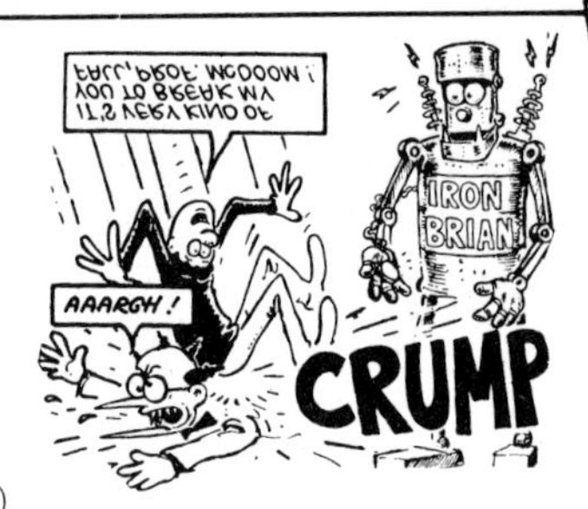

Dick Doobie
Steve Bell
Whoopee 1978 (IPC)
This character was so original he needed a weekly warning from the editor: 'Don't forget, pals, hold this story upside down in front of a mirror to see what Dick is saying!' For Dick Doobie was cursed with an upside-down head, hence his billing: 'Dick Doobie the Back-to-front Man'. Dick was a milkman for the Intergalactic Dairies, zooming through outer space in his Supermoooo dropping yoghurts on the asteroids. Dick's mortal enemy was Professor McDoom, assisted by Iron Brian the Robot, otherwise known as Tinbrain.

Dickory Dock
Peter Woolcock
Dickory Dock 1980 (IPC)
'Once upon a time there was a little dock on the banks of the River Dickory.' This was Dickory Dock, a village full of funny animals, who also filled the sixteen pages of the comic named after it which started on 1 March 1980. Among them, each with their own strip, were Piggles the Postman, Sweet Sue and Big Brother (cats), Clever Dick and Silly Billy (dogs), Bananas Bunny, Goggles and Giggles (cat and mouse), Happy the Helpful Hare, Ferdy Fox and Horace Hound, Fuddy and Duddy and the Disco Kid (bears), and Duke of the Duck Pond.

Dick Hercules
Sydney Jordan
Dick Hercules 1952-53; *Steve Samson* 1954-55 (Sports Cartoons)
'Dick Hercules of St Markham's' was a muscular sixth former who starred in his own comicbook while promoting 'The Gym Gem Pocket Gym', 'Anatomy for the Body Builder', and other items issued by the Body Sculpture Club: 'Muscles like Granite! But Flexible as Whalebone!' His opening adventure, 'The Jet Plane Thieves', introduced him thus: 'Dick Hercules is Captain of St Markham's public school. His magnificent physique and incredible strength allow him to perform amazing feats.' These included holding back a jeep to prevent the escape of a spy.

Dick Turban
Martin Baxendale
Nutty 1980 (D. C. Thomson)
'Dick Turban – Desert Highwayman' rode the sands of the Sahara perched between the double humps of Caramel the camel. Both wore black masks so that the French Foreign Legion should not recognize them. Intent on locking Dick away until the sands of the desert grew cold was big-chinned Capitaine Blownaparte, commandant of the Thirteenth Legion, stationed at Fort Cortina: 'Suffering sandstorms! A thousand curses on zis heat, ze flies, and zat Dick Turban!'

Dickie Duffer
Albert Pease
Joker, 1932-40; *Chips* 1940-53 (Amalgamated Press)
'Dickie Duffer the Dunce' was seldom seen without his classic dunce's cap marked with a 'D', or his subtitle: 'He's Not So Silly As He Looks!' Dickie enrolled in Coshem College in *Joker* No. 259 on 16 October 1932 and remained as the bane of Dr Doughnut's life until the final issue, No. 655, on 18 May 1940. Even the war could not make Dickie graduate: he evacuated to *Chips*, reappearing in No. 2605, 10 August 1940, and was still demolishing Doughnut in the last number, 2997, dated 12 September 1953 – twenty-two years in the same (top) class! Dickie's other enemies were Specky the Inspector and Cecil Sneak.

Dick Turpin/Jack O'Justice
Hugh McNeill
Sun 1951-54; *Radio Fun* 1959-60; *Valiant* 1962-68 (Amalgamated Press)
Hugh McNeill, best known for his highly humorous artwork ('Our Ernie', 'Deed-a-Day Danny', etc), turned his pen to heroic adventure with 'Highway Days', a rousing adventure serial on the two-tone back page of *Sun*. From No. 106 (18 February 1951) the legendary highwayman rode the eighteenth-century roads again astride his faithful mare, Black Bess. By his side rode Moll Moonlight, described as his 'girl companion', or 'girl pal'; on his trail, thief-taker Jonathan Wild. Dick rode again in *Radio Fun*, this time as Jack O'Justice. Moll Moonlight became Velvet his 'girl comrade'.

The Diddymen
Ken Dodd
TV Comic 1967-69 (TV)
'We are the Diddymen who come from Knotty Ash' was the signature song of these high-voiced little fellows who were first heard on Ken Dodd's radio series, and then transferred to stage and television via a team of clever youngsters dressed up in comedy clobber. The tattyfilarious Liverpudlian comedian brought his pocket-sized crazy gang to *TV Comic*, where they starred on the full-colour front page, delightfully drawn by Bill Titcombe. The jam butty miners included Dicky Mint and monocled Ponsonby.

Dilly Dreem
Illustrator unknown
School Friend 1950-65 (Amalgamated Press)
Billed as 'The Lovable Duffer', Dilly Dreem made her day-dreamy debut in No. 1 of *School Friend* (20 May 1950), a page of comic relief to the nineteen other pages of romantic adventure. Madge and Joy were the mischief-making fourth formers whose delight it was to play pranks on the bespectacled Dilly, but usually Dilly managed to turn the tables on them by the final picture. Such as the time when the japers told Dilly the classroom was on fire and headmistress Miss Blunt got doused by mistake. 'Let's laugh at the silly old duffer!', cried the girls, who soon laughed on the other side of their faces.

Digby the Human Mole
Graham Allen
Plug 1977-78 (D. C. Thomson)
'How d'you do?', smiled this fat little fellow with the oversized nose in No. 1 of *Plug* (24 September 1977), 'Digby's the name – robbing's my game!' To demonstrate, Digby dug under the foundations of a firmly closed bank. Unfortunately, he came up in the armed guard's office. Burrowing home in a hurry, Digby emerged through the floor just as Mrs Digby came in with his tea. 'Yorf! How many times do I have to tell you to come in through the front door?', yelled Mrs D, even more upset than the tea things. Digby's problem was that he never quite came up where he intended. Having successfully stolen steak for a beef butty, he came up in a beehive, a puddle, and Colonel Cuthbert's croquet lawn.

Dilly Duckling
Harry Banger
Sunny Stories 1952-58 (Newnes)
'Quacko!' was the cheery cry of Dilly Duckling, star of a long series of stories for nursery-aged children, written by Arthur Groom and illustrated by Harry Banger. Dilly was the son of Mr and Mrs Quacker of Duckweed Cottage, Duckville, and his little sister was called Dimple. The huge popularity of these duck tales, which were eventually published in book form, led to a full-colour strip across the centre spread of *Sunny Stories*, 'The Funny Adventures of Dilly Duckling', as well as regular appearances on the cover.

Dinah Mite/Belle Tent
Reg Parlett
Buster 1965-69 (Fleetway)
'Meet the Little Lady with the Grace of an Elephant!' was the editorial greeting for Dinah Mite on 30 October 1965. As if that was not insufficient description, there was the sarcastic subtitle: 'She's dainty – Ain't she?' Disaster-prone Dinah, a schoolgirl who didn't know her own strength, went for deportment lessons and nearly bashed Clarence Coot's brains in while balancing a book. Then she put her foot on the bar and unbalanced Miss Gumpoyle's ballet class. Dinah Mite was revived in *Whizzer & Chips* (1970) as 'Belle Tent – She's Funtastic!'

Dixon of Dock Green
Ted Willis
Swift 1957-61 (Hulton)
The popular BBC television series created by Ted Willis, built around the character of P.C. George Dixon in the Ealing film, *The Blue Lamp*, was adapted as a serial in *Swift* from 21 December 1957. Jack Warner, the actor who had played Dixon in the film and on television, was recognizably the Dixon of the comic, too, especially when the strip was promoted to the full-colour front page from 9 April 1960, the first issue of the enlarged format. Warner had earlier appeared in *Radio Fun* (1941) in his soldier character from radio's *Garrison Theatre*.

Ding-Dong Belle
Bill Holroyd
Beano 1949-51 (D. C. Thomson)
'The Sheriff with the happy grin – She's always running bad men in!' This was how *Beano* No. 368 billed Ding-Dong Belle when she shot her way on to page three on 6 August 1949. Boosted as the only she-sheriff in the whole wild west, Belle was the opposite of Desperate Dan – in sex only. Just as tough as her *Dandy* counterpart, when Deadshot Daniels quit his job as sheriff of Cactusville, Belle took over. With the aid of her three little kids, she soon had Larry and his hard-boiled hoss Lulu behind bars.

Dinkum the Dog Detective
Terry Wakefield
Tip Top 1934-39 (Amalgamated Press)
Dinkum the Dog Detective solved his first case in No. 1 of *Tip Top*, 21 April 1934. He caught a cat burglar who was literally that: a black cat who tried to spoil a noble hound's party by pinching his bones. For the rest of his six-year career, Dinkum's opponents were dirty dogs, such as Pongo the Purse Pilferer, Bill the Bone Burglar, and Hiram Hooch-hound from Hollywood. Dinkum, whose concession to clothing consisted of a deerstalker and pipe, usually wound up with a suitable reward, such as a tasty hambone.

Dirty Dick
Eric Roberts
Dandy 1960-77 (D. C. Thomson)
Dirty Dick began with a bang: star of the first ever full-colour centre spread in *Dandy* (No. 987, 22 October 1960). He also began with a splash, a splosh, and a whoosh as a day-by-day diary strip depicted a typical week in the life of this filth-prone fellow. On Monday he fell into a pigsty, on Tuesday he was sploshed by a tomato, on Wednesday he fell down a coalhole, on Thursday he was bucketed by water, on Friday he was besooted at bedtime. Seventeen years of similar stuff followed.

Dizzy
Cyril Price
Comic Cuts 1939-53 (Amalgamated Press)
Dizzy, not much more than a filler strip, arrived in *Comic Cuts* No. 2581 and quietly stayed in his place right to the final issue, No. 3006. 'Quietly' is indeed the operative word for Dizzy, because he never spoke. He was that rarity in comics, the star of a 'silent' or pantomime strip. The pictures told the story and, even in the last year of his run, when his space was expanded from four panels to six, and his artist changed to Fred Robinson, Dizzy still kept his mouth shut.

Dr Jolliboy's School
J. MacWilson
Puck 1912-40 (Amalgamated Press)
'Fun at Dr Jolliboy's School', as this strip was later titled, was certainly apt and, if laughter keeps one young, then it may explain why the doctor's pupils aged not one wrinkle in their twenty-nine-year term! Only the school porter changed from thin Peter to fat George, a whim of their last artist, Louis Briault (illustrated). Pupils included slim Sammy and chubby Tubby, plus Miggles Minor, Johnny Jenkins, Tommy Tucker, and Bobby Brown but, as everybody wore shiny toppers and Eton collars, it was hard to tell t'other from which.

Dr Crock's College
Julius Stafford Baker
Sunday Fairy 1919; *Children's Fairy* 1919-21; *Bubbles* 1921-41 (Amalgamated Press)
One of the few funny strips in a failed religious comic, 'Fun at Mr Croc's School', as it was later titled, survived through several comics and artists despite its marked resemblance to the Tiger Tim brotherhood. This is because J. S. Baker had also created Tiger Tim & Co, but the irony is that Herbert Foxwell, who had taken over Tiger Tim, also took over this secondary series (illustrated). The boys: Jumbo Jim, Reggie Rhino, Benny Bear, Dicky Donkey, Charlie Cockerel, Frankie Fido, a rabbit and a frog.

Dr Rhino's Jolly Jungle Boys
Julius Baker II
Sunbeam 1928-39 (Amalgamated Press)
Dr Rhino, pince-nez perched on his horn and mortarboard balanced between his ears, was an ungainly animal to run a comic-strip school. He was no doubt inspired, however, by the popularity of the long-established Mrs Hippo especially when his creator is considered. Dr Rhino's artist was the son of the artist who created Mrs Hippo! Among the doctor's Jolly Jungle Boys were Lennie Leopard, Micky Monk, Horace Hippo, Archie Zebra, Harry Hare, Charlie Kangaroo, and assorted animals never named.

Dr Strange
Steve Ditko
Terrific 1967-68; *Fantastic* 1968 (Odhams); *Avengers* 1973-76; *Spiderman* 1977; *Valour* 1980; *Marvel Action* 1981 (Marvel)
'Dr Strange, Master of the Mystic Arts', was created by writer-editor Stan Lee, in No. 110 of *Strange Tales* (July 1963). He first appeared in Britain in No. 1 of *Terrific* (15 April 1967) where the questions were posed again: 'Where does he come from? How did he get his powers? Who is he?'. Dr Strange turned out to be the once-famous surgeon, Stephen Strange, who journeyed to India, 'land of mystic enchantment', seeking a cure for his nerve-damaged hands. He finds the Ancient One, becomes the old mystic's pupil, and returns to Greenwich Village to combat evil with his white magic.

DODGER & DIDDLE

Two Dogs on the Fiddle

Dodger and Diddle
Roy Wilson
Wonder 1949-53 (Amalgamated Press)
'Dodger and Diddle – Two Dogs on the Fiddle' commenced their canine cadgery in No. 1628 of *Wonder* (11 June 1949). Each issue, they tried to scrounge a meal, sometimes with success. But not in their first caper; the bones being delivered turned out to belong to an extinct diplodizzydial! And, when they helped a GI carry his bags into a restaurant and heard him order a couple of hot dogs, they fled! Another time they put on their best doleful expressions for an old lady. 'I've got something that will make you feel good', she said, producing a bottle of castor oil. They fled again!

Doctor Who
Terry Nation
TV Comic 1965-79 (TV); *Countdown* 1971-72; *TV Action* 1972-73 (Polystyle); *Dr Who* 1979- (Marvel)
Dr Who, the Time Lord, is the hero of the longest-running BBC televison series for children. It began on 23 November 1963. The original actor who played Dr Who was William Hartnell, but a clever plot ploy enabled the role to be taken over by Patrick Troughton (1966), Jon Pertwee (1970), Tom Baker (1974), Peter Davison (1981), Colin Baker (1983) and Sylvester McCoy (1987). This has posed a problem for comic artists, of whom there have been more over the twenty-one years, than doctors! The first was Neville Main, followed by Bill Mevin. The first for *Dr Who Weekly* (17 October 1979) was Dave Gibbons.

The Dolliwogs
Herbert Foxwell
Rainbow 1914-56 (Amalgamated Press)
'The Dolliwogs' Dolls House' was a fascinating strip which started in No. 1 of *Rainbow* on 11 April 1914. All the adventures took place around an outsize dolls' house – four floors and a rooftop which necessitated unusually tall pictures. Teddy Bear lived on the ground floor, pretty Dolly Dimple had the balcony flat, Gretchen the Dutch Doll was on the second floor, and Fuzzy the Golliwog had the top. The tiles were the province of a cheerful cat, although later a parrot took over the roof as a perch. Their later artist was Bert Wymer (illustrated).

The Dolls of St Dominic's
Mike Lacey
Pow 1967-68 (Odhams)
Owing more than a sideglance at Ronald Searle's St Trinian's, the gang at this girls' school (term opened on 21 January 1967 in No. 1 of *Pow*) included Cynthia ('She's always throwing her weight around!'), Marigold the Bulk ('She'd eat anything!'), Judy the Judo Expert ('Gulp!'), Felicity, Penelope, Lavinia, Little Lulu ('She's man daft!'), and the head doll Miss Bolster ('Old Frosty-face!'). The comments come from Harry Migglethorpe, the much put-upon errand boy. Worse was to come when 'The Tiddlers' from *Wham* came to lodge!

The Dolly Girls
Illustrator unknown
Bonnie 1974-75; *Playhour* 1975- (IPC)
'These are such darling Dolls! Their home is a super big dolls house. You'll love the exciting things they do there!' The introduction to the five Dolly Girls who made their debut in No. 1 of *Bonnie* (16 March 1974). There was Baby Doll in her playpen, Dancer Doll who did the dusting twirling on her toes, Rag Doll who tidied up by sweeping everything under the carpet, pretty Fairy Doll who literally flew around doing the cleaning, and Dolly Doll who did the shopping. When *Bonnie* closed, they all moved to *Playhour*, losing one of their full-colour pages on the way.

Donald Duck
Walt Disney
Mickey Mouse Weekly 1936-57 (Odhams); *Mickey Mouse* 1958-59; *Walt Disney's Weekly* 1959-61 (Holding); *Film Fun* 1961; *Donald & Mickey* 1972-75; *Mickey & Donald* 1975; *Donald Duck* 1975-76; *Mickey Mouse* 1976-80; *Mickey Magazine* 1980-81 (IPC); *Disney Magazine* 1982- (London)
Donald Duck made his film debut in the *Silly Symphony* cartoon, *The Wise Little Hen* (1934). From bit-part player, his rise to stardom was rapid and, from 30 August 1936, he appeared in a weekly American newspaper strip drawn by Al Taliaferro. In Britain, Donald was a star from No. 1 of *Mickey Mouse Weekly* (8 February 1936) and was allowed to edit the comic on his birthday (Friday the thirteenth!). His main British artist was William Ward (illustrated), an ex-animator on Bonzo.

Dolly Dimple
Allan Morley
Magic 1939-40 (D. C. Thomson)
'Dolly Dimple – Not So Simple' made her wide-eyed debut in No. 1 of *Magic* (22 July 1939). The two-colour tones of page two suited her to perfection: she wore a red polka-dot dress and had big blue eyes. The top-of-the-page couplet also suited her, describing this angel child's character to perfection: 'She looks as gentle as can be – But Dolly's tough as you'll soon see!' Having blacked the eyes of a couple of apple scrumpers, she deals with their dad by means of a bad banana. Beaming bystanders obliged with a whipround.

Dolmann
Illustrator unknown
Valiant 1966-73; *Vulcan* 1975-76 (IPC)
'The House of Dolmann' stood in a dingy back street of London, a dusty puppet shop run by a master puppeteer. Dolmann had secretly created a fantastic army of mechanical warriors to fight crime and, as a polished ventriloquist, he was able to speak through their mouths. When a masked cat burglar, called the Wildcat, terrorized London, Dolmann fitted Trailer the tracker-puppet with autofocusing telescopic eyes, watching his suspect, Fabulo the escapologist, on a minitelevision screen. Then he sent wrestler-puppet Togo into action.

Don Conquest
H. Winslade
Mickey Mouse Weekly 1954-57 (Odhams)
The crew of the spaceship *Astroquest* wore personalized helmets: Don Conquest was Captain, Bandy was Cook, and Peter and Penny were Peter and Penny. Their dad was Doctor, and the curiously lean creature who said 'Ertmens cuf rockip!' was Ala the alien from Zara. He didn't need a helmet and, fortunately, turned out to be amiable in the end. However, author Kelman Frost hardly had them all safely back on Earth before they were off again to save 'The Young Prisoners of the Planets'.

D

Don Deeds
R. W. Plummer
Comet 1948-51 (Allen)
'Don Deeds and the Racketeers' began in *Comet* No. 51 (24 August 1948), a straightforward picture serial about a bright youngster foiling thieves. But, on 8 October 1949, while saving a Chinese girl from kidnappers, Don was confronted by a weird machine which surfaced on the Cornish shore. It was none other than the Rolling Sphere, piloted by its inventor Hoo Sung, a refugee from a wartime adventure of Sexton Blake in *Knockout*! Soon, they are off across the world on a treasure hunt, but even this paled beside their 1950 adventure – kidnapped by a Martian called Krim!

Doomlord
Heinzl
Eagle 1982- (IPC)
'An Alien Stalks the Earth!' shrieked the headline, in the revived *Eagle* No. 1 (27 March 1982). A midnight meteor streaked over the sleeping town of Cranbridge, crashing in Gallows Wood. 'M-my grief! Wh-who are you?' gasped P.C. Bob Murton. 'I am Doomlord, servant of Nox, master of life,' replied the bat-eared creature in the oriental gown, adding dramatically, 'Bringer of Death!' Absorbing the knowledge of P.C. Murton, and assuming his form, Doomlord set about his assigned task: the annihilation of the whole human race. He also changed from photographs to drawings.

Doodlebug
Gordon Bell
Nutty 1980-82 (D. C. Thomson)
The name was originally applied by the battered British to Hitler's flying bombs, but it was the subconscious habit of cartoon 'doodling' that inspired this little character. He was an artistic mouse who lived in a small world of bugs. These big-headed oddities included the repulsive Uglybug, the fun-loving Chucklebug, and the ill-tempered Humbug who was Doodlebug's main menace. Doodlebug also ran a *Postbag Page* with £2 postal orders for the week's best doodles from readers.

Doubting Thomas
James Crichton
Beano 1940-41 (D. C. Thomson)
Whenever Doubting Thomas was asked if he could do something for someone, his standard reply was, 'I doubt it, but I'll try!' A trier he was, and a trial, too: Tom would try anyone's patience. Helping a short-handed chimney sweep, he was told to come down – and came down the chimney! Disaster struck weekly from the day of his debut, 13 April 1940 in *Beano* No. 90, perhaps best recorded by the headline in rhyme: 'No wonder Tommy's looking sorry – He's broken down a breakdown lorry!'

Doughnut and Rusty
Trevor Metcalfe
Monster Fun 1975-76 (IPC)
'It's Transistorised Trouble when these two Electronic Enemies meet!' promised *Monster Fun* No. 1 (14 June 1975). This two-page tale of two robots was set in the year 2000. Marmaduke Posh, father of young Jamie, was having a spot of pest trouble: mice were overrunning the house and running off with the roast beef pills. A servant was advertised for and two robots applied, Rusty (who prefaced everything he said with a 'Bleep'), who needed the wages to keep himself in oil, and Doughnut (who prefaced everything he said with a 'Whirr'), the most expensive robot ever constructed. Mr Post hired them both, but rivalry led to friction: 'Bleep! Whirr!'

Dracula
Bram Stoker
Scream 1984 (IPC)
'When darkness falls, beware! For in those night hours the vampire seeks its victim!' With these words the most famous vampire in literary history was introduced into a British comic for the first time: *Scream* No. 1 (24 March 1984). Created in a novel by Bram Stoker, dramatized in innumerable horror films (which children were forbidden to see), this strip version was written by Gerry Finley Day and illustrated by Eric Bradbury. 'The Dracula File', lasted fifteen weeks before both the evil Count and the comic were buried. The American Marvel Comics version was reprinted in *Dracula Lives* (1974-76).

Draculass
Terry Bave
Monster Fun 1975-76; *Buster* 1976 (IPC)
Draculass was billed as 'Daughter of Dracula', which must have come as a surprise to Bela Lugosi: in the Universal film, *Dracula's Daughter*, she had been played by the glamorous Gloria Holden! Draculass came over to England from Transylvania on 14 June 1975, in No. 1 of *Monster Fun*, to stay with her cousin Maisie. But the fanged female got a shock when her auntie made her a meal of steak and garlic! Draculass slept in a cosy coffin and proved a pain in the neck to the postman: 'First dogs try to bite me, now it's vampires!'

Drake
Ron Smith
Warlord 1975-76 (D. C. Thomson)
'Into battle against the Germans with the Navy's most daredevil skipper!' This was Lieutenant Drake of the M.T.B.s (motor torpedo boats) or, as he was billed in No. 18 of *Warlord* (25 January 1975), 'Drake of E-Boat Alley'. Drake's seagoing saga started with the saving of Leading Seaman Joe Carter from a make shift raft off Dunkirk in May 1940. Pausing only to sink a U-boat. Drake roars to shore to save Carter's shipmates and sink a few E-boats. The grateful seaman signs on as Drake's torpedo man. The second series, set in 1941, was entitled 'Drake of Malta'.

Dreamy Daniel
George Davey
Lot-O-Fun 1906-22 (Henderson)
'The Delusions of Dreamy Daniel' began on the back page of No. 1 of *Lot-O-Fun*, 17 March 1906. The 'tired tourist' repaired a broken-down motor and was instantly hired as chauffeur at £2000 a year. Treated to 'a gorgeous dinner in several colours and champagne by the quart', D.D. suddenly woke up by the roadside: 'Twas all a cruel dream!' And so it would be throughout his seventeen years of dreaming, his only advance in life being a move to the coloured cover. Among the many he met in his dreams were the magicians, Maskeleyne and Devant, Harry Lauder, Sir Thomas Lipton, and Buffalo Bill.

Dreamy Dave and Dozy Dora
Illustrator unknown
Sparky 1965-68 (D. C. Thomson)
Dreamy Dave and Dozy Dora were a yellow-haired pair whose dreams filled the full-colour centre spread of *Sparky* from No. 1 (23 January 1965). Their exciting adventures, ranging through Hamelin Town with the Pied Piper, to the Crusades with the minstrel Blondel seeking the captive King Richard, always ended with a safe awakening at home. Later their dreams grew less historic and more fanciful: in No. 60 they climbed inside their television set to take part in commercials for Sudzee washing-up liquid and Pussykins cat food (mouse flavoured!).

D

Dredger
Illustrator unknown
Action 1976-77; *Battle Action* 1977-78 (IPC)
'There's only one rule for Dredger – There are no rules!' Secret Agent Breed of DI6 mused over his morose new partner: 'Five years in the Royal Marine Commandos, kicked out for brutality, turned up in '69 as a mercenary in Africa. Beats me why DI6 should use such a man.' Breed soon found out. When Arab terrorists tried to execute an oil sheik, Dredger swung into violent action: 'You're dead, pal, dead!' Smart, crisply dressed, classy Breed and dour, bomber-jacketed Dredger make a fair pair.

Dumbell Fumblebee
Creator unknown
Buster 1960-61 (Fleetway)
'Dumbell Fumblebee and his Loopy Listeners, the Lugg-Holes' was a series which satirized into slapstick the immensely popular BBC radio commentator, Richard Dimbleby. Each week from *Buster* No. 1 (28 May 1960), the fat Fumblebee sallied forth, microphone at the ready, to broadcast some interesting event, and each week disaster struck, so that the most Mr and Mrs Lugg-Hole ever heard was yells of 'Yeeooooow!' followed by such sound effects as 'Splosh!' and 'Kerunch!' Fumblebee's broadcast from a building site was rivetting: 'Brrrrrr!' – 'Yeeooop!'

Dudley Dudd
Harry Banger
Target 1935-38 (Target)
'The Demonstrations of Dudley Dudd the Dud Detective' began in No. 1 of *Target* (15 June 1935), a green penny comic named after its publishers, Target Publications of Lower Weston, Bath. Dudley's first case was to find a farmer's pinched pigs. He trailed them in his car, ran them over, and they popped out of his exhaust pipe as sausages! Later cases were more successful: such as guarding Tottery Mansions while Lord Luvaduck was away for his weekend haircut; collaring Alonzo the Anarchist for blowing up the Town Hall; and locating the lost umbergamp of Montague Moneybags.

The Duke's Spook
Arthur Martin
Shiver & Shake 1973-74 (IPC)
'Helloooo! My comic is haunted!' announced Shiver the Spook as he swanned through the editor's keyhole on the cover of *Shiver & Shake* No. 1 (10 March 1973). Shiver also conducted the 'Cackles from the Cave' cartoon competition and turned out to be the spiritual star of 'The Duke's Spook' strip. The family ghost to a noble old duke, the kind that wore his coronet in bed, Shiver was more than slightly miffed when the small sir hired a big butler named Grimes. This person never batted an eye at the sight of a spook: he batted the spook!

Dunder Ed
Phil Millar
Cracker 1975-76 (D. C. Thomson)
'Things are sure to go wrong – When Ed comes along!' Billed as 'The Wonder Blunderboy', Ed was an above-average accident prone who began wrecking the world around him in No. 1 of *Cracker* (18 January 1975). A simple mission, like taking a lady's Bonzo for walkies, got the hairy hound so smothered in toffee-apples that their removal clipped the poor dog into a soppy looking poodle-cut. Visiting Krumbling Castle, he accidentally unravelled Sir Richard Pyekrust's chainmail and wound up locked in ye olde stocks for safety.

Eagle-Eye
Leo Baxendale
Wham 1964-68 (Odhams)
'Eagle-Eye, Junior Spy' took the oath on 20 June 1964 in *Wham* No. 1 and became Assistant Unpaid Temporary Junior Spy, code-name Eagle-Eye, to his granddad, Colonel Thynne, the gent in charge at M.I.5½. He replaced Agent XYZ who conked out on the doormat from a bad case of bullet-holes. XYZ reported that an inventor had found a formula for altering the atomic structure of treacle. One exploded in Eagle-Eye's face to prove it. Granddad sent him to Doomsday Holiday Camp where he found the proprietor, Grimly Feendish, manufacturing robot housewives. He also had a Hairy Squelch in the cellar.

Edward and the Jumblies
Jesus Blasco
Teddy Bear 1963-73 (Fleetway)
Far and few are the lands where the Jumblies live, according to their ancient creator, Edward Lear, but young Edward found them all right, thanks to the seafaring trio, Og, Gog, and Mog. They arrived in No. 1 of *Teddy Bear* (21 September 1963) and were met by the King of Jumbly Land and his mixed-up subjects. But, by the time they came to Jumbly Town in No. 2, a terrible sound of 'Thump! Thump! Slap!' scared everybody away but Edward. It was the sound made by the big feet and flapping tail of the dreaded Chankley Bore!

Ebony
Magallanes
The Crunch 1979-80 (D. C. Thomson)
History was made when Ebony Jones debuted in *The Crunch*: the first heroine to star in a boy's comic, and a black one at that! Ebony was the only female agent in the British Special Mission Squad, but she was determined to prove that she was the best! A high-kicking karate queen, Ebony went to the north-Italian village of Merando to find her lost partner, Bleak, only to end up chained in a cave of skeletons. The village turns out to be occupied by Nazi war criminals disguised by plastic surgery.

Eebagoom
Albert Holroyd
Plug 1977-79; *Beezer* 1979 (D. C. Thomson)
Eebagoom the Yorkshire caveman and his Uncle Albert were on holiday in Blackpool in 55 BC (actually in No. 1 of *Plug* on 24 September 1977) when up on to the beach came Julius Sneezer. 'I claim Britain in the name of Rome', said Sneezer, adding an 'aah-choo' in emphasis. 'I've come, I've seen, now let's conquer!' The Ancient Yorkies struck back with tripe catties and banners reading 'Home Rule for Wigan', but even their concerted singing of 'Show them the way to go Rome' failed to win the day. Lured by tripe in mint sauce, Eabagoom and Uncle Albert were captured and carted off to Rome as slaves.

E

Electro Girl
Dennis M. Reader
G-Boy Comics 1947; *Whizzer Comics* 1947; *Super Duper* 1947-49 (Cartoon Art)
'Here is the story of the creation and outcome of a crime-fighting force, a gal who strikes terror into the hearts of the minions of evil!' Case No. 1, 'The Slaphappy Safecrackers', introduced the first British superheroine. Dr Flane, eminent electrobiologist, is dead. His daughter, Carol, investigates his laboratory. 'Abruptly there is a terrific bolt of electricity and Carol is thrown high into the charged air – Zap!' She strokes Buster the kitten – and electrocutes it! Weeks later, Burt, Ears, and Windows read in the paper: "To whom it may concern. I, Electro Girl, will give no peace to law breakers. Take heed all wrongdoers!' They jeer, but get zapped!

Elfie
Marjorie Owens
Magic 1976-79; *Twinkle* 1979- (D. C. Thomson)
This merry little elf lived in an old top hat in Dingly Dell. But on 25 September 1976, in No. 35 of *Magic*, there was a fierce storm and Elfie's hat-house was blown away. So the little fairy fellow went looking for a new home, and found one: a house inside a house! It was a doll's house that belonged to a little girl called Mary, and Elfie soon made himself at home. What a surprise next morning when Elfie was taking his bath. He didn't realize that it was actually a water dish for Mary's pet pup, Poochie! Elfie was soon so popular that he was promoted to the full-colour centre spread.

Electroman
King-Ganteaume
Electroman Comics 1951-52 (Scion)
'Electroman only comes forth when the forces of evil are to be conquered. Otherwise he is kind, elderly, New York City newsboy Dan Watkins, who was once an arch criminal! But because of a strange and amazing fate Dan has renounced his former life of crime and has become a staunch ally for the forces of law and order in their unending battle to stamp out evil! What has wrought this great change?' The question was soon answered. Dan, framed for murder, is given 'the hot seat' but survives: 'Warden, the shock has cured his mental disease!' A second shock alters his molecular structure and he becomes – Zzzz! Pow! – Electroman!

Elmer/Wacker
Rafart
Buster 1960-64 (Fleetway); *Smash* 1969-70; *Valiant* 1970-71 (IPC)
'How Stupid Can He Get?' was the caption to Elmer, 'the World Champion Chump' who made his first job application on 29 October 1960. As a trainee bus conductor, Elmer was not just the ticket: in fact, he unreeled a machineful of sixpenny tickets looking for a fourpenny one. Each week, Elmer caused havoc in a different job until, in 1961, he won a cross-channel race, bought an old Naval uniform, and was mistaken for a Grand Admiral of the Subterranian Navy. From then on he was 'All at Sea' with a new artist, Roy Wilson (illustrated). Reprinted as Wacker in *Smash*.

E

Emma
Illustrator unknown
Emma 1978-79 (D. C. Thomson)
'Hi, girls! Emma reporting. Welcome to my mag! This is where it's all happening!' Emma, editor of the new comic for girls, *Emma*, greeted her readers and spelled out her name: 'E for Excitement, M for Mystery, M for Marvellous Free Gifts (the first was an Initial Brooch), A for Action!' Emma was a teenage television reporter running *The Emma Report* with an opening familiar to David Frost fans: 'Hello, good evening, and welcome!' Her first report was diving for treasure off Scotland.

E.T.T. Extra Terrestrial Teacher
David Mostyn
School Fun 1983-84 (IPC)
Hot on the interstellar heels of *E.T.*, the hit sci-fi movie, came E.T.T., a sixty billion light year trip from Planet Freeky. Accidentally abandoned on Earth by his popeyed pupils ('Zeeks! I've pressed the wrong button!'), the Extra Terrestrial Teacher takes a temporary position at Punck Hill Secondary School under the name of Mr Freeky. It took thirty-three weeks to get home again, the length of the run of *School Fun*, thanks to his Freekian Headmaster who grabbed him with a grappling-hook and a cry of 'Borgle thung!'

Erik the Viking
Don Lawrence
Smash 1969-71 (IPC)
Erik the Viking swore to recover a golden helmet looted from the Temple of Thor by Selgor the Wolf, who used it to convince other Vikings that he was the Thor God. Selgor and his followers sailed to conquer the city of Egra in Sicily, while Erik and his companion Ajarn rode to raise men and ships to pursue them. But Berl, chief of the clan, believed Selgor. Erik drove his sword into the earth, crying, 'Odin Allfather, God of the winds and sea, give me a sign that I speak the truth!' And, from out of the sky, a wild falcon dropped like a stone to perch on the hilt of the sword!

Evil Eye
Reg Parlett
Whoopee 1974-77 (IPC)
The oddest of all the oddball characters in comics was this floating eyeball. It first opened in *Whoopee* No. 1 (9 March 1974), talking (!) to itself in an odd-shaped 'thinks balloon'. 'It's a nice quiet Sunday morning with everybody still in bed. Now who can I put the Evil Eye on to ruin it all?' It chose a paper boy delivering the *Sunday Blah*. The lad picked up an old can to throw into a litter bin when the Eye went to work on him making him kick the tin all round an Old Sailors Home. 'Avast!', cried the retired crew, 'All hands on deck!' All hands were about to descend on the lad's end, but all turned out shipshape.

Fabian of The Yard
Robert Fabian
Top Spot 1958-59 (Amalgamated Press)
Fabian of Scotland Yard was the first filmed series on British television (1954), with the famous Ex-Detective Superintendent Bob Fabian played by Bruce Seton. Coming to the new comic for adult males, *Top Spot* No. 1 (25 October 1958), the three-and-a-half-page strip was not adapted from the TV series, but entitled 'Manhunt' presented by Fabian of the Yard. Each week, Detective Sergeant Steve Brady and his veteran colleague Detective Constable Jigs Rafferty 'protected the lambs from the wolves and ordinary plain folk from the crooks'.

Fairy Farm
S. J. Cash
Puck 1920-27 (Amalgamated Press)
'Fun and Adventure at Fairy Farm' was the title of this two-colour, back-page strip in *Puck*. Obviously inspired by 'Tiger Tim and the Bruin Boys', S. J. Cash used a country farm as his setting. Mrs Porker wore a mobcap in the best Mrs Bruin tradition, pince-nez perched on her piggy snout, and her son Percy was ringleader of the animals. These answered to Neddy Bray, Dicky Duck, Rupert Rooster and a dog called Bobby Barker. So successful was Fairy Farm that Cash drew a doppelganger series in *Little Sparks* called 'Funland Farm' (1921).

The Falcon
George Heath
Radio Fun 1947-60 (Amalgamated Press)
'Police Can't Catch Him – All Crooks Fear Him!' That was the billing for the Falcon, the suave Robin Hood of Crime who always got the better of *Radio Fun*'s ace detective, Inspector Stanley. He became so popular that he was awarded a serial story of his own, 'The Falcon – Secret Agent' (25 March 1947), then a back-page picture serial as 'The Man of Many Disguises' (8 November 1947). In 1951, came a two-page serial strip, 'The Land of the Flying Saucers', in which he was whisked to planet Urania by Emperor Ortona. From 1 June 1957, he was promoted to the front page as a sort of superman in a bat-winged flying suit.

Faceache
Ken Reid
Jet 1971; *Buster* 1971- (IPC)
'The Boy with a Hundred Faces' can turn himself into anything by simply scrunge-ing himself. A spot of concentration and – 'scrunge!' – Faceache changes shape all over. He helped a fisherman win first prize by scrunge-ing into a sturgeon, and narrowly escaped being filletted! Scrunge-ing himself skinny to scrump Farmer Brown's orchard, Faceache was mistaken for an oversized stick-insect by mad Professor Schmidt. He escaped by scrunge-ing into a lamp-post! Latterly, Faceache has been the bane of Belmonte School. His real name is Ricky Rubberneck.

Family Trees
Robert Nixon
Wow 1982-83; *Whoopee* 1983-85 (IPC)
This crowd of characters were among the most unusual in comics: a clump of trees who went walkies every week in search of safety from humans – comic conservationists! The walking wood included Poplar, Birch, Scots Pine, Wild Apple, Elm, Weeping Willow, and the Wise Old Oak. One day they cheered themselves up with fun and games: 'Did you hear about the larch who joined a church? They made him larchbishop!' Then they played football: 'Goal! I should be playing for Notts Forest!'

The Famous Five

Enid Blyton

Look-In 1978-80 (ITV); *Enid Blyton's Adventure* 1985-86 (London)

Julian, Dick, Anne, George, and their dog Timmy, made their debut in Enid Blyton's novel, *Five on a Treasure Island* (1942). It was the first of many books written over a span of twenty-one years, and their sales run into millions. When The Famous Five were adapted into a children's television series by Southern TV in 1978, they were turned into a picture-strip serial for *Look-In*, the Junior *TV Times*. Mike Noble illustrated 'Five Have a Mystery to Solve', and others. Later came the full-colour *Enid Blyton's Adventure Magazine* (1985).

Felix the Cat

Pat Sullivan

Modern Boy 1936; *Felix Funnies* 1949; *TV Comic* 1954 (King Features)

The first international superstar in cartoon films, Felix the Cat was also the first to make the crossing from the animated screen to comic strip. Otto Messmer, the animator who designed Felix for producer Pat Sullivan, also drew the newspaper strips, which began on 14 August 1923. British reprints started in the *Illustrated Sunday Herald* and the *Felix Annuals* from 1925. Sullivan produced his last Felix film in 1929, but 'Felix kept on walking' as per his signature tune, into several comics.

Fiends Beans

Gordon Bell

Cracker 1975-76 (D. C. Thomson)

Young Fred's favourite food was baked beans, especially the brand labelled 'Produce of Transylvania'. These were Fiends Beans, a can of which had an unexpected effect on the eater. Fred swallowed a tinful when he went to be measured for a new suit by Mr Soutar the tailor: he grew an extra arm and another head! Fred's Dad was no luckier. His late-night supper of Fiends Beans on toast made him a night-mare: he galloped round the garden all night shouting 'Whinney!' Monstrous!

The Fantastic Four

Jack Kirby

Wham 1966-68; *Pow* 1968; *Smash* 1968-69 (Odhams); *Captain Britain* 1976; *Complete Fantastic Four* 1977-78; *Spiderman* 1977; *Fantastic Four Pocketbook* 1980-82; *Marvel Action* 1981; *Fantastic Four* 1982-83 (Marvel)

The so-called 'Marvel Age of Comics' began in the United States with No. 1 of *Fantastic Four* (November 1961), a team of superheroes written by Stan Lee and drawn by Jack Kirby. When the foursome moved from *Wham* to *Pow*, they were introduced thus: 'There's Reed Richards (Mr Fantastic), the mind-boggling, body-stretching leader of the team. Ben Grimm (The Thing) as handy with a wisecrack as with his fists. Johnny Storm called the Human Torch which is what he becomes when he "flames on". Johnny's sister Sue who can become invisible as well as project a very devastating force field.'

Fiends and Neighbours

Graham Allen

Cor 1973-74; *Buster* 1974-76; *Scream* 1984 (IPC)

Mr and Mrs Alfred Jones, simple suburban souls, did their best to smile bravely when confronted with their new neighbours, the Really-Ghastlies. This frightful foursome (fivesome if one included their pet octo-thing) came carol singing in the *Cor* Christmas Number, but spewed Mr Jones' hot punch all over the carpet. 'Grurrgh! Not enough sulphur!' 'Bleeaargh! More castor oil needed!' 'Not enough bad egg flavouring!' So father sent his son 'Orrid for their own homebrew: 'It's full of carefully distilled creepy-crawlies.' Father hoped 'Orrid hadn't shaken it too much lest the powdered earwig float to the top.

Figaro
Tom Bannister
Topper 1960-68; *Victor* 1974-78; 1986-87 (D. C. Thomson)
The merry Mexican bandito's weekly forays across the border and into *Topper* did him little good, peso-wise. Despite a large measure of help from a trio of incompetent hench-mexes, Figaro failed to fool the local Sheriff and invariably wound up behind bars. By 1965, he was popular enough to be promoted to a colour page but, while this new dimension proved handy when Figaro disguised himself as a redskin, his payoff remained stubbornly the same.

Film Struck Fanny
Bertie Brown
Chips 1925-33 (Amalgamated Press)
Fanny, who addressed her readers as 'Dear Flicker Fanciers', described herself as 'maid, housemaid, kitchenmaid, parlourmaid, and every other kind of maid that was ever made!' On 11 July 1925, she gave her mistress a minute's notice, and determined to break into pictures. Nine years later she was still at it. Fanny's career was anything but saved by the talkie revolution: her sound effects for Stewed Eel Studio's storm scene were a literal washout. Her main artist was Albert Pease (illustrated).

Fireball
Neville Wilson
Bullet 1976-78; *Warlord* 1978-79 (D. C. Thomson)
'He thrives on thrills! He lives on danger! He's Fireball!' His visiting card read: 'Fireball for Hire. Mysteries solved – Problems licked – Lost things found – Crooks straightened out – Anytime – Anyplace – But Only Dangerous Jobs Accepted.' His adventures spread over nine pages a week, starting 14 February 1976 in No. 1 of *Bullet*. And, as if this wasn't enough action, Fireball also ran his own Fireball Agents, a club for readers with a two-page spread to itself, 'Fireball Calling'. His adventures as a youth in training were told as 'Young Fireball' in *Warlord* (1979).

The Fighting Frasers
Bill Holroyd
Topper 1953-56 (D. C. Thomson)
In the wilds of northern Canada lived Big Jim Fraser with his son Dusty and his daughter Jean. After three months panning for gold and coming up with nothing but gravel, they set off in their canoe to reach Fort Gordon before the winter freeze-up. Hardly had they set off on their 200-mile trek when a black bear jumped the canoe, leaving Big Jim with a broken leg. Dusty and Jean soon lashed up a log raft, but many were the perils that lay ahead, from renegade redskins, Running Fox and Black Snake, to claim-jumping Jake Leroy.

The Finkelfeffer Family
Bertie Brown
Radio Fun 1947-59 (Amalgamated Press)
'Issy Bonn Introduces his Famous Finkelfeffer Family' was the actual title of this page which first appeared in *Radio Fun* No. 470, on 11 October 1947, and ran for a lucky thirteen years. Issy Bonn was a Jewish comedian who, besides always ending his act with a tear-jerking ballad, always told a joke or two featuring Jakey Finkelfeffer. It was editor Stanley Gooch's startling idea to build a family strip around Jakey: startling, because ethnic characters seldom appeared in British comics other than in stereotyped supporting roles.

Fireball XL5
Gerry Anderson
TV Comic 1962-64 (TV); *TV Century 21* 1965-67 (City)
Set in the twenty-first century, this serial was adapted from the popular television series created and produced by Gerry and Sylvia Anderson (ATV 1962). On an island in the Pacific Ocean stood Space City, the giant skyscraper headquarters of the World Space Organisation, revolving continuously to obtain a constant view of the Universe. Commander Zero and Lieutenant 90 despatched Fireball XL5 to investigate the silence from Satellite Advance 4. The crew: Colonel Steve Zodiac, Professor Matthew Matic, Venus the doctor of space medicine, and Robert the Robot. Started *TV Comic* 565 (13 October 1962); artist Neville Main.

F

First Ada
Gordon Bell
Plug 1977-79; *Beezer* 1979 (D. C. Thomson)
This is a slapstick variation of 'Nancy the Little Nurse' in *Twinkle*. First Ada is a well-meaning Beryl the Peril, causing more damage with her Little Nurse's Outfit than that tomboy can in a month of *Toppers*. Take her first case, for instance, on 24 September 1977 in No. 1 of *Plug*. 'Yur! Spronged me toe!' moaned a large lad. First Ada zoomed into action, pulled in her prambulance by Barrel her pet Saint Bernard. Ada caused so much physical damage to the man that he was left bandaged and splinted from head to foot – except for his big toe, of course, which remained spronged. First Ada rode off into the sunset singing 'If I can help somebody!'

Flash Gordon
Alex Raymond
Modern Wonder 1939 (Odhams); *Rocket* 1956 (*News of the World*); *TV Tornado* 1967-68 (City)
Flash Gordon, renowned polo player, Yale graduate, and astronaut, made his debut in the American Sunday supplements on 7 January 1934, copyright King Features Syndicate. With girl companion Dale Arden in tow, Flash set forth in Dr Hans Zarkov's home-made rocketship to thwart Ming the Merciless, Emperor of the planet Mongo. His adventures were reprinted in full colour in the prewar photogravure weekly, *Modern Wonder* (20 May 1939) and the postwar strips, now drawn by Mac Raboy, appeared across the centre spread of *Rocket*.

Fishboy
Illustrator unknown
Buster 1968-75 (Fleetway)
'This drama-charged picture-story featuring the fantastic Fishboy, Denizen of the Deep!' started on 20 January 1968. A hundred miles north of the tropical shores of New Guinea lay a tiny, seemingly unhabited coral atoll known as Pandron. A native sponge-diver, trapped by a giant ray, cried out. In answer, a fantastic figure appeared on the cliff top. Bronzed and deep-chested, he wore a costume of closely woven seaweed. He dived, swimming with the speed of a motor boat, thanks to hands and feet webbed like the Mangrove duck, calling to the fish: 'Glaaklush!' This was Fishboy!

Flash Scarlet
Murdock Stimpson
New Funnies 1940-43 (Swan)
Puffing a cigar, brandishing a spy-glass, and pulling a quick trigger, Flash Scarlet was the first British attempt at a tough detective in the Yankee style. Flash dashed into No. 1 of *New Funnies* (February 1940) and, in three pages, recovered the stolen submarine plans by finding a red hair dyed blonde, beating up a gangster until he squeals, tracing a secret hideout, crashing his car into a suspicious monoplane, and shooting down the villainous Red Dilk. Flash's reward was an extra page, which he needed if he was to save a Prominent Millionaire from the Texas Rat's giant python!

F

Flip and Flop
Denis Gifford
Marvelman, Young Marvelman, Marvelman Family 1956-59 (Miller)
Flip and Flop were a peculiar pair of foolish frampolds who filled up the blank bits between the more sensible adventures of Marvelman and Young Marvelman in the Miller sixpenny comic books of the 'Fifties. Narrowly escaping being christened Unk and Punk, Flip and Flop conformed to the classic double-act formula of tall and thin, short and fat, but otherwise were totally nonconformist in their dimwitted doings and dopey dialogue. Drawn by Denis Gifford but signed Belteshazzar Oakworm, Hasteaway Sassoon, Stridington Briskett, Glubtwee Gleeb, Plubby Stunflau, or Whetton Windie.

Fliptail the Otter
Bert Felstead
Jack & Jill 1967-85 (IPC)
Fliptail the Otter lived in Bramble Wood where he romped the days away with his woodland friends. One day, 15 April 1967 to be precise, a little girl called Debbie, who lived in a nearby cottage, came into the wood to play. Naughty Fliptail stole her ball and had a lovely time juggling it in the stream. Then a rabbit told him he must return it, so brave Fliptail rolled it to the cottage, through the cat-flap, and popped it on to Debbie's bed. But her kitten, Snowy, followed Fliptail home. Soon Debbie and Fliptail were great chums.

Flips
Freddie Adkins
Playbox 1939-55 (Amalgamated Press)
'Dear Boys and Girls' began Flips the fluffy white cat, ending up with 'Yours merrily'. Between this regular top and tail, Flips wrote a letter retailing his latest adventure, highlighted by Freddie Adkins' crisp and comic illustrations. Most of Flips' fun came from Peter Puggy, the dog next door, or a spotty hound called Snooker, a dab dog at dressing up. Flips had a girlfriend, too, a kittenish black cat called Boompsie. No wonder it was always 'Yours merrily!'

Flopsy Flufftail
Hugh McNeill
Harold Hare's Own Paper 1959-63 (Fleetway)
'The Funny Ways of Flopsy Flufftail' started in No. 1 of *Harold Hare's Own Paper* (14 November 1959). Flopsy was the female counterpart of Harold Hare, drawn, in fact, by the same artist. She wasn't a tomboy, but managed to get herself into a mess whatever she did. She had only to start cleaning her shoes to take a swipe at a fly in her ear, quite forgetting the polish brush in her paw. Fortunately, Freda Fieldmouse arrived to share her house. 'What with Flopsy making the place untidy, and Freda tidying it up again, they found plenty to do!'

Flossie and Fluffie
Alexander Akerbladh
Merry & Bright 1924-29 (Amalgamated Press)
'The Fascinating Flappers', twin daughters of a portly pa, strolled seductively on to the back page of *Merry & Bright* in the early 'Twenties, disappearing with their decade. Pretty, witty, and very self-possessed, Flossie and Fluffie spent their weeks dealing with bounders, mashers, and cads. One such was Bertie Bonehead who tried to squeeze them both into his sidecar: 'Bai jove, Gals, I'm an awfully wippin' dwivah!' F & F disconnected the doings and kept their date with handsome Tom and Jack – tea and toasties at the café.

F

Football Family Robinson
Illustrator unknown
Jag 1968-69; *Tiger 1969-73; Roy of the Rovers* 1978 (IPC)
Thatchem United, whose emblem was a shield shared by a robin and a football, was a unique family football club, playing in the Fourth Division. It was owned and managed by members of the Robinson family (Ma Robinson, President), and only Robinsons were allowed to play in the team. Small wonder, then, that the team should be known as the Robins. Tich Robinson played inside left, and the hefty ex-lumberjack, Grizzly Bear Robinson, scored most of the goals that got the Robins into the Third Division and on the way to the League Cup.

Footsie the Clown
Leo Baxendale
Wham 1964-68 (Odhams); *Whizzer & Chips* 1975 (IPC)
Footsie the Clown (costarring Wuff the Wonder Dog) was the full-colour, back-page star of *Wham* from No. 1 (20 June 1964). Footsie, so named for his oversized feet, wore a bowler-hat from which sprang all manner of useful props, such as boxing gloves to punch the nose of Fred the Fakir when he pinched Wuff's sausage, or simply a piece of cardboard labelled 'Idea!' Much of Footsie's fun came from other circus folk, such as Zippo the Trapezist, or Ali the Fire Eater, good for breathing on Wuff's sausage.

Flying Flapears
Evi de Bono
Magic 1976-79 (D. C. Thomson)
Flapears was the strongest rabbit in the world. He was also the saddest. 'Everyone laughs at my floppy ears!', he sobbed. But wise old Owl had the answer: 'Won't they flap instead of flop?' So Flapears had a go: Flappity-flap – and 'Whee! Look at me! I can fly!' His first adventure in the air, in *Magic* No. 1 (31 January 1976), was pretty mild, flying Mrs Fox's naughty cubs home in time for their bath. But, by the time of his last adventure, 161 weeks later, Flapears was not only saving Mr Piggy's boat from shipwreck, he was fitting it with wheels and pulling his pals for rides!

The Four Marys
Bill Holroyd
Bunty 1958- (D. C. Thomson)
'Fun at a Boarding School with a Frolicsome Foursome' was the headline that introduced Mary Simpson, Mary Field, Mary Radleigh, and Mary Cotter to the girls who bought No. 1 of *Bunty* (18 January 1958). But, when scholarship-girl Mary Simpson left Grove Street Council School, Ironborough, for St Elmo's boarding school for girls, she could hardly have foreseen the twenty-eight-year plus term that lay ahead of her! On the train she chummed up with fellow 'newt' Mary Cotter ('I'm a real duffer!'), and soon was sharing a study in Bee's House with the other two new Marys.

F

Foxy
Charles Grigg
Topper 1953-75 (D. C. Thomson)
'He's cunning and sly – He's a dangerous guy!' The original introduction to 'Foxy' in *Topper* No. 1 (7 February 1953) outlined this black animal's character, but dark and desperate his deeds may be, his popularity with readers soon promoted him from half page to full page. Foxy was less popular with the farmer on whose lands he prowled, and less popular still with the coopful of chickens upon whom he preyed. But, despite the lengths to which Foxy went, including trailing the farmer on a round-the-world cruise, he invariably ended up with buckshot in his tail.

Fraser of Africa
Frank Bellamy
Eagle 1960-61 (Longacre)
'Fraser of Africa' was one of the few strips in British comics to use colour impressionistically. Althougn the artist, Frank Bellamy, had full use of photogravure, he confined himself to hot, sunny yellows and burned-out browns to create a feeling of Africa in the natural raw. The story of white hunter/guide Fraser and his team, Hash, M'Kuki, and the Masai tracker, Ona, on the trail of ivory poachers, Schagen and Joyce, was scripted by George Beardmore, but it is Bellamy's images that remain burned in the memory.

Frankie Stein
Ken Reid
Wham 1964-68; *Shiver & Shake* 1973-74; *Whoopee* 1974-85; *Monster Fun* 1975-76; *Buster* 1976-86 (IPC)
It was in *Wham* No. 4 (11 July 1964) that Mildew Manor showed the first signs of life for fifty years. Its new tenant was Professor Cube, famous egghead, who was intent on turning custard into uranium. He would have succeeded had not his nosy son Micky interfered just as the vital 2 grams of tomato ketchup were being added. To keep Micky occupied, the prof built him a playmate. Formaldehyde, baking powder, Epsom salts, and a few nuts and bolts, plus a flash of electricity soon created – 'Buzz! Crackle! Phut!' – a creature – 'Burp! Gurgle! Phizzz!' – to which the prof could only remark 'Ee-yulk!' Replied the monster, 'Me Frankie Stein, I fink!'

Freddie Fang
Reg Parlett
Cor 1970-74 (IPC)
Freddie Fang was not just a Wolf Cub – he was a Werewolf Cub! He swore the Werewolf Pack oath: 'Dib-dib-dib! Dob-dob-dob! I promise that I will always cheat, and I also vow to do a bad deed every day!' And his first bad deed, in the first issue of *Cor* (6 June 1970), was to help an old lady across the road. What was so bad about that deed? The old lady didn't want to go! 'There's nothing like the feeling of satisfaction gained from a bad deed well done!', smiles Freddie, until the bad deed turned accidentally good and the old lady rewarded him with a kiss.

Freddie Flipp and Uncle Bunkle
Bertie Brown
Sparkler 1935 (Amalgamated Press)
'The Flighty Pranks of Freddie Flipp and his Uncle Bunkle' took off on the full-colour front of *Sparkler* No. 27, 20 April 1935. Freddie, described as 'the lad with high-speed ideas and an aeroplane to match', piloted while Nunky, all pince-nez and pith-helmet, perched as his permanent passenger. After a few flips to the Far East and elsewhere, they flew to an inside page where, under the new heading of 'Here, There and Everywhere', they were piloted by the pen of Billy Wakefield (illustrated).

Freddie Frog
Peter Woolcock
Knockout 1950-52; *Jack & Jill* 1954-72 (IPC)
'The Funny Tales of Freddie Frog' were told in *Jack & Jill* from No. 1 (27 February 1954). 'Our Freddie has his ups and downs, but he ends up with a smile', said the editor, and he certainly did in his first two-page adventure. Freddie and his good friend Terry Tortoise drove into the country for a picnic. Soon he was bossing Terry about in traditional Mr Toad style (same artist, Peter Woolcock), but got in such a tangle with his new deckchair that he ripped out the canvas. Never mind, Terry turned it into a hammock and they both sat down to tea.

Freddie Fluence
Alex Akerbladh
Favorite 1912 (Amalgamated Press)
'Ladies and Gentlemen, Boys and Girls, Cab-minders, Coke-sifters, Suffragettes, Work-dodgers, Sherbet-shifters, Lamplighters, and other Jolly Old Knuts – allow us to introduce to your notice our latest fun-monger and wonder-worker, Freddie Fluence the Merry Mesmerist!' Thus the editorial introduction to this schoolboy sensation who became the front-page star of *The Favorite Comic* from No. 70 (18 May 1912). For starters, Freddie hypnotized the landlord into scrubbing his poor mum's doorstep, then juggling a dozen shop-soiled eggs until he had earned sufficient spondulicks to cancel the debt.

Freddy the Fearless Fly
Allan Morley
Dandy 1937-54; *Sparky* 1965 (D. C. Thomson)
An odd character for a comic hero, Freddy the Fearless Fly flew into No. 1 of *Dandy* (4 December 1937) and stayed there for no fewer than 667 adventures, surviving constant attacks by his arch-enemy Septimus Spider, irate baldies armed with flyswatters, rolled newspapers, frying pans, flysprays, sticky flypapers, and anything else his ingenious artist could devise. Freddy even survived the real-life 'Swat That Fly' campaign, buzzing comically onwards and upwards in his quest for grub.

Freddie Freewheel
Bert Hill
Rocket 1935-38 (Target)
Freddie Freewheel the Tramp Cyclist may have drawn his inspiration from the several cycling tramps who performed their tricks on the variety stage during the 'Thirties (Slim Ryder; Joe Jackson). He rode into *Rocket* No. 1 (26 October 1935), introduced by the caption writer thus: 'This comical cove is Freddie Freewheel, and he is not the ordinary common or countryside kind of tramp, as you perceive. He flits around on a – well, perhaps you had better call it what you like!' His wooden wonder bumped a boulder. 'Great gravel!', he gasped, 'I've got a puncture!'

Freddy, Teddy, Joe
Illustrator unknown
Little Star 1972-76 (D. C. Thomson)
'Ready, steady, go! It's time to meet Freddy, Teddy, Joe!' announced the editor of *Little Star* in No. 36 (30 September 1972). Closer to the Three Bears of fairy-tale fame than the 'Three Bears' of *Beano* fame, this trio lived together in a comfy little cottage in Lavender Lane. Freddy was a polar bear, Teddy was a teddy bear, and Joe was a koala bear from Australia, and had a boomerang on his bedroom wall to prove it. On their first day, Freddy and Teddy couldn't wake up sleepy headed Joe, so they pushed him to school in his bed! Mr Bruin the lollipop man was surprised, but not so surprised as Joe when he woke up in school: 'Goodness!'

F

Fred the Flop
Tom Lavery
Buzz 1973-75; *Topper* 1975-1986 (D. C. Thomson)
Fred the Flop was well named: as a petty crook, he couldn't have been pettier. Even his clothes were outdated: his snap-brim trilby and checked suit were as old as his hairstyle. With his neat little tash and sideboards, Fred could have been a spiv from the postwar 'Forties. Even his small successes turned to ashes: bagging a briefcase full of banknotes, they turned out to be play money from the Bank of Toytown. Week after week, he wound up in the local cop-shop, clapped in the clink.

Frosty McNab
Sam Fair
Beano 1939-40 (D. C. Thomson)
Billed as 'The Freezy Wheeze Man', Frosty McNab was one of the odder characters to feature in the early *Beano*, even by the decidedly odd standards of that comic. Evidently inspired by the legendary Jack Frost, McNab's nose and hair were spiky icicles, and he wore a pointed hat to match. Frosty's particular gimmick was his icy breath: one puff and anything in its path froze solid. Thus, Frosty was able to do a good turn for some Scottish auld-age pensioners who couldna afford curly walking sticks: he breathed on some eels!

Frog-faced Ferdinand and Watty Wool-whiskers
Illustrator unknown
Coloured Comic 1898-1900 (Trapps Holmes)
Two derivative fat-and-thin tramps, but with a difference: they were the first to appear in full colour. Ferdy (thin) and Watty (fat) were the first front-page stars of the first weekly comic printed in colour, which was called, rather aptly, *The Coloured Comic*. In their No. 1 adventure, dated 21 May 1898, they stole a sailor's box. 'Jumping Johnson!' they cried as out sprang a monkey. 'Good old Monkey Brand!' shrieked Watty when the ape picked Ferdy's pocket, 'Yer one of the boys!' They dressed the animile in their landlady's castoffs and it pinched a masher's watch.

Full O'Beans
Tom Paterson
Jackpot 1979-82 (IPC)
Floppy and feeble Freddie's favourite grub was baked beans. One day (it was 5 May 1979 in *Jackpot* No. 1) his mum ran out of tins, so Freddie ran out to the shop. Selecting a new brand, Ben's Beans, Freddie was surprised to win a prize: as many tins of Ben's Beans as he could carry. To give himself strength, he swallowed a tinful ('Slurp!'). The beans certainly gave him strength – superstrength – 'Ka-Pow!' Freddie was able to carry away every box of beans in the shop, a supply which kept him full of beans for four years.

Fun on Board the Mary Anne
Arthur White
Comic Cuts 1907-21 (Amalgamated Press)
This cosy little craft was captained by a side-whiskered seadog known as the Old Salt. He commanded a crew of three: Bill, the bell-bottomed one, Sambo the seacook, and Chung the Chinee. Their *Comic Cuts'* cruise took them fifteen years, during which time they organized a seals' band at the pole, harnessed giant crabs while becalmed in the tropics, and salvaged a sea-sarpint off the white cliffs of Wapping. It was sad to see them inexplicably replaced by 'Captain Cod's Voyage of Discovery'.

Fury's Family
Denis McLoughlin
Thunder 1970-71; *Lion* 1971-72 (IPC)
'His name was Fury. More than that, they never knew. His father? His mother? Mysteries as baffling as the strange way he had with animals.' Archer Spang, the rich showman with the cruel whip, bought Downer's Circus, little realizing that Fury had learned the language of the animals. 'Aaaarga! Nurrrf! Mrurrr!' he said to Chieftain the lion, 'Throol moopa thurrrg!' he said to Rajah the elephant, and 'Murb thoora jooka nij prakka!' he added to the gorilla. And silently in the night, Fury led his family away from the circus.

The Funny Bunny Boys
Illustrator unknown
Tiny Tots 1927-57 (Amalgamated Press)
'The Fun-ny Bun-ny Boys', to give this pair their correct billing, were the back-page funsters in *Tiny Tots*, a hyphenated comic for the nursery set. They lived in a burrow with Daddy and Mummy Bunny, and their names were Bunny and Bobtail, which must have caused a little confusion for one of them – the one whose full name was therefore Bunny Bunny! They were an old-fashioned family, Mummy wearing a mobcap and pinafore, Daddy a tasselled smoking-cap as he puffed at a lengthy churchwarden pipe.

Fun in Toy Land
Vera Bowyer
Chicks Own 1936-56 (Amalgamated Press)
Tommy Toy Soldier was the leading man in this full-page strip and, although there were pretty dolls galore, his heart obviously belonged to the blue-eyed blonde Belinda. Among the many animated inhabitants of Toy Land were a Dutch Dolly called Wooden Shoes, a Chinese boy called Chinky, a pierrot called Peter, and an elephant called – of course – Jumbo. Then there were the occasional visitors, like Belinda's cousin Dandy Jim, a toff in a topper, and Colin Clockwork-Horse.

Fuss Pot
Norman Mansbridge
Knockout 1971-73; *Whizzer & Chips* 1973-84 (IPC)
'What a fuss pot this girl is – She gets everyone in a tizz!' This sharp-nosed little miss sat down to tea on 12 June 1971 in No. 1 of *Knockout*, and immediately wanted to know why her Dad had three more baked beans than she did! And when he offered her them she screamed. 'Don't you dare let a single one touch my plate now they've been prodded by your fork!' So off she stomped to the shop to buy her own tin of beans which, of course, had to be the one with the untorn label right at the bottom of the pile! 'Rattle . . . . topple . . . clatter . . . clunk!' Fuss Pot's fussing soon promoted her to the full-colour back page.

G

Galaxus
Solano Lopez
Buster 1966-74 (Fleetway)
Borrowing its subtitle from a popular science-fiction film, 'Galaxus: The Thing From Outer Space' landed in England with beings from another planet to carry out a survey of Earth. But the spaceship left unexpectedly and Galaxus was left behind, marooned and frightened: 'Muuu-uuh!' Capable of changing from giant size to a mere 2 inches in height, Galaxus was befriended by two boys, Jim and Danny Jones. Jim found he could understand his thoughts: 'He's saying he's lonely, and means no-one any harm!' But the rest of the world thought otherwise.

General Jumbo/Admiral Jumbo
Paddy Brennan
Beano 1953-74; *Nutty* 1980; *Nutty* 1981 (D. C. Thomson)
'The Cheery Schoolboy who has his own Army, Navy and Air Force' was Alfie Johnson of Dinchester. 'Alfie was twelve years old, a likeable lad, and because of his plump, hefty figure, his chums called him Jumbo.' Kicking his football over a wall, Jumbo was startled to find himself attacked by a tiny RAF jet and a squadron of small tanks! These were the experiments of genial Professor Carter who, when Jumbo saves him from being run over, enlists Jumbo as the General of his radio-controlled troops.

The Gasworks Gang
Frank McDiarmid
Cor 1970-74; *School Fun* 1984 (IPC)
'Are schooldays the happiest days of your life?' queried the headline in *Cor* No. 1 (6 June 1970). 'Ask the teacher of the Gasworks Gang!' This bearded brute with the mouthful of shark-gnashers put no wind up the wild bunch of juvenile delinquents that made up his class. For these were the notorious Gasworks Gang, big fat Tub, zzzz-ing Dozy, inquisitive Nosey, bespectacled Brains, tiny Tich, and, in charge of them all, the bald-headed (save for a sticking-plaster cross) Boss in his sinister sunglasses.

Gay Gus and Shrimp
H. O'Neill
Big Comic 1914-18 (Henderson)
This tall and short combination formed a typical front-page double act from No. 1 of *Big Comic* (17 January 1914) performing such run-of-the-mill stunts as feeding an eel with Fattening Food and selling it in large lumps as shilling sausages. With the declaration of World War 1, all that changed and, as Privates Gus and Shrimp, they waded into the Germ-huns with British gusto. Running out of shells, they blew General Von Muck out of his bath with a well-aimed tin of carbide: 'Donner und blitzen! Vot's dot cosh on mine listenhole?'

General Nitt
Leo Baxendale
Wham 1964-68 (Odhams)
'General Nitt and his Barmy Army', as mercenary a gang of armed idiots as ever speared a sausage, charged into action in No. 1 of *Wham* (20 June 1964) at the airmail behest of Baron Dumff whose castle was currently besieged by Bad Baron Bludgeon. Soon the 'Twang! Pyoinggg!' of arrows were heard in the nearby air so the General sent in a serf disguised as a bush to reconnoitre. A quick bit of hammering in their workshop and Nitt & Co knocked up a cardboard castle to fool the baddies. Their reward: a potato castle with sausage cannons and a gravy moat! 'Yum-yum!'

George the Jolly Gee-Gee
Roy Wilson
Radio Fun 1938-39; *Jester* 1940; *Crackers* 1940-41; *Wonder* 1944-45; *Big One* 1964-65; *TV Fun* 1953 (Fleetway)
Although brilliantly drawn by Roy Wilson, George was obviously the wrong character for the full-colour front page of a comic called *Radio Fun*. A few weeks later Arthur Askey took over, which made more sense – but George was clearly too good to put out to grass. With his creator busy elsewhere, editor Stanley Gooch assigned John L. Jukes (illustrated), who ran George from comic to comic for another six years. Wilson revamped George as 'Hoofer the Tee-Vee Gee-Gee' for *TV Fun* (1953).

Gertie the Regimental Pet
G. M. Payne
Comic Cuts 1906-12 (Amalgamated Press)
'Whiff! Whooster! Plonk!' With these words, the *Comic Cuts* caption writer sought to describe the sound of Gertie's kick. She was a back-firing mule, property of the Thirsty First Regiment (C-in-C Major Musket), in the charge of the youthful Private Raw. In peace and war, Gertie's hind-hoofs could be relied upon to save the day. Indeed, once she was chaired at Bisley for top score on the target range without a rifle! And, when she saved the fort by giving the locals a taste of her horseshoes, she was awarded a life pension of four carrots a day.

Georgie's Germs
Leo Baxendale
Wham 1964-68; *Pow* 1968 (Odhams)
When Georgie said 'Hi, readers!' in No. 1 of *Wham* (20 June 1964), his Mum carted him off to the bathroom for a good scrub. As she washed his hair with antiseptic shampoo, the ensuing battle between the clean-up bugs and Georgie's dirt germs took up the best part of two pages. General Dan Druff led his lads into action: black-head bullets, pimple mixture, muck mortars, and judo germs defended Georgie's scalp against bleach bombers, hair howitzers, and chlorophyll cannons. And when Gen. Druff brought in the bluebottle bombers and red-scalp injun germs, the enemy retreated for ever. Mum gave up!

© 1983 TCFC

Get Along Gang
American Greetings Corporation
Get Along Gang 1985- (Marvel)
Copyrighted by the American Greetings Corporation, and coming to Britain via Tomy Toys and a television cartoon series, Marvel Comics added to the mass merchandizing by publishing No. 1 of their weekly *Get Along Gang* (20 April 1985). 'Enter the Magical World of Green Meadow!' was the enticing headline that introduced the Gang: Dotty Dog the cheerleader, Montgomery 'Good News' Moose the athlete, Portia Porcupine the inquisitive youngster, Zipper Cat the health nut, Woolma Lamb the ballerina, Bingo 'Bet It All' Beaver the gambler, Bernice Bear, Lolly Squirrel, Braker Turtle, Rudyard Lion, Rocco Rabbit, and Flora 'Forget Me Not' Fox. British strips by Barrie Appleby.

Get-Your-Man Gilligan
Jock McCail
Jolly 1938-39 (Amalgamated Press)
'Sheriff of Dynamite City', a subtitle he wore as proudly as his star, Get-Your-Man Gilligan (no other given name known) rode on to the back page of *Jolly* on 15 January 1938. Like all good lawmen, Gilligan had a sidekick, Chick Riley, billed as 'his young assistant', and the saddle pards were soon on the trail of Black Jake and his gang of dangerous bandits. They foiled their plan to rob a bullion train in Dead Man's Gulch by canoeing down Roaring Rapid: 'Dang it! It's the Sheriff and that young cub again!' Then they were off to unmask the hooded White Rider for threatening the boss of Roaring Ranch.

Ginger
Dudley Watkins
Beezer 1956- (D. C. Thomson)
Ginger was the principal page-one star of *Beezer* right from No. 1 (21 January 1956) although, for some years, he was shifted from his rightful site by the triple-threat strip, 'Pop, Dick and Harry'. After his restitution to the full-colour front, Ginger's hair not only grew wilder, it burst into brick red! Ginger's adventures invariably began with him waking up in bed ('Good mornin', readers!') and ended with him retiring for the night ('Good night, readers!'): between, fifteen pictures told of his doings for the day.

Ghastly Manor
Murray Ball
Topper 1974-77 (D. C. Thomson)
'I hope somebody buys this place soon – I can't stand it much longer!' Thus spake the shaky Mr Fear, knocking up a 'For Sale' sign outside Ghastly Manor. He said the same thing every week for years, but there were no buyers, thanks to the family of spooks that lived in the mildewed manse with him. They were ghastly ghosts, including one with his head tucked underneath his arm, a dumpy little witch with a mane of white hair, a vast and decidedly un-jolly green giant, and a skeleton given to loosing a bone now and then to a haunting hound.

Ginger's Tum
Terry Bave
Whizzer & Chips 1969-70; *Buster* 1978-79 (IPC)
Introduced in *Whizzer & Chips* No. 1 (18 October 1969) as 'a cat with an appetite for food and fun', Ginger started his adventures in classic Oliver Twist style, by asking for more. As it was the dog's dinner he'd just scoffed, all Ginger got was a boot up the tail. 'And to think I've only had thirteen tins of Katti-Kit today!', he muttered as he two-legged off with the tummy rumbles. Lured by the pong of a nearby fish restaurant, Ginger was offered a slap-up dinner by the chef, and got it – a slap up the puss with a sloppy cod!

Gip and His Giraffe
Walter Holt
Comic Life 1911-14 (Henderson)
Gip was a jolly Negro gent who addressed his readers thus: 'Deah Mistah Editah an' de Jolly Readahs ob dis Papah!', signing off his weekly adventure with 'Yo's brightly!' His pet giraffe, known as Neckstretch, accompanied him on all his travels, including a trip to the moon courtesy of Messrs Splutter and Fizz, firework manufacturers. It was an early experiment in Air Mail that misfired. In 1912 another odd pet was added to the entourage, Ossie the Octopus, whose tentacles came in handy in a treasure hunt.

The Girls From N.O.O.D.L.E.S.
Illustrator unknown
Diana 1965-70 (D. C. Thomson)
Gale Price and Nicola Main were special agents working for N.O.O.D.L.E.S.: the National Organisation for Order, Discipline and Law Enforcement in Schools. (A secret agency inspired by the popular television series, 'The Men From U.N.C.L.E.'). They received their orders from their chief, Miss Z, at the secret headquarters in a ruined abbey. Typical cases included investigating the electrocution by guitar of a pupil at Alexander's Pop School, and the face-changing masks of the sinister ballet master, Tengali.

Glugg
Gordon Hogg
Wham 1965-68 (Odhams); *Whizzer & Chips* 1975 (IPC)
'He's First in Everything' was the caption for Glugg, a ginger-headed caveboy who made his full-colour entry on the back page of *Wham* No. 33 (30 January 1965). To Glugg it was just another day of boredom, backwardactyls flying backwards and so forth. To pass the time, he invented something but didn't know what it was. When the cavefolks jeered at him, he thumped them all with it, calling it a 'club' after the noise it made bouncing off their bonces! In succeeding weeks, Glugg invented fire (and hence baked beans on toast), and something that displeased his *Wham* readers: the bath.

Gobble-Gobble Gertie
Charles Grigg
Dandy 1954 (D. C. Thomson)
'Gertie is an Eskimo, and Gertie likes to munch – When Gertie meets a monster moose, it's monster moose for lunch!' Luke Smart of the Black Circle Timber Co of Frozen Creek, Canada, described this pesky Esky on 1 May 1954, in *Dandy* No. 649: 'The biggest calamity that ever hit the far north. That calamity walks and eats. Mainly it eats. It eats like a plague of locusts all wrapped up in one huge furry jacket. For this calamity is a dame, the biggest, hungriest whale of a dame that anyone on this earth ever clapped eyes on!'

Good King Coke
Eric Roberts
Beano 1939-46 (D. C. Thomson)
This merry monarch kept smiling despite the patches on his knees, symbols of the poverty-stricken kingdom over which he ruled. Not for nothing was he billed as 'Good King Coke – He's Stoney Broke!' Cursed with a Queen who wore a pinafore and brandished a rolling-pin instead of a sceptre, his troubles were doubled by the later addition of a pair of naughty nephews. When he decreed that gasmasks must be carried, these cruel kids dosed the royal gasmask with pepper!

Good Knight Gilbert
Roy Wilson
Comic Life 1924-26; *Sparkler* 1935 (Amalgamated Press)
'The Good Knight Gilbert and Folio his Funny Page' besported themselves on ye olde back page of *Comic Life* which, for part of their span, blossomed forth into full colour, ye rare honour. Sir Gilbert, never seen out of his shining armour, was given to crying 'Gadzooks!' and 'Out upon thee for a clumsy malapert!' to his portly varlet. Folio, with an 'An' it please ye, sire!' or so, did his plumping best, and oft aided ye knight in his tourneys with bad Sir Roger over ye dainty lilywhite of Ladye Marion. Much mirth-eth!

The Good Ship Funnybone

Louis Briault

My Funnybone 1911-13 (Belvedere)

The crew of the S.S. *Funnybone* consisted of a minimum of three, Captain Hook, Bill the Bosun, and Curly the Cabin Boy, and a maximum of four, if you counted Gertie the parrot. She came in handy for filling up odd corners with the cry of 'Steady, boys!' Their adventures were curiously warlike, considering they flourished well before World War 1 was declared. In 1912 they were chasing a runaway torpedo that escaped from the British boat, *Goalongwithyou*, and were later found trying to capture a German spy balloon.

The Goon Platoon

Illustrator unknown

Whoopee 1974 (IPC)

The Commander-in-Chief of the Army, Major-General Piffleby Pipps, I.O.U., P.T.O., C.D.M., was making his annual inspection. 'Good gad! What's this black blot in the middle of Berkshire?' It was the one blot on the British Army, the 13th Loyal Dragoons, where all the useless, fat-headed, bird-brained twits were posted. In charge was Sergeant-Major Thunderguts (spare-time hobbies: bellowing and lion taming). The Goon Platoon: Corporal Clumper, and Privates 'No Entry' Podge, Blunder Gus, Nutt Shell, Reggie Mental, and the ancient Crack Pop, or, as Sergy called them, 'You loony, loafing, half-baked apologies for soldiers!' An unusual three-page strip.

Goody Gumdrops

Ferguson Dewar

Little Star 1972-76; *Twinkle* 1976 (D. C. Thomson)

Goody Gumdrops lived in Sweetie Town and on 29 January 1972, in No. 1 of *Little Star*, she took her new readers for a turn around the town. She watched Grandma Peppermint chasing the naughty humbugs away from her toffee-apple trees, and said hello to the sugar mice who lived in Farmer Fruitdrop's field of barley-sugar. At last, Goody arrived at the pet shop owned by Mr Mint to buy a puppy. She couldn't decide between a poodle, a terrier, or a dalmatian. So she bought a puppy who was a mixture of all three and promptly named him Allsorts!

Grandfather Clock

Alan Fraser

Magic 1939 (D. C. Thomson)

'Tick-tick-tock! Here's Grandpa Clock – Just you watch him walk and talk!' When Burglar Bill cracked a crib in *Magic* No. 1 (22 July 1939), fully equipped with the traditional footpad's outfit of flat cap, striped jersey, and sack marked 'Loot', he little suspected what lay in store for him. Everything in the house came to life: Money-Box Mick, Arthur Alarm-Clock (who rang for the police), and toughest of the lot, Grandfather Clock, who struck – Bill's bum with a poker!

Grandpa
Ken Reid
Beano 1955-57; 1971-84 (D. C. Thomson)
The chubby old codger with scruffy whiskers, checked waistcoat, and a bag of bullseyes in his pocket, greeted readers of *Beano* No. 680 (30 July 1955): 'Hiya, folks! I'm off to see if the boys are playing in the park!' But Grandpa was due for a disappointment: the benches were full of snoring oldsters his own age. 'Bah! Nothing but a lot of stuffy, dodderin' old fogies!' So, being but a boy at heart, Grandpa put in a spot of practice on his new roller skates. Don't tell Grandpa's dad!

Gremlins
Steve Bell
Jackpot 1979-81 (IPC)
This postwar development of the wartime Gremlins strip concentrated on the evil aspect of the original RAF myth. This black gang of ghastly gnashers included Grasping Granville Gremlin, Greasy Graham Gremlin, Gruesome Greta Gremlin, Grotty Gregory Gremlin, Gormless Gordon Gremlin, and Great Big Grizelda Gremlin who wore plaits and a Viking horned helmet. The cartoonist claimed he drew their doings with a magnifying pen to show what the eye cannot see, such as Gremlins working over a boy's bike: 'This tyre won't get a puncture – unless we sink our teeth into it!'

Greedy Pigg
George Martin
Dandy 1965-71, 1978-82 (D. C. Thomson)
Mr Pigg was a mortar-boarded schoolmaster fond of his food, so naturally his boys nicknamed him 'Greedy' Pigg. Very few lessons seemed to be learned at his school, even by Mr Pigg, whose obsession with adding more padding to his already bulging red waistcoat invariably ended in disaster. Much of Mr Pigg's spare time seemed to be spent lurking around the local tuck-shop, ready to pounce upon Curly and his chums as they emerged with their bags of bullseyes and cartons of cream buns.

Grimly Feendish
Leo Baxendale
Smash 1966-68 (Odhams)
Proudly billing himself 'The Rottenest Crook in the World', Grimly Feendish (when he smiled bats flew out of his fangs) lurked in the cellars of Doomsday House, Tomb Street, plotting plans and planning plots, such as the kidnapping of the Prime Minister, the robbing of the Bank of England, and stealing gobstoppers from the sweet shop. His pets, hairy things, octopussies, and nameless creatures that slithered into corners, had scoffed his supply of suckers, you see. Originally Feendish was the menace to Eagle Eye, Junior Spy in *Wham*.

The Gremlins/The Chuckles
Fred Robinson
Knockout 1943-47 (Amalgamated Press)
'It's the Gremlins!' was the actual title of this popular page which started in *Knockout* No. 201, 2 January 1943. As Fred explained, 'The Gremlins are the elfs of the air, but Pilot Officer Plonk didn't believe in them.' Once Gurch and his gang from Gremlin Grange get cracking, he soon changes his mind! Based on the RAF legend of World War 2, the page changed from a strip to one huge picture, showing the Gremlins up to pranks in best Casey Court style. Revamped as The Chuckles in *Giggle* (1967).

The Group
Mike Brown
Pow 1967-68 (Odhams)
'The toughest kids in our town!' was the way the police sergeant described The Group to newcomer on the beat, P. C. Pratt. Six pictures were pinned up on the station noticeboard: Brain, spotty with specs; Fatso, spotty with schoolcap and lollipop behind the ear; Stupid, spotty with two big teeth; Shrimp, spotty but short; Ringo, a ringer for Ringo Starr; Luvvy, the obligatory girl, pigtails but spotless (except for her conscience). The Group's Place was a wooden shed with a skull-and-crossbones painted on the roof.

Gulliver
Dudley Watkins
Magic 1940 (D. C. Thomson)
Dean Swift's classical character might not have recognized himself from the trailer advertising his first appearance in *Magic* No. 61: 'His merry adventures will make you scream with laughter in this bumper new series of rib-tickling stories!' There was another new twist: 'When you've finished laughing at his adventures in the story, you can watch his antics in a side-splitting cartoon.' Not the Max Fleischer animated cartoon film, but a separate strip which supplemented the two-page text story: a double feature!

Gus Gorilla
Alf Saporito
Cor 1970-74 (IPC)
Gus was a ginger gorilla who sported a school cap. He was the front-page star of *Cor* and, indeed, could be seen shouting the title of this comic, complete with two exclamation marks in red, on all 210 issues. His first appearance (6 June 1970) saw him at the seaside. Finding the water too cold for his toes, he put hot-water bottles on his feet and went for a nice warm paddle. This caused a passing person to comment, 'You can't make a monkey out of Gus!', and this became his regular catchphrase.

Gulliver Guinea-Pig
Philip Mendoza
Playhour 1959-65; *Jack & Jill* 1972-73; *Teddy Bear's Playtime* 1981 (IPC)
Gulliver Guinea-Pig was an inveterate traveller, and his worldwide wanderings (including some which were out of this world) took place across the full-colour centre spread of *Playhour*. His early adventures, including a trip to the Wild West by air balloon, had a realism that turned to pure fantasy after Philip Mendoza turned in his paintbox. The 1961 serial, 'Gulliver Guinea-Pig Saves Summer', featured the Fairy Queen of the Summer and Jack Frost of the North Pole. By 1962, the accent was cartoony as Gulliver explored Nursery Rhyme Land.

Gus Grit
Frank Minnitt
Jester 1932-35; 1937 (Amalgamated Press)
'Gus Grit the Ancient Brit' arrived in *Jester* on 3 December 1932, just in time to fend off a Roman invasion: 'That's the second time this week!' gritted Gus. Having dealt with the invaders ('Go home and tell Julius Caesar we don't like you!') he turned his attention to catching an Oozlum Bird for supper, thwarting Uggug the Stonehenge smash-and-grabbist. Another time, a slab of ancient postcard came in handy to dent the dough of his home-made loaf. After a year's holiday, 'The Return of Gus Grit' (1937) saw our half-baked hero wooing the winsome Wanda, the stone-age belle.

Gums
Robert Nixon
Monster Fun 1976; *Buster* 1976-84 (IPC)
'The Shark Worse Than Its Bite' opened his jaws for business in *Monster Fun* No. 35 (7 February 1976). Unlike his inspiration in the popular film *Jaws*, this outsize shark sunk his teeth in a surfboard sandwich and promptly lost them in a tidal wave: they were dentures! The Australian cobber who copped them used them to decorate his Eats and Drinks Emporium but, with the aid of an unshelled turtle, Gums got his choppers back. Then he lost them again the next week, and so the series swam on.

Guy Gorilla
Tom Paterson
Whizzer & Chips 1982-83 (IPC)
Guy the gorilla was once a great children's favourite at the London Zoo but, when he ate peanuts, nothing much happened to him. When this Guy ate peanuts, he changed from an ordinary scruffy schoolboy into a great black hairy gorilla: 'Snaaarrl! Groowwll! Aaarrrr!' This alarming metamorphosis had the expected effect on bullies, who tended to dash away smartly crying 'Gibber! Gibber!' Guy himself was a bit shy about his special gift, especially when the terrorized township posted a reward for the gorilla.

Hairy Dan
Basil Blackaller
Beano 1938-44 (D. C. Thomson)
Hairy Dan was a bearded old boy who made his unshaven debut in *Beano* No. 1 (30 July 1938). Dan's description by the editorial rhymester ran: 'His Whiskers Neat Reach to his Feet!', although it was a while before this rhyme became regular. Dan's early adventures each had their own comical couplet, from a selection of which can be deduced his specialty: 'How Dan won the Race with his Hairy Face!' – 'Dan makes a Copper come a Cropper!' – 'Dan's Hairy Chin will make you Grin!

Handy Andy
Sid Burgon
Krazy 1977-78 (IPC)
'His Hand Pictures Come to Life!' was the caption to this long-haired lad in the denim suit. When Handy Andy used his torch to throw a hand shadow, the silhouette sprang into life. No rational explanation for this power was given. What was given, however, was a close-up showing how readers could make each week's shadow for themselves. Andy's first shadow shown in *Krazy* No. 1 (16 October 1976) was of a duck. He cast it on the tight trousers of a burglar bending over a silversmith's safe, and it promptly pecked him where it would do most good!

Halcon
Nat Brand
Comic Capers 1942-49 (Soloway)
Halcon (his name rhymes with falcon), subtitled 'Lord of the Crater Land', ruled the front pages of a popular two-colour comicbook of the war years. A blonde Tarzan-type sporting a red waistcoat, he thwarted an invasion of Africa by Nazi paratroopers: with a cry of 'Bwantu!', he ran them down with a herd of wild elephants. In a series unusual for British comics, Halcon rescued a lovely white girl, Karen, from a tribe of nomadic slave-traders (they were planning to sacrifice her to a man-eating tree!), and carried her by camel to his shelter-tree . . .

The Hammer Man
Ted Rawlings
Victor 1973-85 (D. C. Thomson)
'The Hammer Man' was the name given to former blacksmith Baron Chell Puddock, a mighty muscleman who lived and wielded his 'old ironhead' during the reign of King Henry V. Given to odd expletives ('Odds teeth! Odds winks! Odds ribs!') the Hammer Man was accompanied on his adventures by the spry Sir Jack Jinks ('Gadzooks!). Their wild wanderings took in such remote domains as Castle Ratsburg, where Count Krakula hoped to depose them with the Ogre of Drakenstein, and Loch Lorless where they hoped to sell a siege catapult to Angus MacLorless the clan chief: 'Odds gripes!'

Handy Andy
Hugh McNeill
Knockout 1940-48; *Comet* 1949; *Sun* 1951-52; *Big One* 1964-65 (Fleetway)
'The Odd Job Man' was his billing, and an odder job man would be hard to find. This rotund, walrus-whiskered, pipe-puffing old chump was totally incapable of understanding any order. Told to box a brat's ears if he got naughty, Andy went to the woodshed and knocked up some custom-built crates! Hired to cook rock cakes he used real rocks! Told to find some links for a golfer, he loaded him up with iron chains! As with many McNeill creations, Andy was accompanied by a small animal: a snail!

H

Handy Clark
Fred Sturrock
Dandy 1937-39 (D. C. Thomson)
When Major Bryant and his children, Peter and Patricia, were 'plane-wrecked on a plateau in the Andes mountains on 4 December 1937 (No. 1 of *Dandy*), it was the Major's manservant, Handy Clark, who soon emerged as the hero of the hour. Locating a Lost City and saving the kids from giant spiders was all in a day's work in *Lost On The Mountain Of Fear*, a saga which rewarded our hero with a title role in the sequel, *Handy Clark On The Treasure Trail.* Outsize opposition again, only this time in Nigeria.

Hank
Francis Coudrill
TV Comic 1951-58 (*News of the World*)
'Howdy folks! It's sure nice meetin' you on the other side of the TV screen!' Hank, a popular puppet from BBC Children's Television, introduced himself on the full-colour back page of *TV Comic* No. 1 (9 November 1951). He also introduced chief villain, Mexican Pete, his horse Silver King, his nephew Cassy, and other characters created by ventriloquist and artist, Francis Coudrill: Shorty and Slim the cowhands; Big Chief Laughing Gas; Minnie Ha-Ha and Little He-He. Drawn by Ron Murdoch.

Handy Sandy
Arthur Jackson
Beano 1944-45 (D. C. Thomson)
Handy Sandy was perhaps the oddest of all the sideshows of physical freaks that filled up the fun-pages of the D. C. Thomson comics during their early years. Sandy had outsize hands, hence his apt catchline: 'Fun Just Lingers Round His Fingers!' He followed in the footsteps of Tootsy McTurk (big feet) of *Magic*, Barney Boko (big nose) of *Dandy*, and Hairy Dan (big beard), Laddie Longlegs, and Big Fat Joe ('One Ton of Fun') in *Beano*.

Happy Andy/Larry Larks
Roy Wilson
Tip Top 1939-54; *Big One* 1964-65 (Fleetway)
Happy Andy worked at Harker's Stores, located on the front page of *Tip Top.* Andy lodged at Mrs Moggs' boarding house, but whether at home or at work, all the fun came from his two 'playful Pets'. These were called Sugar and Candy, a cuddly little bear and a floppy dog. The pets soon grew so popular that they dominated the action, developed speech, burst into full colour in 1940, and soldiered on, Andy-less, to the final issue (No. 727) as 'Our Playful Pets'.

Happy Bob Harriday
George Heath
Tip Top 1947-49; *Wonder* 1953 (Amalgamated Press)
'The Renowned Rider of the Prairie' mounted on his wonder horse, Rocky, rode on to the red-and-black back page of *Tip Top*, a home-made hero of the west to take the place of such previous cowboy stars as Ken Maynard and Gene Autry. Happy Bob may have come cheaper than his film-star predecessors, but there was nothing cut rate about his trigger finger, as Flash Logan found out. Handsome Happy had a regular greeting for his readers: 'Howdy, pards – here's smiling at you!'

Happy Families
Bill Mevin
Whizzer & Chips 1977-82 (IPC)
This not-so-happy family moved into *Whizzer & Chips* on 1 October 1977: 'Starting today and there's almost a riot – When our noisy lot try to be quiet!' The loud life began when poor old Grandpa was trying to snatch a snooze. First came teenager Sharon with her tranny: 'Be-bop-a-loo-la he's my baby!' Then came the twins, Dicky and Vicki, playing cowboy and injun: 'Whoop! Whoop!' Then it was Mum with her vacuum: 'Whine!' So Grandpa shouted, Mum clouted Dad with the frying pan – 'Clunggg!' – and all six of them wound up at the local library seeking peace and quiet.

The Happy Days
Andrew Wilson
Princess 1960-67; *Princess Tina* 1967-72; *Pixie* 1972-73 (IPC)
'I'm Sue Day! Meet the family! I love the whole crazy bunch, but pheew – sometimes they can drive me nearly out of my mind!' There was Mum ('A darling, but remembering things isn't her strong point!'); Dad, painting Picasso-like pictures of Mum in his attic studio; brother Sid and his messy motorbike; sister Gloria the blonde teenage beauty; and the twins, always squabbling. But, as Dad said, 'You're the brains of the family, Sue, you're the one that's going to go far!' She did, into *Pixie* (1972) where she told stories of her schooldays.

The Happy Family
Don Newhouse
Larks 1928-40 (Amalgamated Press)
Ma, Pop, and Harry, a happy family named Happy, had an unbroken 656-week run in *Larks*, the entire life of that popular penny comic, without once revealing the name of their pet cat. The family dog fared better: he was a terrier called Tintack! Pop Happy was the main butt of the strip, his good intentions towards entertaining his 'little man' ever ending in disaster, much to the despair of Ma and the joy of young Harry-boy. In 1938, the strip was increased from its original six pictures to a full half page: Pop's troubles increased in proportion.

H

The Happy Family
John Jukes
Tip Top 1949-54 (Amalgamated Press)
Horace Happy and his brood who moved on to the full-colour front page of *Tip Top* on 2 July 1949 were quite a contrasting crowd to that other 'Happy Family' from the prewar *Larks*. Drawn in a more realistic style to relate to the home lives of the comic's readers, there was still plenty of slapstick action to raise a smile. Mrs Happy was a pretty brunette, and the children, Sammy and Sue, good-looking miniatures of their parents. Their pets, Ruff and Kim, shared a kennel called the Ruff House. Moving inside in 1950, the strip was taken over by Reg Parlett (illustrated).

Hard-hearted Harriet
Dudley Wynn
Tracy 1979-80 (D. C. Thomson)
This heartrending serial of Victorian times began with the death of Harriet Bond's mother and father from an influenza epidemic, and the teenager's brave determination to care for her younger brothers and sisters, Johnny and Ben, Katie and baby Alice: 'Only 18 months, she was Mama and Papa's pride and joy.' After the funeral, Harriet has a dizzy spell; Dr Bailey diagnoses an incurable disorder of the blood. Harriet, with nine months to live, must find homes for her family. To do so she feigns cruelty to make them happy to leave her, but inside her heart is breaking.

Happy Harry and Sister Sue
Roy Wilson
Crackers 1933-41 (Amalgamated Press)
'The Jolly Adventures of Happy Harry and Sister Sue', with Pa, Ma, and Fido, began when they moved on to the coloured front page of *Crackers*. They ended there, too, in the last issue nine years later although, for a while, they moved again, to an inside plain page. Most of the pair's 'jolly adventures' resulted in poor old Pa taking stick. They caught him in their flour-and-water burglar trap ('Hoo-jolly-old-ray!'), dumped him in a pig-sty while holidaying on Frolic Farm, and smothered him with soot while helping sweep the chimney.

The Hard Man
Illustrator unknown
Roy of the Rovers 1976-86 (IPC)
Johnny Dexter, known as 'the hard man', was a tough mid-field player for the First-Division team of Danefield United. Constantly in trouble on and off the pitch, Johnny's name was seldom out of the newspaper headlines. When he was sent off the field during the first match of the season on 26 September 1976 (in No. 1 of *Roy of the Rovers*), his manager, Harry Telfer, forced him to watch the team lose. Johnny quits, then gets arrested for brawling after angry fans pick a fight in a bar. Suspended, he later makes good and becomes captain.

Harold Hare
Harry Hargreaves
Sun 1950-52; *Jack & Jill* 1954-85; *Harold Hare's Own Paper* 1959-64; *Playhour* 1985- (IPC)
'Everyone in Woody Glade knew Harold Hare, and everybody liked him because he was so jolly.' Harold ('O-me! Oh my!') was born on 1 March and, as a March hare, acted a little haywire. On his first day in *Sun* No. 74 (8 July 1950) he celebrated with a poem:

I'm Harold the Hare and I don't care,
If the North wind blows or whether it snows,
Or if there's a fly on top of my nose,
Or if the bluebells are turning red,
Or the cows slip off their cowslip bed!

As later drawn by Hugh McNeill (illustrated), Harold graduated to his own weekly comic.

Harum-Scarem
Gordon Bell
Buzz 1973-74 (D. C. Thomson)
'Here's a funny fighting pair – A great big hound and a crafty hare!' Harum was the hero, the bunny in the red-and-black striped rollneck; Scarem was the villain, the bulldog in the spiked collar. Between the two lay the farmer's field of carrots, a veritable battlefield thanks to the high-powered war that ranged between the two animals. When Scarem lay a painful trap for Harum with carrots and the farmer's fierce goat, Harum got his own back by starching his long ears and attacking the lunching bulldog in his exposed rear: 'Jab!-Waa!-Oo! Oo! Oo-hoo!'

Harris Tweed
John Ryan
Eagle 1950-62 (Hulton)
'Harris Tweed, Extra Special Agent', began operations in *Eagle* on 4 August 1950, speedily expanding from a half to a full page. A burlesque of *Dick Barton, Special Agent*, Harris Tweed was all monocle, moustache, and chin. His assistant, in best Sexton Blake and Tinker tradition, was a boy but, although he did most of the detective work, the lad's real name was never revealed, his master being content to refer to him as 'boy'. Tweed's cases were usually among the upper bracket, as when he saved Sir Arthur Adenoind-Smith of Pimpole Street from being gassed by his butler's Christmas balloons.

Harry's Haunted House
Reg Parlett
Whizzer & Chips 1969-77 (IPC)
'Hello, I'm Harry!', smiled the spectre in the patched sheet. 'I've haunted this empty house for years and never been bothered by anyone!' Until No. 1 of *Whizzer & Chips* (18 October 1969). Harry's house was sold and an irascible gent moved in, or tried to. Harry soon scared the moving men by shooting through a roll of lino. Next week the council men arrived with mallets, determined to demolish the old edifice. Harry bunged back their dynamite and demolished their van instead. And so for Harry, life (or life after death) goes on.

Harvey
Terry Rogers
Tracy 1979-85 (D. C. Thomson)
'A New Home for Harvey' started in *Tracy* No. 1 (6 October 1979), told in the first person by Harvey himself – a lost dog! 'Girls, get your hankies out, 'cos this is a real sob story. Can you imagine what it's like to be shoved out of a car and abandoned on a cold, rainy night? Well, it happened to me – all because I was growing up and ate too much! Yeeoww!' Harvey soon finds a family to take him in: 'Humans are a pushover for that grateful paw routine – it never fails!', and repays them by warning of an embankment landslide. But no dogs are allowed in their new tower-block flat, so Harvey was on the move again.

The Headhunters
Ken Harrison
Cracker 1975-76 (D. C. Thomson)
Skooldaze was the title of the four-page pull-out in the middle of the new comic *Cracker* (No. 1: 18 January 1975). On the first page were 'The Snookums', featuring Miss Bun and her Little Angels. On the back page was 'Spookum Skool' for ghosts, and across the middle careened 'The Headhunters', otherwise the top class at Skookum School. They got their name from hunting heads: Headmasters, that is! Every week a new one applied for the job, and every week the action was such that they resigned, racing screaming into the distance.

Hellman
Illustrator unknown
Action 1976-77; *Battle Action* 1977-78 (IPC)
Major Kurt Hellman, panzer commander, holds a curious place in British comic history: the first German hero of a World War 2 strip. The date of the first *Action* was 14 February 1976 but, for Hellman, it was 1 May 1940, the first day of Germany's *Blitzkrieg* on the West with his Hammer Force tank first across the Belgian border. At odds with Gauleiter Kastner of the S.S. ('I am a soldier, not a butcher!'), Hellman finds himself on the Russian front where his secret steel jacket of panzer plating comes in handy.

Hetty's Horoscope
Terry Bave
Whizzer & Chips 1969-70 (IPC)
Hetty was a schoolgirl who believed implicitly in her horoscope. Each week from *Whizzer & Chips* No. 1 (18 October 1969) she read her horoscope and then determinedly tried to make it come true. Her first read 'Today will be a good day for solving problems' but, after being accused of babynapping and crashing into her headmistress, Miss Misery, she wound up with extra homework: more problems than she started with. The next week she caused chaos in the sorting office because her horoscope predicted a letter would come her way. One did: a letter fell off the Post Office sign and beaned her!

Hector the Collector
John Aldrich
Cracker 1975-76 (D. C. Thomson)
'Badges, stamps, ties or string – Hector will save anything!' Bespectacled Hector suffered from the same monomania as Little Saver, his female counterpart. Every week, starting in *Cracker* No. 1 (18 January 1975), he developed a new collecting craze. It began with ties, but his Grandpa's bow turned out to be the elastic variety, snapping back on the old boy's adam's apple with a thwak! His bottle collection expanded rapidly: he golluped down brown sauce, vinegar, and lemonade, and wound up with an extra bottle from Mum: castor oil!

Heros the Spartan
Frank Bellamy
Eagle 1962-65 (Longacre)
Superlative saga carried across the full-colour centre spread of *Eagle* from 27 October 1962, with all the cinemascopic sweep of cinematic spectacle. Written by Tom Tully, the adventures of Heros the Spartan and his cohort of Roman soldiers included his capture on the sinister Island of Darkness by the wild subhuman Magus, slavery in the gold mines under the priests of the pagan god Diom, and his search for his friend, the centurion, Septimus, under the spell of an evil Eastern ruler, the Man of Vyah. Frank Bellamy drew the serial for just a year, but his influence remained.

Hi De Hi . . . Hi De Hooooo
Rob Lee
Wow 1982-83 (IPC)
Combining the popular BBC Television comedy series about a holiday camp, *Hi De Hi*, with the popular comic trend towards ghosts and monsters, Hauntin's Holiday Camp opened for business in No. 1 of *Wow* (6 June 1982). The first guests to arrive were the Tuff family, but chalet maids with detachable heads, camp announcers who floated through walls crying 'Rise and shine!', and vampire bats wearing 'Kiss Me Quick' hats failed to faze them. The Tuffs had seen it all before; they were Ghost Train proprietors! A camp specialty was ice scream, petrified peach or vanillaaaagh surprise.

The Hillys and The Billys/The Ruffies and The Tuffies
George Martin
Beezer 1956-58; 1961-64; *Victor* 1972 (D. C. Thomson)
'Jumpin' rattlesnakes!' and other ornery outcries peppered the salty speech of these two feudin' families, just as barrel-loads of buckshot peppered their pants. Based on the classic Kentucky Mountain family feuds as immortalized in the old song, 'The Martins and the Coys they was reckless mountain boys', this full page of quick-fire comedy exploded once a week from *Beezer* No. 1 (21 January 1956). The best way of telling Pappy and the Billys from Zeke and the Hillys was by their hats: the Billys wore red and the Hillys wore black.

Hire a Horror
Reg Parlett
Cor 1970-74 (IPC)
'Service with a Snarl!' was the motto of this monstrous business, an agency that hired out horrors for all occasions. A squire was their first customer on 6 June 1970, in No. 1 of *Cor*. He wanted something to scare the kids away from his private lake. What a shock the kiddies got when their string and bent pin caught the Monster from Forty Fathoms! The monster said 'Rawgh!' and the kids cried 'Skreeek!' Then the squire shouted 'Aaaaagh!' as the monster proceeded to chomp down his apple orchard. When the squire refused to cough up, Hire a Horror sent round the most monstrous monster of all – the rent collector!

The Hippo Girls
Herbert Foxwell
Playbox 1925-55 (Amalgamated Press)
'Mrs Hippo's Boarding School', as the strip was better known, opened for business on the coloured front page of *Playbox* No. 1, 14 February 1925, and closed in the last issue, No. 1279, on 11 June 1955. The Hippo Girls were all twin sisters of the Bruin Boys, but Tiger Tilly never became the star her brother was (Tiger Tim). With Baby Jumbo, Gertie Giraffe, Betty Bruin, Olive Ostrich, Jenny Jacko, Polly Parrot, and Fifi the Pup, Mrs Hippo had her mittened hands full: she was also editor of the comic, occupying Room 178, Fleetway House, Farringdon Street, EC4.

His Sporting Lordship
Barrie Mitchell
Smash 1969-71 *Valiant* 1971-72 (IPC)
Henry Nobbins was always in trouble. He liked nothing better than a scrap and, as a labourer on the building site of T. Bumpton and Sons in the north of England, he found plenty of opportunity to use his fists. When Mr Wimple came seeking a Henry D'Arcy Percival Nobbins who had a star-shaped birthmark on his right arm, Henry found himself hailed as sole legal heir to the late Lord Harbell, 71st Earl of Ranworth, plus five million pounds, and the ancestral home of Castle Plonkton – on condition he became champion at a variety of sports.

H

Hit Kid
Sid Burgon
Krazy 1977-78; *Whizzer & Chips* 1978 (IPC)
The H.K. on his suitcase stood for Hit Kid, his only distinguishing mark. For Hit Kid's face was hidden behind the turned-down trilby, the upturned collar, and the big black glasses. Hit Kid's motto was 'Anytime, Anyplace, Anyone', and his price was a pound of assorted sweets. His first contract was dated 9 April 1977: get rid of a rotten old park-keeper. Picking his spot, a rooftop overlooking the park, H.K. assembled his piece, got a bead on the parky's bent-over bum, and lined up his telescopic lens. The sun's rays did the rest, and the burnt parky was seen no more: 'Sizzle! Yeow!'

Hongree
Frank Holland
Gleam 1902-03 (Brett)
'Hongree the Lady-Killer; or, the Fascinating Frenchman' featured on the front page of *The Gleam*, 'The New Popular Paper for All Classes and All Ages'. M. Hongree was full of himself as a continental lover: 'Ah, here is ze loafly Mees Prettypert! She is simply gone on me! I haf capture her completely! You Englishmens do not undairstand how to sharm ze ladies von leetle bit!' Naturally, he meets his weekly come-uppance, leaving the field clear to such dashing Brits as Dick Brighton. 'Mon Dieu! I am assassinated! Poleece!'

Hockey Hannah
Andy Tew
Sparky 1965-68; *Mandy* 1970-71 (D. C. Thomson)
There were echoes of the *Dandy*'s Keyhole Kate in Hockey Hannah. She was a schoolgirl who wore specs, had her hair in plaits, and wore a gymslip. She also had an obsession: she was never seen without her hockey stick. But where one one-track Kate was a comic heroine pure and simple, Hannah was drawn in a realistic style that made her attractive to girl readers of *Sparky*, and not a laughing stock for boys to jeer at. Her hockey stick came in handy to save kittens from bulldogs, or to collect litter in the park.

Homeless Hector
Bertie Brown
Chips 1909-53 (Amalgamated Press)
'The Tail of a Lost Dog' began its weekly wag in the popular pink-paper comic, *Chips*, in 1909, and only stopped when the comic was discontinued forty-four years later. The original artist, Albert Thacker ('Bertie') Brown, was still drawing the homeless hound, although others, including Arthur Martin, had taken a turn. In his final adventure, Hector jumped bail from a cop-shop and, accompanied by his partner in crime, Moonlight Moggie, beat a retreat murmuring, 'Come on, Mog, we'll fade quietly away into the shadows!'

Hookjaw
Illustrator unknown
Action 1976-77 (IPC)
'When Hookjaw Strikes You Only Scream Once!' – except when he strikes week after week after week. Inspired by the boxoffice success of the American movie, *Jaws*, this centre-spread strip made its own contribution to comic history: for the first time in a British comic, blood was shown in full colour. Set in the Caribbean of 1972, game fishermen make a prize catch of a great white shark. 'The slimy brute' fights back, snapping the gaff so that the hook sticks in its lower jaw. The pain-wracked shark takes its revenge – 'No, no! Uuuuhh!' – 'Th-there's nothing left of Al!' – and ate a victim a week for the rest of its run.

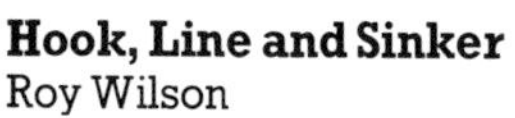

Hook, Line and Sinker
Roy Wilson
Wonder 1949-53 (Amalgamated Press)
Captain Hook, Navigator Line, and Cabin-boy Sinker were the crew of the superjet charter 'plane, Charlie. They took off on the two-colour front page of *Wonder* No. 1628 (11 June 1949), their first mission to deliver a top-secret crate to Juju Island. Professor Whizzo's secret invention turned out to be a bottle of hair restorer for his bald-headed old buddy! Rewards were as odd as their cargoes: safely delivering a ruby to Egypt, Chief Ali Basha gave them the pick of his collection: the only cross-eyed camel in captivity!

Hop, Skip and Jock
Malcolm Judge
Buzz 1973-75 (D. C. Thomson)
These three were the front-page stars of *Buzz* from No. 1 (20 January 1973). Skip wore the black-and-yellow striped jumper, Hop was the scrubby skinhead, and Jock was the little fat one in the wee tam o'shanter. Their first adventure set the style of their strip: they visited a Modern Art Exhibition, reckoned they could do better themselves, and in one large picture staged their own 'fantabulous backyard art exibishun'. The paintings included a line with eyeballs ('Flatfish on its side') and a black square ('Coalman chasing a black pudding in a cellar at midnight'). Next week they ran their own funfair.

Hooky's Magic Bowler Hat
Chick Gordon
Beano 1938-40 (D. C. Thomson)
Hooky Higgs the hiker shared his roadside picnic with an old Indian carpet seller, who repaid the lad's kindness with the gift of a magic bowler hat. One rub and bang! 'The hat gave a pop like a gun and out of it floated a figure like a man made of smoke.' It was Mikki, the slave of the hat, ready to obey Hooky's every command. 'Strike me pink!' cried the surprised boy. 'It shall be done, Master!', said 'the queer joker', and lo! Hooky turned pink! Lucky for him, his strip was printed on a two-tone page of *Beano* No. 1: red and blue!

Horrornation Street
Tom Williams
Shiver & Shake 1973-74 (IPC)
This monstrous skit on Granada Television's soap opera, 'Coronation Street', started on 10 March 1973, at midnight! Residents included Tootin Common the Egyptian mummy, who lived at a pyramid called the Oasis. Next door lived Hoodoo Yudoo the witch-doctor ('Surgery Hours Midnight till Dawn') who was practising a chant: 'Oompah! Oompah! Stick it up your joompah!' At the old castle, Sir Headley Deadley was taking his head for a walk around the battlements, while, for Herr Raisin, the vampire count, fangs weren't what they used to be: 'Zis toothache – I haven't had a bite for days!'

Hopalong Cassidy
Clarence Mulford
Modern Boy 1937; *Radio Fun* 1939; *Knockout* 1954-60 (Amalgamated Press)
'Boss of the Bar 20', Cassidy was created in 1912 by Clarence Mulford in a series of western novels which attained huge popularity when filmed in the 'Thirties by Paramount. Hoppy was played by William Boyd, and his original sidekicks were Windy Halliday (George 'Gabby' Hayes) and Johnny Nelson (James Ellison). Three of the films were adapted as serial strips by Ernest Ibbetson (illustrated) for *Modern Boy*, then C. Montford drew more for *Radio Fun*.

Hot Rod
Alf Saporito
Whizzer & Chips 1969-71 (IPC)
'Run for your lives! Hot Rod the Dragon is heading this way!', yelled a varlet on the back page of the *Chips* pull-out section in *Whizzer & Chips* No. 1 (18 October 1969). The colour helped considerably when Hot Rod let fly with his fiery breath. Little did the lolloping lump realize that, when he heated a knight to boiling point, it was an empty suit of armour. Well, almost empty: a jovial old friar had stowed his kate-and-sidney pie therein and thus Hot Rod had cooked it to a turn. Next week Hot Rod fried the friar.

H

Hot-Shot Hamish
Illustrator unknown
Scorcher 1973-74; *Tiger* 1974-85; *Roy of the Rovers* 1985- (IPC)
Hamish Balfour, the genial, gentle giant in the shaggy, short-sleeved sheepskin jacket, was brought from his small Hebridean island by Mr McBrain to play for Princes Park Football Club. In one short season Hamish helped this struggling team in the Second Division to win the Scottish Cup for the first time in their history, much to the joy of Manager McWhacker. When Princes played the first leg of their European Cup Winners' match, McWhacker put Hamish in against San Martine in Spain. 'Wi' Hamish in the team, mon, anything can happen!'

Hungry Horace
Allan Morley
Dandy 1937-56; *Sparky* 1965-77
Topper 1977- (D. C. Thomson)
For eighteen years, beginning in *Dandy* No. 1 (4 December 1937), when he hid a pie in the cellar and returned to find it covered with coal, to *Dandy* No. 784 (1 December 1956), when the local cake shop only opened when the bank was closed, Hungry Horace suffered pangs in the pinny, much to the amusement of his many readers. The fat boy in the red sweater was so popular that, nine years later, he launched, but seldom lunched, into a whole new career in *Sparky*.

Huckleberry Hound
William Hanna, Joseph Barbera
TV Express 1960; *TV Comic* 1960-61 (TV); *Huckleberry Hound Weekly* 1961-67 (City); *Fun Time* 1972-73 (Williams)
'Well, here we are in jolly old Britain!', announced Huckleberry Hound, the blue-skinned star of Hanna-Barbera television cartoons, on the full-colour front page of No. 1 of his own comic (7 October 1961). Huck was conveniently forgetting that he had already been appearing in another publisher's *TV Comic* for a year or two, drawn by Bill Nevin! His first port of call in London was Scotland Yard, where he helped his cousin, Sherlock Hound, find his mislaid medal.

Hugh's Zoo
Gordon Bell
Plug 1977-79; *Beezer* 1979 (D. C. Thomson)
Hugh, the little lad with the big H on his chest, introduced the readers of *Plug* No. 1 to his own private zoo. First came his pet fiver-pig ('It used to be a guinea-pig, but with inflation the way it is!'), and next his homing pigeon: a bit on the lazy side, it came home by bus! Hugh's rabbits were called Starsky and Hutch, and his pet python Monty: clearly Hugh was a TV fan. Films, too, were his bag: hence Gregory Pecker the woodpecker. But where were Hugh's pet stick-insects? A boy scout was rubbing them together to make a fire!

Hurricane Hurry
William Ward
New Funnies 1940-44; *Topical Funnies* 1948 (Swan)
'Down from the foothills into the Morave Basin, dropped Hurricane Hurry, and made camp in new country with all its promise of fresh thrills and adventures!' But no sooner was this roaming cowpoke camping under a bluff, than bullets were flying. 'Hullo! Now what in the blue blazes!?' Soon Hurry was hightailing it for town. 'Stranger, this is a town of terror! A hooded gang have just killed Kelly to get his ranch, and they're framing his son!' Next morning in court, Hurry unmasks the Sheriff – and the Judge himself! Then it was on Snowball and away: 'I've got a date with some more toughs, wherever they're to be found! S'long!'

The Incredible Bulk
Steve Maher
TV Comic 1978 (TV)
Spotty Herbert, the boy who loved sherbet, was a weedy weakling. One suck of his favourite fizzy sweetmeat and – 'Burp!' – thanks to a dose of his dad's mysterious chemical spray he turned into the Incredible Bulk! This big blue being with the bulging biceps was, of course, a broad burlesque of the American comicbook hero, the Incredible Hulk, who was currently enjoying a popular television series. Most of Bulk's activities were confined to school and playground, however, due to his devotion to Molly Busson.

The Incredible Sulk
James Petrie
Jackpot 1979-82 (IPC)
'One minute he's happy, the next he's a miserable monster! It's the Incredible Sulk!' Taking his name and inspiration from the television series based on the American comicbook hero, *The Incredible Hulk*, this sunny faced, curly haired kid had only to meet the slightest opposition to his will to throw a temper tantrum. With a cry of 'Yuuuuuulk!', his lower lip pushed out in a pout so peculiarly prominent that it seemed to swallow his entire face. Then all he could mumble was 'Hmmp! Hmmp! Hmmp!', and the odd bit of babytalk, 'Wah! Me's got wetted!'

The Indestructible Man
Jesus Blasco
Jag 1968-69 (Fleetway)
'What is the connection between the mysterious man who called himself Mark Dangerfield and the captain of the royal cavalry during the reign of Pharaoh Rameses the second of Ancient Egypt? The astounding, unbelievable answer is that they are both one and the same man!' So began the strange saga of a young Egyptian, buried alive for the false murder of his father, the High Priest of Osiris, and reawakened on 4 May 1968 (in No. 1 of *Jag*) by Professor Abercrombie the archaeologist. Sacred scrolls give him the secret of eternal life and the power of invisibility.

The Incredible Hulk
Jack Kirby
Smash 1966-68 (Odhams); *Marvel* 1972-79; *Hulk Comic* 1979-80; *Hulk Pocketbook* 1980-81; *Spiderman* 1980-84; *Incredible Hulk* 1982 (Marvel)
Stan Lee (writer) and Jack Kirby (artist) designed No. 1 of *The Hulk* (May 1962) as a follow-up to *The Fantastic Four*. It told the strange story of Dr Bruce Banner who, in trying to save young Rick Jones from the explosion of his new gamma-ray bomb, was himself exposed to the rays. This had the effect of turning him into a decidedly un-jolly green giant, a chunky look-alike to the Frankenstein Monster. Never seen without his Incredible, Hulk came to Britain in No. 19 of *Smash* (11 June 1966).

Inky, Binky and Fluff
Harry Banger
Magic 1939-40 (D. C. Thomson)
Three little kittens in a row!
There's Inky, Binky, Fluff!
One, two, three and off we go!
Just watch 'em do their stuff!
Harry Banger based his kitten triplets on the old nursery rhyme, 'The Three Little Kittens': Inky was the black one, Binky the grey, and Fluff the snowy white. Visiting the seaside in *Magic* No. 1 (22 July 1939), they donned their bathing suits, illustrating an odd convention among comic-strip animals who normally appear au naturel. Tougher than their nursery-rhyme originals, the kits turned the tables on Tom-Cat Tim by filling a paddling pool with crabs.

Invisible Dick
George Ramsbottom
Dandy 1937-39; *Sparky* 1968-77 (D. C. Thomson)
'Even every tiny tot'll . . . Soon be talking of Dicky's bottle!' Dick was on his way to play footer with his pals in No. 1 of *Dandy* (4 December 1937) when he bumped into a solid lump of nothing. 'Ouch!', gasped Dick, and gasped again as a one-legged sailor called Peg-Leg Pete slowly materialized. 'One sniff at the queer liquid in this bronze bottle turns anyone invisible!', explained Pete, presenting the ancient Egyptian relic to Dick, who promptly faded away and chucked eggs at a 'proper rotter' called P.C. Peeler. Dick first appeared (and disappeared) in a *Rover* serial (4 March 1922).

Iron Hand
Paddy Brennan
Cracker 1975-76 (D. C. Thomson)
'Ker-runch! With the dull crunch of splintering timber, a steely fist came bursting out of a crate lying on a Caribbean quayside. British Agent 041, otherwise known as Iron Hand, had arrived on Kalagar!' The only adventure hero in the new comic *Cracker* (No. 1, 18 January 1975) had arrived, and in panel one, demonstrated exactly why Agent 041 was known as Iron Hand: at the end of his right arm he had an iron hand! This came in handy for ironing out a reported build-up of nuclear weapons in a Caribbean island fortress.

Iron Barr
Michael White
Spike 1983-84; *Champ* 1984 (D. C. Thomson)
Charlie Barr, a scrap-metal dealer, brags he can do better than the Darbury Rangers' goalie. Given the chance to silence his big mouth, he astounds Limp-along Leslie by saving every goal and playing bare foot, to boot! 'Listen, mate, in my goal I'm king, and anyone who gets in my way had better look out!' Charlie's boast earns him the nickname of 'Iron' Barr and a contract with the team. Sixty-seven weeks later, when his comic, *Spike*, closed, Iron Barr was transferred to another team, United, in another comic, *Champ*.

The Iron Man
Illustrator unknown
Boys World 1963-64; *Eagle* 1964-69 (Odhams)
As the editor of *Eagle* explained when that comic absorbed *Boys World* and continued the story of Iron Man: 'Only young Tim Branton knew that the famous Iron Man was really a wonderful robot, dressed in clothes and special plastic skin to appear human. And not only was the all-steel robot stronger than 100 men, he was capable of absorbing and understanding even the most complicated information'. In his *Boys World* days, Iron Man thwarted the fleeing 'Doctor' by grabbing hold of the whirling screw of his midget submarine. In *Eagle*, he battled Dr Fear and his Titans of Terror, 100000 giant robots!

The Iron Fish
Bill Holroyd
Beano 1952-67; *Buddy* 1981-82 (D. C. Thomson)
'Through the light green waters of the Pacific Ocean glided the silvery shape of the Iron Fish, the wonderful mechanical swordfish invented by Professor Jim Gray.' It glided into the pages of *Beano* No. 367 on 30 July 1949 but, as a serial story, it made its plunge into picture strips in No. 506 (29 March 1952). The Iron Fish was propelled by a powerful electric motor which made its tail beat like that of a real fish. Seated in its snug little glass-domed cockpit was Deep-Sea Danny, the Professor's young son.

Iron Man
Don Heck
Fantastic 1967-68 (Odhams); *Spiderman* 1974-76; *Captain America* 1981-82; *Big Ben* 1984 (Marvel)
'Watch his awesome approach! Listen to his ponderous footsteps as he lumbers closer . . . closer . . . for today you are destined to encounter the Invincible Iron Man!' The 'today' was March 1963 in the United States (No. 39 of *Tales of Suspense*) and 18 February 1967 in Britain (No. 1 of *Fantastic*). Created by editor-writer Stan Lee, Iron Man was in reality Anthony Stark, 'rich, handsome, known as a glamorous playboy. Both a sophisticate and a scientist' he is wounded in Viet-Nam where captured Professor Yinsen instals him into a new body built of iron.

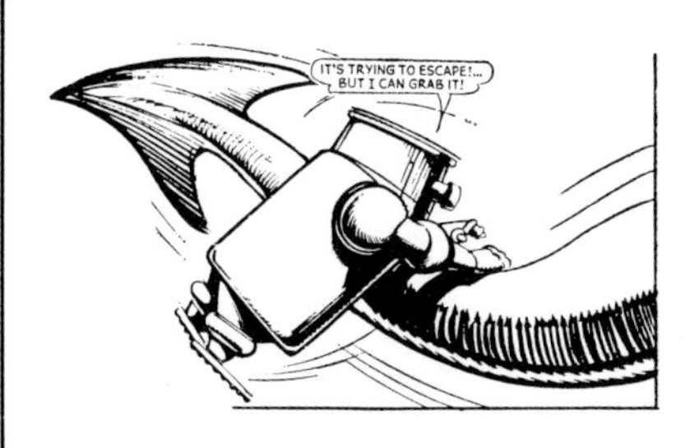

The Iron Teacher
Terry Patrick
Hotspur 1972-74 (D. C. Thomson)
'The Iron Teacher Speaks' was a long-running serial which started in *Hotspur* No. 412 (19 July 1941) in the days when it was a boys' story paper. *Hotspur* was revamped in to a comic in 1959 and, in 1972, it was the Iron Teacher's turn to be turned into a picture strip. Changed considerably in appearance, the Teacher was now revealed as a robot controlled by Special Agent Jake Todd. Soon, their adventures ranged far and wide, including a sensational serial set in the South American jungle where they were 'plane-crashed into a lost valley of prehistoric monsters.

The Iron Warrior
William Ward
Thrill Comics 1940-45; *New Funnies* 1948 (Swan)
'The Iron Warrior in Darkest Africa' began in *Thrill Comics* No. 1 (April 1940), the most violent and bloodiest strip ever seen in British comics to this time, and for several decades to come. Rodney Dearth, seeking the Jewels of Junius, arrives at the site of the Temple of Sloth in Central Africa, accompanied by his robot, the Iron Warrior. Captured by a White Princess, he summons the Warrior ('Wavelength 60, impulse 400'). Crying 'I come, Master!' and also 'Ahr-rr! Whoo-roo! Roar!', the Warrior's built-in chopper slices up the Sloths, cuts up a giant crocodile, and pulls the head off an outsize eagle.

I. Spy
Les Barton
Sparky 1969-74 (D. C. Thomson)
'Meet I. Spy the "Sssshh!" Guy!' was the headline in *Sparky* on 1 February 1969, introducing an hilariously mysterious character clad totally in black. With hat-brim pulled down to meet his upturned collar, and hands permanently plunged into his pockets, I. Spy's features remained totally obscured throughout his comic career. His was a major success story, spreading from one page to two before the end of the year, and from two to three in 1970. He needed room in his unending battles with Mr Mastermind's Amazing Machines, and the dreaded Mr X.

It's a Nice Life
Reg Parlett
Jackpot 1979-82; *Buster* 1982-85 (IPC)
With a plot borrowed from BBC Television's popular situation comedy, *The Good Life*, and with its heroes' names borrowed from Laurel and Hardy, this strip started as the full-colour centre spread in *Jackpot* No. 1 (5 May 1979). Stan at No. 12 began by giving up his office job to become self-sufficient, much to the amusement – and annoyance – of Oliver at No. 13. Ollie, his wife Maddie, and their spoilt child Roddy, decided to buy new bicycles for exercise, and wound up pulling farmer Stan's plough – which was the rudder of Ollie's expensive boat, anyway!

Ivor Klue
Bertie Brown
Chips 1925-28; 1936-46 (Amalgamated Press)
'The Dud Detective' opened up for business on the back page of *Chips* on 11 July 1925, and finally shut up shop on 11 May 1946: a run broken by an unexplained eight-year gap. Klue had two assistants, Curley the Comical Pageboy and Napoleon the Perky Parrot: 'baffling mysteries unravelled while you wait, tricksters tracked, trapped and tripped up at shortest notice.' His later cases, as depicted by Albert 'Charlie' Pease (illustrated), were less successful, his final bag being none other than Chief Inspector Coppem himself.

Ivor Lott and Tony Broke
Reg Parlett
Cor 1970-74; *Buster* 1974- (IPC)
The comedy contrast between rich and poor was the basis for this long-running strip which started in No. 1 of *Cor* (6 June 1970) and soon expanded to a double-page spread. Tony Broke, an average penniless schoolboy, was much miffed to see young Ivor Lott arriving at school in his chauffeur-driven Rolls, with a butler, Grimes, to carry his satchel. While Tony had to do his best to swallow school dinners, Ivor tucked into a private pile of turkey with jelly to follow. Small wonder Tony seethed when Ivor called him riff-raff.

J

Jack Flash/Jackie Flash

Dudley Watkins

Beano 1949-58; *Nutty* 1980; *Mandy* 1973 (D. C. Thomson)

'Jack Flash the Flying Boy' flew into *Beano* No. 355 on 19 February 1949. 'Crikey'!, gasped a sailor, 'E's got wings on 'is ankles!' Jack Flash was no ordinary boy; a sturdily built youngster in a one-piece suit, he was the son of the leading scientist of the planet Mercury. Setting off in his father's rocket-ship, Jack had crash-landed off the south coast of England, where his flight from the wreckage astounded local lifeboatmen. Even more astounding, perhaps, was Jack's reworking as a supergirl, Jackie Flash, for *Mandy*!

Jack and Jill

Hugh McNeill

Jack & Jill 1954-85 (IPC)

'Jack and Jill of Buttercup Farm' were the front-page stars of No. 1 of *Jack & Jill* (27 February 1954), the first of the modern-style nursery comics in full-colour photogravure. Delightfully painted by Hugh McNeill in a departure from his knockabout *Knockout* style, the twins were introduced thus: 'Jack and Jill are the children of Farmer and Mrs Honey. Their little puppy, who loves a piece of sugar so much, is called Patch.' From No. 2 their captions were couplets: 'The funny hat the children catch – And there inside is little Patch!'

Jackie and Sammy The Terrible Twins

Percy Cocking

Comic Cuts 1918-37 (Amalgamated Press)

Modelled in everything but their accents on the Katzenjammer Kids, Hans and Fritz, Jackie and Sammy first crept on to the front page of *Comic Cuts* as subsidiary mischief makers in 'The Side-Splitting Adventures of Jolly Tom the Menagerie Man'. These naughty nevvies drove their Uncle Tom doolally with their pranks, tying a wild dog to his nose, then hiding the hound in the pelican's pouch at feeding time, and painting the penguins as Easter eggs. When Professor Noah took over the Zoo in 1936, they soon showed him who was boss.

Jack O' Lantern

Robert Ayton

Eagle 1955-61 (Hulton)

Jack Rorke starred in a spectacular period serial that switched beween the England and France of the early nineteenth century and took seven years of fine, full-colour pages to tell. Written by George Beardmore, it began on 28 January 1955. Soon young Jack was rescuing his father, Captain Yorke, and a prize-fighter, Jem Slammer, from the gallows, in an attempt to prove that his villainous Uncle Humphrey has falsely accused his father of treason. Then Jack and his cousin Rufus, a secret service Lieutenant, set about unmasking Captain Zero, who engineered the escape of French prisoners of war from Camp 9.

Jack Pott
Joe McCaffrey
Cor 1971-74; Jackpot 1979-82; *Buster* 1982- (IPC)
Jack Pott lived at No. 2 Lucky Street, Cortown, and was the first British comic hero to break a long moral tradition and rely on gambling for his weekly wheeze. When Jack's uncle sent him a globe of the world, his dad thought it would keep him away from the gambling arcades, Jack's usual playground, but the boy sent him into a spin by getting his buddies to bet on which country the globe would stop turning at. Jack Pott was so popular that he later starred in a comic called *Jackpot*.

Jack Silver/The Fizzfist
Bill Holroyd
Dandy 1973-81 (D. C. Thomson)
Curly Perkins was kidnapped and whisked right out of this world, but he didn't mind in the least! For his kidnapper was Jack Silver, a cheery chap with outsized ears who whizzed the Earthboy off to his wacky world of Marsuvia, where pigs mooed, chickens oinked, and snapper-flappers were after Farmer Neep's quackers! Jack and Curly took a load of Earth toys with them, and they came in handy among the Marsuvians. When Jack came back in 1975, he had the whole of the full-colour centre spread at his command – and nasty Captain Zapp on his tail.

Jack Ransom
Ley Kenyon
Rocket 1965 (*News of the World*)
Professor Jack Ransom was the star of the science-fiction serial, 'The Seabed Citadel', which filled the full-colour back page of *Rocket* from No. 1 (21 April 1956). Drawn and written by an expert in the underwater field, Ley Kenyon, one of Jacques Cousteau's aqualung explorers, the strip had an unusually authentic look for all its fantastic theme. The grey-haired Professor invited his newphews, Tom and Jeff, to join him in testing a new pressurized diving suit made of a plastic designed to stand ultradeep water. It was also fitted with radar, radio, an infrared headlight, a jet motor, and an atom-gun for fishing: 900 fathoms in no time!

Jack Sprat and Tubby Tadpole
Roy Wilson
Jolly 1935-37 (Amalgamated Press)
'The Sailors Who Don't Care' signed aboard H.M.S. *Hotpot* on 19 January 1935, front-page stars of the first issue of *Jolly*. 'Two bells had just bonged when Admiral Onion decided on a drop of drill.' Our merry matelots began as they would continue: on the command right turn they left-turned right off the deck ('Oo! The floor's slipped!') and into the drink! Chance in the form of a forgetfully flung match ignited a box marked 'Bangee Stuffee' and blew Hot-Cha and his Chinkee nicknack snatchers sky high, winning the men a bushel of yen.

Jack of United/Jimmy of City

Barrie Mitchell

Score'n'Roar 1970-71; *Scorcher* 1971-74 (IPC)

'Jack of United' was the star of *Score*, the first half of a two-part sports comic, *Score'n' Roar*, which kicked off on 19 September 1970. Jack Chesley and his younger brother, Jimmy, both top-class amateur footballers, were offered a trial by the First-Division team, Castleburn United. Jack soon caught the eye of manager, Eric Mills, and got himself signed. The dejected Jimmy joined in a game on the way home and was spotted by Ian Clark, Manager of Castleburn City. He was signed right away and starred in the second half of the comic, *Roar*!

Jake's Seven

Tom Paterson

Jackpot 1980-81 (IPC)

Taking its title from the BBC Television science-fiction series, *Blake's Seven*, Jake's Seven was a gang of Earthkids including the black boy, Fuzzy, and a beanpole of a schoolgirl in a gymslip. Stuck somewhere in futuristic space, they palled up with a planet kid called Plook who helped them in their narrow escapes from Narky the villainous mad genius. He chased them radiating the curious phrase, 'Half-daft cackle!', while letting fly zaps from his paralyzing ray-gun. Jake turned the tables by reflecting the ray back with a hover-mirror.

Jak the Dragon-Killer

James Fisher

Dandy 1941 (D. C. Thomson)

'On a high cliff stood a giant figure of a man, over eight feet tall and with broad muscular shoulders.' This was Jak the Dragon-Killer of Thrace, a man with a mission. His three sons had been carried off by the King of Turkan, who had left a trail of clues for Jak to follow. Each was hidden in the lair of a different monster, each of which had to be slain before the clue could be solved. Luckily, Jak was armed with a mighty club, the thigh-bone of the first dragon he had slain.

Jake Jeffords

Denis McLoughlin

Wizard 1975-77 (D. C. Thomson)

Jake Jeffords was an X-Agent in the British Secret Service. He was also the Karate champion, which made him perfect choice for tough assignments in exotic climes. His chief was Sir Ralph Cowper-Dacier, better known as the Fat Man. Jeffords' name never appeared in the titles of his cases as depicted in *Wizard*. 'Sign of the Shark' began on 14 June 1975 with a 'phonecall from Agent XE-21, the first message from him for thirty years! Jeffords traced him to dismal dockland where XE-21, just in from dodging death-quoits in Sandakan, was instantly killed by a Shark Man's crossbow bolt.

Jak of The Jaguars

Patrick Nicolle

Sun 1952-53 (Amalgamated Press)

'Beginning the Strangest Story Ever Told – the Boy who was Brought Up by Jaguars!' It began in blue ink on 29 March 1952, across the centre spread of the new comicbook format *Sun*, No. 164. A baby floated ashore in its cradle after a ship was wrecked off the storm-lashed coast of South America. Riga, King of the Jaguars, heard the boy's weak cry and fed him, fighting off Akra the giant snake. The boy grew up to play with his foster brother Tika, but one day was caught by natives and forced to become their slave. Escaping, he and Tika save Queen Karina of the Lost City.

James Pond
Gordon Hogg
Buster 1965-67 (Fleetway)
This lampoon of James Bond (Agent 007 – licensed to kill) was billed as James Pond (Agent 008½ – licensed to laugh). The elegant agent strolled into *Buster* on 6 November 1965, dressed, if not licensed, to kill in his bowler, brolly, and cigarette holder. Little did he know that, on his trail, were Tiny Ivan and Lofty Lenin the Ruskovian spies, after the secret plans. This gruesome twosome proved to be Pond's perpetual nemeses, as they made regular but doomed attempts to steal the Crown Jewels from the Tower of London.

Jane Green
Illustrator unknown
Debbie 1973-75 (D. C. Thomson)
'Jane Green's Schooldays began in No. 1 of *Debbie* (17 February 1973), 'The tale of the girl who wanted to go to the school on the hill'. Hill Grange was a big, expensive girls' school which stood high above the village of Weston. Everyone in the village knew Jane and liked her, whether it was Sir Robert whose paper she delivered at the top of the hill, or rheumaticky Mrs Carter whose grocery was at the bottom. Then the mysterious letters started to arrive: Jane was to sit the Hill Grange entrance exam (she passed), she was to go to Clarrods for a school uniform, her £400 fees were paid. Who was responsible?

Jane Bond
Michael Hubbard
Tina 1967; *Princess Tina* 1967-70 (Fleetway)
'Look out! Here she comes! Crashing through with a thousand thrills!' Jane Bond, Secret Agent was the leading lady of *Tina* (25 February 1967), the first international comic. Jane was described as 'cool as an early morning rose, and as deadly as a nightshade. Born in the United States, educated in Italy, dressed by Zior (*sic*) of Paris – and hated by every crook in the world.' At least her artist was English, the excellent Michael Hubbard, who blessed Miss Bond with the kind of legs he had lavished on another Jane (of *Daily Mirror* fame).

Jane: Model Miss
Pamela Chapeau
Diana 1963-73 (D. C. Thomson)
'The story of a schoolgirl in the exciting world of fashion modelling' started on the full-colour back page of *Diana* No. 3 (March 1963). It started unhappily, with Jane Morgan's father failing to survive an operation and her mother getting the sack when Gordon's Dress Salon sells out to Mr Bossman. But soon teenager Jane saves the day by becoming, not only a successful model, but opening her own gown salon in Carchester. Soon Princess Tina of Slovia comes calling for a specially designed wedding dress and by 1965, Jane and her model team are globetrotting for World Wide Beach Wear.

Janie's Jeannie
Illustrator unknown
Lindy 1975 (IPC)
The popular sport for girls, tennis, and magic were combined in this serial which started in *Lindy* No. 1 (21 June 1975). When Jane Martin's father died, her mother was forced to take a job as caretaker at St Margaret's Academy for Girls, where Jane was allowed to attend as a pupil. On her first day, she made an enemy of Cynthia Delisle, but also acquired a strange friend, who popped out of an old tennis racket! 'You can call me Jeannie, and I'm jolly grateful to you. It's been an awful drag hanging about in that racquet all these years!' Jeannie helps Jane beat Cynthia and win the Schools Championships.

Jasper the Grasper
Ken Reid
Wham 1965 (Odhams)
Back in the bad old, good old days, when you could buy 5000 jelly-babies for a ha'penny, and a penny was worth four farthings, there lived in Stingy Street in the village of Muddling-on-the-Mire, the meanest old miser in the world. The name of this tight-fisted old skinflint was Mr McGrabb, but everyone called him Jasper the Grasper. His house was equipped with directional ear-trumpets so that he could hear the tiniest chink of dropped farthings and grab them while they were on the rebound. Every night he counted his hoard, all £15,002 2s 4¾d of it!

Jeff Arnold
Charles Chilton
Eagle 1950-62 (Hulton)
Riders of the Range was a radio serial about the Old West, written and produced by enthusiast, Charles Chilton. It began broadcasting on 13 January 1949, with Paul Carpenter in the lead as cowboy, Jeff Arnold, and Charles Irwin as his sidekick, Luke. The strip adaptation started in *Eagle* No. 37 on 22 December 1950, with the title accent on Jeff Arnold. The full-colour page was drawn by Jack Daniel. Daniel's impressionistic way with colour did not suit the editor, who preferred the brighter style of Angus Scott.

Janus Stark
Solano Lopez
Smash 1969-71; *Valiant* 1971-73 (IPC)
'The Incredible Adventures of Janus Stark' started on 15 March 1969 as 'the dark silence of midnight lay over Victorian London'. Inside the orphanage of Hemlock Hall the brutal hand of Simon Tragg fell on the thin form of young Jonas Clarke. Flung into a rat-infested cellar, Jonas used the strange rubbery quality of his bones to wriggle through a six-inch gap. Befriended by blind Largo he learned light-fingered trickery and soon became Janus Stark, escapologist, son of the unknown, master of illusion.

Jay R. Hood
George Martin
Nutty 1980-85 (D. C. Thomson)
'Jay R. Hood – He's Anything but Good!' was inspired, of course, by the popular television soap-opera series, *Dallas*, with its antihero, J. R. Ewing. This Junior Jay R. was a bad-hat, too, and, to prove it, always wore an outsize stetson. Jay R. had nothing but contempt for the boy he called 'my goody-goody drip of a kid brother', Robby. Robby was a good lad with a penchant for the bow and arrow (Robby Hood, get it?). And as for the love-struck Sue-Helen and her talking Lucy Doll, Jay R. had but one word: 'Yeeargh!'

Jeff Hawke
Sydney Jordan
Junior Express 1954-56 (Beaverbrook)
'Jeff Hawke, Space Rider' became the First Citizen of the Space Age after his experimental aircraft, the XP5, took off (in the *Daily Express* on 15 February 1954) and he wound up among the Lords of the Universe 3000 miles beyond the Moon. One of the first newspaper strip heroes to transfer to comics, Squadron Leader Jeff Hawke relived his experiences in *Junior Express* from 4 September 1954. At first in simple red and black, his strip filled the full-colour photogravure centre spread from 18 February 1956, as drawn by Tacconi (illustrated).

Jerry, Jenny and Joe

Reg Parlett

Tip Top 1934-39 (Amalgamated Press)

'The Adventures of Jerry, Jenny and Joe' started with a bang on the front of *Tip Top* No. 1, 21 April 1934. Joe, an orphan, catapulted the hat off Jerry Jackson! By the end of the episode, Jerry had adopted Joe and his sister Jenny, and they were off on their first adventure, by steamer to the South Seas. Soon Roy Wilson took over and sent them to India to encounter untrustworthy Marcus Carstairs. Their main artist was W. D. Davies (illustrated) who drew their battle with the Green Dragon Tong, winding up at episode 261 with 'Three cheers for Jerry, Jenny and Joe!'

Jet Jordan

Illustrator unknown

Champion 1966; *Lion* 1966 (Fleetway)

The Red Bisons, a crack Canadian aerobatic team, were returning to their base in France after licking the American Skyblazers at an aerial display in North Africa. Their leader, Red One, was Squadron-leader Jet Jordan. Suddenly, from 5000 feet above them, four gleaming Super Sabre jets went into a powerdive and, with a roar like a thousand thunderstorms, left the Bisons shuddering in their slipstream. A gag attack by the Skyblazers, and the begining of new adventures in a new comic, No. 1 of *Champion* (26 February 1966).

Jessie Joy

Bertie Brown

Jester 1923-32 (Amalgamated Press)

'Jessie Joy – Just Like a Boy': her full title tells it all. She was just the kind of girl for a comic, a tomboy who would cheerfully get up to any slapstick prank of the kind usually perpetrated by the predominantly male heroes of her prewar era. She made sure she included her own sex in her captions: she addressed *Jester*-ites as 'Dear Lads and Ladesses' or even 'Dear Readers and Readeresses'. But 'The Jolly Jinks of Jessie Joy', as her strip was later headed, were reserved for men such as mingy Mr Nevergrin or toothy Algy Allnut.

Jet Morgan

Charles Chilton

Express 1956-57 (Beaverbrook)

Captain Jet Morgan made his first *Journey Into Space* on the radio, in a serial of that title which began on 21 September 1953. Immediately popular with space-minded youngsters, other serials followed, all written and produced by Charles Chilton. The first strip adaptation rocketed across the full-colour centre spread of *Express* No. 84 (28 April 1956), illustrated by Tacconi. Set in 1976, Jet and his crew (Lemmy, Doc, and Mitch) left Lunar Base bound for Mars in the serial entitled 'Planet of Fear'.

Jet-Ace Logan

John Gillat

Comet 1956-59; *Tiger* 1959-68 (Fleetway)

In the year 2056, RAF space cadet Jim Logan, known as Jet-Ace to his chums, is aboard one of twelve long-range spaceships bound for the planet Jupiter, which has been mysteriously invaded by unidentified objects and green fog. Commented Jet-Ace wryly, 'Dear Mum, I may be a little late for supper. Don't bother to keep it warm for me, love, Jim.' Jet-Ace and his comrades, Flight-Lieutenant Cobb and Plumduff Charteris, sort out Zor Horus, self-styled Master of the Earth, and then save the Mars satellite from Straiker's space pirates.

Jill Crusoe

Roland Davies

School Friend 1950-59 (Amalgamated Press)

'It was 50 years ago when the sailing ship Arepathus was wrecked in the Indian Ocean. A small boat with a lone exhausted survivor, drifted to a desert isle. She was Jill Blair who, in the care of the Captain, had been on her way to Australia.' Now her serial strip started in *School Friend* No. 1 (20 May 1950) with Jill removing a thorn from a leopard's paw and naming her new friend Katzi. The episode ended on a familiar note: a footprint in the sand! Soon she was saving little M'Lani from a witch doctor: 'Me belong you', she said.

J

Jilly of Jingle-Bell School
Bob Dewar
Twinkle 1972-80 (D. C. Thomson)
The playmates from Primary One of Jingle-Bell School made their debut in one large picture which filled a full-colour page of *Twinkle*: a kind of cleaned-up 'When the Bell Rings' for little girls. The merry capers of these mixed infants, under the watchful eye of their teacher, Miss Jolly, were miles away from the Bash Street Kids. Yet, like their *Beano* counterparts, they, too, changed from one big panel to a standardized strip. This occurred on the back page in 1975, when Jilly emerged as the star of the strip, supported by Mr Lockett the caretaker, Mr Mould the sculptor, and Miss Cook the cook.

Jimmy Jeckle and Master Hyde
Terry Bave
Whizzer & Chips 1970-73 (IPC)
Inspired by the classic horror story of *Dr Jekyll and Mr Hyde* by Robert Louis Stephenson, this junior variation began on 21 February 1970, Jimmy Jeckle's birthday. His over-loving mum gave him a chemistry set and the lad began mixing right away ('Blop! Bloop! Blap!'). Tasting a test-tubeful, Jimmy went through an amazing metamorphosis – 'Kerpow! Gloop! Gulp! Grooo-heh-heh!' – and changed into a hairy horror: 'Wow! I feel wicked but great!' His Auntie Aggie was the first to flee from the sight, but he changed back in time for a slobbery kiss from mum.

Jimmy and his Grockle
James Clark
Dandy 1937-39; *Sparky* 1966-76 (D. C. Thomson)
'Queerest Beast to Walk on Land – Jimmy's Grockle Beats the Band!' was the introductory headline to this pictorial version of a serial story which had run in *Rover* from 1932. Now it was in *Dandy* No. 1 (4 December 1937) that Jimmy Johnson once again received a parcel from his Uncle Bill in South America. It contained a giant egg, which Jimmy promptly popped in the oven to hatch. Out came 'the queerest animal you ever saw, right from its funny grin to its spiky tail.' It ate everything in sight, including pa's boots and, as all it ever said was 'Grockle', that's what Jimmy called it.

Jimmy Jinx
Ken Harrison
Buzz 1973-75; *Topper* 1975-85 (D. C. Thomson)
'Jimmy Jinx and What He Thinks' was the full title of this strip. Jimmy Jinx was your average male comic reader, always in trouble with his teacher. The unusual aspect of Jimmy's adventures was that his thoughts were visualized as double bubbles. One depicted his good nature: Goodie the angelic cherub complete with wings and floating halo; the other his bad side: Baddie the imp with horns and pronged tail. Between the pair of them, they seemed to get Jimmy into more trouble than ever.

J

Jimmy Joy the T.V. Boy
Albert Pease
Chips 1952-53 (Amalgamated Press)
'In Ye Days of Ye Knights' was ye title of Jimmy Joy's first adventure into television, in *Chips* No. 2948 dated 6 September 1952. When Maid Marian cried 'Oh, would some brave hero save me from ye Bad Baron!', Jimmy responded with a cry of 'To the rescue!', diving into his TV screen and doing a duel with his mum's mop! Owner of an unexplained magical telly, Jimmy jumped into all kinds of exploits, such as Roman Games with Julius Sneezer ('Helpius! Thou hast put ye horses back to frontius, thou chumpus!'), and trying to help telly-cook Philip Heartburn toss a pancake.

Jingle's Jolly Circus
Walter Booth
Puck 1930-36 (Amalgamated Press)
'Fun and Frolic with the Merry-makers of Jingle's Jolly Circus and Joy Camp' was the full and flowery title of this series which spent six years on the full-colour front page of *Puck* before moving inside. The merry-makers were a crowd of circus kids – Merry Max the boy cowboy, Laughing Eyes the Red Indian, Smiling Sambo the pageboy, Sing Song the Chinese juggler, Nip Nimble the acrobat, and Trixie the trapeze girl – who spent most of their time playing pranks on the two old clowns, Tim Titter and Joey.

Jo and Co
Brian Delaney
Diana 1974-76 (D. C. Thomson)
This 'Super new series about Three Girls and a Menace called Mitzi' started in the first combined edition of *Diana and Romeo* (21 September 1974). Jo, Haze (a black girl), and Mary all lived together in a large flat, 'and with three crazy girls there is never a dull moment'. Smiled Jo: 'Living the sweet life in this fabso flat! Do what I like, when I like, and peace, purr-fect peace to do it in! Um, s'bliss! Everything's luvverly in my luvverly life in this luvverly flat!' Even when Mary cooked chicken surprise and Haze used mustard instead of custard! Then in moved kid sister Mitzi.

Jimmy and his Magic Patch
Dudley Watkins
Beano 1944-59 (D. C. Thomson)
'Cheerio, Mum!' shouted Jimmy Watson, 'I'm off to school!' It was New Year's Day, 1944, and *Beano* No. 222: a fateful day indeed. Jimmy was badly delayed: first he rescued an old gypsy's kitten from a fierce bull terrier, then he tore the seat of his short trousers. The gypsy patched them up for him with a piece cut from the corner of her carpet. 'Maybe I should have told him that was a magic carpet!', she mused. Meanwhile Jimmy, late for a history lesson, was wishing he had lived in the days of Drake and – 'swoosh!' – he was whisked back in time to Plymouth Hoe! It was the first of many adventures in the past.

The Jocks and the Geordies
Jimmy Hughes
Dandy 1975- (D. C. Thomson)
The battle of the border broke out on 1 November 1975, in *Dandy* No. 1771. 'We're the Jocks!', cried a clan of cloth-capped kids, 'We live north of the border and we're cocks of the walk!' The gang in school caps and black blazers had an answer to this. 'We're the Geordies!' they yelled, 'We live south of the border and we're always knocking spots off them Jocks!' To prove it, they splatted a suet pudding all over the Jocks, and the war was on. Despite cries of 'Ooyah!', 'Ooof!', and 'Gloob!', the war continues to this day.

Joe Bones
Carrion
Victor 1975-86 (D. C. Thomson)
Private Joe Bones known as 'The Human Fly' was known to his Sergeant as a military disaster. He returned from leave to Portsea to find the town in ruins. The Germans had mounted a long-range gun on the French coast. 'Channel Charlie', as it was nicknamed, was reducing convoy ports to rubble. Joe took off his army boots in case the broken glass should cut them, then climbed a tottering wall to rescue a child. Lord Percy Plimpton, the Prime Minister's representative, saw the deed and speedily enlisted Joe into climbing the French cliffs to destroy Channel Charlie. It was the first mission of many.

Joe 90
Gerry Anderson
Joe 90 1969; *TV 21* 1969-70 (City); *Countdown* 1971 (Polystyle)
Nine-year-old Joe 90 was adopted by Professor Ian McClaine, and became the youngest special agent in the World Intelligence Network (W.I.N.). Joe lived with Professor Mac at an antique cottage in Dorset, underneath which was hidden a huge laboratory. Here was the Big Rat, a computer able to induce the recorded brain patterns of experts into schoolboy Joe, via his special electrode spectacles. In No. 1 of his own comic, *Joe 90* (18 January 1969), Joe used an aquanaut's expertise to save sunken missiles from Russian frogmen. Keith Watson and others illustrated this T.V. series.

John Brody
Colin Andrew
Boy's World 1963-64 (Longacre)
'What Is Exhibit X' was the title of the first case for John Brody, science investigator of the *Daily Newsflash*. Introduced in No. 1 of *Boys World*, John Adam Brody 'is 26, and was educated at Leeman's Grammar School, Doncaster, and Leeds University, where he took the best B.Sc. that any of his professors could remember. He has written two books, *Science and Crime* and *Climbing to High Adventure*. His hobbies are judo, reading detective novels, and mountaineering. His pet hates are snobs, blood sports and untidiness.' Exhibit X was an odd object found in the sea at Tollworth.

Joe Soap
John Dallas
Cracker 1975-76 (D. C. Thomson)
'Joe's soapy bubbles bring lots of troubles!' Joe Brown was his real name, but all the folk in Sudsbury called him Joe Soap because he was forever blowing bubbles. One day, 18 January 1975 to be precise (in No. 1 of *Cracker*), Joe's genial old Grandpa, an eccentric inventor, made some special bubble mixture in his potting shed. When Joe blew, he made bubbles so big and strong that he could bounce around Sudsbury inside one. Each week Grandpa had a go at making fresh mixture, and each week Joe had different bubble trouble.

John and Joan
R. W. Plummer
Sun 1948-49 (Allen)
'Voyage to Venus' was the title of their first adventure: 'An exciting picture adventure of a boy and girl on a great planet far away from Earth.' John and Joan Randall took off in panel one, page one, of *Sun* No. 7, 3 February 1948, and landed on Venus in panel two! The shortest space-flight in comic-paper history, thanks to their father, Professor Randall, and his discovery of 'how to conquer gravity and soar anywhere in space'. They came home on 15 February 1949 and then they were off to 'The Forgotten Land'.

Johnnie Wingco
Illustrator unknown
Knockout 1954-60 (Amalgamated Press)
'*Knockout*'s Ace of the Skies – the Greatest Pilot of Them All!', that was 'Johnnie Wingco, Master Pilot' who flew in a double-page picture serial for six years, including a spell on the full-colour cover (1958). Johnnie was a peace-time pilot in exotic lands: he cleaned up Algernon Kersh's slave-worked uranium mine in Borneo, test-flew a vertical takeoff fighter for Anywhere Airways, and was joined by Molly Wilson in an endurance flight to Australia in an ancient biplane. 'By glory!', was Johnnie's catchphrase.

Johnny Jones
J. H. Bleach
New Hotspur 1962-70
(D. C. Thomson)
'Johnny Jones at School' was a series remarkably similar to 'Smith of the Lower Third' (see Tom Smith). Johnny Jones was a working-class lad who won a scholarship to Kingsleigh College, a big public school. Johnny, too, was in the Lower Third, under form-master Mr Squall, and was put into Drake's House. His chums were Sandy Wilson and Sleepy Sam Simson, while the unpopular boy in the form was Ken Crowther. He it was who sneaked into the rifle club armoury and twisted a sight so Johnny would lose the silver cup.

Johnny Cougar
Geoff Campion
Tiger 1962-84; *Roy of the Rovers* 1985-86 (IPC)
'The Man with the Iron Grip' was discovered by Ed Spiro, manager of all-in wrestlers, who was on a fishing holiday in the Everglades with his trainer, Lou Rossi. He was Johnny Cougar, a Seminole Indian, who saved the men from animal attack and, in return, was given a chance in the grapple-and-grip game. Palling up with ex-wrestler Bill Maclean, the Fighting Seminole soon becomes a champion. But always there is the call of his blood, as when Chief Nahzav sends a message: 'Come quickly, a demon walks our land!'

Johnny Jett
Dudley Watkins
New Hotspur 1959 (D. C. Thomson)
Readers of No. 1 of *New Hotspur*, a comic converted from the long-running story paper, were invited to 'Meet the Most Amazing Boy in the World – the boy that every boy would like to be'. It was 24 October 1959 and he was Johnny Jett the Super Boy. He had lived on Signal Island for ten years, ever since a liner had run aground on the reef. Samuel Holmes, a brilliant scientist, had taken a liking to Johnny and developed him into the world's first superboy. Now it was time for Johnny to go into the world, to be schooled at Manton College. The professor's parting gift was an energy belt: he would need it in the adventures to come.

Johnny Red
Joe Colquhoun
Battle Action 1977- (IPC)
'Blazing Aerial Action with the Pilot who can't Fly for Britain!' His name was Johnny 'Red' Redburn. Unjustly discharged from the RAF, he now flies a British plane with a Russian squadron, the Falcons. As the refugees from Leningrad cried when Johnny's bullets brought down a Stuka: 'They say that even the Fritzies live in fear of the Hurricane that strikes out of nowhere!' Alex, leader of the Falcons, showed Johnny a Russian newspaper: 'Even the children paint your nickname amongst the ruins! You have become a legend!' Their word was 'Djavol – the Red Devil.'

Joker
Sid Burgon
Knockout 1971-73; *Whizzer & Chips* 1973- (IPC)
'You'll laugh at this one – A boy who likes fun!' Joker pulled his first gag in *Knockout* No. 1 (12 June 1971) and, although it was the oldie of the squirting-flower-in-lapel joke, it started him on a comic career that has filled fifteen years of fun. The old gags are the best ones, although it's true that Joker manages to give them a twist. For instance, the fake ink-blot joke: he pulled this one with a hard pool of tar on mum's carpet. Unfortunately, Joker came unstuck when the fire melted the tar.

Jolly Jumbo
A. W. Browne
Bumper 1946-49 (Barrett)
'Jolly Jumbo' had started as a children's strip in *Home Notes* magazine as early as 1909, drawn by G. Sidney. By the 'Thirties, A. W. Browne had taken on the feature, and his strips were reprinted in *Jolly Jumbo's Annual*. When the war discontinued the series, Browne developed the characters as stars of *Bumper Comic Book*, with Jumbo and his chums, the Jungle Boys, Tim Tiger, Mickey Monkey, Piggy Porker, George Giraffe, and the rest. Surprisingly, Tiger Tim and the Bruin Boys never sued!

Jolly Jack Robinson
Fitzpatrick
Comic Home Journal 1904; *Butterfly* 1904-06 (Amalgamated Press)
'The Merry Sailor Lad' sailed on to page one of the Easter Holiday Number of *Comic Home Journal* (2 April 1904) offering undersea trips in his tight little submarine: 'I'll show you how the winkles wink, the lobsters lob, the bloaters bloat and the kippers kip!' But, before the month ran out, he was in far-flung seas wreaking havoc among the warring Japs ('That must be Yack Yobinson') and Russes ('I am toldovitch you havitch an ironclad'). Later some gay Geisha girls said 'Nagasaki-hakodati' to him, to which Jack murmured, 'I dare say!' Transferring to *Butterfly*, Jack embarked on new conflicts with pirates.

Jonah
Ken Reid
Beano 1958-62; *Hornet* 1971-73; *Buddy* 1981-82 (D. C. Thomson)
'Once in a lifetime a guy like Jonah turns up. He means well, but he's so full of bad luck that when people see him coming they go round the world the other way, just to avoid him!' Entering *Beano* No. 817 (15 March 1958) by the back page, this paunchy, buck-toothed matelot's cap blew off. In the fifteen pictures it took to regain it, he managed to sink three cargo ships. The fourth was hardly Jonah's fault: it sunk under the weight of the survivors! Still, Jonah was happy: 'That hat cost me five bob!' It was the start of a voyage of disaster unequalled in the sagas of the sea.

Jolly Joe Jinks
Bertie Brown
Puck 1911-14 (Amalgamated Press)
'The Merry Adventures of Joly Joe Jinks and his Pocket Pierrots' made a striking full-colour front page for *Puck*. The series developed from Joey, a wandering clown (G. M. Payne 1910); Bertie Brown gave him four little kiddie-clowns and, in 1913, a baby elephant to boot. These chucklesome additions helped lower the age-appeal of the old clown when it became obvious that *Puck* was read by younger children than originally anticipated. Poor old Joe was further degraded when his strip was taken over by an infant called Angel.

The Joyland Express/Sunbeam Cinema
Don Newhouse
Sunbeam 1928-37 (Amalgamated Press)
'The Joyland Express' puffed its way across the entire centre spread of *Sunbeam*. A pixie stoked the engine, and each of the eight little carriages formed one picture of each week's adventure of 'The Piggy Pierrots'. These two fat clowns were called Piggy and Trotters, Trotters being the one who wore black. Whether this choice of costume made him the automatic villain or not, it was usually Trotters who played the painful pranks, like substituting fireworks for Piggy's sausages. In 1938 the strip was retitled 'Sunbeam Cinema'.

Judge Dredd
John Wagner
2000 AD 1977- (IPC)
'He is the Law – and you'd better believe it!' was the catchphrase that trailered Judge Dredd in No. 1 of *2000 AD*. He arrived, law-giver gun set on high explosive dispensing instant judgement and execution, in No. 2 (5 March 1977), and British comics have never been the same since. Dredd, implacable lawman of the twenty-second century, has become the top cult hero of the 'Eighties, the very antithesis of Dan Dare, hero of the 'Fifties. The year is 2107, the location Mega-City One, vast metropolis of 400 000 000 citizens trapped in a nightmare of unemployment and rampant crime. Artists include Brian Bolland (illustrated).

Julius Sneezer
Allan Morley
Dandy 1946-49 (D. C. Thomson)
Julius Sneezer the Sneezing Caesar was advertised thus: 'Honk! goes his conk – He always has a cold – And in funny coloured pictures – His story will be told!' And so it was, beginning on 26 October 1946 in *Dandy* No. 330, when the Roman emperor's noble nose blasted red-inked 'ah-tish-oos' in three out of six pictures. No cure seemed to work: a mustard plaster was so hot it brought the fire brigade, whose hose only made Sneezer's cold worse. Advised that standing on the head stoppeth sneezing, Julius turned upside down only to sneeze backwards: 'Oo-tish-ah!'

Julius Cheeser
George Martin
Topper 1958-68 (D. C. Thomson)
This black mouse in red shorts spent a decade of half pages in his search for chunks of cheese. Inspired by the long-running animated cartoon film series, *Tom and Jerry*, by Hanna-Barbera, Julius Cheeser's nemesis was also a cat called Tom. This Tom, however, played safe by being a ginger moggie with stripes, unlike his black counterpart from Hollywood. Nor was the human lady of the house black, either: she was pleasantly plump, but pink. Otherwise the chases between pantry and mousehole were much the same.

Jumbo Jim and Brother Tim
Bertie Brown
Sunbeam 1928-39 (Amalgamated Press)
Elephant lovers (and which prewar child was not?) must have delighted in this *Sunbeam* strip. Not only were the stars a pair of young jumbos, but so was everyone else! They lived with Uncle Jumbo, who wore pince-nez spectacles – perhaps pince-trunk would be a better word! – and, when not playing tricks on him, there was always Mr Tusker the Lamp-lighter, or an elephantine policeman. Jim and Tim were a trunkload of laughs.

Jumping Jiminy

William Ward

Dandy 1939-40 (D. C. Thomson)

'The Kangaroo Who's Always On The Hop', as he was subtitled, bounded into *Dandy* No. 78 in the Spring of 1939. Jumping Jiminy was often put down but always bounced back, thanks to his big feet and bigger tail which soon put paid to bullies. Jiminy's resiliant rubberiness owed a lot to his artist's early career as an animator: Billy Ward had made the *Bonzo* cartoon films in the 'Twenties.

Junior Rotter

Trevor Metcalfe

Whizzer & Chips 1980- (IPC)

'He's the pest of the west with his sneaky tricks!' Junior Rotter – J. R. for short – moved into *Whizzer & Chips* on 4 October 1980 and, if his initials and tall ten-gallon hat weren't clues enough, his dirty tricks would have switched on any telly-fan to his inspiration: J. R. in the popular T. V. soap opera, 'Dallas'. Junior Rotter lives way out west on a vast ranch where he spends his time, and his pa's dollars, in an unending feud with his little sister, Sue Helen. Typical trick: switching the Easter Bunny's eggs for a stack of stinky bad'uns.

Jungle Lord

R. Beaumont

Comet 1947-48 (Allen)

'Gosh, I feel more like Tarzan every minute!' says Dick Seymour as he parachutes into the treetops of impenetrable Africa on the front page of *Comet* No. 12, 21 February 1947. Three weeks later he remarks, 'Gee, I'm a real Tarzan now!' as he swaps his tattered shirt and shorts for an off-the-shoulder leopard skin. Like all good British heroes, Dick was nothing if not honest! Dick is saved from a snake by Bibi, a half-caste native girl, and proclaimed Lord of the Jungle People by Baki the High Priest.

Justine

Illustrator unknown

Sally 1969-71 (IPC)

'The Justice of Justine' was the title of this serial starring the supergirl, Justine Jones. Her saga began in *Sally* No. 1 (14 June 1969) where she was identified as a 'generous-hearted girl but excessively timid'. Holidaying on a remote Greek island, Justine saved an old man from drowning. Leading her into a deep cave, the grateful Greek presents her with the legendary cloak of Icarus. 'Take also the bow with its arrows of sleep, and the wondrous lenses that give magic vision. You will fly like an eagle and your courage will know no bounds.' Becoming the Winged messenger of Justice, Justine was timid no more.

Kaloo: King of the Tigers
Arthur Mansbridge
Golden 1939-40 (Amalgamated Press)
'Lost in the jungle while a baby, Kaloo, a white boy, is brought up by a tigress. All the animals of the jungle obey him because he conquered fire. He rides on Sandra, a tiger, and rescues a white girl from the river.' So much for the synopsis. The white girl is Betty Baker, an explorer's daughter, who soon has to be rescued again, this time from her unkind guardian, Mr Krantz. Kaloo summons Yama the great ape and Bomba the big elephant, and soon has Betty safe in his treehouse. 'You play with Wawa while I'm gone', he says. And she does.

Karl the Viking
Don Lawrence
Lion 1961-64 (Fleetway)
'The Sword of Eingar' was the title of the original serial saga of Karl, Son of Eingar the Manslayer. Karl led the Vikings in their longboats to Saxon Britain in search of the stolen Sword of Eingar. Commanding the army was his rival for the throne, the sneering Skurl, doing his best to dispense with the young heir. The sacred sword was in the possession of Earl Gyrth of Eastumbria, from whom it was duly regained. Then Karl was off in his serpent-ship to explore and plunder North Africa.

Katie Country Mouse
Philip Mendoza
Harold Hare's Own 1959-64; *Jack & Jill* 1964-73 (IPC)
'The Stories of Katie Country Mouse' filled the full-colour back page of *Harold Hare's Own Paper* from No. 1 (14 November 1959). Katie lived in a house made from a barrel in Bluebell Lane, by Bluebell Down, whither she went to pick buttercups for her famous Buttercup Broth. This always won the prize at the village fair, a large cheese which lasted her the whole year round. Once, on her way to the fair, a mouse bounced out of a car and drank all her broth to recover. Luckily, though, he turned out to be the judge, so she still won the cheese! 'Oh my tail and whiskers!', as Katie regularly remarked.

Kangy the Bush Boy
Colin Merritt
Flash 1948-49 (Marx)
Kangy the Bush Boy was the front-page star of *Flash*, publisher Philipp Marx's first regular comic. The photogravure printing in attractive orange and green suited the strip which retailed the action-packed adventures of Kangy, who rode on the back of his pet Kangaroo, Karoo, through the outback of Australia. In his first three-page outing, Kangy called on the kangaroo herd to help stop a raging bush fire, caused by a careless cigarette smoker. From No. 10 Kangy and Karoo jumped to the full-colour centre spread.

Kathy
Illustrator unknown
June 1961-69 (Fleetway)
'Kathy at Marvin Grange School' was the full title of this 'heart-warming story of an orphanage girl at Britain's most famous school', which started in No. 1 of *June* (18 March 1961). It was a strange day for Kathy Summers, 'the happiest girl at Tolliver Orphanage', for, suddenly, it turned out to be her last. A mysterious person was paying for her to become a boarder at the most famous girls' school in England. Could it be the beautiful lady standing watching her in the corridor of the train? If so, why? Soon Kathy settled in, chumming up with Mary while, in the offing, was Jemima Carstairs, the Terror of the Third.

Kat and Kanary
Charles Grigg
Beano 1952-57 (D. C. Thomson)
Inspired by the popularity of the brilliant Warner Brothers' cartoon films featuring Sylvester the lisping cat and Tweetie Pie the canary-bird, Kat and Kanary began their fur *v.* feather feud in No. 526 of *Beano* (16 August 1952). The battle raged for years, despite a 'rest period' which began on 12 October 1957 when the comical combatants were reduced to playing rival hosts of 'Kat's Krazy Korner', a puzzle feature. 'A clever bird whose name is Dicky – and a crafty cat who's not so tricky!'

K.B.R.
David Mostyn
Wow 1982-83; *Whoopee* 1983-85 (IPC)
The craze for Citizens Band Radio spawned this spin-off, Kids Band Radio, whose strange new language was first heard in the land on 6 June 1982 in No. 1 of *Wow* 'Jammy Jim to Fruit-face. I've murkled the buzz-which, 7-14 and bats pyjamas!', cried a boy on a bike, 'I'm putting the juice on the funny bunny!' Answered a breaker on a skateboard, '7-4 tangleweed, let's ronday at the shiver-show!' Meanwhile something snapped: 'All the sevens from Steamy Sid! The fairycakes have gonked on my chunker! I'm fruiting down Summerside Hill!' Luckily Clanger Kid was on the beam: 'Keep it on ice, Steamy!'

Ken and Katie
Illustrator unknown
Sparks 1918-20 (Henderson)
'The Adventures of Ken and Katie' became the front-page serial of *Sparks* when that comic changed its format to become a coloured comic for the younger age group (5 October 1918). The regular introduction read: 'While on a visit with Katie to his uncle, Professor Mossy Knut, Ken tampers with some scientific instruments with the result that the whole party, house, cat, and butler included, are shot to the moon!' The butler, Billy Bluemole, soon bounces down a crater crying 'Flee, fly, flow, flum for your lives!' A monster chases them, they find Snowball the cat, and meet the Man in the Moon.

Kelly's Eye
Solano Lopez
Knockout 1962-63; *Valiant* 1963-71; *Vulcan* 1975-76 (IPC)
Tim Kelly arrived in South America to claim the vast fortune left to him by his late uncle, owner of the Los Solos mines. Captured, to be sold into slavery by police chief Pedro Garcia, Tim saves an old native from piranhas. In gratitude, the Indian guides Tim to the Temple of Zoltec where, lit by eternal fires, shines the everseeing Eye of Everlasting Life, whose mystic powers will protect he who possesses it from death in any shape or form. Tim uses the Eye to fight injustice anywhere in the world.

Keyhole Kate
Allan Morley
Dandy 1937-55; *Sparky* 1965-74 (D. C. Thomson)
'Keyhole Kate's a little sneak . . . See her on this page each week!' was the comic couplet that introduced this classic character in No. 1 of *Dandy* (4 December 1937). A beak-nosed, four-eyed beanpole in gymslip and well-holed stockings, Kate was the only girl in a gallery of nineteen strips – typical tokenism of the time. Her snoopings invariably rebounded via Uncle's cane, much to the joy of a boy, Cousin Cuthbert. Kate's obsession was crystallized in her favourite reading: *Keyhole Topics* by O. Howie Peeps!

Kelpie
John Burns
Wham 1964-65 (Odhams)
'Kelpie the Boy Wizard' was the youngest assistant to Merlin the Magician at the Court of King Arthur. When a mistake with the pine juice ruins Merlin's liquor of strength, the chastisement leads to the ancient one's incapacitation. Thus, Kelpie is charged by the King to weave a magic spell to help him defeat the evil Knight of the Raven. Unfortunately, Kelpie gets the incantation twisted ('Accandra Dundo' instead of 'Dundo Accandra') and the King is defeated. Changing into a cat, Kelpie sets forth to thwart the evil sorceror.

Kicks
Graham Allen
Pow 1967-68 (Odhams)
The kid who'll do anything for kicks made his first mistake in *Pow* No. 2 (28 January 1967). Stating his creed in the first picture, 'I'm fed up! I wish I was old enough to go to dances, ride a motor bike, and things like that!', and kicking his toy train to bits, Kicks swiped one of his Dad's cigarettes. 'I feel all growed up now!' he said, lighting up the deadly weed, but, by the next picture, his speech balloon read 'Aagh! Gasp! Grooh!' Dad, assuming where there's smoke there's fire, chucked a bucket of water over him.

The Kicktail Kid
Ferrer
TV Comic 1978-79 (Polystyle)
Riding along on the skateboard craze came 'The Kicktail Kid', 'The Space-age Skateboard Sensation' who shot into a full-colour serial in *TV Comic* No. 1377 (5 May 1978). Buzz Blaze, 'the kid who works as a slop-jockey at Joe's Pizza Palace', took his plywood skateboard to Skatkat City in Thunder Bay, L.A., hoping for a crack at the novices slalom, and was chucked out. In return for helping an old hobo, Buzz is given an amazing skateboard. Leaping on, his heel kicks a button 'S' and – 'var-r-r-oom!' 'Waah! I'm accelerating with the speed of a racing dragster!'

Kid Comic
Martin Baxendale
Wow 1982-83; *Whoopee* 1983-85 (IPC)
'I'm going to be a comedian when I grow up, just like them!' announced Kid Comic in No. 1 of *Wow* (6 June 1982), indicating his idols, Morecambe and Wise, Benny Hill and the Two Ronnies. To get into practice, he tried to tell his first joke to his Grandad. 'Danny had a little drum, given him by his mum, he slipped on some mud, and with a thud, landed on his –'. Fortunately, Mum censored the last word by shouting 'Tum!' Next week it was Aunty Mabel who was asked 'What's green and slimy and lives in a hankie?' The answer, of course, was Kid's pet frog! Moving to *Whoopee*, Kid teamed up with Smiler as a double act.

Kid Chameleon
Joe Colquhoun
Cor 1970-74 (IPC)
Years ago, in the burning wastes of the Kalahari Desert, when Tagasee the Wise One was young, an iron bird crashed into the desert. One passenger survived, a baby lily-skin. When Tagasee found him, chameleon lizards were attending him. Their sticky tongues had coated his body, giving it a protective skin. So the boy lived and, as he grew, all reptiles became his friends. He wove a suit of scales to cover his body, giving him the power to change colour at will, a power that came in handy when he pursued the man who shot his parents.

Kiddo the Boy King
Frank Minnitt
Knockout 1939-40 (Amalgamated Press)
'Kiddo the Boy King and his Posh Prime Minister' – known as Primey for short – reigned in *Knockout* from No. 1, 4 March 1939. King Kiddo wanted to do all the things a boy should, while Primey did his best to stop him (cries of 'Tut-tut!', 'Disgraceful!', etc). Primey's A.M.P. (Anti-Marble Precautions) Proclamation read 'Warning! All marbles, aniseed balls and gob stoppers must be handed to the police. Penalty for trying funny business, a good hard slap!' All the kids in the kingdom obeyed the law, then went round to the Cop Shop with Kiddo for a jolly good game!

Kid Dynamite
John Wheeler
Kid Dynamite 1954-60 (Miller)
'The Gunslinging Marshal of the Old West' rode into sixpenny comicbooks at the height of the western boom, mounted on his faithful horse, Lightning. 'Ever since the day Kid Dynamite began packing hardware, his flaming thundersticks have blazed across the western plains and rockrimmed hills on the side of the law!' As Leslie Turner, U.S. Marshal, remarked after Kid beat up a bunch of baddies, 'Man, you're a greased-lightning terror with them fists!' Kid's real identity is unknown: a last-minute editorial change dubbed him Kid Dynamite.

Kid King
Reg Parlett
Jackpot 1979-82 (IPC)
'Kid King Rules Okay!' was the contemporary title of this series which reigned in *Jackpot* throughout that comic's run of 141 weeks. As with his *Knockout* ancestor, Kiddo the Boy King, this mischievous monarch had an adult overseer in the shape of Lord Claude. Kid King soon won over his sceptical subjects when he knighted Arnold Scroggit, headmaster, by giving him six of the best with a cane and a chestful of chocolate medals!

Kid Gloves
Geoff Campion
Valiant 1962-64 (Fleetway)
'You had to be tough to live in a neighborhood like the Shambles, the local name for the poor district of Hillchester. Young Kid Gloves was tough, all right, and as strong as an ox!' Also, pointed out the headline in *Valiant* No. 1 (6 October 1962), Kid had Fists of Iron and Heart of Gold. Billed as 'the Hard-Hitting, Soft-Hearted Heavyweight', Kid won thirty bob by ko-ing a fairground boxer, but only when Kid's dad, Sam, shouted to spur him on. Soon Kid was training at Jim Smith's Gym as sparring-partner for heavyweight Hank Neilson.

Kid Kong
Robert Nixon
Monster Fun 1975-76; *Buster* 1976-81 (IPC)
'Meet our Number One Monster Mirthmaker – He's a King-size Kid!' howled the headline in *Monster Fun* No. 1 (14 June 1975), the first horror comic to feature comic horrors. Shouted the showman: 'Roll up! Roll up! Come and see the biggest gorilla in the world – Kid Kong, son of the famous King Kong!' Forgetting perhaps that this very same outsize ape had already been seen in (and seen to drown in) *Son of Kong*, the sequel to the original film of *King Kong*, cartoonist Bob Nixon, had his jolly monster escape from a Fun Fair, steal a school uniform, and be adopted by short-sighted Granny Smith: 'My, you have got a big appetite, but don't speak with your mouth full!'

K

Kid Pharaoh
Illustrator unknown
Valiant 1973-75 (IPC)
Zethi, a young Egyptian Pharaoh, emerged from a pyramid many centuries after lying in a deep coma. Thothek, an evil High Priest, had entombed Zethi under a terrible curse of darkness, and was now reincarnated as Baron Munsen, a cruel-faced nobleman served by an ill-tempered butler called Kramp. In his search for Thothek, Zethi uses his physical skills to become a champion Greco-Roman-style wrestler under the name of Kid Pharaoh, with crippled Jerry Smith as his second. Zethi was given to uttering such ancient oaths as 'Scarlet scarabs!' and 'Purple pyramids!'

Kids' Court
Mike Lacey
Whoopee 1976-78 (IPC)
'Oh, law! Adults are for it . . . A court run by kids – Judge for yourself!' The caption to this unusual strip of 'Legal Laughs and Courtroom Comedy' described it well. Each week, an offending adult was pounced upon by a Kid Cop wielding a truncheon, or tracked down by Constable Kink-Konk the detective dog, and hauled before a slightly spotty His Honour, who handed down an appropriate sentence. A sweet-shop swindler who charged tuppence for a penn'orth of sweets was sentenced to fourteen days gob-stopping, while a nasty was had up for impersonating Santa Claus and sentenced to hanging – the kids' stockings!

Killer Kane
Colin Andrew
Warlord 1977-84 (D. C. Thomson)
'War in the Air with the Scourge of the Luftwaffe!' was the headline that introduced Squadron-Leader 'Killer' Kane in *Warlord* No. 121 (15 January 1977). 'Achtung! Schpitfeuer!' was the cry of the Jerries as Killer's Spitfire roared over the U-boat pens of Virelle. Killer had got his Flight-Sergeant to fit cameras to his Spit for a recce job and buzzed across the drink despite specific orders to the contrary from Group-Captain Cobb. But the snaps he brought back enabled Bomber Command to make a sortie with Blenheims, and Killer and his Spits went along for the ride.

Kids' Army
Maureen & Gordon Gray
Tops 1981-82 (D. C. Thomson)
'You've heard of *Dad's Army* – now meet Kids' Army' was how the new-style comic *Tops* introduced this four-page serial in their No. 1 (10 October 1981). But there the resemblance ended, for Dave Smith and Sammy Benson were evacuees from blitzed London who organized their chums into a junior and highly unofficial version of the Home Guard, in the south-coast town of Beachcombe. Joining them in their salvage drives and spy hunts were the bespectacled Boffin, the patriotic Winston, ever ready with a speech, Lofty, and two reluctantly admitted girls, Olive and Jean.

The Kids of Stalag 41
Tony Goffe
Jet 1971; *Buster* 1971-73 (IPC)
Stalag 41 was a prisoner-of-war camp in Nazi Germany during World War 2. It was filled with British boys, including Nipper Long, Winston, Dinger Bell, Muscles Miller, and the bespectacled Judge Jenkins. These five spent their days planning tricks to play on the camp commandant, Colonel Klaus Von Schtink, old Schtinky for schort. Their personal German guard was Fat Hans, fond of his black sausage, who called his charges 'der liddle pig-boys', but who soon yelled for der help when the kids rigged up the ghost of Vilhelm der Vicked of Vaisburg.

Killer Kennedy
Ibanez
Victor 1968-77 (D. C. Thomson)
The saga of wartime motor-torpedo boats starring Lieutenant-Commander Kennedy, known as Killer to his second-in-command, Sublieutenant Bill Doyle, was unfurled in *Victor*. Starting in 1968 with a serial called 'Under Two Flags' in which Killer sailed a captured German E-boat full of commandos to the French coast, many more maritime adventures were recorded. 'Strike First, Strike Hard' (1971) saw the M.T.B. sneaking into Bremerhaven to torpedo the battleship, *Mannheim*, while 'The Strange War of Killer Kennedy' (1972) told of his exploits as a lorry driver in prewar Germany.

King Arthur and his Frights of the Round Table
Robert Nixon
Whoopee 1974 (IPC)
'This was Camelot Castle, home of the legendary King Arthur, whose knights were famous for their brave deeds. But Arthur had fallen on hard times. All his knights were out on quests, and only a handful of loyal subjects stayed behind – and they were either too old ("Ohh-me-lumbago!") or too ugly to be any use. Except the watchtower lookout.' This was a tatty looking raven. 'Hey, Kingy! The Vikings are invading!' Kingy did his best, fighting back with the only available weapon: hot porridge! Then Windy the Castle Ghost came to the rescue, and next week Milly the Moat Monster saved Kingy from a dragon. An unusual three-page strip.

King of the Jungle
James Clark
Dandy 1943 (D. C. Thomson)
Known as 'King of the Jungle', Bill King was a world-famous animal tracker and big-game hunter who operated deep in the heart of Darkest Africa. King's quarry was generally of the bizarre variety: golden-tusked elephants whose graveyard was concealed behind a stone door operated by a tune blown through their trunks; the missing link, or the rare snow leopard of Kamchatka. Opposing King in all his ventures was cruel Carl Hertz, a rascally Boer whose methods were less civilized.

The Kings of Castaway Island
James Walker
Beezer 1956-58 (D. C. Thomson)
In 1943 a freight 'plane carrying the King family from Ceylon crash-landed on a lost island in the Indian Ocean. Tom King, Mrs King, and their children, Rob and Jill, turned the fuselage of the freight 'plane into a house, calling it King's Castle. They soon made a pet of a friendly ape, and named him Baldy. A tribe of chimpanzees also became their friends, as did a mysterious Jungle Boy, who rode a young elephant named Jumbo. In their second serial, the Kings' island was invaded by Japanese soldiers.

King Cobra
Ron Smith
Hotspur 1976- (D. C. Thomson)
Bill King, the famous world-roving reporter, had a secret identity. By pulling on secret cords in his specially made suit, Bill transformed it into the amazing outfit of King Cobra, the scientific superhero feared by law breakers everywhere. Trapped on the island of Jerak in south-east Asia, he was able to escape Dr Klarg's remote-controlled robots with the aid of his power-packed gauntlets which could deliver electric shocks. Then it was a simple matter of using his inflatable hood to fly free.

Kit Carson
Geoff Campion
Comet 1950-53; *Big One* 1964-65 (Fleetway)
Kit Carson, the world-famous Indian scout, came riding through Arizona blazing a trail for the wagon-trains that would follow. He rode straight into the two-tone pages of *Comet* No. 113 (16 September 1950), accompanied by his young pardner, Johnny Scott, where they encountered Chief Grey Moose on his way to the Happy Hunting Grounds. In return for Kit's kindness, the dying redskin gave him a golden arrow, key to the tribal treasure. As White Dove translates the secret symbols, the arrow is snatched by Hawkeye, an outlaw Indian.

Kitty Clare's Schooldays
Bertie Brown
Crackers 1931-41 (Amalgamated Press)
When Kitty Clare signed on at Coffdop College in 1931, little did she guess that term would last ten years! Kitty was the pretty one, of course, the other girls being less fortunate. There seemed to be but two of them, the skinny Skittles and her pal Podgy, but this pupil shortage didn't seem to bother the headmistress, Miss Allchin. Visits from school inspectors were the regular headache, including a wartime call from H.M. Inspector of Potherbs.

Koko the Pup
Barry Banger
Magic 1939-41 (D. C. Thomson)
'Full of tricks and full of fun – Koko's a pal for everyone!' This black-and-white bulldog was the full-colour, front-page star of *Magic*, from No. 1 on 22 July 1939 to the last issue, eighty weeks later. As originated by Harry Banger, Koko was a silent star, being limited to radiating 'idea' or 'revenge' in glow-marks about his head. Later artists added speech, which detracted from the visual quality of Koko's activities. Another later addition was a black pullover embossed with a big red 'K', which half-covered the pup's plump nakedness.

Kitty Hawke
Ray Bailey
Girl 1951-52 (Hulton)
'Kitty Hawke and her All Girl Aircrew' flew on to the full-colour front page of *Girl* No. 1 (2 November 1951). 'Well, here we are again, gang!', smiled Kitty, daughter of the owner of Hawke Air Lines, 'One more job chalked up to the all girl aircrew to prove to Dad that we can operate his 'planes as efficiently as the glorious males!' Senior Captain Smedley was less certain: 'After all, gels are only gels, aren't they? In emergency one needs the steadier qualities of the male, what?' Kitty's gels: Second Officer Winifred 'Windfall' White, Radio Officer Jean Stuart, Navigator the Hon. Patricia D'Arcy.

Koo Koo Klub
Denis Gifford
Whizzer & Chips 1969-73 (IPC)
Koo Koo Klub was konducted by Kuthbert Koo Koo K.N.I.T., a not-too-distant relation of Cuthbert McCoo-Coo who conducted Cuckoo Column (later Corner) in *Sun* (1951). Komical kartoons included Koo Koo Kops ('Oho! Just as I suspected! This window is broken on both sides!'); Koo Koo Kwiz ('What has web feet, horns and gold teeth? A duck, a brass band, and a dentist's surgery!'); Koo Koo Kids ('How old are you, lickle boy?' 'I'se not old, I'se nearly new!'); Koo Koo Kourt, Koo Koo Zoo, and others as kontributed by Kids in the Koo Koo Kontest (prize: one kwid!).

Korky the Cat
James Crichton
Dandy 1937- (D. C. Thomson)
Korky was a front-page feline from the first issue of *Dandy*, a black-and-white cat on a full-colour cover. Korky's reign ran from 4 December 1937 to 10 November 1984, when a promotion for *Desperate Dan* pushed the puss to an inside page. In the early years Korky's capers were of the pantomime variety, wordage being limited to the regular radiation of 'revenge!' around his head plus a caption in rhyme: 'Poor old mice are filled with gloom, when the plum duff goes off boom!' Cat chat arrived in 1942, and none of Korky's human antagonists found a talking cat the least bit odd. His nephew, Copycat, appeared in *Magic* (1976) while three more, Nip, Lip and Prip, turned up ten years later.

K

The Krazy Gang
Ian Knox
Krazy 1976-78; *Whizzer & Chips* 1978-85 (IPC)
Closer to *Beano*'s Bash Street Kids than the Crazy Gang of stage and screen fame, this mob was the supposed staff of *Krazy*, running all seventy-nine editions of that comic from 16 October 1976, then transferring their actionful activities to *Whizzer & Chips*. Leader was Ed the eye-shielded editor, who had a pet parrot called Blue. Out in the Gang Hut, there was Brainy the bespectacled printer of *Krazy News*, Showbiz Liz the square-eyed telly-watcher, Sporty the token black, Freaky the token alien from space, and Cheeky. Their arch enemy was the evil-smelling Pongo Snodgrass, a proper stinker.

Krakos the Egyptian
William Ward
New Funnies 1941; *Thrill Comics* 1941-44 (Swan)
'O Tanis, give me strength to reach your secret tomb and burn in the sacred herbs! My palsied hands can scarcely strike the fatal match!' But they did, and in *New Funnies Autumn Special* the wizened old man turned into a tall, youthful Egyptian. Changing his traditional costume for a snap-brimmed trilby and cigarette in holder, he says 'I can arrive in London now without attracting too much attention!' – and promptly flies through the skies – without an aeroplane! On the way, he explodes the rifles of a Nazi firing-squad. 'Who are you?' 'Nemesis to you, worshipper of stone gods!' says Krakos, setting the officer on fire with a touch. 'The angel of the burning death walks among you!'

Krazy Krockitt
Denis Gifford
Davy Crockett, Daniel Boone, Jim Bowie, Annie Oakley 1956-59 (Miller)
A batty burlesque of Davy Crockett, King of the Wild Frontier, was Krazy Krockitt, Thing of the Mild Front-rear, who capped (coonskin, of course) a cracked crowd of wacky westerners who filled up the odd corners of the posse of cowboy comicbooks that stampeded through the 'Fifties. Also around: Wild Bill Hiccup, Dan'l Goone, Jim Pooey, Granny Croakley, Wynott Burp. All drawn by Denis Gifford, but signed by Isidore Oping, Freda Prizner, Hack R. Tist, Unctious Ung, Muncher Lunch, N. 'Doc' Kreengland, Willoughby Derned, and Puffer P. Shewter, to name but a few.

L

Lady Penelope
Gerry Anderson
TV Century 21 1965-66; *Lady Penelope* 1966-69 (City)
'Elegance, Charm and Deadly Danger' was the motto given to Lady Penelope Creighton Ward, heroine of the television puppet series *Thunderbirds*, created by Gerry and Sylvia Anderson (she was also Lady P's voice). She was chauffered through her adventures by reformed burglar 'The Nose' Parker, who became popular enough to have his own strip, 'The Perils of Parker'. After her debut in *TV Century 21* No. 1 (23 January 1965), she escalated to her own comic, *Lady Penelope* (22 January 1966). Artists included Frank Langford (illustrated).

Lanky Larry and Bloated Bill
Tom Browne
Comic Home Journal 1897-1903 (Harmsworth)
'The Adventures of Lanky Larry the Lancer and Bloated Bill the Bobby' might be considered a Victorian comment on the status of the Army and the Police. The skinny soldier and plump constable spent their front-page pictures in sundry shady schemes, such as stealing the family plate from the Duchess of Sloshborough's fancy dress ball, or posing as a giant 'too big to work'. Their early adventures were accompanied by a nameless hound, but their later artist, Tom Wilkinson, introduced a weird, tentacled creation called Moses the Oomph (1901).

Lags Eleven
Illustrator unknown
Scorcher 1970-74 (IPC)
Willie Smith, known to his pals as 'Brilliant Genius', was the mastermind behind countless bank raids, jewel robberies, and wages snatches. The greatest supercrook in Britain, he was currently serving a ten-year stretch in Bankhurst Prison. From the comfort of his armchair in Cell 27, Willie plots with his henchman, Nutcase, to form a convicts' football team. His idea is that, when they play an away match, they will escape under the very nose of Chief Warder 'Bad-news' Benson. As Willie was wont to remark, 'Stone me sideways!'

Larry the Lamb
S. G. Hulme Beaman
Okay Comics 1937-38 (Boardman); *TV Comic* 1954-60; *TV Land* 1960-62 (TV); *Playland* 1968-75 (Polystyle); *Toytown* 1972-73 (Williams)
Larry the Lamb ('Baa – I'm only a little la-a-amb, sir!') emerged as the star of *Toytown*, a BBC Children's Hour favourite on the radio from the 'Thirties, adapted from the books by S. G. Hulme Beaman. Larry was played by Uncle Mac (Derek McCullouch). The first strip version was drawn by Harry Parlett in the otherwise all-American *Okay Comics*. Larry's postwar appearances on television brought him into *TV Comic*, drawn by Lovell (illustrated), and his own *Toytown* (No. 1: 7 October 1972).

Lancelot Lake
Hugh McNeill
Sun 1949-51 (Amalgamated Press)
Once upon a time, to be exact 26 November 1949 in No. 54 of *Sun*, there lived in the greenwood a young fellow named Lancelot Lake. He knew only one tune, 'London Bridge is Falling Down', so sang words to fit it, such as 'I'm off to build my little boat' and, having built it, 'And now to see what fate may bring' as he sailed to seek his fame and fortune. Soon he was promising jolly King Egbert of Avalon to deal with the local giant in return for a knighthood, 50 000 pieces of gold, ten castles, and the hand of Princess Pamela.

Larry the Larky Legionnaire
Reg Parlett
Jester 1932-39 (Amalgamated Press)
Larry, known as 'O white maggot' to Ali Ben Yoyo, the desert dad of the fair Fatima, signed on for a sand-filled slog that ran from 3 December 1932 to 11 February 1939. A long haul but a laughing one, despite all the dirty looks from Sergy the Sergeant-Major, and all the dirty deeds from such Arabian badlads as Ali Ben Banana, Ali Razz Beri, and Ali Ben Veri Tuffstuff, Chief of the Riffraffs. Larry's latterday larks were with Serafina the Shiek's daughter behind the Sahara Gasworks.

Laser Eraser
Robert Nixon
Jackpot 1979-82; *Buster* 1983 (IPC)
It all started when a survey ship from the 13th Dimension parked a few thousand miles above the Earth and sent Spaceman Splod down to beam up some examples of our technology. 'Dokey Hokey!' said Splod, zapping away a builder's hod so that a batch of bricks bounced on his bonce. At this point, Ernie Oddsocks, Earthkid, entered the scene and took charge of the alien's outer-space equipment, the Laser Eraser that made objects vanish. One-hundred-and-forty-one weeks later, Splod let off a zap that wiped out the entire *Jackpot* comic!

Laurel and Hardy
George Wakefield
Realm of Fun & Fiction 1929; *Film Fun* 1930-57 (Amalgamated Press); *TV Comic* 1968-84 (Polystyle); *Laurel & Hardy* 1969-76 (Williams); *1979-82* (Byblos)
'Everyone has roared at the comical adventures of this famous couple on the screen, and I promise you a real good laugh when you see them in *Film Fun*!' This was Eddie the Happy Editor trailing Stan Laurel and Oliver Hardy's debut in *Film Fun* No. 563 (1 November 1930). 'The Comical Capers of the Screen's Cutest Couple' moved from the centre spread to the front/back pages in 1934 and there they remained until 16 November 1957: a twenty-seven-year run, longer than their screen partnership!

Lazy Bones
Martin Baxendale
Whizzer & Chips 1976- (IPC)
Benny Bones was bone idle, a boy who would do anything to get out of work: 'Of course Benny has but one idea – To take it easy year by year!' Benny arrived home yawning: 'I've just done up my shoelace. I must have a lie down after all that effort!' Dad thought otherwise and laced the armchairs with barbed wire. Benny won in the end: he was so naughty Dad sent him to his room for the rest of the day. When Benny read in the paper that the British are the laziest nation in the world, he waved a Union Flag crying, 'I'm proud to be British!'

Laser Eraser and Pressbutton
Steve Dillon
Warrior 1982-85 (Quality)
A double act totally unlike the traditional comic-strip double act as formulated by Weary Willie and Tired Tim, Laser Eraser and Axel Pressbutton teamed up in No. 1 of *Warrior* (March 1982), the latter moving in from earlier appearances in *Sounds*. The scene was the fifty-second century, Laser (Mysta Mystralis) was female, Axel was male – or what was left of him: he was partly human, mostly mechanical, editorially described as 'a psychotic cyborg'. Between the pair of them, they formed a deadly team of legalized exterminators.

Laurie and Trailer
Albert Pease
Chips 1935-53 (Amalgamated Press)
'The Secret Service Lads', later 'Our Extra Special Agents', enlisted in *Chips* No. 2352 dated 5 October 1935. They spent most of the next eighteen years trying to snatch back the Secret Plans, stolen from General Sir Bloater Blazes by the fiendish spies from Socko-Suspenda, Crown Prince Oddsockz, and his minions Serge Pantz and Nick Splitz: 'Gif us ze plans or into ze drinkovitch you goski!' Oddly, Oddsockz's accent changed to der German during der Var; even oddlier he became a postwar Mexican bandit! The lads' last enemy was a hooded crook called the Shufflin' Shadow.

Lazy Leonard and Lively Laurence
G. M. Payne
Firefly 1915-17 (Amalgamated Press)
'The Lads of the Village', this pair of tramps formed the page-one double act of *Firefly*, a ha'penny comic which ran from 20 February 1915 to 31 March 1917, when World War 1 shot them down after 111 issues. No. 1 described them thus: 'Laurence is the human hairpin with the patriotic top-hat [it flew the Union Jack!] and the cherubic smile on his whiskers. The pretty one with the expansive grin and ditto waistband is Leonard.' In their first adventure, they plucked the unstrung wires of a busted-up telegraph pole like a harp, winning enough coinage with their version of 'Tipperary' to retire to Brighton for a week.

Lazy Sprockett
Illustrator unknown
Buster 1960-61 (Fleetway)
'The Tiredest Man in Tennessee' was Lazy Sprockett, who sleep-walked his way through the mountains starting in No. 1 of *Buster* (28 May 1960). Also billed as 'The Horizontal Hill-Billy', Sprockett was, of course, a langorous lampoon of Davy Crockett, the American folk hero popularized by Walt Disney's film. Ma Sprockett sent her half-asleep better half to the fur woods to git a b'ar: 'My coat's more wore out than you are!' But he fell asleep on the job and on the b'ar, too, who carried him home in disgust.

Lefty
Illustrator unknown
Action 1976-77 (IPC)
'Look Out for Lefty!' was the title of the serial strip starring Kenny 'Lefty' Lampton, sixteen-year-old footballer for the Third Division team of Wigford Rovers. Winning goals apart, Lefty has his place in comic history: it was an incident in his strip which sparked off an outcry that virtually killed off his comic. His teenage girlfriend Angie helped Lefty score by clouting his rival with a well-aimed Coca Cola bottle! 'Appalling and brainless!' cried Alan Hardaker, secretary of the Football League.

L-Cars/Krazy Kops
Bill Hill
Sparky 1968-77; *Spike* 1983 (D. C. Thomson)
This bright burlesque of the BBC Television series, 'Z-Cars', starred a team of learner-cops called Cedric and Frederic. Cast in the classic comic double-act mould, Cedric was tall and skinny, Frederick short and fat. Whizzing around town in their bashed-up police car, they were the bane of their Inspector's life. Prowling about in the traditional plain-clothes' uniform of trench-coat with the turned-up collar, and puffing the obligatory pipe, the Inspector often ended up in hospital at the end of two pages of high-speed slapstick. Revived in *Spike* as 'Krazy Kops' (1983).

Legge's Eleven
Illustrator unknown
Valiant 1964-70 (Fleetway)
Billed as 'Britain's Strangest Soccer Team', Rockley Rangers were an outfit of misfits formed by the lean and lanky Ted Legge. The full team: monocled Lord Darcy Lozenge, wild Welshman Griffith Jones, dapper Frenchman Pierre Gaspard, the Tearaway Twins, Les and Ron, overweight Chubby Mann, Nippy Norton, bespectacled Algernon Simms, tough guy Badger Smith, and bearded Scot Angus MacPhee. Their uncanny football won them into the Second Division and, in 1966, they played and beat the Brazilian World Cup holders, Grazia.

L

Lemon and Dash
Louis Briault
Sparks 1914-17; *Big Comic* 1917-19 (Henderson)
Lemon (fat) and Dash (thin), a pair of tattered tramps, were the front-page funsters of the new halfpenny comic *Sparks* (21 March 1914). Their serialized slapstick took them around the world, acquiring Cocktail the Parrot en route: 'Oorah for a sailor's life, tra-la!' Their seafaring did them in good stead: the declaration of war found them with the British Fleet, 'Cruising off . . . . . . in the vicinity of . . . . . . near . . . . . . just the other side of the straits of . . . . . . !' Then they went to Flanders and exploded the Crown Prince of Schleswig-Havanother.

Lieutenant Daring and Jolly Roger
Roy Wilson
Sparkler 1935-37; *Golden* 1937-40 (Amalgamated Press)
'Fun and Thrills with Lieutenant Daring and Little Jolly Roger' began on the full-colour front of *Sparkler*, a fascinating mixture of thrills and comedy as only a master like Roy Wilson could draw. H.M.S. *Joybelle* steamed to an inside page, where their new title was 'All Aboard with Jolly Roger and Captain Daring for a Fun Trip', a curious combination of promotion and demotion. Douglas Daring was back to Lieutenant when, as 'The Bold Sea Rovers', they took command of the black-and-orange cover of *Golden* No. 1, 23 October 1937, right to the last issue.

The Leopard from Lime Street
Mike Western
Buster 1976-85 (IPC)
'The whole strange, spine-chilling business began in the bike-shed at Selbridge Secondary School where, as usual, 13-year-old Billy Farmer was providing some fun for Ginger Moggs and his bullies.' Snapping photos of Professor Jarman's Experimental Zoo for the school magazine, Billy gets scratched by a loose leopard, one being treated with radioactive serum. When he gets home to bullying Uncle Charlie, Billy is baffled by his sudden strength. 'Why am I bounding up the stairs with the speed and agility of next door's cat? My whole body seems to be throbbing with energy!' Wearing a pantomime cat costume, Billy springs into the night . . .

Limp-along Leslie
Vandeput
New Hotspur 1962-74; *Buddy* 1981-83; *Victor* 1983 (D. C. Thomson)
Fourteen-year old Leslie Thomson (no relation to D.C.!) had lived at Low Dyke Farm with his aunt and uncle, Lucy and Arnold Smith, since the death of his parents in a car crash ten years previously. The accident had caused a shortening of Leslie's left leg, but this did not prevent him cherishing an ambition to play professional football for the Darbury Rangers, his dad's old team, or training his sheepdog, Pal, to be a champion. One of this publisher's story-paper heroes successfully transferred to strip format.

Lettice Leefe
John Ryan
Girl 1951-64; *Princess* 1964-67 (Hulton)
'The Greenest Girl in the School', all plaits and giglamps, was Lettice Leefe. The school, an all-girl establishment, of course, was Saint Addledegga's: Head Mistress Miss Froth, form mistress, Miss Tantrum. This long-running strip was not always set in the school: Lettice blew it up too frequently for that. The summer of 'Sixty-one was spent in a sunny cruise with her bearded Uncle Timothy, while Miss Froth made a play for millionaire shipowner Popthelotoulos. Miss Tantrum chanced her bony arm, too.

Lion Boy
Jack Glass
Dandy 1949-50 (D. C. Thomson)
'This is a strange land, Rajah, a land of much smoke and many smells.' Thus, spake Raboo the Lion Boy, an English-speaking lad in a leopard skin who had been captured by a South African hunter and sold, with his lion, to Silas Martin, owner of Martin's Mammoth Circus of Freeburg, U.S.A. But the lad and his lion soon break loose from their cage and, pursued by police, are off on the hunt for food and the way back to their African jungle home. The trip took from 13 August 1949 to 22 April 1950.

Lisa
Geoff Jones
Debbie 1973-82 (D. C. Thomson)
'Lisa the Lonely Ballerina' was the story of young Lisa Blake who wanted to become a dancer like her mother, a famous ballerina. Unfortunately, her mother was killed in a 'plane crash, and Lisa had to live with her unpleasant Aunt Edith. She was determined to stop the girl from dancing so that she would inherit Mrs Blake's fortune instead. But Lisa had a mysterious friend. Whenever she returned to her mother's empty house, her ghost appeared in the mirror to help her. Or was it an electronic effect operated by the mystery man upstairs? Could he be her father, long believed dead?

Little Angel Face
Ken Reid
Dandy 1954-55 (D. C. Thomson)
Cute as the polka-dots on her outsize hair-ribbon and matching skirt, this little mummy's darling made her bow in *Dandy* No. 676 (6 November 1954). She began as she was to continue, with much fluttering of her long eyelashes and many a sickly simper, only to turn into a terror behind mumsie's back. Most of her pranks were directed against bully boys, however, saving Porky the fat boy from back-alley pirates, or Mr Wong the laundryman from a ragging by Bert Bragg. Small wonder they called her 'that pesky little horror'.

Little Adam and Eva
Paul Ailey
Jackpot 1979-80 (IPC)
The first characters in a children's comic to appear totally and regularly naked, these youthful versions of the Genesis legend were born on 5 May 1979 in No. 1 of *Jackpot*. 'It's a new world for Adam and Eva' noted the editor, 'Will they live apple-ly in it?' They certainly did on the first day, despite the serpent who tempted them to eat of the fruit of the Tree of Knowledge, despite a 'Keep Off' notice. One munch and Eva started jumping up and down, a second crunch and Adam completed their knowledge: to skip they needed a skipping-rope. Ropes not having been created, the used the serpent!

Little Elf
George Parlett
Funny Wonder 1936-42 (Amalgamated Press)
'The Wag of the Wigwam' made his reservation in *Funny Wonder* No. 1153 on 2 May 1936 and settled in for a happy hunting-ground of many ha-has which would last until 24 January 1942. Elf was a papoose of the Sawnee Tribe, ruled by Big Chief Mighty Mutt, and his main opposition was Big Stiff the Medicine Man: 'Waugh! Heap big stingum insect wiping hot tootsies on um nose!' In 1938, the editor changed the Medicine Man's name to Murky, and on 23 March 1940 George's brother Reg took over the strip, giving Little Elf a Magic Tomahawk to mark the occasion: 'One Wave and he Gets His Wish!'

Little and Large Lenny
Norman Mansbridge
Jackpot 1979-82 (IPC)
Little Lenny discovered his strange power in No. 1 of *Jackpot* (5 May 1979). Inspired by the comedians of the same name (Little and Large), Lenny found he was able to grow in either direction, up or down, just by thinking hard. As a baby, he objected to his play-pen so he thunk till he shrunk! Then a bird flew him up to the roof, where he thought himself into a giant and stepped down to the ground. His mum got a fright when Lenny's big eye looked in the window. Next week, aged nine, Lenny did his small/tall tricks to get his ball back from Moany Mannering's garden.

Little 'Orror
Illustrator unknown
Cracker 1975-76 (D. C. Thomson)
"Orrors' proud boast – Is that he's a ghost!' Inspired by the legendary vampire, Count Dracula, this spectre sported a battered top hat, a flowing black cloak, and fangs. The only way you could tell he was younger than Dracula was that he wore short trousers and droopy red socks! In his early adventures 'Orror was accompanied by a little black bat but, on his rapid promotion to the full-colour back page of *Cracker*, his pet vanished. 'Orror's Christmas prezzies for his *Cracker* pals included a castor-oil-flavour lolly for Slojak.

Little Plum
Leo Baxendale
Beano 1953-86 (D. C. Thomson)
'Little Plum – Your Redskin Chum!' arrived in *Beano* No. 586 on 10 October 1953. Starting in a small way with the standard pranks on um medicine man and um Big Chief Eaglebeak, plus the occasional foray with um big brown bear, Plum's strip slowly spread from six pictures to um half page (1954) to um full page (1959). This expansion gave artist, Leo Baxendale, a huge happy hunting-ground for whole herds of heap hungry hairy bears.

Little Mo
Bob McGrath
Beezer 1964- (D. C. Thomson)
'Here's Little Mo – She's not so slow!'. This cool, calm and collected kid wearing a big red bow and dungarees to match has been clocking up quite a career in her own quiet way. It's twenty-three years since she started doing her own comic thing in *Beezer* No. 457 (17 October 1964), yet nobody seems to have noticed. Never one to be put upon, this diminutive girl with the oversized head (perhaps she needs it to hold her well-developed brain) showed her style in her first strip. A bully swiped her toffee-apple, so Mo built a staircase, brick by brick, until she was tall enough to splat him!

The Little Piccaninnies
Vincent Daniel
Bubbles 1921-41 (Amalgamated Press)
'The Little Piccaninnies and Their Tricks' was a favourite feature of the nursery comic *Bubbles*, back in those innocent days between the wars. Foreigners were funny folks, and none funnier than our coloured brothers, 'our nigs' as the caption writer called them. Their names were Sambo and Tambo, and they lived with fat old Uncle Eph in a wooden house, perhaps on some Southern plantation (their neighbour was a Mr Rastus). Eph was the butt of their pranks, but all ended happily: 'Well, I nebber did! Yo' shall hab some cake, boys!'

Little Saver
Terry Bave
Whizzer & Chips 1969-73 (IPC)
Susie Saver's mum cleaned out her daughter's wardrobe in *Whizzer & Chips* No. 1 (18 October 1969). She found 150 bottle tops, eighty-nine detergent bottles, 300 pebbles, ninety-nine halfpennies, 102 sea shells, sixty-six cotton reels. 'Why don't you collect something more interesting?', she suggested. Words she would live to regret, for Susie became a compulsive collector and, because her mum told her not to put anything else in her wardrobe, Susie put her first collection in her mum's. It was a collection of moths!

Little Snowdrop

Frank Jennens

Tiny Tots 1927-59 (Amalgamated Press)

'The Girl Who Had No Mummy' started her heartbreaking adventures in No. 1 of *Tiny Tots*. The 1930 synopsis read: "The fair-ies find a lit-tle girl who has no mum-my. They give her in-to the care of a kind wo-man, Mrs Da-vis. Snow-drop has a doll who is real-ly the Queen of the Fair-ies. Snow-drop gets ta-ken a-way by gip-sies but she es-capes with Lit-tle Jim the boy clown.' By the final issue (No. 1334), they had found happiness: the strip was retitled 'Snowdrop and Jim of Sweetshop Corner.'

Little Snow White

Treyer Evans

Bimbo 1961-72 (D. C. Thomson)

When the pictorial adventures of Little Snow White started in No. 1 of *Bimbo* (18 March 1961) the publishers were careful to label them 'From the Grimm's Fairy Tale'. That the Walt Disney feature cartoon was not being infringed became even more apparent when the fleeing Princess came face to face with the Seven Dwarfs. They were called Bossy, Nosey, Thumpy, Chuckles, Dozy, Dumpy, and Mumpy! After the original story unfolded itself, the series was too popular to drop, and new fairy-tale adventures were devised. The strip also moved to the full-colour centre spread.

Little Teddy Tring

Bertie Brown

Tip Top 1940-51 (Amalgamated Press)

'Little Teddy Tring – He Walks Through Anything!' began life as 'Tommy Tring' in *Jester* just a few weeks before that comic closed on 18 May 1940. Editor Stanley Gooch, knowing a novel idea when he saw one, quickly transferred him with a slight name change to *Tip Top*, where Teddy continued to startle the world with his strange power for another twelve years. Teddy could not only walk through walls, much to the amazement of his teacher, Dr Dogsbod, but, as his later subtitle explained, 'Pop Through Anything!'

Lizzie and Her Comical Courtiers

Reg Parlett

Jester 1928-40; *Tip Top* 1940 (Amalgamated Press)

Ye place was Merrie England, where ye throne was satupon by Queen Elizabeth, 'Liz' to her Comical Courtiers, Sir Wally Rally and Sir Francis Hake, whose rudest oaths were cries of 'Ye corks!' and 'Ye crumbs!' Lizzie was wont to give forth with the occasional 'Ods socks and suspenders!', especially when confounded by such scurvies as Sir Rasher Bacon, Sir Sid Knobblyknees, and Sir Halibut Skate, who had foul designs on ye privy purse. Deposed in 1936 when a real Queen Elizabeth was crowned, they returned in 1938 as 'Queenie and her Comical Courtiers'.

Little White Chief of the Cherokees

George Ramsbottom

Dandy 1939-41 (D. C. Thomson)

Harry Martin, mourned for dead by his mother and little sister Nancy when he had been swept away in his canoe over Death's Mouth Rapids, survived to be made Chief of the Cherokee Indians. They discovered a strange birthmark on his chest that matched the carved raven on their totem-pole. But a White Chief's life was no picnic: there was the Grim Dwarf to be dealt with, not to mention the Lord of the Big Sea Water, who had an otter's skin, webbed hands, and a fish face.

Lolly Pop
Sid Burgon
Shiver & Shake 1973-74; *Whoopee* 1974-85 (IPC)
'Where thar's luck thar's brass!' was Lolly Pop's motto. He was the richest dad in the world (and the meanest) and he made his mark in *Shiver & Shake* No. 1 (10 March 1973): 'Gasp! It's a tough life being a millionaire – counting money's hard work!' It was a tougher life for his young son, Archie, who pleaded for some money to buy a football. 'You can 'ave a penny and lump it! That's all I got when I was a kid! I'm going to bring you up the hard way, just like I was!' Complaining that a penny would barely buy a pingpong ball, Pop promptly bought him a dented one for a ha'penny.

Longlegs/Wingfoot
Paddy Brennan
Beano 1954-59; *Wizard* 1973; *Buddy* 1981 (D. C. Thomson)
'Longlegs the Desert Wild Boy' was tall, brown skinned, wore only a loin-cloth and a head-band around his jet-black hair. He lived beside a water-hole in the Hungry Desert, a grim, sun-drenched spot in Arizona where he spoke as a friend with the desert creatures who came to drink there. As Sheriff Bill Barclay put it, 'That Longlegs is a terror – a nameless terror. Ain't never seen the likes o' him before!' Longlegs raced into *Beano* No. 642 on 6 November 1954, and reappeared in 1980 as Wingfoot in *Buddy*.

Lonely Nan
H. C. Milburn
Bubbles 1921-41 (Amalgamated Press)
'The Cinderella of the School', as she was subtitled throughout her twenty-year term, was described by the synopsis thus: 'Nan is a poor girl who has no parents. She is at the Grange School where Miss Grim is the school-mistress. Miss Grim does not like her because she has no money. Ronnie Grant is her chum. Another chum is Sue. All the boys and girls like Nan because she is so jolly and unselfish.' Nan was a bit selfish when it came to troubles, though. She was always the one who found lost babies in the snow, got run over by a motorbike while saving a puppy, or had to scrub out the schoolroom while the class went to the pictures.

The Lone Ranger
Fran Striker
Mickey Mouse Weekly 1939-46 (Odhams); *Comet* 1957-58 (Amalgamated Press); *Express* 1959-60 (Beaverbrook); *TV Comic* 1961 (TV); *TV Tornado* 1967-68 (City)
The Lone Ranger's cry of 'Hi-yo Silver! Away!' was first heard on an American radio serial. It was adapted as a King Features' newspaper strip from 10 September 1938, drawn by Ed Kressy, and reprinted in the British *Mickey Mouse Weekly* from 8 April 1939. 'The Lone Ranger' television series prompted *Comet* to reprint more American strips from 1957. Then the first original Lone Ranger strip by a British artist, Mike Noble (illustrated), was introduced into *Express* as a full-colour page in 1959.

Lop-Ears
James Clark
Magic 1940 (D. C. Thomson)
Lop-Ears was the big-footed bunny in the red-and-black checked trousers who starred in a long-running series of stories in *Fairyland Tales*, D. C. Thomson's pocket-sized weekly for tinies. When the war put an end to his regular magazine, Lop-Ears transferred to *Magic* as a full-page comic strip in red and blue entitled 'Leave It to Lop-Ears'. Unfortunately for the big bun, the banes of his life, little Bobbity and Lollop were transferred, too, not to mention Flopsy and hungry Muncher: quite a large family, the Rabbits.

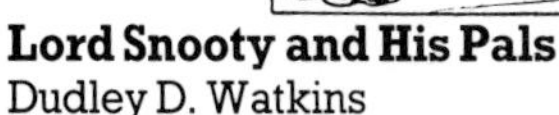

Lord Snooty and His Pals
Dudley D. Watkins
Beano 1938- (D. C. Thomson)
The young Lord Marmaduke Bunkerton, 'Snooty to you', and his Pals first appeared in No. 1 of *Beano* on 30 July 1938. They are still running, but no longer drawn by their late creator, Dudley Dexter Watkins. The constitution of the Pals has changed, too. The originals, known as the Ash Can Alley Gang, were Hairpin Huggins, Scrapper Smith, Happy Hutton, Skinny Lizzie, Rosie, and Gertie the Goat, soon to be joined by the twins in rompers, Snitchy and Snatchy. Current Pals include Swanky Lanky Liz, who had starred in her own strip back in 1948.

Lucky Logan
Illustrator unknown
Knockout 1953-54 (Amalgamated Press)
'Look Out for Lucky Logan!' cried *Knockout* No. 766 on 15 August 1953. 'The first of a smashing new 4-page picture adventure series begins next week!' Hero of the first postwar strip to run to such a length was Lucky Logan, 'hard-riding, fast-shooting Range Rider', supported by his sidekick, Hashpan, 'his fat, jovial and surprising pard'. Perhaps to protect his investment in a period western strip, the editor added an up-to-date comment: 'You're going to get a supersonic kick out of their amazing adventures each week!' Billed as 'The Laughing Cowboy', Lucky's lingo was slightly off: 'This is where I make a nitch (*sic*) on my gun butt!'

Loser
Tony Goffe
Whizzer & Chips 1971-78 (IPC)
Loser was a doomed soul with a permanent shrug, fatalistically accepting all the sorrows that were heaped upon him. He made his debut on 2 January 1971 and promptly lost his roller-skates. Dad found them, luckily for Loser, unluckily for Dad: 'Slip! . . . . . Neee-aarr!' The skates shot down the stairs, out of the house, narrowly missing Grandma, but bearing the milkman's horse down the hill and into the river: 'Sploosh! Glurb!' The horse caught cold and the milkman made Loser pull his cart in the horse's reins. Loser promptly got lost, of course!

Lucky Luke/Buck Bingo
Morris & Goscinny
Film Fun 1960; *Giggle* 1967 (Fleetway)
This Belgian hero of the Old West first rode into action in the weekly *Spirou* (12 June 1947), drawn by Morris (Maurice de Bevere) and scripted by René Goscinny. Luke's theme song (sung in English!) is 'I'm a poor lonesome cowboy', and he tops and tails his serialized adventures by riding in/out singing it astride his faithful horse, Jolly Jumper. His popularity elsewhere has not been echoed in Britain and, after a run in *Film Fun*, he tried again in *Giggle* under the new name of Buck Bingo.

Luck of the Legion
Martin Aitchison
Eagle 1952-61 (Hulton)
Sergeant 'Tough' Luck of the French Foreign Legion began his highly coloured adventures in *Eagle* on 9 May 1952. Written by Geoffrey Bond, the serials all had separate titles. 'Death by the Dawn' had Luck and his comrades, Corporal Trenet and Legionnaire Bimberg, unmasking the mysterious El Fagr who was causing riots among the natives. 'Brotherhood of the Bat' was a secret Arab society out to paralyze North Africa by raiding the caravans. 'The Shadow of the Scimitar' featured the mad Commander of Fort Lebel.

Lucky's Living Doll
Robert MacGillivray
School Friend 1963; *June* 1964-74 (Fleetway)
Everybody called Lucinda Ursula Cynthia Kate Yolande Smith 'Lucky', simply because those were her initials. But even Lucky's mother didn't know how lucky she really was, for her doll, Tina, had come to life one day when Lucky had made a wish. But if anybody ever guessed that Tina was alive, the spell would be broken and Tina would become an ordinary doll again. One sad day Tina hid from Mrs Smith in a box, not knowing it was about to be sent to a repair shop 168 miles away. There was plenty of heartbreak before girl and doll were united again.

McCoy

Jack B. Yeats

Big Budget 1898 (Pearson)

'Signor McCoy the Wonderful Circus Hoss' had a short but significant career: he was the first funny animal hero in British comics and the undoubted ancestor of such later haybags as 'George the Jolly Gee-Gee' (1938). McCoy literally bucked off the pages of *Big Budget*, causing such celebrated chaos as the revenge he took upon the schollards of Spankbourne when they fed him a peppered bun. Small wonder his owner, the Circus Man, referred to McCoy as 'that sagacious quadrupedlar!'

The Magic Bus

Tom Kerr

Little Star 1972-74 (D. C. Thomson)

Every summer Jim Grant's Funfair came to the home town of Bill and Bunty Martin. It was on 29 January 1972, in No. 1 of *Little Star*, that the children heard the sad news. Their favourite ride, the red bus on the roundabout, was too old to be used again. They went home heartbroken, but then a carrier arrived with a big crate. In it was the old red bus, a present from Mr Grant. After painting it bright red again, the children took their first ride in the bus. To their great surprise there was a 'Click! Whirr!' and the bus soared up into the sky! In *Little Star* No. 2 it landed – in America! It was the first of many worldwide adventures.

The McTickles

Douglas Jensen

Beano 1971-74 (D. C. Thomson)

'The Ha-ha-happy Highlanders who live in Lonely Glen Tickle' arrived en masse in *Beano* No. 1522 (18 September 1971). Chieftain of the clan was Big Jock McTickle, a bearded giant who wore a badge marked 'Sir'. Then there was Tubby Tam McTickle, the local haggis-guzzling champion, Cooky McTickle the clan chef, Murdo McTickle, ninety-five years old and still going strong, and at the end of the line, the Wee McTickles. The McTickles spent their time in pursuit of the wild McHaggises, wee timorous beasties also sought by the hairy McNasties, poachers to a man.

The Magic Lollipops

Allan Morley

Beano 1941-47 (D. C. Thomson)

An old catchphrase came in handy as the caption to this amusing series: 'Suck 'Em and See!' It was about a boy who wandered the world clutching a jam-jar full of red, white, and blue lollipops. One lick and they worked their magic, a transformation often as unexpected to the reader as to the victim. A burglar's look-out licks a lolly, turns into a policeman, and arrests his partner. Once in the cop-shop the magic wears off, much to the baffled rage of both parties. The little lad was never named.

Major Eazy
Carlos Ezquerra
Battle 1976-78 (IPC)
'July, 1941. High summer in the Libyan Desert as troops of Rommel's Afrika Korps shelter from the heat of the day, just beyond the heavily guarded perimeter of the besieged port of Tobruk!' Suddenly a powerful car roared out of the desert. It was Major Eazy, coolest and deadliest member of the Eighth Army's Long Range Desert Group, and his murderous Bedouin guide.' 'Show 'em your teeth, Tewfik!' 'A pleasure, El Eazy!' And the Bedouin lobbed a few grenades at close range. 'Der crazy Englander swept through like a demon from Hell!' – Eazy was on a personal mission – capturing beer!

Manix
Carmona
Eagle 1983-84 (IPC)
'He is the Ultimate Secret Weapon!' – a robot secret agent known as Manix. His uncovering of a deadly terrorist organization known as S.M.O.G. (the Society for the Militant Overthrow of all Governments) was originally told in photographs, but the fair-haired fellow who played the role looked anything but robotic. Keith Law's script became immediately more exciting when Carmona started to draw the strip from 24 September 1983, the day the new *Eagle* went from class litho to cheap newsprint.

The Mantracker
Salinas
The Crunch 1979-80; *Hotspur* 1980 (D. C. Thomson)
'Bounty hunter! Hated by law-breakers and despised by society! A man who tracks down other men for the price of their heads! This is the story of Bearpaw Jay, the Indian warrior who became a bounty hunter!' This was the original introduction to a bullet-ridden, blood-spattered serial starring the highly decorated ex-Green Beret and Blackfoot brave who went on the warpath in No. 1 of *The Crunch* (20 January 1979), and was still on it when that comic merged with *Hotspur* fifty-four weeks later.

Major Jump
Ian Knox
Monster Fun 1975-76 (IPC)
'Major Jump, Horror Hunter' opened for business in No. 1 of *Monster Fun* (14 June 1975) by advertising for a willing lad. Cosmo Crump applied for the job provided he could bring his pet, Meredith. The Major liked animal lovers, so Cosmo got the job helping him stock his stately home as a Monster Menagerie. The Major meant 'monster' as 'big', but changed his mind when pet Meredith turned out to be a midget monstrosity: 'Great wobbling walking-sticks!' Off they flew to Loch McSporran armed with a giant gorgonzola to catch a monster mouse around the house. But, being Scotland, it turned out to be a monster moose around the hoose!

Mark Fury
Paparella
Junior Express 1955-56 (Beaverbrook)
Brought up by gypsies, heir to a fortune, Mark Fury, handy with his fists, fought his way to fame and fortune with the help of Tom Finnegan, a battered old prize-fighter. Convinced that the languid Lord Trentwater is a highwayman, and on the dodge from the Bow Street Runners, Mark dons a mask to meet milord's champion, the burly Black Ned. Then Mark moves on to Olde London to become a sparring partner at Jackson's Boxing Academy, bursting into a full-colour page from 18 February 1956.

Mark Sabor
Alcatena
The Crunch 1979-80 (D. C. Thomson)
'Arena' was the title of the science-fiction serial starring Mark Sabor, a saga that was completed in fifty-four weeks, in time for the final issue of *The Crunch*! Sabor, a twenty-first century pamphleteer, is sentenced for infringing Article 29 of the Public Order Code and criticizing the government. With all rights of citizenship revoked, he is condemned to the twilight world of the Arena. Here, under Alexis Powers, he is trained to kill as a Styx Company gladiator, but finally destroys the Great Brain, the computer that rules the world.

Martha's Monster Make-Up
Ken Reid
Monster Fun 1975-76 (IPC)
Martha's Dad was the caretaker of Mallet Horror Films studio, and on 14 June 1975 (in No. 1 of *Monster Fun*) he found an old jar of make-up while sweeping out the dressing room. He gave it to young Martha, his pig-tailed moppet but, instead of it making her look pretty, it did just the opposite. 'Yikes! It's made my hands go all scaly and horrible!', cried Martha, running off to show her Mum. 'Shriek!' shrieked Mum, who was off to a party but, as the sight made her hair curl, she was quite delighted. So was Martha, who found the make-up changed her into a different monster every week.

Marmaduke and his Ma
Freddie Crompton
Funny Wonder 1922-49 (Amalgamated Press)
'Marmy and his Ma' (as they were later called) were the original one-parent family in comics: in all their twenty-eight-year run, there was never a sign of Marmaduke's Pa! Ma, a scrawny harridan in bun and button boots, lost only her pince-nez as a concession to changing fashion, while poor Little Marmy had to wear his sailor hat and Eton collar the whole of his naughty life. Many of their 'Merry Moments' concerned jovial uncles, school inspectors, and 'that cat Mrs Stingy', the nextdoor neighbour.

Martin's Marvellous Mini
Illustrator unknown
Tiger 1971-84 (IPC)
Martin Baker bought his first car, a mini, and christened it George. With the help of his mechanic pal, Tiny Hill, Martin determined to become a racing driver. The pals set up as 'Odd Job Drivers; Any Driving Job Done, Good Speedy Service, Guaranteed Cheap' to raise money to pay for modifications to George. Hired to take a lucky mascot to the Italian racer, Enrico Mapiletti, they deliver it during the race at Brookton! 'Never before have I seen the teeny-weeny mini driven so fast-a!' cried Mapiletti, entering George for a mini race. They were on their way.

Marsalla of the Mists
John Woods
Debbie 1973-75 (D. C. Thomson)
'The Wild Girl of the Welsh Hills' lived alone in the misty mountains with her faithful dog, Rex. Marsalla first walked out of the mists in *Debbie* No. 33 (29 September 1973) to help a rescue party save a crashed pilot but, before a reporter could take her photograph, she was back to the mists again. Swimming with her friends the otters, Marsalla was startled by a nearby explosion. Mining engineers were surveying the river bed for minerals. Marsalla warned: 'The mountains will resist you! Thunder and lightning! It is a warning! Do not defy the mountains!' Nonsense? The miners were caught in a flood. Never defy the Welsh mountains.

Marvelman
Mick Anglo
Marvelman 1954-63 (Miller); *Warrior* 1982-85 (Quality)
Created more out of necessity than invention, Marvelman was the British continuation of Captain Marvel, when that superhero was suddenly cut off in his powerful prime by a suit for plagiarism. Micky Moran, crewcut copyboy on the *Daily Bugle*, is rewarded with super powers when he saves Guntag Barghelt, recluse astroscientist, from crooks. By shouting the Keyword to the Universe, 'Kimota!' (atomic spelled backwards), Micky is transformed into Marvelman, the Mightiest Man in the Universe: Woof! Many pens drew Marvelman, the best being Don Lawrence (illustrated). He was revived by Garry Leach in *Warrior* (1982).

Mary Brown
Illustrator unknown
Diana 1967-73; *Debbie* 1980-81 (D. C. Thomson)
'Mary Brown's Schooldays' started on 11 March 1967 in No 212 of *Diana*. 'The first day at a new school can be an ordeal for anyone, but 11 year old Mary Brown was to find life particularly hard when she went as a Scholarship Girl to the exclusive boarding school of St. Winifred's.' As the Head, Miss Drake, said, 'A scholarship to St. Winifred's is awarded only once in five years. It is a rare distinction.' Mary chummed up with Liz in Tennyson Dorm, but soon fell foul of the Hooded Ones for breaking one of the Twelve Taboos – walking on the front lawn.

Masterman
Joe Colquhoun
Masterman 1952-53 (Streamline)
Mr Fletcher, the oil magnate, introduced his son, the bespectacled Bobby, to Professor Whitehead. 'He's a bit on the thin side, isn't he?' said the Prof. If only the venerable scientist could have read Bobby's thought balloon: 'Little does he know that I can transform myself into the mighty Masterman by rubbing my Ring of Fate and saying, "O Ring of Fate, I call upon you to help me fight for freedom and justice!"' Fortunately for the western world, Bobby found time to utter his long-winded oath and change into Masterman, thus foiling the Dictator of Demonacia's plot to melt the icecap.

Marzipan the Magician
Ernest Webb
Rainbow 1914-56 (Amalgamated Press)
Although a late arrival in *Rainbow* – he made his debut in No. 9 on 11 April 1914 – Marzipan (Marzi for short) lasted right through to the final issue, No. 1898. His popularity was entirely due to his magic wand, a black-and-red striped walking-stick which could enlarge everyday items with a single tap. His first trick was to cross a river by sitting in an enlarged matchbox and getting a tow from a small boy's enlarged clockwork dreadnought. 'Dat not such a bad business, eh?' cried Marzi.

Master Mind
J. Edward Oliver
Buster 1981-83 (IPC)
Inspired by the BBC television quiz series *Mastermind*, this superhero was, in real life, a long-headed lad called Alf Witt. When danger threatened, all Alf needed to do was to nip into the nearest telephone box, shout the magic word – 'Pass!' – and 'boom!', magic lightning transformed him into the world's brainiest superhero, Master Mind. Among his many enemies were Natasha the Basher, and her equally sinister sister, Natasha the Dasher. Bones the Wonder Dog helped him, but Master Mind's main assistants were *Buster* readers, who were asked to solve the puzzles that beset him.

Matt
Louis Gunnis
Bubbles 1921-41 (Amalgamated Press)
'The Boy with the Merry Heart' began twenty-one years of serialized adventures at the bottom of the back page of *Bubbles*, in twelve stock-cube-sized boxes a week. Promoted to bigger pictures in 1927, Matt soon became 'The Merry Circus Boy', joining a travelling show run by Queenie's daddy. Here he had fun with Sniggers the Clown, Professor Quicko the conjurer, and Crusoe the monkey until, in 1936, he was sent to Africa with Fuzzy to trap zebras for the circus. Matt finally made it to a full page.

Maxwell Hawke
Eric Bradbury
Buster 1960-66 (Fleetway)
'The House of a Thousand Secrets' was the exciting title of the first case for Maxwell Hawke, Britain's Greatest Ghost-Hunter: *Buster* (20 October 1960). Hawke, holidaying up a sheer rock face in the Lake District, was called in to find Carol Masters, who had vanished the day afer Hawke's old friend, Sir Charles De'ath, died – yet her face has been seen crying for help at the windows of empty Grimstone Grange! Hawke and his assistant, Jill Adair, set off for mist-cloaked Yorkshire and the first of many mist-cloaked mysteries.

The Merry Boys of Dingle School
Bertie Brown
Comic Life 1923-26 (Amalgamated Press)
Dr Dingle, 'the dear, delightful old gentleman', was head of Dingle School, a front-page establishment that needed all its full colour to cope with the Merry Boys. There was Billy Britain, Wee McToots the Scots Boy, Ching Wung Too the Chinese chappie, Dutchy the fat boy ('Vot-ho!'), and Ebenezer Ebony,' the lively little lump of blackness from Africa'. 'Where am Timbucthree, Billyum?', he asked the Britisher. 'Second on the left past the Spanish onion factory', answered our lad. Alphonse, the top-hatted tadpole from France, arrived in 1925.

Max Bravo
Eric Parker
Sun 1954-57; *Swift* 1962 (Fleetway)
Max Bravo the Happy Hussar, headlined as 'The Rousing Adventures of a Gay Young Cavalryman', spread his historic exploits across the full-colour centre spread of *Sun*. Max was a trooper in the Ninth Hussars of the French Army. He travelled to Egypt with General Bonaparte, who afterwards became the Emperor Napoleon. But, for the present, his campaign was being starved out by jealous Paul Barras. Max, made to stand night guard by Sergeant-Major Slashtrap, wakes up in time to save Napoleon from the assassin's sword: 'Ho-hah! Up the Ninth Hussars!'

Meddlesome Matty
Sam Fair
Dandy 1938-42; 1948-49; *Sparky* 1968-69 (D. C. Thomson)
Second of D. C. Thomson's schoolgirl obsessionals, Meddlesome Matty never quite reached the star status of her forerunner, Keyhole Kate. Devised as a Nosey Parker in gymslip and plaits, Matty's curiosity would have killed a cat. Even when she tried to do good, her interference ended in pain. She swept away some broken milkbottles from a road, thus unwittingly spoiling a police trap for a car thief. The regular payoff was 'Maybe that'll teach you not to meddle!' It never did.

Merry and Bright/Muffin and Crumpet
Roy Wilson
Merry & Bright 1932-35; *Sparkler* 1936 (Amalgamated Press)
'Our Jolly Wandering Clowns' came jogging along the country lane and on to the front page of *Merry & Bright* on 20 February 1932. The surprise was that it had taken 766 issues of the comic before anyone thought of using its title as names for its heroes. 'I hope you're feeling merry, Bright?' smiled Merry, and Bright replied, 'I am, and you look bright, Merry!' Their cluttered caravan was drawn by Neddy the moke, assisted by Bunty the pup, both wearing clown's hats, of course. In 1936 they were reprinted in colour in *Sparkler*, rechristened 'Muffin and Crumpet'.

Merry Margie
Frank Minnitt
Knockout 1939-40 (Amalgamated Press)
'Meet Our Merry Margie the Invisible Mender' was the full title of this strip which started in *Knockout* No. 1, 4 March 1939. Margie, one of the few full-page females in prewar comics, was a smartly uniformed lass who worked for the Ritz Invisible Mending Co. Accidentally splashed with Mr Smart's patent invisible mending fluid, she faded away and was thus able to thwart Mr Grabber's plans to evict Mrs Miggs and her young Miggses. 'Yah boo!', they cried, while Margie said 'Ha-ha!'

Merry Marvo
Allan Morley
Dandy 1942-46 (D. C. Thomson)
Merry Marvo and his Magic Cigar puffed up five years of fun in the days when smoking was no sin. In the 'Eighties, Marvo's smoke-clouds, magic or not, would never pass an editor's blue pencil, but, in the 'Forties, tobacco was good for more laughs than coughs. Marvo, a top-hatted, tail-suited magician, had but to blow a smoke ring at a suitcase to turn it into a wireless set, while a tramp who stole the cigar found himself firing bullets from it and smashing a tough nut's window.

Merry Merlin
Joe Hardman
Bubbles 1921-28 (Amalgamated Press)
'Merry Merlin the Wonderful Wizard' waved his wand in No. 1 of *Bubbles*, a coloured nursery comic, on 16 April 1921, and continued to make magic for eight years. Some of his tricks were vengeful, such as turning a surly sweep's bundle of brushes into a wild African warrior, but most of his metamorphoses were kindly. Merry Merlin turned a clothes-horse and washing into a Punch and Judy show to cheer up a lonely little lad, and made another child happy by changing his cushions into a pair of dancing imps.

The Merry Mischiefs
Freddie Crompton
Sunbeam 1926-40 (Amalgamated Press)
'The Merry Mischiefs' were a group of nursery-rhyme characters who attended Mother Hubbard's school. There was Little Jack Horner (he of the corner), Simple Simon (he of the pieman), Humpty Dumpty (he of the wall), Little Boy Blue (he of the horn), Johnny Stout (he who pulled it out), Little Red Riding Hood (she of the wolf), and Dog Toby, who wore a red ruff instead of a collar. What with Lord Mayor's Shows, Easter Eggs, Whitsun Fairs, and Fireworks Day, life on page one of *Sunbeam* was full of fun.

Mickey the Monkey
Dudley Watkins
Topper 1953-86 (D. C. Thomson)
This cheerful little chimpanzee was chosen as the full-colour front-page star of the first issue of *Topper* (7 February 1953), D. C. Thomson's first venture into large-size tabloid comics. After a few swift changes – Mickey learned to speak in No. 2; his yellow shorts turned permanently red from No. 3 – he settled down to a long run of 1074 weeks before relegation to an inside page in black and red. Mickey's pal, a pet parrot called Polly, shared most of his adventures from *Topper* No. 2.

Mickey's Magic Book
James Crichton
Dandy 1941-48 (D. C. Thomson)
Mickey was a very ordinary boy in a striped pullover, but the old book he always carried under his left arm was anything but ordinary. It was a magic book and, whatever page Mickey opened it to, the fairy-tale character depicted thereon came to life, stepping out of the pages to save the day. When a nasty copper stopped Mickey playing football in the street, Mickey produced Ali Baba and all his Forty Thieves. So much robbery on his beat caused the cop to get the sack.

Micky Midge
Louis Diamond
Merry Midget 1931-32 (Provincial)
When *The Midget*, a half-size comic, failed, the publishers expanded the format to full tabloid and, in an attempt for continuity, called it *Merry Midget*. To justify the title, a new front-page hero was created – a merry midget! 'Hello everybody, here's a new pal for you!' wrote editor Jack Long in No. 1 (12 September 1931), 'Micky Midge, the lad with the big feet and dome, he's a oner and no mistake!' A large panel in Casey Court style topped the back page, with Micky and all the other characters from the comic having fun. The title read, incorrectly, 'Micky Midget's Family'.

Mickey Mouse
Walt Disney
Modern Boy 1933 (Amalgamated Press); *Mickey Mouse Weekly* 1936-57 (Odhams); *Mickey Mouse* 1958-59; *Walt Disney's Weekly* 1959-61 (Holding); *Donald & Mickey* 1972-75; *Mickey & Donald* 1975; *Mickey Mouse* 1975-80; *Mickey Magazine* 1980-81 (IPC); *Disney Magazine* 1982- (London)
Mickey Mouse made his talkie cartoon film debut on 19 September 1928 in *Steamboat Willie*. A newspaper strip followed on 13 January 1930, drawn by Floyd Gottfredson, and this was first reprinted in Britain as a weekly page in *Modern Boy* from No. 302 (18 November 1933) and in the newspaper supplement, *Boys & Girls Own Evening World*. Mickey's own comic, *Mickey Mouse Weekly*, started 8 February 1936 and ran 920 issues. It was the first in full-colour photogravure.

Micky Mimic
Alf Saporito
Krazy 1976-78; *Whizzer & Chips* 1978 (IPC)
'He can impersonate anybody!' was not just boastful bill-matter for this skilful young impressionist. Inspired by a visit to the *Mike Yarwood Show* in *Krazy* No. 1 (16 October 1976), Micky tried his talent on a mean old park-keeper. Using his suitcaseful of disguises, Micky impersonated Columbo in his raincoat, Kojak with a fistful of lollipops, and even Billy Bunter, in a centre spread of full-colour fun. Next week, the star parade included footballer Jimmy Hill, rugby commentator Eddie Waring, and a glittering Liberace.

Micky Mouse
Harry Rountree
Playtime 1919-28 (Amalgamated Press)
'Coral Island; or, Jill and her Jungle Friends' was the original title for this centre spread of full-colour pictures in the new nursery comic *Playtime* (20 March 1919). 'Oh, please, I've been wrecked and I don't like the sea!', cried little Jill as she was washed ashore on Coral Island. 'By my feathers, it's a girl!', exclaimed Oswald Ostrich and, in no time, Jill numbered his animal pals among her chums: Harold Hare, Hubert Hippo, Billy Bear, Roy Rhino, Kate Kangaroo, and Max Mouse who would shortly take over the strip as 'Micky Mouse and his Jungle Friends'.

Mighty Moth
Dick Millington
TV Comic 1959-84 (Polystyle)
The unending warfare between Dad, the head of the family, and his indestructible enemy, Mighty Moth, provided a pageful of knockabout slapstick in *TV Comic* for a record twenty-six years (although the latter end of the run consisted of reprints). The character was even popular enough for the publisher to issue a couple of *Mighty Moth Specials* in 1980-81. Whatever weapon Dad used on Mighty Moth failed miserably, including a splat on the conk with his elasticated bow tie. But there was the odd truce, notably the Christmas when Dad served M.M. with slices of roast tweed!

Midge and Moocher
Arthur Martin
Joker 1934-40 (Amalgamated Press)
Midge wore a bowler hat, a bib marked 'Baby', and, just to make sure, an outsized safetypin in his pants. Moocher was easily spotted: he was the doleful dalmatian. Together, with Midge often riding on Moocher's back, they brought their unique relationship to the centre spread of *Joker* for seven years, during which time Midge grew just big enough to abandon his dummy for limited speech: 'Giddyap Moocher!' and so forth. Oddly, Moocher started to talk, too, and in 1935 abandoned doggie wuffles for 'I'll soon make that cat scat!' and similar statements.

Mighty Mouse
Schiaffino
Roy of the Rovers 1979- (IPC)
Kevin Mouse, nicknamed Mighty, was a medical student and overweight winger for Alftown Hotcakes, a non-league football club. He made such an impression in a Fifth-Division match with Chelbury Athletic that he was bought for half-a-million pounds by London's superteam, Tottenford Rovers. Meanwhile, as a medical student at Saint Victor's, he is forced to play in the hospital team. More amusing perhaps was Mouse's tour with the Rovers' Reserves, playing against convict teams in prisons!

The Mighty Misfits
Jack Pamby
Buster 1965-67 (Fleetway)
Major Ripper of Ripper's Raiders was cursed with an odd couple, a pair of privates called Albert 'Bomber' Briggs and Socrates Smith. Known collectively as the Mighty Misfits, these two represented the brains and the brawn of World War 2 soldiery. Although the best of buddies, Bomber's names for Socrates were not always polite: 'Bird brain' and 'You barmy little newt!' He saved his naughtiest names for the enemy, however: 'Crop-heads', 'Snivelling whelps', and 'You sausage-eating square-heads!'

Mike/Smiler
Eric Roberts
Knockout 1945-57; *Sun* 1957-59; *Big One* 1964-65 (Fleetway)
Mike Dobson, in his red roll-kneck sweater and check trousers, was the first 'ordinary boy' hero in *Knockout*, a comic hitherto packed with eccentrics. he started as a half-page filler but soon expanded to the full-colour front, thus enabling his poor old Dad to get an even bigger share of the slapstick. Mike's best pal was the yellow-haired Curly-boy, but from 1952 his strip was shared with a blonde girlfriend called Dimps. This didn't seem to embarrass Mike and probably did wonders for *Knockout*'s neglected girl readers. Later reprinted as *Smiler*.

Mike, Spike and Greta

Walter Bell

Pilot 1937-38; *Knockout* 1939-40 (Amalgamated Press)

'Our Krazy Gang', Mike, Spike, and Greta, were three wild westerners who began with a bang on the full-colour front of *Pilot* No. 76 (13 March 1937). Mike was the sawn-off shrimp, Spike the lanky Yankee, and Greta their hopeless hoss who never said anything but 'O-my, o-my!' Moving to the back page of *Knockout* No. 1, 4 March 1939, as 'The Goofs of Ragbag Ranch', their artist changed to John Jukes (illustrated), whose style drew them further away from their American inspiration, Castor Oyl and Ham Gravy in Segar's *Thimble Theatre*.

Milly O'Naire and Penny Less

Sid Burgon

Jackpot 1979-82 (IPC)

Miss Milly O'Naire lived at Moneybags Mansion in Rich Road, a palace with dozens of rooms, central heating, and an indoor swimming pool. Down-town Penny Less lived in a propped-up shack with two rooms (if you count the coal shed), central heating (a candle in the middle of the floor), and indoor pools (thanks to the holes in the roof). The clash between the two ends of the social scale – 'Hello, ragbag!' – 'Hello, toffee-nose!' – provided a double-page spread of fun from No. 1 of *Jackpot* (5 May 1979) but, when that comic joined *Buster*, the girls joined Ivor Lott and Tony Broke.

Milkiway

Illustrator unknown

Buster 1960-61 (Fleetway)

'Milkiway: the Man from Mars' flew to Earth in No. 1 of *Buster* (28 May 1960), in his one-Martian flying-saucer: 'Fftoomm!' His encounters with Earthlings caused considerable confusion – and comedy. Mistaking an 'I Speak Your Weight' machine for an Earthling, he gave it greetings from Mars. 'Eight stone four pounds!', replied the machine, a remark a policeman didn't think funny when Milkiway repeated the phrase on being booked for illegal parking of his saucer! Each Earthling encounter ended with Milkiway resolving to 'try again next week!'

Minnie the Minx

Leo Baxendale

Beano 1953- (D. C. Thomson)

'She's horrid! She's awful! She's dreadful! She's Great Fun!' She was the feminist answer to 'Dennis the Menace; and she started her tomboy career in *Beano* No. 596 (19 December 1953). At first, she had only six small pictures in black and white, compared with Dennis's sixteen in two colours but, by the following week, her matching pullover was in black-and-red stripes, too, she was up to half a page by 1954, and a full page by 1957. Tam o'shanter and pigtails apart, Minnie is no mere menace in skirts, but, being a girl, she is less likely to end up with a walloping from dad.

Minnie's Mixer
Rafart
Whizzer & Chips 1969-73 (IPC)
'No-one mixes it with Minnie and comes off best!' That was because little Minnie found a food-mixer in the rubble of a demolished house on the back page of *Whizzer & Chips* No. 1 (18 October 1969). The house belonged to an inventor, and evidently he had magicked up the mixer because, when Minnie tried it, it immediately mixed a dog with a Belisha beacon! Quickly unmixing them – 'Can't have a pup wagging a beacon all over the place!' – Minnie went on to mix a painter with his ladder. 'Heh! Heh!', laughed Minnie, 'I'm going to make this a crazy mixed-up world!'

Moko the Monk
Robert MacGillivray
Sun 1950-52 (Amalgamated Press)
Originally billed as 'Moko the Baby Monkey', this lovable little chimpanzee made his debut in *Sun* No. 59 (4 February 1950) in a short strip entitled 'Moko and the Boomerang'. He found one, threw it, it whizzed back, broke a window, and Moko hid in a dustbin! It was a 'silent' strip, and this tradition was continued when, with a change of format, he was promoted to the new full-colour front page from No. 163 (29 March 1952). Hugh McNeill (illustrated) now drew 'Moko the Mischievous Monk', but changed the title to 'Moko and Boko' from 17 May, after introducing a parrot pal.

Molly Mills
Illustrator unknown
Tammy 1971-81 (IPC)
'The year was 1926. A train stopped at a small country station in Devon, and out stepped Molly Mills, late of the East End of London.' And straight into *Tammy* No. 1 (6 February 1971) and a sad period serial entitled 'No Tears For Molly'. 'Coo, the air here ain't half fresh after smoky old London!' mused Molly as she wondered about her future as maid to Lord and Lady Stanton, 'I can still hardly believe my luck: £25 a year! I'll be able to send all of six bob home to Mum every week!' She gets off on the wrong foot with Pickering the butler, and Kitty the upstairs maid, but soon makes friends with crippled Clare, daughter of the house.

Moira Kent
Ron Smith
Bunty 1958-64 (D. C. Thomson)
'The Dancing Life of Moira Kent' began in *Bunty* No. 1 (18 January 1958) with the following foreword: 'Moira Kent lived in London with her grandfather, Matthew Martin. They were looked after by her Aunt Jane, who had brought Moira up since she was a baby. It was a happy household except for one thing – Moira loved dancing and her grandfather hated it!' Trouble was, it reminded Matthew of Margaret, Moira's mother. Up in the attic were Margaret's ballet shoes, the tutu she wore when she danced her first solo, and a photo taken six months before she died in poverty. But at Holsworth School, Miss Jordan was giving Moira dancing lessons for the concert: the first steps of a career.

Molly and Mick
Roy Wilson
Butterfly 1931-34 (Amalgamated Press)
'The Terrors of Little Tittering' were a boy-and-girl double act, brother Mick and sister Molly, who went everywhere and then some in their tiny two-seater, the Mighty Midget (number plate: WE 2). They lived at The Wurzels where their watch-hound, Bingo, shared his kennel with their car. Soon there hove a band of masked desperadoes in black masks and school caps: 'twas Wallie Waffles and the Sekrit Six, sworn to carnap the Midge or else. Molly and Mick saw they got the 'or else'. Deposed from page one on 15 October 1932, they moved merrily inside for two more years.

Monster
Redondo
Scream 1984; *Eagle* 1984-85 (IPC)
What was the terrifying secret of the locked room? Twelve-year old Kenneth Corman soon found out. First, he buried his murdered father in the garden, then he unlocked the door. Inside was the most hideous horror ever unleashed in a British comic, a shambling, drooling, deformed creature that made Quasimodo look like Tyrone Power: Kenneth's Uncle Terry! The plucky youngster determined to take the malformed monster to Scotland where a doctor dwelled who could cure him: 'Goodee! Terr like bee bedderr!', but left a trail of terror in their wake: 'Terr kiilll!' 'Uuurgk!'

Monty Carstairs

Cecil Orr

Mickey Mouse Weekly 1951-56 (Odhams)

'Red for Danger' was the title of the first case for the Hon. Monty Carstairs, Special Agent, which began in No. 562 of *Mickey Mouse Weekly* (17 February 1951). The monocled, moustachiod manhunter leaped from the Scots Express and into the Scarlet Runner, the high-powered sports car which his Oriental servant, Mr San, had waiting for him. Thus, he eluded his pursuers, while Pip the pup hid under the seat ready to carry a vital message to Monty's young assistants, Johnny, Taffy, and Andy Mac, boys of the Springfield Club.

Moonlight Moggie

Bertie Brown

Jester 1909-25 (Amalgamated Press)

'The Musical Mouser' was a (sometimes) lucky black cat who wandered the pages of *Jester* looking for lunch some years before her Yankee cousin Felix. Moonlight Moggie was a female feline counterpart to Homeless Hector the hungry dog who hounded *Jester*'s pink partner, *Chips*. Indeed, in the 'Fifties, she turned up out of the blue to share Hector's declining years – still drawn by the same Bertie Brown. Most of her mooching took place by night and she took special pleasure in serenading slumberers from fence or rooftop.

Monty Monk

Albert Pease

Chips 1930-40 (Amalgamated Press)

'The Comic Jungle Capers of Monty Monk' was quite a breakthrough for the funny animal fraternity. Obviously influenced by the animated antics of American cartoon characters, Monty, in his little bowler hat and spotted trousers, arrived in a twelve-picture series in *Chips* on 29 March 1930. Hitherto, balloon-talking animals had been confined to nursery comics like *Rainbow*. Monty's girlfriend was Minnie Monk and his rival, rather oddly, was Hippo! Other animal pals included Ted Tiger, Gerry Giraffe, and Jumbo.

The Moonsters

Bill Ritchie

Sparky 1965-68 (D. C. Thomson)

Peter and Penny Pleasant were examining the inside of a rocket at a Space Travel Display on the full-colour back page of *Sparky* No. 1 (23 January 1965), when Peter pressed a button and – 'whoosh!' – in *Sparky* No. 2 they landed on the moon! 'Golly! Look at these funny moon folk!', they cried; 'Gosh! Look at these funny Earth folk!', cried the Moonsters. In next-to-no-time they were all promoted to the front page where, week by week, in one large panel, the Moonsters got up to all kinds of interplanetary pranks.

Moony

John Donnelly

Harold Hare's Own 1959-64; *Playhour* 1964-82 (IPC)

On 14 November 1959, Moony the Moon Man fell off the Moon, slid down a moonbeam, and landed safely on page ten of No. 1 of *Harold Hare's Own Paper*. By No. 2, he was feeling hungry! Seeing a little girl posting a letter in a pillar-box, he thought she was feeding it. So, quick as a wink, Moony turned himself into a pillar-box, albeit a spotty one, and soon a boy came along and popped a letter in his mouth. It tasted horrid but, when a postman tried to turn a key in his tummy, it tickled so much Moony ran away!

Mowser

Reg Parlett

Lion 1964-74; *Valiant* 1974-76 (IPC)

'Mowser the Priceless Puss' was the much-pampered moggie of Crummy Castle. Much loved by Lord and Lady Crummy (never seen without their coronets), quite the reverse was true when it came to James the butler. James tended to refer to Mowser as 'that tatty old kipper-stealer', so perhaps it was no surprise that, for much of Mowser's run, the title of the strip was changed to 'Mowser the Priceless Puss and his enemy James the Butler'.

Morgyn the Mighty

Kearon

Beano 1938; *Victor* 1963- (D. C. Thomson)

'The Strongest Man in the World' made his serial-strip debut in *Beano* No. 1 (30 July 1938), but readers with long memories recalled 'Morgyn the Mighty' from his many adventures in *Rover*, the boys' story paper, which started in No. 304 (11 February 1928). Sole survivor of the shipwrecked schooner *Hebrides*, Morgyn ('over six feet in height and broad in proportion') made his home on Black Island, where his superior strength soon dominated the denizens, be they goats, eagles, or sharks. The map appended to his strip showed a mountain labelled Morgyn's Seat.

Mr Benjamin Bumchowder

Oliver Veal

Best Budget 1902; *Larks* 1902-04 (Trapps Holmes)

'Mr Benjamin Bumchowder in Search of Fame and Glory' was the full title of this front-page strip. The search began in No. 9 of *The Best Budget* (10 May 1902) and continued when that comic changed its name to *Larks* (7 June 1902). Mr Benjamin Bumchowder rushed home crying 'I've chucked it!': after twenty years of sausage-roll making, he had decided to seek Fame and Glory, to the fury of his Missus and the joy of his offspring, Horatio. But all his efforts ended in anguish, especially when he put up for Parliament and called for three cheers for Kruger!

Motherless Mary

P. J. Hayward

Sunbeam 1926-40 (Amalgamated Press)

Another of the many orphan waifs who found their way into the prewar comics, Motherless Mary spent fifteen years in the company of her best friends, Sadie and Topsy. They all went to Dainton School where everyone wore school uniform, except Topsy, who was a different colour to the rest of the girls. She also spoke differently, and had a pet lion: 'Rex am getting quite big now!' Rex escaped. 'Oh dear!', said Topsy. Then the school burned down, and the girls were sent to Revelstone Castle. 'It am a ghostess!', cried Topsy.

Mr Bubbles

Pam Chapeau

Sparky 1970-75 (D. C. Thomson)

'Hi, folks! My name's Mr Bubbles and I'm a bubble imp. I live in a plastic bottle, and every time someone squeezes it, I pop out and grant them three wishes!' This explanatory speech balloon was the standard opening, setting the scene for a two-page fantasy adventure in which a magic manikin made of washing-up liquid brought a little wish-fulfilment into the lives of those who chanced to squeeze his container. Among the many, were Brian, who wished to be a cowboy, and Colin, who wanted to win the Monte Carlo Rally in his pedal car.

The Mr Men/The Little Misses
Roger Hargreaves
Playhour 1975-; *Jack & Jill* 1981-85; *Playgroup* 1984-85 (IPC)
Roger Hargreaves, an advertising executive who couldn't draw, invented the simple Mr Tickle to amuse his children. Soon it was the first of a series of never-ending *Mr Men* books, amusing the children of Britain, then the world. From the first book in 1971, then a television series, the Mr Men arrived in comics on 1 February 1975 in *Playhour*, and, true to tradition, the first Mr Man in strip format was Mr Tickle 'and his extraordinary long arms'. Bowing to feminist pressure, Hargreaves introduced his 'Little Misses' series into *Jack & Jill* from 1981.

Mr Pendragon
Mike Dorey
Champ 1984-85 (D. C. Thomson)
'The Sinister World of Mr Pendragon' was unveiled in No. 1 of *Champ* (25 February 1984); readers were invited to step into it 'if you dare!' Each week Mr Pendragon tells a story of the strange and sinister, starting with 'The Meddler'. 'I am he, and my world is that of the dark forces of the supernatural. Happily, few of you are ever touched by them. But young Jimmy Lester made a terrible mistake when he dared to dabble.' Jimmy stages a fake seance with his pal Des dressed as a ghost, but a boy called Gary faints, believing it to be the spirit of his dead dad. Later, in Cornwall, Jimmy's body is possessed by a wrecker's ghost. 'Be warned! Play not with the supernatural!'

Mrs Tabby and her Tibbies
Charles Gill
Tiger Tim's Weekly 1929-41; *Rainbow* 1941-53 (Amalgamated Press)
This popular pussy-cat strip soon grew from a single row to a half page. The three Tibbies were called Tinker (the tabby one), Snowball (the white one), and Nigger (the black one), and such was the merry mischief they got up to that poor Mrs Tabby was wont to cry, as did Mrs Hippo and Mrs Bruin before her, 'What is the meaning of this?' As who would not when returning home with the shopping to find the floor flooded! The Tibbies, having broken their schoolroom window with snowballs, replaced the glass with a square of ice sawn out of the pond! Naughty kittens!

Mr Pastry
Lunt Roberts
TV Comic 1951-58 (News of the World)
Richard Hearne, the comedy actor, created his 'old man' character in prewar stage revues and films, bringing him to postwar television in a popular series for children as Mr Pastry (signature tune: 'Pop Goes the Weasel'). He was an obvious choice for a colour strip in *TV Comic*, starting with No. 1 (9 November 1951). His typically slapstick adventures involved his neighbour, Mrs Twiggle, the well-meaning Mr Timblethwaite, the helpful lad Mortimer, and the High School at Upper Lowly for whom he tossed pancakes.

Mrs Sudds
Oliver Veal
Picture Fun 1912-18 (Trapps Holmes)
'The Adventures of Mrs Sudds the Charlady' formed a sordid saga of sackings: the plump pummice-person made such a mess of things that she was forcibly ejected from her job at least once a week. Her terrible temper took much of the blame, flaring up at the slightest excuse, such as when a forgetful old gent called her 'Mrs Soapsuds', 'Mrs Dustpan', 'Mrs Dishcloth', 'Mrs Slop-pail', and Mrs Soapdish'. Who could blame her?

Mr Toad
Kenneth Grahame
Harold Hare's Own 1959-64; *Playhour* 1964-82 (IPC)
Kenneth Grahame's ever-popular book, *The Wind in the Willows*, was originally picturized by Hugh McNeill for *Sun* (1950). New adventures of the leading characters, Toad, Ratty, and Mole, began in the full-colour centre spread of *Harold Hare's Own Paper* No. 1 (14 November 1959), drawn by Peter Woolcock (illustrated) under the title of 'Here Comes Mr Toad'. Mr Toad, Toady to his riverbank chums, inspired by his great-great-grandfather, Captain Long John Toad, bought a luxury motorboat: 'Other boats can all be blowed – Make way, make way for Mr Toad!'

Muffin the Mule
Annette Mills
TV Comic 1951-60 (News of the World)
'We want Muffin, Muffin the Mule!' This much-loved signature song was first sung on BBC television in 1946 and, on 9 November 1951, Muffin made his debut as the full-colour, front-page star of No. 1 of *TV Comic*. Muffin was a puppet designed by Ann Hogarth of the Hogarth Puppets, but it was Annette Mills as presenter, story-teller, and singer, that made him so popular with young viewers. Neville Main drew the strip adventures, and another character from the T.V. series, Peregrine the Penguin, starred in a separate strip drawn by Ron Murdoch.

The Mummy's Curse
Reg Parlett
Whizzer & Chips 1969-70 (IPC)
Inspired by the Universal horror film of the same name, this serialized strip was anything but horrible. Professor Potts discovers the Tomb of the Cursing Mummy in Egypt, and translates the heiroglyphics for his servant, Abdul. 'Whoever opens this parcel before Xmas will be cursed and haunted forever!' Being British, the Prof promptly prises it open whereupon the mummy roars into life. 'Can't a chap have a couple of thousand years nap without some inconsiderate clot disturbing him?' Soon defilers and pursuers (the mummy and a spider who hangs from his bandaged nose) are chasing across the Sahara.

Mummy's Boy
Norman Mansbridge
Monster Fun 1975-76; *Buster* 1976- (IPC)
Mummy's Boy arrived by pram in *Monster Fun* No. 2 (21 June 1975). 'I want to enter the cartie race, Mum!', he said. But his Mum was the most possessive Mum in the world. 'Carties are for big boys', she said, 'Drink up your milky-wilkies for Mumsie-wumsie!' 'But Mum!', yelled Mummy's Boy, 'I'm nine years old!' Squirting his bottle into her face, the bonneted and nappied lad whizzed off to win the race in his pram, but was too embarrassed to collect the prize. Never mind; Mumsie had a big kiss for her naughty precious: 'Slobber! Slobber!'

Musso the Wop
Sam Fair
Beano 1941-42 (D. C. Thomson)
As an anonymous cartoonist in the comics, Sam Fair did more than his share of propaganda during World War 2. Having lampooned Der Farderland with 'Addie and Hermy the Nasty Nazis' in *Dandy*, he had a bash at the Italian Eye-ties in *Beano*. The result was 'Musso the Wop – He's a Big-a-da Flop!', a burlesque of Benito Mussolini. When Musso begged *Beano* readers to send him something to help him sleep, they obliged with a clothes-peg ('Clip this on your nose and don't breathe'), rat poison, and an old sock ('Stuff this in your big mouth!').

Mustapha Million
Reg Parlett
Cheeky 1977-80; *Whoopee* 1980-85; *Whizzer & Chips* 1986 (IPC)
It all began in Arabia on 22 October 1977 in No. 1 of *Cheeky*. Young Mustapha Million pitched his tatty tent and up shot oil: 'Thwack! Rumble! Splooosh!' Swiftly swapping his camels for a Rolls Royce, Mustapha's delighted dad sent his lad to England to be educated. The boy was so rich that a busload of teachers came round to his house every day. When the local boys were late for school, Mustapha drove them down in his super train set. And, when a prospective playmate had to wash his dad's car, Mustapha helped hose it down with his private fire engine. At Christmas he played Santa Claus using his camels as reindeer!

My Pal Baggy Pants
Ken Hunter
Dandy 1956-59 (D. C. Thomson)
Baggy Pants arrived with a 'Whoom!' on 7 January 1956 – in young Johnny Grant's bedroom, and in *Dandy* No. 737. Johnny had been chuckling at a picture in his *Book of Magicians*: 'Hee-hee! Look at old Baggy Pants!' Then came the 'Whoom!' and old Baggy Pants himself! It turned out that Johnny had unwittingly spoken the magic word – 'Bagee' – that had unlocked the turbanned magician from the picture in which a rival magician had trapped him. 'Little master, I am thy slave!', beamed Baggy Pants, taking Johnny to school in a chariot.

Mustava Bunn
Percy Cocking
Merry & Bright 1926-31; *Tip Top* 1934-35 (Amalgamated Press)
'Frolics and Fun with Mustava Bunn' was an unusual serving of Eastern delight beginning on 13 March 1926. Bunn and his dainty daughter Sultana spent their sultry days thwarting the evil intent of a bearded nogood called the Jam Sponge, 'a nasty old cake'. 'By the whiskers of a whelk!', and other Eastern oaths uttered the lord of the Bunneries, while the Jam Sponge, dosing the old boy's curry with a jugful of Desert Dope, hissed 'The cold-hearted son of a saveloy needs warming up! Eesh!' Sultana, 'fair apple of my peeper', turned the tables, of course.

Mytek the Mighty
Eric Bradbury
Valiant 1964-70; *Vulcan* 1975-76 (IPC)
Looking like a cross between King Kong and a caveman, 'Mytek the Mighty' was the biggest robot in the world. Inside its realistically hairy head rode its inventor, Professor Arnold Boyce, and game warden Dirk Mason. Mytek battled with and defeated another super robot, controlled by the evil dwarf Gogra, saving America's gold reserves, and then walked to London, straight up the River Thames. Convincing the government he was on their side by building a skyscraper block in minutes, Mytek then had his brain stolen by Gogra, who put it into a giant robot in his own image.

N

Nancy the Little Nurse
Sabine Price
Twinkle 1968- (D. C. Thomson)
'In Sunshine Street there is a very special little hospital. It is special because the patients are dollies. The dolly doctor who takes care of them is kind old Mr Jingle. The doctor has a nurse. She is his grand-daughter, Nancy.' Nancy the Nurse is the leading strip of *Twinkle*. *Twinkle* is a comic for little girls. Nancy has been its star since No. 10. No. 1 was published on 27 January 1968. Nancy is now nineteen years old. She has not grown one inch. Isn't Nancy a lucky little girl?

Nelson Twigg
Roy Wilson
Merry & Bright 1933-35
(Amalgamated Press)
'Nelson Twigg the Boy Detective', assisted by his pet bloodpup Wellington, opened his comical casebook as a six-picture strip, but became so popular with *Merry & Bright* readers that he was promoted to page one in 1934. Young Nelson, clad in a voluminous check overcoat several sizes too large (it needed to be: it concealed his spyglass, telescope, handcuffs, and divers disguises), solved bafflers such as the purloined picnic chicken. But his greatest cases concerned the Pernicketty Six, a masked gang led by Billy Bifbat.

Nap and his Bonny Bodyguard
Reg Parlett
Funny Wonder 1929-32
(Amalgamated Press)
Nap, known to his Froggie mates as Boney, employed a one-man bodyguard called Nick. Nick's job was to ward off evil in the shape of Talleyman and his hireling, Andre Uglimug. 'Leave it to me, Emp!' Nick would cry, sharpening his conkers or soaking his sword in vinegar. Before you could say Jacques Robinson, the terrible Talley would bite the dust with a wallop that made his tonsils rattle. But readers knew jolly well that next week the old usurper would be back again, ready to spoil Nap's picnic with a dose of Nasty Stuff in his teapot.

Napper Todd
Illustrator unknown
Hotspur 1965-75 (D. C. Thomson)
For a typical tousel-haired youngster, Napper Todd had plenty of ups and downs in his years as a football hero. Shooting up fast, Napper was the star player for First Division Riverport United in a practice match, but was sacked by the sinister chairman, Falke Werner, in case he remembered seeing him burning the 1939 record book. It held a secret that concerned Werner and the supposed suicide of one, Henry Sanderson. Meanwhile Napper signed on for Riverport Casuals, a top amateur team, but Werner's minion, Stanley Sinclair, was bribed to frame him. In another serial, Napper was boot boy for the United but playing centre-forward for the South End Rovers.

Nemesis the Warlock
Kevin O'Neill
2000 AD 1981- (IPC)
Surely the strangest strips ever seen in comics are the series depicting the totally alien worlds and ways of Nemesis the Warlock, from the planet Gandarva, and leader of the alien resistance organization, Credo. Assisted by his familiar, Grobbendonk, who speaks only the fringe world dialect of gibberish ('Skrunkies! Schnorkles! Ork trogged and trugged and waggled my fangles for yaft! Doop de boop!'), Nemesis smashed the evil regime of Torquemada, Grand Master of Termight. But the torturer's fanatical hatred lived on.

N

Nero and Zero
Allan Morley

Wizard 1930-40; *Buzz* 1973-74 (D. C. Thomson)

'Nero and Zero the Rollicking Romans' first appeared in the comic centre spread of *Wizard*, a boys' story paper, on 1 November 1930. Two centurions of Ancient Rome, Nero was addressed as 'O fat one' by Zero, while Zero was known as 'O thou skinny nitwit' by Nero. The pair were Caesar's bodyguard, but that Noble One's body needed guarding from his bodyguard. After thirty-three years of retirement, the boys came back as a full-page strip in *Buzz* No. 1 (20 January 1973). Things had not improved. Their theme song was 'Keep the Rome fires burning!'

The Nibblers
Ron Spence

Beano 1970-84 (D. C. Thomson)

This gang of hungry mice moved into *Beano* and undermined the floorboards of one, Porky, a fat fellow fond of his cheese. To guard the tasty stuff, Porky had a pet cat, a black-and-white moggy called Whiskers. This did little to worry the Nibblers, who numbered eight: the muscular Enor Mouse, the twins Scritch and Scratch, Gordon Zola who wore a Scottish tam o'shanter, the ever-hungry Cheddar George, the bespectacled Chiseller, the long-snouted Sniffler, and the born leader known as His Nibs.

The Nervs
Mike Brown

Smash 1966-68 (Odhams)

The Nervs are the wacky looking weirdos that keep the human body going, 'make us do all the things we do and so on and so fifth!' The Nervs illustrated in the weekly treatise known as *Smash* (5 February 1966) had the misfortune to live inside the rather rotund body of Fatty, 'as fit as a fiddle with no strings!' Gobbling down a sausage sandwich in great lumps, Fatty blocked his internal mincer. Luckily the Nervs rang for the fire brigade and sent smoke signals to their boss's brain to wash things down with a drink of water.

Nick Smith
Llampayes

Hornet 1965-76; *Hotspur* 1976-80 (D. C. Thomson)

'It's Goals That Count' was the continuing title of the story of Nick Smith, England's famous inside-left. Although originally told in words in *Rover*, starting in No. 1119 (29 September 1945), the strip version ran for fifteen years. Young Nick, an orphan, was brought up by his Auntie Maud who worked for Hatton's Circus. While wintering at Hamcastle, Fleed Manton, the new manager of Hamcastle United, a Fourth-Division team, advertised a pre-season trial for local lads. Nick was first in the queue and was tried out as inside-left. Soon he was signed as a professional and gave up his circus career with Horace and Hector, the sealions, for £3 a week as a reserve.

Never-Never Nelson
Jack Glass

Dandy 1938-39 (D. C. Thomson)

Big Bill Nelson had one of the world's most dangerous jobs. He was hired by circuses to search the world for new star-turns to thrill their audiences, hence his subtitle: 'The Circus Scout Who Never Never Fails'. His first task, as depicted in *Dandy* No. 53 (3 December 1938), was to search Burma for the world's biggest white elephant on behalf of Manzoni's Circus. Naturally Never-Never made it, despite being roped to the wild elephant's head by vicious natives. Then it was off to capture a sacred sealion.

Nicky Nobody
Illustrator unknown

Swift 1954-61 (Hulton)

'The Story of a Boy and his Dog' began in *Swift* No. 1 (20 March 1954) with young schoolboy Nicky ordered off to deliver groceries. 'It's not fair! Why does Aunt Ethel always pick on me? Just because I have no Mum and Dad!' On the way Nicky saved a scruffy pup from some stone-throwing ruffians and soon his one-and-only pal shared the title of his strip: 'Nicky Nobody and his dog, Chum'. His adventures were just beginning. Caught in the rain, he was given a lift by Sir Giles Horton, a private detective on the track of the Black Opal gang, and later Nicky chummed up with Jenny, daughter of Colonel Rowse, and saved a village from flooding.

Nigel Tawny
Redvers Blake
Zip 1958-59; *Swift* 1959 (Odhams)
Sir Nigel Tawny, Explorer (he received his correct title billing only when his comic, *Zip*, was taken over by *Swift*), was the epitomy of British upper-class pluck, and one of the few strip heroes to sport a bristling moustache. With his research team, Taffy Jones (Welsh) and Angus MacKay (Scottish), he journeys to the Arctic where they discover a petrified mammoth which shows evidence of modern bone-setting! Rescuing Professor Peter Dean from a crevasse, they find themselves in a lost world under the ice cap where mammoths still roam.

Nippi the Jap
P. J. Hayward
Bubbles 1924-38 (Amalgamated Press)
'Nippi the Jap Visits Britain' was the original title of this strip, which came complete with an explanatory synopsis: 'Nippi has come to stay for a holiday. He does not understand all our ways and does some quaint things.' Among Nippi's quaint things were mistaking Santa Claus and his sack for a burglar, and riding on a train by sitting on the funnel. Small wonder he let out a cry of 'Nokio pokio!' In 1929 the strip was 'Nippi the Jap and his Baby Austin' (he motored around Britain), and in 1934 it became 'Nippi and Rosebud the Happy Japs'.

Nobbler and Jerry
Charles Genge
Funny Cuts 1908-12 (Trapps Holmes)
'The True History of Nobbler and Jerry' was, of course, anything but. Nobbler and Jerry were the characters played in the Music Halls by Lew Lake and Bob Morris. Their act was entitled *The Bloomsbury Burglars*, and it gave the world the once familiar catchphrases of 'Go it, Nobbler!' – 'Stick it, Jerry!' Their knockabout pursuit from the police might have been made for comics, and their page-one strip in *Funny Cuts* soon developed into a serial. 'Swallered we wos by a blessed sea-serpint! Did we ekscape? Well, buy nex week's and sea! Yours merrily, Lew Lake.'

Nipper
Eric Bradbury
Score'n'Roar 1970-71; *Scorcher* 1971-74; *Tiger* 1974-84 (IPC)
'He's a real Zipper, the lad known as Nipper!' In the sprawling Midlands estuary town of Blackport, the boys of Stoneleigh Secondary School were looking forward to watching Blackport Rovers beat Cranmere. All except the shabbily clad young scruff, Nipper Lawrence, who worked spare time at the docks, saving money to clear his dead dad's name. He lived in a slum terrace with his only pal, Stumpy the mongrel, occasionally visited by his guardian, Nat Munger, who wanted the orphan's savings. Then Andy Stewart, manager, saw the wiry lad playing football. . . .

Nip and Rrip
George Martin
Nutty 1982-85 (D. C. Thomson)
'Meet the lad with the Wildest Cat in the World!' was the headline in *Nutty* No. 135 (11 September 1982). The lad was Nip and the cat was Rrip – a fat, furry freak far from the furry felines that more frequently fill the odd corners of comic frames. Rrip's line of descent was more likely via Gnasher, Dennis the Menace's devilish dog. Rrip hisses his thoughts thus: 'I'll ssharrrpen my clawss on thisss!', as he 'ssscratches' his way through mum's washing pole, a colonel's shooting stick, and a window-cleaner's ladder.

Nobby and Pip
Harry Banger
War Comics 1940-43; *Cute Fun* 1950 (Swan)
'Over There with Nobby and Pip' was the original title of this four-page strip which started in No. 1 of *War Comics* (April 1940). Nobby was the Old Contemptible, the regular who was put in charge of Pip, the New Reinforcement. Their adventures were redolent of World War 1: trench patrol, cutting barbed wire, spotting snipers ('Ach! Der ammunition haff all used up, don't it!'). But Dunkirk changed all that, and from No. 4 the title became 'Over Here', with Nobby and Pip guarding the White Cliffs of Dover, snaffling birds' eggs, and sinking U-Boats by accident.

© 1986 Noddy subsidiary rights

Noddy
Enid Blyton
TV Comic 1956-69 (Beaverbrook); *Noddy & his Friends* 1974-75 (Hudvale); *Noddy Time* 1975 (Woman's Way); *Rupert* 1982 (Marvel)
Noddy, the happy little chap with a bell on his cap, lives in Toyland. Among his chums are jolly bearded Big-Ears, Bumpy Dog, Mr Jumbo, Miss Kitten and, of course, the legendary constable, P.C. Plod. A series of small strip books drawn by Harmsen Van Der Beek was published by Sampson Low from 1949, and once Noddy had transferred to television, he starred on the front page of *TV Comic*. He eventually graduated to his own weekly comic, *Noddy & his Friends* (9 March 1974) with a title change to *Noddy Time* (10 May 1975).

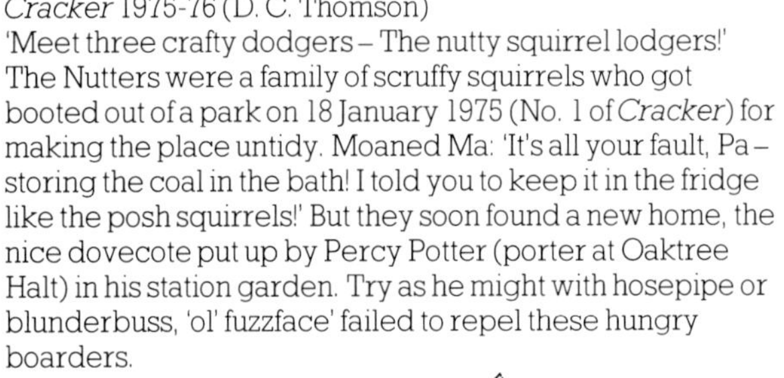

The Nutters
John Geering
Cracker 1975-76 (D. C. Thomson)
'Meet three crafty dodgers – The nutty squirrel lodgers!' The Nutters were a family of scruffy squirrels who got booted out of a park on 18 January 1975 (No. 1 of *Cracker*) for making the place untidy. Moaned Ma: 'It's all your fault, Pa – storing the coal in the bath! I told you to keep it in the fridge like the posh squirrels!' But they soon found a new home, the nice dovecote put up by Percy Potter (porter at Oaktree Halt) in his station garden. Try as he might with hosepipe or blunderbuss, 'ol' fuzzface' failed to repel these hungry boarders.

Nosey Parker
Allan Morley
Rover 1925-47; *Beezer* 1956; *Sparky* 1966 (D. C. Thomson)
'Our Prize Busybody' began his twenty-three-year career of poking his long nose into other people's business in *Rover* No. 172, on 3 June 1925. His usual beat was the back page, twelve neat little panels, but during the war, he was promoted to fill the full-colour cover, from 1942 to 1946. Then he returned to the back, this time in tasteful two-tone red and blue. It was Nosey's nose that usually bore the brunt of his inquisitiveness: 'The gent didn't like Nosey nosing around so he slammed the door shut. Wham! It biffed Mr Parker a hefty one on the proboscis!' Ouch!

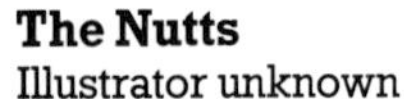

The Nutts
Illustrator unknown
Valiant 1962-71 (Fleetway)
'Our Funny Family are Tough Nutts to Crack!' claimed No. 1 of *Valiant* (6 October 1962), 'The family with nuts in the belfry!' There were eight Nutts in all, from Nora Nutt and her daughter, Hazel Nutt, down to the pet parrot who was posted on the chimney to keep an eye out for Silas Snatch, the landlord. The house, by the way, was named the Nuthatch. Dad Nutt, never one to waste money on such nonessentials as rent, once bought a car instead. When he got it home he found it had no engine – the dealer lived on top of a hill!

The Numskulls
Malcolm Judge
Beezer 1962- (D. C. Thomson)
One of the oddest crowds in comics, the Numskulls inhabit the head of a gent known as Unk (short for Uncle). A cross-section of his skull shows the sections inhabited by this gang of six. There is Brainy who lives in his brain, and Blinky who operates the telescope in Unk's eyeball. Then there is Luggy who operates his earhole department, Sniffy who lives in his nose, and a pair who manage the food and drink department in the man's mouth. This section gets a bit tangled when Unk tries a tongue-twister!

Nutty Noddle
Hugh McNeill
Robin 1961-69; *Playhour* 1969-73; *Jack & Jill* 1977-81 (IPC)
'The Funny Adventures of Nutty Noddle' started in the full-colour centre spread of *Robin* on 21 October 1961, another delightful animal creation of Hugh McNeill. 'Deep in the heart of Greenwood Forest stands a big chestnut tree. And high in its branches is – guess what! – a cottage – yes, of all things, a cottage – a dinky little cottage with a red roof. And now you will be asking: "Who lives in the little cottage in the tree?" Well, this is the home of Nutty Noddle, the funny little red squirrel. He is called Nutty not only because he likes nuts, but also because he is just a tiny, tiny bit "nutty"'!

Odd-Ball
Mike Lacey
Whizzer & Chips 1969- (IPC)
Two spring-heeled inhabitants of the planet Bounco were enjoying a ball game ('Blip-googly-goal!') when an outsize header ('woompf!') shot their ball into space ('Iddly-idiot!'). Bouncing off the helmet of an orbiting astronaut, the ball shot down to Earth and was caught by a kid called Nobby Noodle. He was playing goalie at the time but soon guessed something was wrong when the ball grew an arm and tweaked his nose! 'Coo! I've got me a real odd-ball! It's alive, and it won't cost me anything to feed it! It eats grass!' ('Chomp!')

Old Father Time
Sam Fair
Magic 1940 (D. C. Thomson)
'Meet Father Time, who as you'll see – Can make things what they used to be!' This bearded old boy made his bow in *Magic* No. 43 (11 May 1940), complete with traditional scythe and hourglass. It was the latter that gave him his special powers, especially when accompanied by a suitable chant:

O Sands of Time, O Sands of Time,
O please now backwards flow,
And make this pup like its grandad
Of a million years ago!

Instantly a teased tailwagger turned into its prehistoric ancestor and put paid to the bully who tied a tin can to its tail.

Olac the Gladiator
Brian Leigh
Tiger 1957-68 (Amalgamated Press)
Olac, a British slave in Ancient Rome, had ambitions to become a champion gladiator. A nobleman, Senator Durbio, helped him in return for his keeping watch on Pendor, who was plotting against him. Olac is befriended by Claudius, a gladiator, and they discover Pendor is a member of the mysterious Brotherhood of the Sword. After passing his tests, Olac becomes a gladiator and enters the annual championships at Pompeii, once again saving Durbio, this time from General Branda. Then, by the bolts of Jupiter, it was tyrannical Tarquin the Proud threatening all Rome.

Old Hooky
William McCail
Topical Funnies 1940-46 (Swan)
'Heave away m'lads! There's plenty o' loot an' grog when she's ours!' With these stirring words Captain Moonlight, or Old Hooky as he was named by his buccaneers, slashed his way into the first of many six-page adventures in *Topical Funnies* No. 2 (June 1940). Cannons roared, cutlasses slashed, and many a man would walk the plank during the exciting years that lay ahead. Artist William McCail, himself a moonlighter from D. C. Thomson, signed himself 'Ron' lest his comic bosses spotted him! 'Pirate Gold', the original title, became 'Adventures of Old Hooky' in 1941.

Old MacDonald's Farm
Turnbull
Bimbo 1964-72 (D. C. Thomson)
This strip for young readers was based on the popular old comedy song. Each week it was introduced by a burst of verse containing the name of the animal featured:

Old MacDonald had a farm,
E-I-E-I-O!
And on that farm he had a cockerel.
Read about it below!

Of course, the rhyme worked better when the animal was a lamb, or a horse. However, when Charlie Cockerel failed to wake the farmyard animals with his usual cock-a-doodle-do Old MacDonald visited the village clockmaker. Next morning at six o'clock, a specially adapted cuckoo clock woke Charlie on the dot.

One-Eyed Jack
John Cooper
Valiant 1976; *Battle* 1976-77; *Eagle* 1983-84 (IPC)
'The New York cop with his own brand of justice' was Detective Jackson McBane of the 94th precinct. With a black patch over his left eye, One-Eyed Jack was the first character to bring American-style violence into British comics. As he told Lieutenant Carelli, 'I lost an eye bein' soft with a thug, now I'm going to do it my way!' With his partner, Willy Novack, McBane waged war on crooks using their own tough methods. 'The law's fine as far as it goes, but sometimes it takes a man with his own kind of law to see justice.'

Old Ma Murphy
Allan Morley
Dandy 1944-49 (D. C. Thomson)
Originally christened Miss Prim, Old Ma Murphy arrived in the Christmas 1944 edition of *Dandy* complete with descriptive subtitle: 'The Strong-Arm School-Marm'. A mistress of the old school, Ma Murphy ruled her class of boys (Basil Binks, Jimmy Jinks, Charlie Chickweed, and Curly Kelly) with a rod of iron and a whangee cane. One of her pupils, Donald Dope, wore a dunce's cap. Small wonder for, when he was told to write an essay on a horse, he couldn't find one, so did it on a donkey instead.

One-Eye Joe and Two-Toof Tom
Hugh McNeill
Knockout 1946-47; *Sun* 1958 (Amalgamated Press)
'This Priceless Pair of Pirate Pals' stepped ashore in *Knockout* No. 404 (23 November 1946) in search of a new pair of trousers. Buying a secondhand pair for ninepence (borrowing 8½d from his toothy pal), Joe soon discovered that one of the buttons was boiled down from Aladdin's lamp. 'Blow me down!' he cried – and he was! Whoosh! All seems set fair but then they run afoul of Duss-bin-lid, the pirate chief who snatches the button. Murky work on the high seas ensues.

Ollie/Tib O' the Tiles
Harry Hargreaves
Sun 1951-52; *Big One* 1965-66 (Fleetway)
Originally entitled 'The Alley Cat – Our Playful Puss', this character was drawn in best animated-cartoon style by a former animator from Gaumont British, Harry Hargreaves. The line of the plot was simple if familiar: cat chases bird, bird gets best of cat. Again the influence on the animation is clear: Sylvester and Tweety from the Warner Brothers cartoons. Popularity promoted the puss to the front page as from *Sun*'s 1951 Christmas number, when Alley Cat's name was revealed to be Ollie. Soon he was chasing a new prey, which led to a new subtitle, 'The Merry Mouser'. Revamped as Giggle in *Giggle* (1967).

Oor Wullie
Dudley D. Watkins
Sunday Post 1936- (D. C. Thomson)
'Oor Wullie', Scottish dialect for Our Willie, is the front-page-strip star of the *Sunday Post Fun Section*, and has been since that pull-out comic was introduced on 8 March 1936. The original cartoonist, Dudley Dexter Watkins, was not a Scot. The dialogue was scripted for him in dialect. Wullie's homely and mischievous adventures always begin and end the same way: with Wullie seated on his upturned bucket. Pals include Fat Boab and Jeemy the Wee Moose (Jimmy the little mouse), with friendly opposition from P.C. Murdoch.

OUR BRAINS TRUST
PROFESSOR PIFFLE, DR DUNBROWN, ADMIRAL PENNY-FOREM AND – THE QUESTION MASTER, IVOR POSER

Our Brains Trust
Alex Akerbladh
Radio Fun 1942-50 (Amalgamated Press)
Radio Fun's burlesque version of the BBC 'Brains Trust' was called to order in No. 185 on 25 April 1942. The original team of Professor Joad, Dr Julian Huxley, Commander Campbell, and Question Master Donald McCullough were parodied as Professor Piffle, Dr Dunbrown, Admiral Penny-Forem, and Ivor Poser. Their first challenge was from Willie Snodgrass of Wigan who wanted to know why you should never let your braces dangle! When they were asked the difference between a left hook and a right uppercut, Joe Louis turned up to show them!

Our Gang
Dudley D. Watkins
Dandy 1937-47 (D. C. Thomson)
Hal Roach's famous juvenile troupe from his Hollywood film series made their comic strip debut in No. 1 of *Dandy* (4 December 1937) and ran for 340 issues. The kiddies, excellently depicted by Dudley D. Watkins, were Alfalfa Switzer, Scotty Beckett, Darla Hood, Billy Thomas, Patsy May, Porky Lee, Spanky McFarland, and Buckwheat Thomas, not forgetting Pete the Pup. Their main rivals were a bunch of toughs called the Kelly Gang, and their teacher was Miss Frump.

Our Kinema Couple/Our Screen Screams
Bertie Brown
Funny Wonder 1919-31; *Jester* 1935-37 (Amalgamated Press)
Our Kinema Couple were not, as you might expect, Handsome Harry the Hero and Mildred the bobbed-hair beauty, but Handsome Harry the Hero and Vernon the Vile Villain. Mildred was the object of their rivalry, which led to much machination from Vernon, accompanied by hisses of 'Phwists!', shrieks of 'Merciful powers!' from the maid-ern, and last-minute rescues by the even fairer-haired Harold. Clutching a friendly welt on the dome, Vernon would stagger off crying 'Curses, foiled again!' Reg Parlett revived them four years later in *Jester*.

Our Ernie
C. E. Holt
Knockout 1939-60; *Big One* 1964-65 (Fleetway)
'Mrs Entwhistle's Little Lad' was the first provincial comic hero, a Lancashire Lad from Wigan inspired by 'Albert Ramsbottom', the naughty boy of Stanley Holloway's popular monologues. This connection was consolidated by the funny four-line verses that appeared under each of the strip's twelve pictures. Ernie's weekly wanderings grew even weirder once Hugh McNeill (illustrated) took over the artwork from episode twelve. In No. 61 McNeill introduced Charlie the Caterpillar, a Jiminy-Cricket-like conscience given to commenting in corners. The first strip had catchphrases: 'What's for tea, Ma?' and Pa Entwhistle's 'Daft I call it!'

Our Gang
Illustrator unknown
Swift 1954-61 (Hulton)
Inspired by the series of short films of the same title, this particular Our Gang consisted of a more manageable trio, Tubby, Teena, and Tich. They started in a small way, half a page of *Swift* No. 1 (20 March 1954), but, when *Swift* increased its page size as from 9 April 1960, Our Gang expanded to fill a whole page. Their first exploit was to go in for the local soapbox derby: they won by fixing firework rockets to their cartie. They celebrated their expanded space by Tubby's Dad buying the house next door to Teena and Tich. Tubby devised a quick way to join his pals – spring-heeled shoes: 'Spling! Splang! Splonk!'

Our Merry Mannikins
Percy Maycock
Comic Cuts 1906-12 (Amalgamated Press)
Later as 'Our Merry Midgets', these three, Mandy, Monty, and Marmaduke, were identical triplets, from their single corkscrew curls down to their spats. Occasionally referred to as 'our tricky trio' or 'our artful atoms', M, M, and M were a variety act and thus spent much of their seven-year engagement on stage or behind the scenes at such variety palaces as the Colidrome, playing pranks in triplicate on stars like Hoodwinky the Handcuff King.

Paddy Payne
Mark Ross
Lion 1957-70 (Amalgamated Press)
'Paddy Payne, Warrior of the Skies' was the new full-colour, front-page star of *Lion*, replacing the fantastic adventures of Captain Condor. Squadron Leader Patrick Payne was an ace RAF fighter pilot of World War 2, and was considered their top troubleshooter. His buddy was Flying Officer Dick Smith. Their air adventures included investigating Nazi activity at the Maudais marshalling yards, protecting convoys to Russia from Hitler's secret weapon, and flying against the Japs in the Pacific.

Pam of Pond Hill
Bob Harvey
Jinty 1979-81; *Tammy* 1981-84 (IPC)
Reflecting the popularity of BBC television's school series *Grange Hill*, *Jinty* introduced its own comprehensive school, Pond Hill. Jay Over's script centred around the short-haired Pam and her pals in Miss Peebles' class, who found themselves bussing to the posh St Dorrit's at Eversfleet when Pond Hill's foundations started to shift. The working-class kids at comprehensive school were greeted with fresh-air sprays: 'Suddenly there's an awful pong around here!' Pam narrated the stories, and regulars included Mr Gold the head, Miss Phillips the sports mistress, and Goofy Boyle.

Paddywack
Jack Clayton
Cheeky 1978-80; *Whoopee* 1980-84 (IPC)
The craze for 'Irish Jokes' came to comics with the adventures of Paddywack, supposedly a strip drawn by Doodle Doug, one of Cheeky's pals. Aroused on 8 July 1978 by his old Mum shouting, 'Wake up! I told you to put the alarm clock on!', Paddywack replied, 'I did, Ma, but it fell off me wrist!' *Cheeky* readers were offered £2 per Paddywack joke, and the first was won by Sarah Lynch of Woking: 'I'd like a sheet of wrapping paper two inches wide by 100 feet long. I need to wrap the clothesline I've bought my Ma for her birthday!' When *Cheeky* combined with *Whoopee*, Paddywack became a comic strip again.

Pancho Villa
Illustrator unknown
Pancho Villa 1954-59 (Miller)
Billed as 'The Robin Hood of Mexico', the historical hero was introduced in No. 1 of his own sixpenny comicbook thus: 'Rising from a lowly peon to a bandit general who, by right of might, ruled all of Northern Mexico, Pancho Villa had become the legendary 'Robin Hood of his country. Cruel, vicious and a ruthless killer, his exploits made him the greatest bad man of the 20th century.' On the run from the rurales for supposedly shooting Don Lopez for kissing Dolores, Pancho Villa's sister, Pancho takes over an outlaw gang when their leader is killed: 'We shall steal only from the oppressor and give to the poor. I have spoken.'

Pansy Pancake
Bertie Brown
Comic Cuts 1912-29 (Amalgamated Press)
'The Comical Cook', also known as 'our pantry pet' and 'our bun burner', was the plump queen of the kitchen range at Marmalade Villa. She stayed in service for some eighteen years despite jaw from her Missus 'for the way I cooked the boots and cleaned the steak!' Seldom lost for a winning wheeze, when she forgot the plums in the Master's duff, she shot them in with a blunderbuss! When her beau, a bluebottle named P.C. Robert, demolished Master's pet pie, she replaced the crust with a handy tortoise! It was enough to make Mrs Beeton laugh.

Pa Perkins and His Son Percy
Bertie Brown
Chips 1922-53 (Amalgamated Press)
'A most useful old person about the house was Pa Perkins. He could make a noise like a cheese and catch mice!' He could also do his weekly best to amuse his chubby little offshoot, Percival (Percy for short, which he certainly was), amusing even more the young readers of *Chips* – who weren't so young if they followed Pa's entire thirty-two-year career. Pa's educative efforts invariably landed him up to the scrawny neck in hot water, or even cold ditto: when he flopped into the seal pond, Percy cried to the keeper: 'Please rescue Pa – he's the one with the hat on!'

Pansy Potter
Hugh McNeill
Beano 1938-54; *Sparky* 1965-75 (D. C. Thomson)
'Pansy Potter the Strong Man's Daughter' – perhaps the first fighting feminist in British comics – bashed her way into the first Christmas number of the *Beano*. A last-minute name change by editor George Moonie spared her from being christened Biff Bang Bella! Pansy, with her sunburst of corkscrew curls and Popeye-type forearms, was female and fearless. Her wartime adventures, under artist Basil Blackaller, were legend: 'Pansy's having fun galore – Sinking U-Boats by the score!'

Patch-eye Hooker
Illustrator unknown
Giggle 1967-68; *Buster* 1968 (Fleetway)
'Pirates ahoy! Meet the fiercest pirate who ever flew the Jolly Roger!' Patch-eye Hooker, subtitled 'the Terror of the Seas', sailed into a four-page serial in the Christmas 1967 number of *Giggle*. Feared by all who used the sea, Patch-eye sailed his ship, *The Firebrand*, among the islands of the Caribbean in pursuit of his sworn enemy, Peg-leg Palmer. 'By the great turtle of Tortuga!' cried Hooker, 'I'll blow him to bits from the cannon's mouth and feed the pieces to the seagulls!' Will Barber was Hooker's clean-living cabin boy.

Pat the Pirate
Anton Lock
Tiger Tim's Weekly 1929-40 (Amalgamated Press)
Pat the Pirate and his chums – John, Jim, Michael, Boko the monkey, and a raven-haired young lovely called Marie – set sail on the red-and-black back page of *Tiger Tim's Weekly*. It was a voyage that would take them twelve years and still be uncompleted: their comic was cut off in its prime by the paper shortage of World War 2, something their evil enemy Blackbeard was never able to accomplish. Pat's sailing ship was called the *Flying Scud*, and his most awful oath was 'My goodness!'

Patsy and Peter Panda
Bob Dewar
Twinkle 1968-76; *Bimbo* 1968-72 (D. C. Thomson)
Known collectively as the Perky Pandas, this brother and sister did not team up until 5 June 1971 in No. 534 of *Bimbo*. By this time, the panda pair were so popular that they were given the complete full-colour centre spread for their big-picture adventures. Both bears had begun in separate strips in separate comics during 1968, both drawn by the same artist, Bob Dewar. Patsy Panda, being female, was featured in *Twinkle* 'The Picture Paper Specially for Little Girls', while Peter, being a boy, was in *Bimbo*.

Patty
Illustrator unknown
Girl 1981- (IPC)
'Patty's World' was that of a young teenager, still at school, and the love/hate relationship she had with her elder, sexier blonde sister, 'Our Carol'. Plus, of course, her relationship with Sharon and the gang, her school set, and Doreen Snyder and Co down at the disco. Then there were Mum and Gran and her baby sister, and, of course, the boys. Not to mention her stepdad, and Gran's old gentleman caller. Occasionally, Patty's World serialized itself into adventures, such as when she became dogsbody for Carol's boyfriend, Kenny, who made a home movie in a haunted house.

Patriotic Paul
H. O'Neill
Lot-O-Fun 1908-20 (Henderson)
Billed as 'The Boy Cadet', Patriotic Paul was one of the few comic heroes to reflect the spirit of his times. He went into action on the full-colour front of *Lot-O-Fun* on 14 November 1908, ready 'to die for Peckham, home and gooseberries'! Week two opened with a caption that tells a lot about the sentiments of 1908: 'Patriotic Paul couldn't stand Germans.' He summons the fire brigade to hose down Herr Schwinks, a street musician, and ends up dancing on the busker's belly, playing 'Rule Britannia' on the poor man's trombone! By 1909 he was a militant member of Baden-Powell's Boy Scouts.

Patsy and Tim
Eric R. Parker
Knockout 1940-43; *Sun* 1949 (Amalgamated Press)
'The Queer Adventures of Patsy and Tim' began in *Knockout* No. 81, 14 September 1940. Their scottie dog Scrubby swallowed some of their uncle's patent Dwindling Pills and promptly shrank in size! They found some instructions: 'Every pill you eat will halve your size. To get back to right size, sniff the Sniffing Salts. They are in the tiny glass tube.' Naturally, the kids couldn't wait, and soon they were riding on Scrubby's back, off on their Queer Adventures. In Africa, they were thought of as Little Gods from the sky.

P

Patty Pickle
Tom Kerr
Twinkle 1971-79 (D. C. Thomson)
Patty Pickle was a little girl in big spectacles who started in *Twinkle* No. 195 (16 October 1971). Patty always tried her hardest to do things right, but somehow always managed to get into a muddle. She dutifully wrote thank-you letters to all her aunties and uncles after her birthday, but the wind blew all the envelopes out of her hand. It took her ages to collect them all up but, after she had posted them, Mummy found she had forgotten to put the letters into the envelopes. 'Skipetty-skip!' said Patty Pickle, but then she always did. It was her catchphrase. All that Pongo, her puppy, said was 'Wuff!'

P.C. Copperclock
Bert Hill
Sunshine 1938-39 (Target)
'P.C. Copperclock, the Desert Cop', clocked in for double-page duty in No. 1 of *Sunshine* (16 July 1938). His beat was across the bottom of the centre spread and, when not being harassed by his portly Sergeant, he was tapping bad-lads' beans with his truncheon and popping them off to the cop shop. Some of the dusky do-badders included the Sly Sheik of Slipshod and Mustapha Jujube, who fancied the jools which Copperclock was conducting from the Sultan of Sulphur to His Fatness the Rajah of Hoopla.

Paul Power
Colin Merritt
Chips 1948-53 (Amalgamated Press)
'The Fastest Flying Man the World Has Ever Known' was the headline for Paul Power and his Speed Shell when he burst on to the red-and-black back page of *Chips* on 25 September 1948. Paul, his Speed Shell 'blazing like a lightning flash', rushed to the rescue of Captain Branson, somewhere at sea, in a complete ten-picture story, but was soon involved in full-page serials such as 'The Treasure Planet' and 'The Menace from Mars'. He finally foiled his main enemy, Dr Gec, in the last issue of *Chips*: 12 September 1953.

P.C. 49
Alan Stranks
Eagle 1950-57 (Hulton)
The Adventures of P.C. 49 started on radio on 24 October 1947, with Brian Reece playing Police Constable Archibald Berkeley-Willoughby. By 14 April 1950, Archie was sufficiently popular with young listeners for him to be adapted as a strip for No. 1 of *Eagle*. The original artist was Gould, but it was John Worsley (illustrated) who took the character over and made the strip his own. Rejected for plain clothes work ('Putting you in plain clothes would be like sending out the police band in full regalia!') P.C. 49 was condemned to uniformed patrol ('Still a beat basher – all feet and no brains!').

P

P.C. Penny
Cyril Price
Comic Cuts 1938-44 (Amalgamated Press)
P.C. Penny, neatly billed as 'Our Bright Copper', went on the beat in No. 2504 of *Comic Cuts*. His early adventures were not much different from any other comic-paper policeman, collaring such bad hats as Crafty Chris (the lad with taking ways: umpteen quid reward), nabbing Naughty Ned and Percy the Pillar Box Pilferer, or taking the prisoner for his morning walk around the Cop Shop. From No. 2579 (21 October 1939), however, Penny went on war duty, swapping his helmet for a tin titfer, keeping blacked-out Britain safe from Basil the Bank Buster and Ted the Ticker Taker.

Peggy the Pride of the Force
Reg Parlett
Larks 1931-40 (Amalgamated Press)
'You will all love Peggy and will roar with laughter at her adventures!' wrote the editor (Stanley Gooch) of *Larks*, announcing the arrival of the pretty policewoman (No. 188). A comic heroine who was easy on the optics was a rarity in prewar comics, although Peggy's bossy boss, Commander Clara, more than made up for it with her lack of looks. Among Peggy's bag of arrests were Tiny the Ticker Taker, and Sam the Stickjaw Snatcher. Although Peggy was created by Reg Parlett, it was his brother George who brought her to full feminine fruition.

Peggie, Peter and Nunky Noah
George Jones
Fairyland Tales 1924-39 (Leng)
Peggie and Peter, the twins, and their uncle, Nunky Noah, were the stars of the longest-running comic strip in *Fairyland Tales*, the nursery weekly published prewar by John Leng. The threesome started their larks in No. 126 (31 May 1924) and continued to the final issue, No. 902 (25 November 1939). Never once in those sixteen years did the bearded old boy in the fancy smoking-cap and jacket learn his lesson: week after week those naughty kidlets caught him with their jolly japes. 'Ha-ha! Poor old Nunky!'

Penny Dreadful
Michael Green
Wow 1982-83 (IPC)
The colloquial name for Victorian story papers for children made a perfect one for this awful schoolgirl. Penny Dreadful made her debut in No. 1 of *Wow* (6 June 1982), her explosion of blonde curls doing little to conceal the spots on her face or on her character. No mere traditional comic tomboy she, Penny was all her name suggested. Rather than take a bath, she removed all traces of soap from home, filling duckponds with foam and cleaning up a policeman's beat: 'Argh! She's persilled our peepers!' When Dad lost his temper she told him to count to ten: he did – on her botty with his slipper!

Penny Wise
Norman Pett
Girl 1951-53 (Hulton)
'The Adventures of Penny Wise, Private Detective' began in No. 1 of *Girl* (2 November 1951). Mileson Horton's script was illustrated by Norman Pett, creator of Jane of the *Daily Mirror*. Teenage Penny, fresh out of school, talks her brother Bill, enquiry agent, into taking her on as his secretary. She soon proves her worth by calling the police to save him from capture by armed blackmailers. She guessed he was in trouble when his note to her was signed with his full name, William K. Wise.

Pest of the West
Leo Baxendale
Wham 1964-68 (Odhams)
Hank Coot was Sheriff of Powderkeg Gulch ('I've got a star pinned on my chest, 'cos I'm a lawman of the West! Yea-yea-yeah!') and his son was Sam, better known as the Pest of the West. This black-clad little gunslinger was known to hit a man at one yard – with his water-pistol, and this while aiming elsewhere at a bluebottle! When the Rattlesnake Kid came to town for a showdown at high noon, the Pest swung into action. Although he beat the Kid to the draw and thoroughly soaked his six-guns with well-aimed water, it was Pest who wound up behind bars.

Percy the Problem Child
Roy Wilson
Valiant 1962-64 (Fleetway)
This little lad with the big specs was unusual in that, instead of having adventures, he presented a page of pictorial puzzles which were arranged as a traditional strip. The reader was invited to pencil in answers to such posers as 'What instrument is this man playing (a) a bun (b) a bassoon (c) a harpoon?' and check them with the right answers which were 'spoken' upside-down at the end of the page. Each week a different character tried to beat Percy, beginning with Noel Knowall in *Valiant* No. 1 (6 October 1962).

Pete Madden
Roland Davies
Knockout 1961-63 (Amalgamated Press)
Ace detective Pete Madden and his young assistant Steve were modernized substitutes for Sexton Blake and Tinker, replacing the venerable pair in a two-page serial in *Knockout*. Much more the man of action ('Pete launched himself forward, his fist swinging in a jarring punch!'), Madden still favoured the dated turn of phrase ('What the deuce could he have been up to? Some devilish plan of the Otter's, I'm sure!') in 'River Raiders', but graduated to outer space in 'The Moon Rocket Mystery': 'I hope you can fly that heli-jet, Guv'nor!' He could, of course.

Percy's Pets
Illustrator unknown
Smash 1966-67 (Odhams)
Most readers of *Smash*, when very young, had rattles to play with, but not little Percy Potts. 'Surprise! Surprise! Me got a spider!' And from that fateful moment, little Percy's life was influenced by his animal friends. His pet parrot read him bedtime stories; when he was naughty Rover the dog fanned his red-hot rump with his tail; at school his adders helped him with his sums! Of all his thousand-and-one pets, on 5 February 1966, the day No. 1 of *Smash* came out, Percy chose to take his spiders for a walk. They went for a skate on Mr Webb's bald head.

Peter the Paleface Brave
Anton Lock
Bubbles 1925-41 (Amalgamated Press)
'In Red Eagle's Care' was the original title of this long-running serial, which took its young hero's name in 1936. As the standard synopsis put it, 'Peter, the lost son of a sailor, has been found by Chief Red Eagle and is brought up in the Indian camp. The Indians are proud of Peter's bravery and make him a brave.' So 'Petah', as the Chief's young daughter, Redflower, called him, became, if not the last of the Mohicans, then the first of the pink ones. The medicine man snorted 'Awaugh!'

P

Peter and Peggy in Jungle-Land

Walter Bell

Tiny Tots 1927-56 (Amalgamated Press)

Pe-ter and Peg-gy lived a hyphenated life in Jun-gle-land and *Tiny Tots*: thirty years without learning to read properly! Perhaps they were too busy having fun and games with the talking animals! There was Jumbo Jim, an elephant of course, Kenneth Kangaroo, Georgie Giraffe, Sammy Seal, Charlie Crocodile, Mickey Mouse, Willie Woodpecker, and lots more. And, once in a while, there were even one or two lady animals, like Lettie Lion and Rosie Rhino, who fought to be the jungle May Queen, 1930.

Peter Piper

Dudley Watkins

Magic 1939-40; *Sparky* 1965-77; *Topper* 1986 (D. C. Thomson)

'Picking People Out of Pickles' was Peter Piper's subtitle, and his way of doing this was explained by the rhyme at the top of his first appearance in *Magic* No. 1 (22 July 1939): 'Statues wake up at the toot – Of Peter Piper's magic flute!' Strolling through the park one Thursday, Peter is pounced on by a pair of bullies. Incensed at the unfairness of it all, the statue of Pan the Piper comes to life and presents Peter with his magic pipes. 'One blow and any statue will come to life!' Peter toots, Cupid lets fly with his arrows, and the bullies are routed.

Peter Pest

Tom Williams

Nutty 1980-85 (D. C. Thomson)

Romance seldom gets a look-in in British comics, especially those with titles like *Nutty*. Thus, teenaged Doris should have known better than to try to get a little going with a kid brother like Peter Pest hanging around. Boyfriends seldom lasted a week out, let alone a page, once Peter got busy. This curly headed kid had no other aim in life than to disrupt, destroy, and otherwise ruin his big sister's love life. And Catty the pet cat lent a paw, too.

Peter Pye

Dudley Watkins

Dandy 1942 (D. C. Thomson)

Peter, the ten-year-old son of a poor woodcutter, was the apple of Mrs Pye's eye. 'I'd like to be a cook, the finest in the world, and perhaps cook for the King one day', he told his mother on 7 February 1942, and sure enough, twenty issues of *Dandy* later, there was young Peter receiving his royal appointment as Chief Cook, direct from the hand of King Francis II. Mum's tuition had helped, but so had the magic utensils given to him by his pals, the jolly dwarfs of the forest.

Peter Quiz

Arthur Martin

Chips 1946-53 (Amalgamated Press)

'The Lad Who Wants to Know' arrived in *Chips* No. 2784, 25 May 1946, and was still asking questions in the last issue, No. 2997, 12 September 1953. Corny Chips, the editor, introduced him thus: 'Peter Quiz is quaint, queer, and full of questions. He wants to know things and the way he tries to find out will make you laugh until you bust the buttons off your waistcoats, or ladder the fronts of your jerseys!' Peter was also trailed in rhyme:

When first you gaze at his phiz,
You'll wonder whoever he is,
Though he's only quite small.
He wants to know all,
And that's why he's called Peter Quiz!

Pete's Pockets

Mike Lacey

Knockout 1971-73; *Whizzer & Chips* 1973-77 (IPC)

Pete's pockets perhaps owed their inspiration to the capacious coat of Harpo Marx. But whereas that screen comedian produced nothing more unlikely than a candle burning at both ends, Pete was able to produce an endless variety of objects – large and small. They usually took Pete by surprise, such as the time when a bully mocked his stamp collection and Pete's pockets produced a herd of mooing cows – the nearest they could get to a stamp was a stampede! When Pete had sore feet, his pockets produced powder, but of an increasingly wrong kind: itching, sneezing, and gun!

The Phantom Viking

Illustrator unknown

Champion 1966; *Lion* 1966-69 (Fleetway)

'Introducing the Meek Schoolmaster with the Mysterious Power!'; Olaf Larsen, bespectacled weakling, was taken to task by Mr Grimsole, headmaster of Woodburn School, for his lack of control over the boys. Wandering homeward past an old Viking burial ground, Olaf chances on a helmet bearing the legend: 'Only Larsen the Liberator and his descendants shall have the power of this helmet, the secret of great strength and flight.' Trying it on, Olaf leaps to the top of the school clocktower, vowing to destroy evil wherever it may be found.

Pete's Pocket Army

Illustrator unknown

Buster 1973-78 (IPC)

Six tiny aliens, Litluns from the planet Liturnus, are stranded on Earth when their star-ship crashes near the town of Whitford. Commander Kon-dar and his crew, Dokk, Grunf, Moonie, Tigg, and Zapp, adopt freckled, bespectacled Peter Parker, who soon shares his secret with his mischievous cousin, Julie. Using their Liturnian power-tools, the Litluns fit an atomic battery into one of Pete's toy cars, and help Peter become a star footballer against his will. Trouble came when the Litluns were determined to celebrate their Festival of Frenzybane.

Phantom Force 5

Illustrator unknown

Buster 1960-62 (Fleetway)

'During World War II', whenever a task arose so danger-packed and perilous that it was called impossible, they sent for Phantom Force 5.' Captain Clive Carter was in command, with Lieutenant Dicky Bird as pilot, Sergeant Chalky White, explosives, Sergeant Mick Morgan, boats, and Corporal Smiler Gray, radio. They set off on their first mission in *Buster* No. 1 (28 May 1960): to land their Lancaster in Germany, pick up the world's biggest bomb, and drop it on a vital target. 'Sacré bleu! Les Boches!' or, as Chalky White put it, 'Swipe me! The Jerries!'

Phil the Fluter

Illustrator unknown

Thunder 1970-71; *Lion* 1971-72 (IPC)

Inspired by the old Irish song. *Phil the Fluter's Ball*, Phil Taylor certainly had a ball with the magic flute he found in No. 1 of *Thunder* (17 October 1970). On his way home from Claythorpe village school, a storm broke out and the old abbey ruins were struck by lightning. Investigating, Phil found only an old tin-whistle. Tootling his flute – 'Pleee-eeep! Wheeeeh!' – as he strolled through the high street, Phil was startled to see everyone and everything freeze like stone statues. Obviously the flute was magic!

The Pickles of Pepper Street

Moira & Colin McLean

Pepper Street 1985- (D. C. Thomson)

The Pickles family – Mum, Dad, Sally, Colin, and their dog Tuppence – moved into Pepper Street on 12 January 1985, in No. 1 of the comic called *Pepper Street*. Subtitled 'The Read-with-Mum Weekly', this nursery comic was constructed around a community, taking in Pepper Street School with Mr Trimble the Lollipop Man, Pepper Street Zoo with Bimbo the Bear, Mrs Blink's Bakery, the weekly visit of the Playbus, and the Old Oak Tree where Sammy Spider lived above, and Wiggles the Worm down below.

Ping the Elastic Man

Hugh McNeill

Beano 1938-40 (D. C. Thomson)

'Here Comes Ping the Elastic Man' was the full title of this strip which began in No. 1 of *Beano*, 30 July 1938. 'There's nobody like me – I'm the only elastic man in the world!' boasted Ping. The ensuing action was described thus by the *Beano* versifier: 'The crowd tied poor Ping in a knot – To prove he wasn't talking rot!' Ping's unique twangability enabled him to tie his legs around a bucking bronco and win first prize at a rodeo, squash inside a tortoise's shell to keep dry in the rain, and stretch his arms long enough to replace a broken tightrope!

The Piggywigs

Bertie Brown

Tiny Tots 1927-57 (Amalgamated Press)

Bertie Brown seems to have been fond of pork: he ran 'Piggy and Wiggy' in *Bubbles* from 1921, and drew the entire thirty-one-year career of 'The Piggywigs' in *Tiny Tots*. The only visible difference between these chubby brothers and their predecessors was their names: Piggy and Porky (and their hyphens – *Tiny Tots* was a comic for beginning readers). The Piggywigs lived, not as you might suppose with Mummy and Daddy, but with Uncle and Auntie. Perhaps this was because Uncle Jack the editor considered mothers and fathers not suitable persons upon whom to work japes.

Pinhead and Pete

Bertie Brown

Comic Cuts 1940-51 (Amalgamated Press)

Introduced by Clarence Cuts the editor as 'The screamingly funny adventures of a prize pair of fun-makers, and the lively larks and comical capers of these two crazy comics will make you roar with laughter!', Pinhead and Pete appeared as back-page stars of *Comic Cuts* from No. 2623 (24 August 1940). Pinhead, described as 'the good-looking goof' and his pal Pete, described as 'the diminutive darkie', were room-mates and rivals for the hand of pretty Pamela. After a scrimmage with a cement spreader, Pete won the day: 'How about a stroll round de park, Missy?' Innocent days!

Pike Mason

Illustrator unknown

Boys World 1963-64 (Longacre)

Leading man of the new comic *Boys World* (26 January 1963) was Pike Mason, introduced at length by the editor. 'Pike is a man worth knowing, especially if you ever need someone at your side in a tight corner. His full name is Robert Wentworth Mason, and he acquired his nickname when he landed a 32-pound pike from Hornsey Mere when he was nine. Before his eighteenth birthday, he had been three times round the world. He hates soft beds, stuffy offices, and pompous people,' Pike's first serial, 'The Sea Ape', took his motor cruiser, *Sabre*, to Sumatra.

Pinkie and Patsy

Herbert Foxwell

Tiger Tim's Tales 1919; *Tiger Tim's Weekly* 1920-38 (Amalgamated Press)

'Pinkie and Patsy of Pat-a-Cake Palace' were a royal pair, but that didn't seem to stop them acting just like any other young readers of comics: playing practical jokes on their elders. The Queen, known as 'Ma', was nice enough to be an exception, but the King, known as 'Pa', was plump enough to deserve any prank. It was inevitable that a cork which had been stuck down the herald's royal trumpet should pop the King on the royal conk! Pinkie and Patsy's pet was a blackbird in a crown (evidently leaving only twenty-three for the royal pie!).

P

Pinkie Puff
P. & R.
Bobo Bunny 1969-73; *Hey Diddle Diddle* 1973; *Playhour* 1973-85 (IPC)
Biled as 'The Little Elephant with the Long Trunk', this cute character was a pink elephant, but obviously far from the usual run of such creatures. Just as Disney's Dumbo had oversize ears, so Pinkie Puff had trouble with his tremendous trunk. Usually he kept it neatly rolled like a hosepipe, but once a week he would find just cause to unroll it to lend a helping hand. Such as when Firemen Ned and Nod broke their ladder and couldn't rescue a kitten, Pinkie unfurled his trunk and won a friend for life called Purr.

Pitch and Toss/Chish and Fips
Joe Hardman
Comic Life 1920; *Funny Wonder* 1922-44; *Big One* 1964-65 (Fleetway)
'Our Saucy Shipwrecked Sailors' sailed into the centre spread of *Comic Life* on 3 April 1920, but it was not until they shipped aboard *Funny Wonder* on 22 October 1922 that their classic combination of thin (Pitch) and fat (Toss) really caught on, thanks to a change of cartoonist. Roy Wilson remade them into 'Our Merry Mariners', signing them on *The Saucy Sal* to make things decidedly unshipshape for Cap'n Codseye. They moved to page one in 1932, where they stayed for twelve years, adding to their popularity with pets Pengy the Penguin (1936) and Occy the Octopus (1937). Reprinted 20 years later as Chish and Fips.

Pip the Penguin
Bill Ritchie
Bimbo 1961-72; *Little Star* 1972-76 (D. C. Thomson)
Pip the Penguin made his debut in No. 2 of *Bimbo* (25 March 1961) and stayed in Snowland right to the last issue of *Little Star* (24 January 1976). Pip was *Little Star*'s mascot: he was depicted on the Grand Free Gift in No. 1, a balloon toy called the Pip-Squeaker, and also was given away in the guise of a glove puppet in No. 60 (17 March 1973). Pip was only a little penguin, but at least he was black and shiny, unlike his younger brother, Squeak, who was still a fluffy yellow chick. Pip's pals included Sammy Seal, Peter Polar Bear, and Koko the Eskimo.

Plug
David Gudgeon
Plug 1977-79 (D. C. Thomson)
Percival Proudfoot Plugsley, Plug for short, is the all-ears-and-teeth member of The Bash Street Kids. But his popularity as 'World Champion Sporting Supergoon' was such that he soloed into his own full-colour comic, called *Plug*, of course, from 24 September 1977. 'Greetings to all Funpersons!' was his welcome, 'You are now entering the Plug-age! It's Plugnacious! It's Trendifferous! Everybody switch to *Plug*!' But the sporting accent of the comic proved too much to take and, after seventy-five weeks, it merged with *Beezer*.

Plum and Duff
Albert Pease
Comic Cuts 1926-53 (Amalgamated Press)
'The Boys of the Bold Brigade', Plum (the dark one) and Duff (the fair one) signed on for the duration plus when they joined *Comic Cuts*: they were still the bright-eyed, buttoned-up bane of beefy Sergeant Suet and blustery Colonel Bogey when the comic capitulated twenty-eight years later, on 5 September 1953. A monocled Captain Cackle was also involved and, during World War 2, a certain A. Hitler and B. Mussolini: the lads had a plum job duffing them up! Their comic career was topped and tailed by 'Charlie' Pease, but their promotion to page one (1930) was via Roy Wilson (illustrated).

Plunk
John Mortimer
Buster 1965-67 (Fleetway)
'Our Monster Mirth-Maker!' was a nice, gentle dinosaur named Plunk, but the Ancient Brit-Nits seemed not to realize it. In fact, King Brit-Nit spent a page a week of *Buster* doing his darndest best to get rid of the poor thing. Perhaps it was because Plunk had a propensity for treading on him and denting his crown. The King imported an Ancient Chink from Ancient China, along with a pet dragon. The dragon breathed fire, Plunk squirted water, and the Brit-Nits got parboiled for their pains.

Pongo Snodgrass
Ian Knox
Krazy 1976-78; *Whizzer & Chips* 1978 (IPC)
Pongo was originally the sworn enemy of The Krazy Gang, but grew so curiously strong with readers that, on 4 December 1976, he started his own rival gang: Jim the stable lad, Fishface the fishmonger's assistant, Rumbletum Tom the human dustbin, famed for his oniony breath. They called themselves The Stinkers and, of course, Pongo was boss as he was the biggest stinker of the lot! Their first adventure was called 'Kicking Up a Stink': 'Hum! Pong! Niff!' On 9 April 1977 Pongo produced a double-page muck-spread entitled 'Pongalongapongo', complete with 'Niff of the Week' and 'Fun with Old Socks'.

Plum MacDuff
Bill Holroyd
Dandy 1948-52 (D. C. Thomson)
'Plum MacDuff – the Highlandman who Never Gets Enough' arrived in *Dandy* on 9 October 1948. As Hungry Horace, who had been feeding his face in the same comic for 380 issues already, had recently expanded from six pictures to nine, you might think *Dandy* readers would have suffered from a surfeit of stuffing. Obviously the editor thought otherwise; perhaps the continuance of wartime food rationing had something to do with it. At any rate MacDuff laid on feeds and laughs aplenty.

Podge
Eric Roberts
Dandy 1937-45 (D. C. Thomson)
Podge was a pioneer among comic heroes, an 'ordinary boy', if a trifle overweight, living in a standard lower-middle-class suburban environment, with a Mum to feed him and a Dad to spank him when he came home from work. Created by a former joke-cartoonist, the later episodes of Podge's 290 appearances were drawn by Walter Brown. When Roberts returned from the war, he created a new character called Smudge, a feminized Podge.

Pop, Dick and Harry
Carmichael
Beezer 1956- (D. C. Thomson)
'Laughs with a Dad and his Tricky twins' was the billing for this family of funsters who began in *Beezer* No. 1 (21 January 1956). Their slapstick antics were so popular that they soon shifted Ginger from his full-colour front, only to move house to the back page after some years. All three sported similar hairstyles, Dick's being the only variant: yellow. The family pets were Darkie the cat and Towser, a spotty dog. Mum's appearances were limited to the occasional photo on the piano.

P

Popeye
Elzie Crisler Segar
Jolly Comic 1937; *Film Fun* 1959; *TV Comic* 1961-84 (King Features)
Popeye the Sailor Man (motto: 'I yan what I yam!') made his American debut in *Thimble Theatre* on 17 January 1929, and is still going strong, thanks to spinach. He took over the strip from hero, Castor Oyl, and set sail on an unending saga with sweetie Olive Oyl, moocher J. Wellington Wimpy, and 'adoptid boykid' Swee'pea. The strips were reprinted in *Jolly* from 1937, but the twenty-four-year run in *TV Comic* were British originals, drawn by Chick Henderson, Neville Main, and Bill Mevin (illustrated).

Portland Bill/Butterfly Bill
G. M. Payne
Butterfly 1907-26 (Amalgamated Press)
'The Champion Smile Raiser and Laughter Merchant' was the front-page star of *Butterfly* for twenty years, although he reformed and changed his name in mid-career. Beginning as an ex-convict in search of employment, from 1917 he was known as 'Butterfly Bill', cheery victim of some early clean-up-the-comics campaign. Bill responded to any kind of job, such as the 1910 notice in Periwinkle Park: 'Wanted, a young man fond of children, kind to sparrows, ten bob a week and as much grass as he can eat!' Barrow-boy, busker, or sandwich-man, Bill's last-panel success never lasted more than a week.

Popgun Pete
John Jukes
Jester 1939-40; *Funny Wonder* 1940-46 (Amalgamated Press)
'Popgun Pete, the Back-Alley Cowboy', cantered into the centre spread of *Jester* No. 1984 (18 November 1939). A cowboy-crazy kid in cricket-pads for chaps, he soon got into trouble when he popped his corks at Mrs Bagwash. However, a bang-up spot of shootery saved the day when a well-placed cork caused a pawnbroker's brass ball to bounce off Bill Bashem's bonce and save P.C. Jellyknees from a nasty knock. 'Good old Popgun!' cheered the kids. 'Don't mench!' parped Pete, popular enough to transfer to *Funny Wonder* when *Jester* popped off.

Pop and Mick
Roy Wilson
Jester 1931-32 (Amalgamated Press)
'Pop and Mick the Monkey Knuts' – not just plain nuts, but knuts, please note – were a pair of chatty chimps that arrived in the Grand Whitsun Holiday Number of *Jester*, 30 May 1931. Talking animals were a rarity in English comics of the slapstick kind, especially when drawn by a master. In the opening epic, Ma Monk tells pipe-puffing Pop to amuse their offspring. He sets up a game of leapfrog, an odd pastime for monkeys. It gets even odder when Eddie Elephant joins in: 'Never had the old dad been so downtrodden!'

Pot and Pan Tales
Philip Swinnerton
Chicks Own 1920-56 (Amalgamated Press)
This long-running strip for the tinies went through several changes of title in its thirty-seven-year lifetime. It started as 'Tales of Billy Pot and Percy Pan' in No. 1 of *Chicks Own*, 25 September 1920 (Jimmy Jug pours water on a flaming match), then expanded from three pictures to the full-page 'Pot and Pan Tales' in 1937, and in 1950 was taken over by a shaggy dog and called 'Rags and His Friends'. By this time, the animated kitchen folk included Bertie Broom, Vernon Vase, Reggie Rake, Charlie Coffee-pot, Ken Knife, and Sammy Saucepan.

Pot T. Pot and Piecan
Louis Diamond
Golden Penny 1927-28 (Fleetway)
The unlikeliest character for a comic: an escaped lunatic! Pot T. Pot and his Pet Patient Piecan were the front-page stars of *The Golden Penny Comic*, and may well have contributed to its decline. Each week Piecan ('our puddin' head') broke out of the asylum, wreaked a little havoc, and was duly nabbed by his keeper, Pot T. Pot, and locked up in his cell in time for the final picture. Typical was the time he sold boot blacking as beauty cream and was battered about by brollies. 'The director of dithering doughnuts directed his darling in the direction of the daft'uns dump!'

Prince
Sep E. Scott
Playhour 1954-55 (Amalgamated Press)
Prince, 'The Wonder Dog of the Golden West', was the front-and-back-page star of *Playhour Pictures* No. 1 (16 October 1954). Illustrated in seven large, hand-painted, full-colour pictures by the famous artist, Sep E. Scott, the series, all too soon to be relegated to interior monochrome and another hand, was a landmark in high-class comic art. Prince was the pet of Texas Jack, 'the famous Wild West scout', who rode the prairies on the faithful Duke. Their first adventure was to save White Moon, an Indian girl, from a cliff.

Powerman
Dennis M. Reader
Super Duper 1946-49 (Cartoon Art)
'Our story opens on Christmas Eve in a city in Illinois, the apartment of Kerry Lattimer, Britisher and crime reporter.' This determined attempt to produce an American-style superhero opened with a mysterious stranger giving Kerry 'a seasonal present from the mists of time' – a copy of Dickens' *Christmas Carol* from which emerged the Ghost of Christmas Yet to Come. 'On Christmas Day you will become a crime fighting force endowed with super human gifts! Fight evil and injustice! Use this strength to bring about good in this upset world!' And Kerry turned into Powerman!

Prince Whoopee
Charles Grigg
Beano 1955-58 (D. C. Thomson)
Billed as 'Your Pal from the Palace', Prince Whoopee gave *Beano* readers a right royal time from No. 680 (23 July 1955). So much so that his original half page was expanded to a full page in 1957. Young Whoopee was the son of a fiercely whiskered King, heir to a kingdom that mixed the medieval with modern times. Lacking the requisite penny to play an arcade football game, Whoopee ordered two aircraft carriers to steam side by side so their flight decks formed a super-size football pitch.

Professor Crazy Klew

Illustrator unknown

Merry Moments 1919-22 (Newnes)

'The Adventures of the Happy Twins and Professor Crazy Klew the Dud Detective' was the full-colour front page of *Merry Moments* No. 1 (12 April 1919). Cyril and Gladys were the Happy Twins, a mischievous pair who spent their weeks playing pranks on the curious Klew, who was forever on the trail of crime equipped with cloak, spy-glass, and top hat crowned with a talking canary. In 1922 the strip suffered a switch to nursery readership: the Prof lost his detecting licence and was saddled with a crowd of talking animals including Sammy Seal, Ken Kangaroo, and Tommy Tusker the elephant.

Professor Peek and Phuzzy!

Harry Banger

Topical Funnies 1940; *Slick Fun* 1940-45; *New Funnies* 1941; *War Comics* 1941; *Fresh Fun* 1941; *Comicolour* 1947; *Cute Fun* 1948 (Swan)

'Exploring with Professor Peek and Phuzzy' began in *Topical Funnies* No. 1 (April 1940), but soon moved to *Slick Fun* No. 3, settling down for a long run usually from the assorted wild animiles and fierce fellows who inhabited Bungholand and environs ('Keep on de path'). The Prof, benign and bespectacled, was almost as rotund as Phuzzy, a pint-size pygmy who showed faint respect for his fat baas: 'Yo' shuah makes me laugh, Massa!' When asked to find a big native rising, Phuzzy found one – yawning as he rose from his hammock!

Professor Jolly and his Magic Brolly

H. E. Pease

Chips 1940-44 (Amalgamated Press)

'He's a Regular Champ with his Magic Gamp!' This little stalwart of the Conjurer's Club had only to tap with the tip of his gilly-gilly gamp to cause any everyday object to enlarge or reduce, according to whim. This led to much mirth for all, save his victims: a crib-cracker trapped in wax from an outsize candle, a pop-snaffler swallowed by a gigantic glass, a ratty park-keeper stumped by a whacking great cricket wicket, and Walter Wobble the Waiter dished by serving a posh diner shrunken soss-and-mash!

Professor Radium

Tom Wilkinson

Puck 1904-16 (Amalgamated Press)

'Professor Radium the Scientific Man' was the two-colour star of the back page of *Puck*, but more than once he strayed to the full-colour front, such was his popularity. His inventions were legion during his thirteen-year career: an unlucky number, perhaps, for most of them ended in explosions! Some were simple, like the skates for Pluto his pet donkey; others advanced, like his Actinic Polarised Concordescent Spectacles for reading minds. He tried them on his cook: 'Old Radium ought to be in some 'ome for the 'opeless mad, he isn't fit loose!'

Professor Noodle's Natty Notions

Don Newhouse

Funny Wonder 1940-43 (Amalgamated Press)

'Proffessor' (his title was misspelled for the first two weeks!) Noodle was the epitome of all comic-strip inventors, a barmy old brainbox whose wacky wheezes invariably brought high-explosive disaster upon his skull-capped bean. His premier patent (22 June 1940) was an egg-beater ('anything from an ant's egg to an ostrich's'), his final fling (Christmas Day 1943) a snow-jeep. Between, he did his best for the war effort with such foredoomed failures as his Patent Gun that Shoots Backwards at any Enemy Creeping up Behind, and his Patent Tune-playing Siren for Cheering Up Air Raids.

Professor Switch and Zipp

Arthur Martin

Jolly 1936-38 (Amalgamated Press)

Introduced on 24 October 1936 as 'our prize professor', Prof. Switch, a whiskery old whizbang, had an unusual pet of his own design: a wireless watchdog called Zipp. This tin-can canine, operated via an aerial atop the professor's tall topper, said 'whir-r-r!' rather than 'woof!' When accidentally dognapped by Oscar the Old Iron Man, Zipp sent out a wireless warble for S.O.S.-istance. Tuned in to sing, Zipp so huffed Colonel Custard that the old buffer boomed him with his blunderbuss. Zipp, black in the face, promptly changed his tune to 'Swanee Ribber'.

Puck, Pot and Pan
Joe Hardman
Puck 1920-36 (Amalgamated Press)
Three little characters whose pranks filled three little pictures in *Puck*. They stayed for sixteen years, so their small-time escapades must have pleased the younger readers of that coloured comic. Exactly what breed of fairy folk they were was never quite clear: pixies, elves, gnomes, dwarfs, they were tiny enough to use toadstools as handy umbrellas. Their later adventures, lengthened by one picture, bore the title 'Fun in the Forest with Puck, Pot and Pan', and were narrated in verse.

Pup Parade
Gordon Bell
Beano 1967- (D. C. Thomson)
Also known as the Bash Street Dogs, the Pup Parade bounded into *Beano* No. 1326. A gang of outcast hounds living in a dustbin outside Bash Street School, home of the famous Bash Street Kids, their leader is Bones, a black pup branded with a skull and crossbones and wearing a Bash Street School cap: bashed-up, of course. Den mother is the only bitch in the bunch, Peeps. Rest of the Parade: Sniffy, 'Enry, Tubby, Wiggy, Manfrid, Blotty (he's spotty), and Pug, a buck-toothed, canine equivalent of Bash Street's Plug.

Puss and Boots
John Geering
Sparky 1969-77; *Topper* 1977-79 (D. C. Thomson)
'They Fight like Cat and Dog!' was the apt caption for this pair; Puss was a black tomcat, and Boots a typical tripehound. They had other names for each other, like 'puddin' headed pooch' and 'that half-baked welly-boot!' Forever feuding ('Now for my super-super-never-get-up-from-this-one-karate-chop!') and fighting ('Have a taste of my super-Boots-is-it-a-bird-no-it's-a-moggie-knuckle-bruiser!'), their madcap mayhem promoted them from the full-colour back page to the entire full-colour centre spread of *Sparky*.

Punch and Jimmy
David Jenner
Beano 1962-67 (D. C. Thomson)
This quarrelsome couple bashed their way into *Beano* No. 1046. A battling pair of twin brothers, Punch was the one in the black pullover and red shorts, Jimmy the one in the red pullover and black shorts. 'Will I ever find a way to stop them fighting?' mused their Mum in panel one. She never did, of course: the boys averaged three scrimmages a page for the next six years! As if there was not enough mayhem among the humans, a pet mouse and cat echoed the carnage in the corners.

Pyjama Percy and Balmy Bill
Pip Martin
Comic Life 1908-16 (Henderson)
Percival and William were a pair of seaside entertainers by trade, which made them even more hard-up than usual during the winter. When singing on the sands, they were assisted by Smoky the Moke, but were on their own when busking with a barrel-organ in the gutters of London. Their brains were a little dim: helping a professor of entymology, they used his butterfly net and killing bottle to capture a pretty damsel. He'd asked them to catch a 'painted lady', you see. When the old boy called for the cops, Percy and Bill hopped it, crying 'There's ungratefulosity!'

P

Q-Bikes/Q-Karts

Sandy Calder

Beano 1963-71; *Buddy* 1981-82 (D. C. Thomson)

A junior, two-wheeled version of the popular televison series, 'Z-Cars', Q-Bikes raced into the red-and-black pages of *Beano* No. 1072. The regular heading read: 'Six expert young cyclists with radio bikes have formed themselves into a Flying Squad to help anyone in trouble.' The leader was Johnny Masters, known as Q1; the others were Billy Brown (Q2), Alfie Thomas (Q3), Tom Steptoe (Q4), Judy Baxter (Q5), and Buzz Taylor (Q6). In 1970 they went to Australia and became the Q-Karts.

Queen of the Seas

Ken Reid

Smash 1966-67 (Odhams)

The *Buoyant Queen*, known colloquially as 'the heap', was owned by Captain Enoch Drip who, with his one-man crew, Bertram Bloop, ran her as a ship-of-all-trades. 'Strewf! One more mouthful o' cockles an' cocoa an' I'll go right rahnd the perishin' bend, mate!' quoth the cap'n as he read his *Maritime Monthly*. But, as the sun sank low over Sludgewater-on-Sea, the old heap nosed her way from the jetty on the start of her 450-mile voyage to Cape Clam (at 1½ knots), seeking a sunken Spanish treasure ship as pinpointed by Prof Herman von Schnoogle, 'renowned harkyhologist'.

Quackie the Duck

Albert Pease

Tiny Tots 1927-56 (Amalgamated Press)

Quackie was really no more a duck than his inseparable chum Egbert was a chicken. They were duckling and chick, a fluffy pair of barnyard buddies who spent their few pictures a week in getting up to mischief in *Tiny Tots*. This hyphenated comic for young readers spelled their names Quack-ie and Eg-bert, and so the parental butt of most of their little jokes was known as Dad-dy Duck. Mum-my Duck seemed permanently absent, as did Dad-dy or Mum-my Chick-en, something which never seemed to worry Uncle Jack the editor. Later artists included Fred Robinson (illustrated).

Quick Nick

Jack Glass

Dandy 1958 (D. C. Thomson)

Back in London, 1758, Mr Morrow bound his young son, Nick, apprentice to a blind locksmith called Tappity John. For two years Nick learned his trade, sleeping under his bench by night. When John, who was Captain of the Watch, chained Nick to his bench to stop him attending a secret meeting of the oppressed apprentices, Nick made a key and escaped. His quick fingers saved the apprentices from capture by the Watch, and he was back home, chained to his bench again, when John returned. No wonder he was called the 'Lightning Lock-picker of London'!

Raggy Muffin

James Crichton

Dandy 1948-50 (D. C. Thomson)

The first four-legged friend to be billed as 'The Dandy Dog' (the second such was Black Bob), Raggy Muffin wagged his way into the *Dandy* on 11 September 1948, heralded with the traditional editorial verse: 'Raggy is a warrior – Raggy is a toff – Raggy's tricks will make you – Laugh your head right off!' Raggy, 'a towsy little wandering dog', chased a rabbit through a magic stream and came out the other side walking on his hind legs and talking like a boy! A comic-strip mystery solved!

Raven on the Wing

Illustrator unknown

Valiant 1968-72 (Fleetway)

Highboro United, a First-Division team, had lost their seventh match in a row, to the despair of new manager Baldy Hagan. Then the chairman of the board, Sir Mortimer Child-Beale, sent him to sort out a gypsy tribe camping on Noakes Heath, the team's training ground. There Baldy saw a barefooted boy scoring goal after goal, to the wrath of his mates: 'My father says he's wafferdy – evil!' Baldy saved the boy from his bullying Uncle Joe and gave him a trial in a third-team game. 'Swipe me, if it ain't a bare-footed wonder!' they sneered, but the Lengro lad was soon a brilliant left-winger.

Red Devil Dean

Desmond Walduck

Junior Express 1955-56 (Beaverbrook)

Red Devil Dean was a carrot-topped ex-commando specially designed to exploit the two-tone red-and-black printing of *Junior Express*. Set in the Sahara during an Arab uprising, Red and his partner Jerry, who wore spectacles and a small moustache, go to Tamanrasset with attractive Sally Reid, who is looking for her missing father. Soon Sally disappears too, and the adventurers discover that Monsieur Costa, chief of the Special Force, is the traitor behind the troubles. As Red is wont to remark, 'By Crippen!'

Rat Pack

Illustrator unknown

Battle 1975-76 (IPC)

In the Maximum Security Wing of Wessex Military Prison, 1941, were four dangerous men: No. 37021 Kabul Hasan of the Cyprus Rifles, known as the Turk; No. 37194 Ronald Weasel of the Kent Infantry, expert safebreaker; No. 36616 Ian 'Scarface' Rogan, Highland Infantry, athlete and deserter; No. 34024 Matthew Dancer, Commando, marksman with the knife. One night they break jail with the assistance of a man called Taggart. He is Major Taggart, and the breakout was a test. 'You men are rats, nasty crooked rats! But rats with special skills the Army needs.' They become convict commandos; first job – Operation Big Karl.

The Red Lion Scouts

H. O'Neill

Comic Life 1910-20 (Henderson)

The boys of the Red Lion Patrol took over the front page of *Comic Life* from an earlier outfit called 'The Scouts of the Wild Cat Patrol'. Tom the Tracker and his pals only lasted a year (1909) before Punch Baker and his chums (Curly, Rubberneck, Specs, and Bristles) came on the scene and stayed for ten. They were named for their publisher, James Henderson, who produced his comics in Red Lion House, Red Lion Square. The Scouts' great days were during the 1914-18 war, when scarcely a week went by without the capture of a Teuton or two. By disguising a squirrel-cage as an 'underseasboat', they soaked some escaping Hunnies.

Red Ray
Roland Davies
TV Comic 1954-56 (News of the World)
'The Adventures of Red Ray, Space Raynger, with Philip and Anne' began on 16 October 1954 in No. 154 of *TV Comic*. Visiting Earth from the planet Tevada, Red Ray takes two young children, Philip and Anne, for an adventurous voyage in space. They meet Rosva and Destin from Tevada, and see Venusians taking off in their Flying Saucers. Back on Earth, Red Ray helps them rescue Prince Gay from kidnappers. From 22 October 1955 readers could join the Red Ray Space Rayngers, with badge, Space Passport, and Magic Space Pencils, all for 1s.6d.

Reggie and Roger
Alexander Akerbladh
Larks 1927-38 (Amalgamated Press)
'The Rollicking Rambles of Reggie and Roger' set sail on the back page of *Larks* No. 1 (29 October 1927), described thus: 'Yo-ho! Heave-ho! Tally-ho! Float up, lads, and meet our jolly sailors. That's Reggie, the captain, with the "pane" (i.e. monocle) in his eye!' Roger was the entire crew, equipped with toothbrush, brolly, and anchor, all tucked in his seabag. The strip was a twelve-picture comedy serial, landing the merry mariners in France. ('Pay ze bill or go to ze clink!'), the province of Pye Khan the Posh Pasha of Plonk, and elsewhere on Earth.

Red Rory of the Eagles
Paddy Brennan
Beano 1952-62 (D. C. Thomson)
One day in 1746 (or 7 June 1952, if you happened to be a reader of *Beano* No. 516), a red-headed Highland lad in a Macpherson kilt watched a column of Redcoats marching thro' the glen. This was Red Rory of the Eagles, so called for his pets, Flame and Fury, the golden eagles he had trained to do his bidding. Within a picture or two, the boy and his birds were helping an outlaw chieftain, Callum the Piper, and Black Angus on the way to Tobermory, France, and freedom.

Rent-a-Ghost Ltd
Reg Parlett
Buster 1969-78 (Fleetway)
Horrible haunts for all occasions were supplied for hire at reasonable rates by Rent-a-Ghost Ltd. A simple 'phonecall, and the head of this unlikely agency (it was, of course, tucked underneath his arm!) despatched a suitable spook by return. The Laird of Loch Lummy, plagued by salmon poachers, got the ghost of Old McDuff – but the spivs let fly with their shotguns and McDuff got a punctured sporran! An unimpressed audience watching 'The Thing from the Gasworks' was chilled when a rent-a-vampire shot ice lollies down their necks!

Red Star Robinson
Escandell
Hotspur 1969-73 (D. C. Thomson)
'The Ace Crime-fighter with the Red Star Trademark' was actually seventeen-year-old Tom Robinson. He had thwarted a bank raid in Brickfield and thus attracted the attention of a mysterious crime-fighter called The Watcher. This mystery man had developed amazing electronic equipment and techniques, including a gun which could show up criminals by marking them with a red star. This he gave to Tom, who soon donned a tight-fitting uniform which was also emblazoned with the red star on front and back. Tom was assisted by Mr Syrius Thrice, a bowler-hatted robot.

Rex Keene
Harry Bishop
Express 1956-57 (Beaverbrook)
Rex Keene, Texas Ranger, was the first front-page hero of the newly revamped *Junior Express Weekly*, which blazed into full-colour photogravure from No. 74 (18 February 1956) as *Express Super Colour Weekly*. Rex was the son of Jeremy Keene, a settler from England who had built up a cattle ranch in Sunset Valley, Texas. When the Commanche Indians, led by a notorious outlaw called the Raven, destroy the Keene homestead, only Rex is left alive. On his noble steed Stryder, Rex sets out to avenge his parents and become a Texas Ranger.

Richard Lion
Maria Jocz
Robin 1953-67 (Hulton)
Richard Lion, no relation to but obviously inspired by Richard Lyon, the radio-star son of Bebe Daniels and Ben Lyon, was the cute little cub in red school-cap and shirt who starred on the full-colour back page of *Robin* from No. 1 (28 March 1953). The caption which originally introduced him read: 'Richard Lion lives with his mother and father in a pretty thatched cottage in the village. The village is called Gay and everyone is happy.' Mrs Lion wore a pretty pink mob-cap about the house, while his Daddy was a doctor. A magic fish that tastes of ice cream, chocolate, and fruit drops whisks him off on his first wonderful adventure.

Rick Random
Ron Turner
Super Detective Library 1954-61; *2000 AD* 1978 (IPC)
The First Detective of the Space Age and Head of the Interplanetary Bureau of Investigation (I.B.I.), Rick Random solved his first space case in the pocket-sized *Super Detective Library* No 37, *Crime Rides the Spaceways*. For the next eight years he circumnavigated the universe in pursuit of such intergalactic criminals as John Jolson, who used a matter transmitter on Venus to heist gold bullion from the Interplanetery Bank in London (*The Frozen World*). Fair-haired Rick was seldom seen without a cigarette or the attractive Detective Superintendent Andi Andrews.

Rip Van Wink
Eric Roberts
Beano 1938-48 (D. C. Thomson)
'Poor Rip Van Wink is all at sea – There's something wrong, he fears – He doesn't know he's been asleep for Seven Hundred Years!' This bald, bearded, big-eared old boy went to sleep on 24 July 1238 and woke up on 30 July 1938, to find himself on page 20 of *Beano* No. 1! He promptly shot a hiker with his bow and arrow, mistaking him for a deer, and ate a banana with the skin on. Finding a tin of corned beef tough on his teeth, Rip put it on the fire to cook. The explosion shot him back to the safety of his cave: 'Zounds!'

Richie Wraggs
Mike Lacey
Jackpot 1979-81 (IPC)
The first front-page funster of *Jackpot* arrived with many an 'Aar!' on 5 May 1979. A country bumpkin complete with haystack and a straw tucked between his two buck teeth, Richie Wraggs was a much-patched pupil of the village school in Little Drudgebury. But his schooling lasted no more than six pictures before he was expelled for eating pongy cheese in class. 'From now on it's Wraggs to riches!' he cried as he hit the road in traditional Dick Whittington fashion, accompanied by Lucky, his fat black cat.

Rip Van Tinkle
Illustrator unknown
Cracker 1975-76 (D. C. Thomson)
This noble knight of yore did his best at deeds of derring-do in the up-to-date world of Crackertown. When he tried to hire a squire, characters from *Cracker* applied for the job, but Little 'Orror was put off by the thought of helping do good deeds, and Hector the Collector promptly added Rip's armour to his collection. Rip's mount, which he insisted on calling his Trusty Steed, was an Iron Horse with such useful appurtenances as an extendable neck – handy for winning races.

Rip and Van Winkle
Wally Robertson
Jester 1922-26 (Amalgamated Press)
'Our Double Dutch Chums' arrived in *Jester* on 2 December 1922, and were introduced thus: 'Welcome to our little Dutch doughboy Rip, and his portly pa, Van Winkle.' Another of the one-parent families so popular in prewar comics, these two had a distinct advantage in the smile stakes – they spoke with a funny accent. Told by Van not to let his liddle brudder's hands get into der mischief, Rip said: 'Joost plump doze paws on dis!', giving the baby a flypaper to play with! 'Gootness!' cried pa, reaching for a handy clog.

Robbie of Red Hall
Roy Newby
Girl 1952-56 (Hulton)
Robbie MacFyle, an orphaned Scots girl, found herself the mistress of the neglected Fyle estate. She soon chummed up with young Duncan, and had all sorts of highland adventures, as scripted by George Beardmore. In 'The Ghost of Craigie Keep' the youngsters set out to explore the deserted village of Vaegan. Why is the village empty? 'Och, it was built by the lumbermen in your grandfather's time, and when they'd cleared the mountain side of trees, they just packed up and went.' It was now reclaimed by wildlife. They save a hind's calf from hungry foxes.

Robin Alone
E.O.
Mickey Mouse Weekly 1950-57; *Zip* 1958-59 (Odhams)
Billed as 'The Wild Boy of the Forest' and subtitled 'He lived with the Forest Creatures and Knew their Language', Robin Alone swung through the trees and into No. 524 of *Mickey Mouse Weekly* (27 May 1950). Exactly where the forest was situated was unclear, but Robin soon saved Guetta the fawn from a fierce wildcat, while Kauna the King Stag raced to the rescue. Robin lived in a house built into a hollow tree 'twisted by a thousand storms', and it was a dull week when he wasn't saving the likes of Mimi the beaver from Growsa the bear. He also ran the Jungle Club; a badge cost 1s.6d.

Robert Rabbit
Walter Holt
Chicks Own 1920-57 (Amalgamated Press)
Each week's 'Tale of Robert Rabbit' began with this rhyme:

Jol-ly Rob-ert Rab-bit,
Loved by ev-ery one,
Full of mer-ry jokes and tricks,
Join him in his fun!

He was the chubby bunny in check trousers who cheered up *Chicks Own*, the hy-phen-a-ted com-ic, throughout its entire thirty-eight-year life. Jol-ly Un-cle Whis-kers was an occasional guest, but Er-nie Elf and the Elves made frequent appearances, up to all sorts of elf-in mis-chief. 'Ha! Ha!' laugh-ed Mum-mie.

Robin Good
J. Edward Oliver
Jackpot 1980 (IPC)
Robin Good (the Daring Outlaw with the Nerves of Steal!) and his Outlaw Band started to play in the New Year 1980 number of *Jackpot*. The band consisted of Friar Tuckshop, Little Jim, Will Scarelot, Ellen-a-Dale, and Maid Marian, with Robin on guitar. The scene was Olde England: 'It is 1145, or to put it another way, a quarter to twelve!' While R. Hood helped the poor peasants, R. Good championed the peasant kids. 'I'm fair feddeth up with ye Sheriff of Nuttingham's son and his greedy gang!' quoth he, so he set up a secret hideout in Sure-would Forest.

Robin Hood
Various artists
Merry & Bright 1930; *Sparkler* 1937; *Knockout* 1947; *Comet* 1949; *Sun* 1952 (Amalgamated Press); *Swift* 1956 (Hulton); *Robin Hood* 1957; *TV Heroes* 1958 (Miller)
The legendary outlaw of Sherwood Forest has been a favourite hero in comics since he first appeared in 'The Children of the Forest' in *Bubbles* (1922) drawn by Vincent Daniel. The serial in *Knockout* (1947) was adapted from the Warner Bros film, 'Adventures of Robin Hood', and the first *Sun* serial (1952) was also an adaptation, of Sir Walter Scott's *Ivanhoe*. This and succeeding original serials, 'Lord of Sherwood' and 'Robin Hood's Quest' were by Patrick Nicolle (illustrated). Funny Robins: Reg Parlett in *Merry & Bright* (1930), Roy Wilson in *Sparkler* (1937).

Robot Archie
George Cowan
Lion 1952-66; *Vulcan* 1975-76 (IPC)
'The Jungle Robot' was the original title of this long-running series which started in No. 1 of *Lion* (23 February 1952). Archie was the world's most powerful mechanical man and possessed giant strength. He was invented by Professor C. R. Ritchie, and was in the charge of his young nephew, Ted Ritchie. Ted and his pal, Ken Dale, arrived with Archie in M'Lassa, Africa, in search of the treasure of Kaal, which lay somewhere beyond the Crouching Lion Hills. Trailing them was Bwana Pugg and his servant, Umbala.

Robinson Crusoe
Tom Browne
Comic Cuts 1899-1906 (Amalgamated Press)
'The Comic Adventures of Robinson Crusoe Esq and his Man Friday' commenced on the cover of *Comic Cuts* on 24 December 1899. 'As told to us by himself' continued the headline, adding 'Mr R. Crusoe will receive 8½d a week salary so long as he continues to give truthful accounts of his life among the savages.' Actually the tale was told by Mr T. Browne, who received considerably more than 8½d for his six large pictures a week. Crusoe, it seems, was wrecked on the *Saucy Codling* while kipper-fishing off the coast of Birmingham. He calls Friday 'an elongated piece of liquorice and no mistake' and catches a small elephant called Jumbo Junior in his butterfly net.

Rob the Rover
Walter Booth
Puck 1920-40; *Sunbeam* 1940 (Amalgamated Press)
Rob the Rover gave his name to the first adventure-strip serial in British comics. He floated in from the sea and on to a page of *Puck* on 15 May 1920, and was found by a grizzly old fisherman, Dan, who became his constant companion during the next twenty years. 'The Picture Story of a Brave Boy who was All Alone in the World' became an unending saga of travel and adventure taking in the seabed, the North Pole, several Lost Cities in several jungles, and a trip aboard Professor Seymour's submarplane, the *Flying Fish*.

R

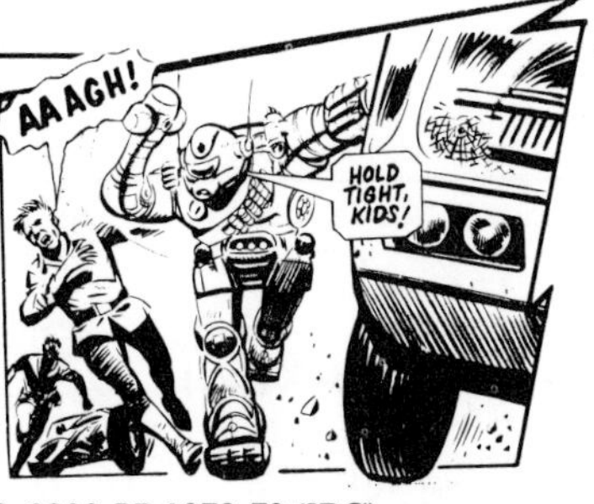

Ro-busters
Carlos Pino
Star Lord 1978; *2000 AD* 1978-79 (IPC)
By the year 2078 man has created many wonders of engineering. But the bigger his achievements, the bigger the disasters. Hence the origin of the Ro-busters, a very special kind of International Rescue team: a team of robots! Organized by their chief, Howard Quartz, from his base on Devil's Island, the Ro-busters roar into action whenever and wherever required. The team includes a partnership called Ro-jaws and Hammerstein, always arguing: 'You've got your hammer arm, laser arm, phaser arm and heck knows what. All I've got is me gnashers!'

Roger the Dodger
Ken Reid
Beano 1953- (D. C. Thomson)
'Here comes Roger! Always scheming! You will never catch him dreaming!' This was the headline over the first Roger the Dodger strip in *Beano* No. 561 (18 April 1953). The previous week an unusually large preview promoted Roger as 'The World's Craftiest Dodger – Trickier than a cageful of monkeys!' The claim seemed justified, although the editor's sense of morality usually made sure Roger's chubby mum or walrus-whiskered dad came out on top in the final panel.

Rocky Mountain King
Colin Andrew
Rocky Mountain King 1955-59 (Miller)
One of a series of western heroes published in sixpenny comicbooks during the 'Fifties' craze for cowboys. Like his comicbook pardners, Rocky Mountain King started out as some other personality and suffered a last-minute editorial change of name (see Colorado Kid, Kid Dynamite). In his original appearance he is saddled with a girl companion, Annie Oakley (another Miller comicbook star), while his name is badly relettered wherever it appears in the strip. His horse was called Prince.

Rogue Trooper
Dave Gibbons
2000 AD 1981-85 (IPC)
Nu-Earth, a war-ravaged planet at the edge of the galaxy with much of its atmosphere poisoned by chemical attacks, was the site of fierce battles fought by Rogue Trooper, last of the G.I.s – the Genetically Engineered Infantry. Helping him in his one-man war against the evil alien Norts were the biochips of his three dead buddies: Bagman, his backpack, Helm, his helmet, and Gunnar his gun, with whom Rogue Trooper held a continuing conversation. Rogue later voyaged to the planet Horst in search of antigen to regene his biochipped buddies. Script: Gerry Finley-Day.

Rodney Flood
Uggeri
Junior Express 1955-56 (Beaverbrook)
Rodney Flood was sailing his schooner *Silver Cloud* to the South Sea island of Taro-Tiki when he rescued three youngsters, Tim, Terry, and Midge, from a 'plane crash. He hoped to leave them in the care of Doc Wessell and his niece Gail Lester, but arrived to find the island had been taken over at gunpoint by Conrad Jago and his rascally crew who were seeking buried treasure. Italian artist Uggeri introduced the sexiest girl then seen in British comics.

The Rolling Stones
Cecil Orr
Swift 1954-61 (Hulton)
The Stones (Mr, Mrs, and their three children, Johnny, Pam, and Midge) were a family of acrobats who travelled around the country in their brightly painted lorry. Called the Rolling Stones because they never stayed in one place for long, they began what was to be an eight-year career in *Swift*'s full-colour centre spread by joining a circus. When clown Bambo's performing dog Bimbo fell ill, Johnny put on a pantomime dog's outfit and helped out. When they packed to move on, the girls got Jummy the elephant to sit on their trunk to close it: he squashed it flat!

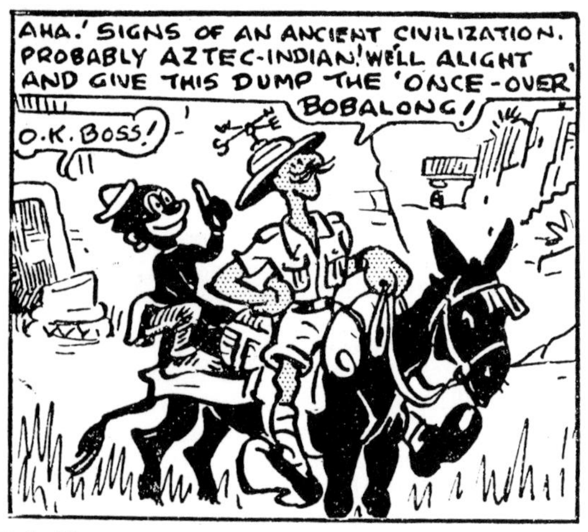

Roly Stone
Bertie Brown
Comic Cuts 1951-53 (Amalgamated Press)
'Down in the jungle something stirred. 'Twas Roly Stone the explorer, and Bobalong his bearer.' They found their way into *Comic Cuts* No. 2917 (10 February 1951), a dot-tint tanned bwana with a windvane atop his solar topee, backed up by his black manservant carrying tent and teapot on his bald bonce. Last of a long line of Empire builders to trek their way through British comics, Roly's speech was typical: 'Good show! Oh bothah! Deuced awkward, what?', as was Bobalong's: 'Dis am de laziest camel I'se neber ridden, Boss!'

Ronnie Roy
Harry Parlett
Funny Wonder 1940-50 (Amalgamated Press)
'Ronnie Roy the Indiarubber Boy' bounced into *Funny Wonder* No. 1356 (23 March 1940), having been previewed the previous week by the editor as Reggie Roy! Ronnie's extraordinary abilities were explained in the couplet: 'Meet Ronnie Roy, our funny new chum – Who stretches as easy as chewing gum!' Ronnie demonstrates by extending a leg to kick a bully from the far side of the road. The bruised bully responds by pulling Ronnie's leg, but our boy catches him on the rebound: Bing!

Ronnie Rich
Gordon Hogg
Smash 1966-67 (Odhams)
For young Ronnie Rich, 5 February 1966, the day No. 1 of *Smash* came out, began like any other day. A chauffeur-driven ride to the sweet shop to load up for the week. Then came the shock: his great-great-grandmother left him a million pounds, but only on condition he was penniless! Giving away a private fortune should be easy, thought Ronnie, but nobody would take his free bags of money. The more he gave way, the more he earned, just like the hero of the famous play and film, *Brewster's Millions!*

The Rooky Racers
Alan Rogers
Buzz 1974-75 (D. C. Thomson)
Inspired by the popular American television cartoon *Wacky Races*, this silly serial boiled the field down to two, a dauntless British inventor, Dan Druff, versus an evil German inventor, Herr Oyle. Over a weekly double-page spread in *Buzz*, these two battled it out in their ingenious machines in a round-the-world race. When they got to the Alps, Herr Oyle had a surprise for Dan. 'Der's snow business like snow business!' he sang as his extendible arms bunged giant snowballs at Dan. But – 'Doppeldrat! Der little maggot iss catching up!' – Dan's ejector nodule with parachute attachment got him to the finish first: 'Hup, hup and away!'

Rory Macduff
Reg Bunn
Lion 1959-65 (Fleetway)
'Danger Wanted' was the subtitle for Rory MacDuff, ace stuntman and private investigator, and his young assistant, Barney Lomax. 'To Rory, anything strange, or better, perilous, was a challenge! His craggy, square-jawed face widened into a grin!' Barney knew that grin only too well: 'Don't look so happy! I come out in a danger rash when you grin like that!' There was a good deal of grinning during the case that took them to the lonely laboratory of Milo Demain, eccentric scientist, who created an electrical cylinder to conquer time.

Roy Carson
Denis McLoughlin
Roy Carson 1948-53 (Boardman)
Inspired by the radio success of *Dick Barton – Special Agent*, 'Roy Carson – Special Agent' opened for business in his own two-tone comicbook in 1948. Unlike his broadcasting role-model, Carson was a tough 'tec of the Yankee school complete with a sexy blonde secretary called Silk, and a bizarre series of opponents ranging from the bird-costumed Condor to the masked Cheetah, Queen of the Spies. Dialogue was by the artist's brother, Colin McLoughlin.

Roy of the Rovers
Joe Colquhoun
Tiger 1954-85; *Roy of the Rovers* 1976- (IPC)
Roy Race, centre-forward of the Milston Youth Club team, scored his first goal on the coloured cover of *Tiger* No. 1 (11 September 1954), was spotted by Alf Leeds of the Melchester Rovers First-Division team, and given a chance in the Juniors on the back page. He was on his way to the longest career in football strips, and, most probably, in football. After twenty-two years, by which time he had become manager of the Rovers (and grown his hair long), Roy was rewarded with his own weekly comic, which he also edited. Roy's creator was writer Frank S. Pepper using the pen-name, 'Stewart Colwyn'.

Royal's Rangers
Illustrator unknown
Scorcher 1970-71 (IPC)
No. 1 of the new sports comic *Scorcher* (10 January 1970) kicked off with Royal's Rangers, actually Caxford Rangers football team managed by Ben Royal. Rod Roper, the Caxford skipper, had a clear shot at goal but threw it away! Why? Then Ben spotted the Man with the Hook Nose in the crowd. It was Grymes, the man who had the star centre-forward in his power, for Rod's brother Jim had helped him rob a bank and Grymes had photos to prove it. The story of Rod Roper was the first of many as Ben Royal told a reporter the tale of his team.

Roy Rogers
C. Montford
Wonder 1944-52 (Amalgamated Press); *TV Comic* 1952-56 (*News of the World*); *Sun* 1957-58 (Fleetway)
Roy Rogers, billed as 'The Cowboy Film Star' rather than his more familiar 'King of the Cowboys', rode on to the red-and-black back page of *Wonder* No. 1498 on 24 June 1944. 'Hello, *Wonder* Chums!' wrote Roy, 'I am real glad to meet you all and hope we shall be good pards. I know you will all love my pony pal, Trigger! Ride with us along the danger trail and share our thrills!' Roy's first complete adventure was 'A Fugitive from Justice'. His 1950s strips were all American reprints.

Rubberman
Illustrator unknown
Smash 1966-67 (Odhams)
Cursed by an Indian fakir and turned into rubber (and evidently inspired by the American stretchable superhero, Plastic Man), Rubberman twanged into action against the evil Jonas Sleech, a midget of monstrous strength. Rubberman's fantastic powers were stretched to the limit by this mad midget. 'Power! Power! I have the strength of a thousand men! I could become the richest man in the world!' cried Sleech, ripping a steel door off a jewellery store on his way to the Happy Home boarding house. As a bystander remarked, 'What is the world coming to?'

R

Rudolf the Red-Nosed Ranger
Arthur Martin
Chips 1951-53 (Amalgamated Press)
This half-pint hero rode on to the back page of the new twelve-page series of *Chips* which began with No. 2920 on 11 August 1951. Equipped with a star badge, high-heels, and a hoss named Hilda, not to mention a nose that glows, Rudolf soon turned the tables on a whole posse of badlads, beginning with Ned Narkit and his Knock-kneed Nag. He knew he was on the right trail by the sound of knock-kneed hoof-prints! Others duly dealt with included One Gun Willie, Jughead Jake, and Big Chief Chumpchops.

Rupert the Chick
Arthur White
Chicks Own 1921-57 (Amalgamated Press)
This fluffy little yellow fellow wore nothing but an outsize in knitted bobble-hats – except, of course, in Grand Holiday Numbers, when he put on a bathing costume to go swimming! He was the full-colour front-page star of *Chicks Own* for most of that nursery comic's life, replacing the same artist's Dicky Duck. Uncle Dan, the editor, obviously had the belated thought that a chick on the cover would be more suitable than a duckling. Rupert's pal was a black chick (called Nigger, I'm afraid), and along with Stripey Tiger, Piggy, and Golli they all attended Mrs Quack-Quack's school.

Rupert
Mary Tourtel
Pippin 1974-80 (Polystyle); *Rupert Weekly* 1982-84; *Storyland* 1984 (Marvel)
Rupert Bear – who lives in the village of Nutwood with Mummy and Daddy Bear, and his chums Bill Badger, Algy Pug, and Edward Trunk – is the star of the longest-lived children's strip in the UK. He made his debut in the serial, 'The Little Lost Bear', in the *Daily Express* (8 November 1920) and his adventures, as unchanging and as magical as ever, continue to this day. Originally drawn by Mary Tourtel, Rupert was continued after her retirement in 1935 by Alfred Bestall, and it is mainly his work which is reprinted in comics.

Rusty
Paddy Brennan
Dandy 1950-54 (D. C. Thomson)
Rusty moved into the red-and-blue back page of *Dandy* No. 445 on 3 June 1950, but, despite his name and the colour process, his hair was blue, not red. Slapstick in style but realistically drawn, Rusty was a forerunner of the 'reader-identification' type of character which would gradually take over the Thomson comics. Ever ready with swift fist or a quick twang of his catapult, Rusty was as tough as they come and his language was tough, too: 'Yah, you're a red-haired ape!' and 'Scram, wartface!'

Saber
Denis McLoughlin
Tiger 1967-69; *Vulcan* 1975-76 (IPC)
'Saber, King of the Jungle', was a blond, bronzed giant reared in the African wilds, 'as proud and untamed as nature herself'. He was friend to all the animals, including Cheeki the chimp and a pet parrot useful for shrieking alarm-calls. He also had a Zulu companion, Umbala, and was given to swinging through the trees via vines while venting his war-cry. 'Awarreeeeee!' Saber had a nice turn of phrase: he addressed crocodiles as 'O scaly one', called his knife 'my steel fang', and motorized vessels 'chuck-chuck boats'. Any resemblance to Tarzan was, of course, purely coincidental.

Sally in our Alley
Bertie Brown
Funny Wonder 1922-32; 1936-42 (Amalgamated Press)
'A bright little lass is Sally, as you'll see before long, dear readers.' Thus spake the editor of *Funny Wonder* on 14 October 1922, many years before Gracie Fields sang the song that gave her a signature tune. Sally, a sweet but ragged slum girl, opened her long innings by devising a warm coat for her mongrel puppy Ruff, out of a much-holed sock. 'What swank!' cried a tatty urchin. Sally's rival, Liz Lobdob, disappeared when the girl was pensioned off on 28 May 1932. But she was back on 2 May 1936 as 'Sally the Sunshine of Our Alley', and Liz was back, too, both being drawn by Reg Parlett.

Sally Sweet of Sunshine Street
Illustrator unknown
Twinkle 1968-76 (D. C. Thomson)
Sally Sweet lived at Honeysuckle Cottage, which was No. 1, Sunshine Street, just up the road from Nancy the Little Nurse. How odd, then, that Nurse Nancy was not invited to Sally Sweet's fifth birthday party, especially as they both starred in the same comic, *Twinkle*. Perhaps it was because they were drawn by different artists? Anyway it didn't stop Sally having a lovely time with her little friends, and after Mummy played the piano for a game of 'The Grand Old Duke of York', they all had a slice of Sally's birthday cake, baked by Mr Bran the Baker. Well, you can't expect Mummy to do everything.

The Saint
Leslie Charteris
TV Tornado 1967-68; *TV 21* 1968-71 (City)
Simon Templar, the modern-day Robin Hood of crime and detection, was created by novelist Leslie Charteris and first appeared in the novel *Meet the Tiger* (1928). His early exploits were printed in the boys' paper, *The Thriller*, but it was the television series which began in 1963 that brought the Saint (as played by Roger Moore) into weekly comics, although some of his American comicbooks had been reprinted in the 'Fifties. Artists included Harry Bishop, who drew a sight better than the Saint (vide his famous stick-figure signature).

Sally Sunshine
Albert Pease
Chips 1951-53 (Amalgamated Press)
'Sally Sunshine and her Shadow' ('A fun star that's new – with her shadow she's two!') were among the new characters introduced into the expanded twelve-page *Chips* on 11 August 1951. Cunningly contrived to appeal to girl readers, Sally lived with a slightly nasty Aunty: 'No, you can't go to the Festival Funfair! Stay in and tidy the house!' Sad Sally chances to switch on the light, and her shadow springs to life. 'Well, crumple my curlers!' cries the child as her shadow proceeds to wreck the old homestead. A masculine variant, 'Me and My Shadow', ran in *Whizzer & Chips* from 1969, drawn by Terry Bave.

Sammy and Shrimp
Arthur Martin
Comic Cuts 1938-51 (Amalgamated Press)
'The Castaways of Crusoe Island', as they were originally billed, were washed ashore on the front page of *Comic Cuts* on 15 October 1938. The good ship *Goozgogge* had foundered in the tropics, and Captain Robbie Crusoe and crew, consisting of Salty and Porky the mates, and Sammy and Shrimp the cabin boys, soon knocked up a shack. The kids adopted Mick the monkey, an invaluable aide in their wars with Big Chief Chumpo. From 12 August 1939 they went to sea again as 'The Cruise of the Crusoe Kids', and from 11 August 1945 settled ashore as 'Sammy and Shrimpy'.

Sammy Shrink
David Jenner
Wham 1966-68; *Pow* 1968; *Smash* 1968-70 (Odhams); *Whizzer & Chips* 1973-86 (IPC)
'He's Tiny but Great!' was the descriptive caption for this little character. A modernized version of Tom Thumb, Sammy was a curly topped kid who never grew up. He slept in the top drawer of a chest, and had problems at Christmas hanging up his extra-small sock for Santa. However, Dad came to the rescue with one of Mum's old elastic stockings! The following Christmas was less successful: it ended up with Sammy being stuck on top of the tree dressed as the fairy. Sammy was later revived for a different comic, drawn by a different artist, Terry Bave.

Sammy and his Speedsub
Illustrator unknown
Swift 1954-59 (Hulton)
Sammy started in a small way, just half a page of *Swift* No. 1 (20 March 1954), but in it he went underwater in his Speedsub to save a lady's handbag. Soon he was filling a full page, thanks to Professor MacDonald who fixed wheels and wings on the Speedsub so it could travel on land, sea, or in the air. Sammy repaid the Prof. by saving his dog, Jock, from drowning. His adventures grew more exciting in 1957 when, with his chum Jill, Sammy went to Space Cadet School and saved test pilot Ace Silver from kidnappers.

Sammy Smile
Louis Diamond
Chuckler 1934-38 (Target)
Sammy Smile was one of those cheery, chubby chumps who bowled about beaming their way through life. Billed as 'The World's Champion Chuckle Maker', Sammy was the first front-page hero of *Chuckler* (31 March 1934), a penny comic printed on orange paper and published in Bath, Somerset. Originally drawn by the slapdash Louis Diamond, who was also editor of the comic, Sammy smiled more brightly under the slapstick Bert Hill, who took him over. Later Sammy shifted to the back page when Diamond introduced 'Harry Coe, Our Has-Bean' in 1936.

Sammy Sprockett
Denis Gifford
Chips 1953 (Amalgamated Press)
'Sammy Sprockett and his Pocket Rocket' promised 'All the Fun of the Future' when he zoomed into the Easter Number of *Chips* (4 April 1953). Unhappily, Pilot Pobjoy of the Space Squad arrived eggless, his Easter cargo of eggs having been spacejacked by Skowle the Sky Pirate. Colonel Cloudhopper was quite cut up, but Junior Cadet Sprockett soon saved the day by disguising an antimagnetic meteorite as an Easter egg and flummoxing Scowle good and proper. As Giggle the Gremilin remarked: 'Ploob!' Sammy, reflecting the 'Fifties' fascination with sci-fi, was the last new character to appear in the venerable *Chips*.

Sammy Specks
Harry Banger
Topical Funnies 1940; *New Funnies* 1940; *Thrill Comics* 1940; *Fresh Fun* 1940; *War Comics* 1942; *Slick Fun* 1945 (Swan)
'Sammy Specks, Our Extra Special Constable' reported for duty in No. 1 of *Topical Funnies* (April 1940), smartly turned out with his tin helmet marked 'Police', his official armband, gas mask slung over his shoulder, and natty bow-tie. His first case turned out like most of his cases to come: badly. A boy told him a man was beating a lady ('That'll be enough from you old girl!' Slap!) but it was a farmer milking a cow! And while Sammy was being kicked, the boy bagged his motorbike wheels for his soapbox car! Sammy had better luck with spies.

Sammy's Scribbles
Gordon Bell
Buzz 1973-75; *Topper* 1975-76 (D. C. Thomson)
This ingenious series started in *Buzz* No. 18 (19 May 1973). The entire full-colour centre spread was designed to look like a blue-lined exercise pad covered with cartoons and scribbles by a talented lad called Sammy. The boy began with a portrait of the editor: 'He doesn't have false teeth – just false hair, eyebrows, lashes and nose!' Next came some doodles: 'an arrow escape' was an arrow breaking jail! There were some cartoons built around Sammy's thumbprints including Thumbody and Thumbthing, portraits of Dad before and after the football match – 'guess who's team lost!' – and even some photos of pop stars 'pasted down'.

Samuel Creeps
Bob McGrath
Nutty 1980-81 (D. C. Thomson)
'Meet the Snivelling Schoolboy who's Softer than a Marshmallow!' That was Samuel Creeps the Teacher's Pet whose pictures were decorated with furry caterpillars and other suitable creepy-crawlies. Samuel, never seen without his kiss-curl, his gig-lamps, and his pimple-like school cap, sat at his own neat little desk, while the rest of his class glowered, an unruly mountain of spotty pupils, from their ink-spattered pen. Samuel's favourite film was *The Lone Flower Arranger*, and on occasion he sallied forth in disguise (including hair-ribbons) as Supersofty!

Sandy Dean
Barry Nelson
Lion 1952-56 (Amalgamated Press)
'Sandy Dean's First Term' started on 23 February 1952 in No. 1 of *Lion*. Actually it was the middle of the term for Tollgate School when the new boy arrived, but the bullies of the Fourth, Bossy Bates, Spider Jessop and Gus Trevor, didn't let that stop them preparing a welcome: 'There's an awful smell of new kids around here!' But their sooty trap backfired on them, thanks to Sandy's wit, and after an encounter with Mr Mallory, the breezy housemaster, Sandy was hailed as a hero and treated to lashings of tuck. Title changed to 'Tales of Tollgate School' in 1963.

Sandy and Dusty
George Wakefield
Jester 1928-32 (Amalgamated Press)
'The Regimental Rascals' signed on the centre pages of *Jester* for five years' panel-bashing. Sandy was the sawn-off Scottie in the sporran, while Dusty was the walrus-whiskered cockney with the back-to-front cap style. The bane of their barracks was Sergeant Major Rorter, as red-faced as artist 'Billy' Wakefield could make him using bags of black ink shading. For the record, their regiment was the Royal Standbacks, and the ossifer in charge, Colonel Crackpot. As Sandy often said, 'Och, hoots, the noo!'

Sandie
Guido Buzzelli
Romeo 1970-74 (D. C. Thomson)
Sexy Sandie was the star of the teenage romance comic, *Romeo*, a chirpy cockney girl with an eye for the boys, although it might be truer to say the boys had an eye for Sandie – especially when she strolled the streets as a sandwich-girl for Herbert's Happy Dashery. This boutique's boards read 'Herbert's Hot Pants will Light your Fella's Fire', and a porthole in the stern revealed why: a devil dancing on Sandie's pert botty! Sandie's reward was a pair of scarlet Popsie Peepers to wear under her miniskirt, but dad objected. So she wore her maxiskirt over them and took it off when she got to the Fireman's Ball.

Sandy and Muddy
Norman Ward
Knockout 1939-43 (Amalgamated Press)
'The Two Terrors of the Terriers' – i.e., the Territorial Army – joined up in *Knockout* No. 10, 6 May 1939. Sandy, the skinny Scottie, and Muddy, the chubby cockney, were the first shadow of impending war to cloud the comic which would in time subtitle itself 'The Victory Comic'. Their early activities were limited to war games, which they played on their Sergy the Sergeant, a bully who sported a brolly. Once the war was under way, they did useful things like pitching their tents – over a cliff and on top of a Nazi invasion force.

Sandy's Steam Man
Joseph Walker
Knockout 1939-40 (Amalgamated Press)
Originally billed as 'The Steam Man on Treasure Island,' this two-page serial which started in *Knockout* No. 1, 4 March 1939, was soon changed to 'The Adventures of Sandy's Steam Man'. Sandy was the pipe-puffing old Scots engineer of the *Shamrock*, wrecked on the reefs of a tropical island. Sailor Sam was the entire crew, and Rob and Jill were the schoolchildren passengers. To help them battle gorillas, Sandy knocked up a Steam Man out of the ship's engine, and named it Steve!

Scamp
Harry Hargreaves
Comet 1950-54; *School Friend* 1962; *Big One* 1964-65 (Fleetway)
'Old Scamp's the sort of happy tyke – That any of you kids would like!' This couplet introduced the loveable great lolloper of a ginger dog when he moved to the front page of *Comet* from No. 95, just a few weeks after his first appearance in No. 88 (28 January 1950). Such was Scamp's swift rise to success. He moved back inside the comic later, where he was given the subtitle of 'Our Happy Hound' to cheer him up! Scamp's young master was a lad called Sonny, and his pet menace was Pip the puss.

The Sarge
Mike Western
Battle Action 1977-80 (IPC)
'A rock may crumble, but a good sarge'll never fall!' Sergeant Jim Masters, his old pipe clenched between his teeth, led his men into action on 23 October 1942 (and into *Battle Action* on 19 November 1977). The place was El Alamein, North Africa, British infantry versus the German Afrika Korps. When the smoke cleared, the Grenadiers and the Coldstreams were cut down, but the Sarge's platoon made it, thanks to his old soldier's cunning. His right-hand men were Corporal Tom Savage and Private Sid Strong, but Private Kidd was a problem: under Sarge's training he had become a ruthless killer.

Scared-Stiff Sam
Mike Lacey
Whoopee 1974-80 (IPC)
If ever the phrase 'big baby' applied to anyone, it was to Sam Smith. This hulking great lump looked tough enough to duff Desperate Dan, yet the least little thing reduced him to a shivering jelly. At the age of six months he was frightened by the noise of his rattle, and scared of heights until Dad sawed the legs off his high-chair. Hilda Smith, his Mum, called him her little Sammikins, but occasionally got exasperated enough to call him a big cowardly lollop, especially when he wouldn't go shopping for her on account of 'that awful, death-defying drop' – the front doorstep.

Scaredy Cat
Terry Bave
Krazy 1976-78 (IPC)
This frightened feline was just a bundle of nerves. Seldom seen without the shivers, Scaredy Cat went one better than the usual quota of nine lives. He had an amazing trick of being able to turn into anything with a 'catty sound' to it, whenever he was really frightened. His first appearance in *Krazy* No. 1 (16 October 1976) was typical: knocked into a river he turned into a catamaran to float free, and then, when a fisherman caught him, he became an octo-puss! On 14 May 1977 he lost his powers, teamed up with Squeeky the mouse, and inherited Doompussy Hall and an enemy in Boswold the Butler.

The School Belles
Evi de Bono
Nutty 1980-83 (D. C. Thomson)
The belles of St Onion's Finishing School for Young Ladies started their term of terror in No. 1 of *Nutty* (16 February 1980). This gym-slipped quartette formed a floral foursome: Daisy, the one in the glasses, non-shrinking Violet, Rose with the rope-like pigtails, and unblushing Marigold, the biggest in the bunch. Their headmistress was in the tradition, too: her name was Miss Buttercup. In mortarboard, bun and specs, she was shortsighted enough to miss most of her minions' mayhem.

The Scareys of St Mary's
Terry Bave
Whizzer & Chips 1970-77 (IPC)
The new school term opened on 21 February 1970, and while ordinary kids were queueing at the bus stop, the girls of St Mary's were flying high – aboard the school broom! Zooming into a cave in the side of Wookey Hill, the girls arrived in the deepest cave, St Mary's School for Would-be Witches: headmistress and sole prop., Miss Fizz. She used her crystal ball to contact little Ivy, a latecomer ('Say after me, I'm late for school, naughty ghoul!'), but Ivy was bad at spelling – the magic kind. Spelling lessons were in order, especially for the little one, Titchy Witchy.

Schoolditz
Frank McDiarmid
School Fun 1983-84 (IPC)
The year 1939, and war had broken out while Baker Street School was touring Germany in a bus. Blocked at the border, Commandant Gunther has the master and his pupils carted off to Schoolditz Castle, a menacing pile plastered with such signs as 'No readink in bed', 'Sweeties must be shared with the guards' and 'Last one in switch off the lights'. Gunther runs over the rules: 'I'm in charge und efferybody does vot I say or gets punished much! No sveeties for a veek und two extra pieces of garlic sossie in der cornflakes!' But under the guise of the debating society, the boys are organizing an escape committee.

School Belle
Tom Paterson
School Fun 1983-84; *Buster* 1984- (IPC)
School Belle is the belle of the school, a blonde baggage forever preening and posing on the full-colour back page of *School Fun* from No. 1 (15 October 1983). Put out when Dishy Derek ditches her for a disco date with Soppy Sonia, Belle gets busy with a sneaky snigger. First she squirts Sonia with spare hair spray, then shows the girl her pet spider. 'Shriek!' shrieks Sonia, her hair standing on end and instantly setting solid. But Belle's cunning wheeze turns to ashes. Dishy Derek actually likes Sonia's sunburst of spikes. 'Wow! What a fantastic futuristic hairdo! Let's go!' All Belle could say was 'Dooohhh!'

Scientific Silas
Illustrator unknown
Comic Life 1907-20 (Henderson)
Scientific Silas was the first of those crazed inventors who would cause comic-strip chaos throughout the century. The old saw about pigs flying was proved true as early as 1909 when Silas fitted one out with flapping wings. The same year he cured a hunger marcher on sit-down strike with his electrified training suit. He reconstructed the extinct *Odontosaurus* from bones dug up by his gardener, and provided comfort for accident-prone pedestrians with his pneumatic cowcatcher. He helped win World War 1 by selling the Kaiser a multi-barrelled backfiring gun. 'Himmel!' cried Wilhelm; 'Ditto!' cried his son.

Scoop Donovan
Geoff Campion
Film Fun 1959-62 (Amalgamated Press)
'Scoop Donovan, War Cameraman', was the first non-film star hero in *Film Fun*, a character created for the first modernized series of the comic which started on 13 June 1959 as *Film Fun and Thrills*. Billed as 'the ace trouble-shooter of World War Two', Roy 'Scoop' Donovan was a freelance newsreel cameraman caught in Berlin on the day war broke out. After filming the invasion of Poland, Scoop hijacked a Jerry plane, bombed the rest of the squadron, and hightailed it for home. Soon he was back at the warfront filming the news in the making.

Scream Inn
Brian Walker
Shiver & Shake 1973-74; *Whoopee* 1974-77 (IPC)
'We're Only Here for the Fear!' was the sign which swung outside Ye Scream Inn. Pinned to the wall with daggers was a notice: 'One Million Pounds to anybody who can stay all ye night in ye Haunted Bedroom!' The first to accept the challenge was Champ the boxer, on the night of 10 March 1973 in No. 1 of *Shiver & Shake*. Although he braved the series of spooks sent against him, he lost by bashing his way through the wall with only a minute to spare. Readers were invited to nominate someone to spend a night in the Inn and win £1. See The Spooktacular Seven.

Scoopy
Gordon Bell
Nutty 1980-85 (D. C. Thomson)
'The Runaround Hound with a Nose for News' dashed into No. 1 of *Nutty* (16 February 1980), slipped on the cleaning lady's soap and crashed into Cornelius the editor's cat ('Slip! Wheeee! Crump! Blech!'). This proved to be par for the course for the over-enthusiastic news-hound, a talkative dog who wore a press pass in his hat. Sent to cover a big greyhound race for *Nutty News*, he had all the dogs posing for a photograph so that slowcoach Fred Rum crawled home to win his first race in ten years of trying. The punters weren't pleased.

Screwy Driver
Bill Holroyd
Dandy 1955-59; 1975-84 (D. C. Thomson)
'The Tricks of Screwy Driver' started on 12 November 1955, in *Dandy* No. 729. In a packed page of pictures, twenty in all, readers were presented with a biography of disaster which began when Screwy was two. To stop his yelling, Grandpa Driver gave the babe a hammer. The boy showed his innate mechanical genius by using it to smash a teapot. Grandpa's fifth birthday present was a Junior Carpenter's Outfit. Screwy removed the bathroom tap as a return present and flooded the house. From then on Screwy and disaster were inseparable.

Scribbler
Terry Bave
Whizzer & Chips 1970-73 (IPC)
Scribbler was a boy cartoonist who ran Scribbler's Page in *Whizzer & Chips*. The idea was for readers to write in with suggested sketches for a comic strip, the ones selected by Scribbler winning a £1 prize. Young David Hackwell of Billericay set Scribbler a task when he asked for a story about two rival gangs, the Mucky Kids versus the Scruffy Kids. The battle scene featured forty-four fighting figures! A bit easier on the ink was Stephen Ward of Hoddeston with his hairy caveman called Stoneage Doff, not much more than a fur-ball with eyeballs.

Send for Kelly
George Martin
Topper 1961-; *Champ* 1984-85 (D. C. Thomson)
His card read 'Nick Kelly, Special Agent: Dangerous Missions Undertaken'. He originally worked for the Ministry of Secret Information, donning disguises in his search for Fritz Von Splosch, the international diamond smuggler. Unfortunately, Von Splosch donned better disguises than Kelly! Moving into full colour, Kelly's pulled-down hat and turned-up trenchcoat were revealed to be green and red, in that order. Instead of disguising himself so much, Kelly dressed up Cedric, his bespectacled assistant, thus saving the King of Khandibah from rebel Rhansid Buttah.

The Secret Seven
Enid Blyton
Penny 1979 (IPC)
The popular heroes of a series of novels for children written by the late Enid Blyton first came to comics in No. 1 of a new girls' weekly, *Penny* (28 April 1979). Peter and his sister Janet were the leaders of the Secret Seven, a gang who met in a garden shed. The others were Colin, George, Pam, Barbara, and Jack, whose sister Susie was a rotten outsider who caused them trouble. The Seven's secret password was 'Holidays', and the Secret Eighth was Scamper the spaniel. Drawn by John Armstrong.

Sergeant Rayker
Salinas
Warlord 1979-84 (D. C. Thomson)
Moses Rayker was more than a sergeant in the U.S. Army: he was the first black hero to star in British comics. His story began in *Warlord* No. 232 (3 March 1979) in Italy, with the German counterattack on Anzio in 1944. 'Chew on that, Squareheads!' shouted Rayker, tossing a grenade into a pillbox. 'Not bad thinking for a black boy!' commented a G.I. 'Cut that kinda talk!' snapped his officer, 'His blood spills out the same colour in this man's war!' But Dallas, a G.I. from the South, thought differently; 'About face, Sergeant Sambo!' Sgt Rayker had more than one battle to fight.

Seezum and Squeezum
Bertie Brown
Jester 1924-31 (Amalgamated Press)
'Our Artful Arabs' were modelled on the classic comic double-act formula: Seezum was skinny ('Thou hop-pole!') and Squeezum was not ('Thou slab of fat!'). They operated as guides for odd archaeologists. When Professor Stingey hired them to show him some waving palms, they betook him to the bazaar. Plenty of waving palms there as merchants cried 'Yoi! Yoi!' S & S cried other things, like 'By the ten sacred toe-bones of the sphinx!' when confronted by their enemy, P.C. Ali Bazooka. Their main artist was Louis Briault (illustrated).

Sergeants Four
Illustrator unknown
Jet 1971 (IPC)
Going one better than Rudyard Kipling's *Sergeants Three*, Sergeants Four told their story in as many pages a week, starting in *Jet* No. 1 (1 May 1971). They were Sergeants Alf Higgs from London ('Scarper, mates!), Taffy Jones from Wales ('Indeed to goodness, lookyou!'), Jock McGill from Scotland ('Hoots! They're headin' this way, laddies!'), and Paddy O'Boyle from Ireland ('Bejabers, ye sausage stuffin' spalpeens!'). They joined forces to return to Dunkirk after the evacuation to recapture the British Bulldog Banner, the Army's most treasured war souvenir.

The Seven-Foot Cowboy
James Walker
Magic 1939 (D. C. Thomson)
'The Adventures of the Tallest, Toughest Cowboy in the Wild West' started in No. 1 of *Magic* (22 July 1939). His name was Shorty Bill Brand: 'in spite of his nickname, Bill was a huge, good-natured chap who stood over seven feet in height and was as broad as a barn door'. Having lassoed a trio of baddies and slung them up on a signpost, and saved the Circle S herd from stampeding by steering a steer with his horns, Shortly settled down as sheriff of Boulder Gap wearing a special super-sized star hammered out by the local blacksmith.

Shari King
Juliana Buch
Dreamer 1981-82 (IPC)
'Shari King – Shark Girl' swam into No. 1 of *Dreamer* (19 September 1981). Daughter of the owner of King's Aquarium, she soon showed the girls of Tide Street School that water was a second home to her. Shari was determined to be best in her year's swimming team, by fair means or foul. Fair enough was the trick she used to help her cut through the water: she piled her shaggy-cut hair into the shape of a shark's fin. Fouler were the tricks she pulled on Dawn the diving champion, and once she had made team-captain she trained them in trickery to win at synchronized swimming.

Sexton Blake
Hal Meredith
Knockout 1939-60; *Valiant* 1968-70 (Amalgamated Press)
'The World's Greatest Detective' first appeared in a complete story written for *The Halfpenny Marvel* (20 December 1893) by Harry Blyth, using the pen-name 'Hal Meredith'. 'Sexton Blake and the Hooded Stranger' was the first strip adaptation, commencing in *Knockout* No. 1 (4 March 1939), drawn by Jos Walker. Blake was supported by Tinker, his faithful boy assistant, and Pedro, his equally faithful bloodhound. Of several artists, the favourite was Alfred H. Taylor (illustrated), who introduced Hoo Sung and his Rolling Sphere.

Sheerflop Soames
Douglas Lovern West
Thrill Comics 1940; *Topical Funnies* 1940-46; *New Funnies* 1946; *Cut Fun* 1946; *Fresh Fun* 1948 (Swan)
'Bumping Off Lord Bunglefoot' was the first Crazy Case of Sheerflop Soames and Bottson, a burlesque of Conan Doyle's detectives making their debut in *Thrill Comics* No. 3. After much mulling over such suspects as a suspiciously foreign piano-tuner ('Ja! I gom to tuneski der pianovitch! Where ees eet, moosewer?'). Soames solves the case: 'In searching for Lord Bunglefoot's wealth, the bewitching Lady Bunglefoot knifed the bogus piano-tuner, then tripped over his body and broke her neck. The butler fell over Lady B and shot himself. These two gents killed each other, so there's no evidence, no prisoners, and no use staying!'

Sheerluck and Son
Trevor Metcalfe
Whoopee 1978-79 (IPC)
Bearing an uncanny physical resemblance to the television comedians The Two Ronnies (Barker and Corbett), rather than any family likeness to Sherlock Holmes, these two detectives set up shop on 29 July 1978. Their first case was to get enough money to pay their back rent. Donning a pantomime horse disguise they saved a racehorse from doping – by getting jabbed themselves. They did a week as house detectives at the Hotel de Poshe, saving Sir Geoffrey Spark's sample case from a snatcher and getting a reward: 50 pence tip for carrying the case.

The Sheikh of El Bashan
'Gil'
Tip Top 1945-49 (Amalgamated Press)
Hamid, the boy sheikh of El Bashan, astride the black Moonbeam, wonder-horse of the desert, rode into *Tip Top* in a series of complete picture-stories. But wonder-horses were not the only things he could ride. With a cry of 'Billah!' he leaped into a jeep, or on to a motorbike, and roared off after scurvy Arab spies with gay abandon. He was equally handy with boats and soon stopped the smugglers of El Zora Bay.

Sheriff Fox
William Ward
New Funnies 1940-49; *Slick Fun* 1945; *Fresh Fun* 1948 (Swan)
'The slickest robber in the badlands turns lawman because a lady shooed off the hounds and hid him under the bed! See him in action against grizzly Pete, the terror of Lone Valley!' William Ward, a former animator, introduces his well-drawn pair, a fox and a bear, in No. 1 of *New Funnies* (February 1940) – the first comic strip to run six pages. Ward's dialogue was in best pseudo-Yankee style, as were his plots. Pete strings Foxy up by the neck ('Haw! Haw! That's finished that pesky sheriff! Now I kin hold up Pugg's saloon!'), but Foxy wiggles free ('Whut's he think I am, a cissie?') and poses as his own ghost.

The Sheriff of Sherbet City
Reg Parlett
Merry & Bright 1929-32 (Amalgamated Press)
Known only by his rank, this nameless lawman rode on to the back page of *Merry & Bright* on 12 October 1929. He made such a hit bagging the baddies that he was soon promoted to page one. His first capture was Tough Tex, whanged in the waistcoat via an accidental slip on a banana's pyjamas. Then it was Big Chief Chunkabeef (Minniehaha's papa) engineering the Injuns on to the warpath. Getting the whiphand over Piebald Pete, the Undertaker's Friend, was a snap, as was handcuffing the feet of Red Razzo in the Duck and Stuffing Saloon. Small wonder big men cried 'Great galloping gazookas!'

Shiner
Mike Lacey
Whizzer & Chips 1969- (IPC)
The front-page star of the *Chips* pull-out comic section which forms the centre section of *Whizzer & Chips*, made his debut in No. 2 (25 October 1969). 'And remember, Shiner, don't come home with a black eye!' warned Mum. 'Righto, Mum, I'll be careful!' shouted Shiner, but – thwack! – right in the second picture he trod on a rake and had to spend the rest of his page trying to disguise his eye. And this is how poor old Shiner has walked through the world ever since: getting one eye blacked every week for over sixteen years.

Strong-man and ape grappled and a tremendous struggle took place.

The Shipwrecked Circus
Dudley Watkins
Beano 1943-47; 1951-58; *Buddy* 1981-82 (D. C. Thomson)
Samson's Circus was originally shipwrecked in No. 372 of *Adventure* (15 December 1928). Then history repeated itself, this time in pictures, in *Beano* No. 200 (27 February 1943). Once again Samson the strong man paddled a lashed-up raft towards Crusoe Island in the South Seas, with a precious cargo consisting of young Danny, Trixie the girl acrobat, Gloopy the clown, and Horace the educated ape. Salvaging the wreckage of the cargo ship *Margo* was no problem for Samson, even when an angry octopus lurked in the hold.

S

Shipwreck School
Mike Lacey
Wow 1982-83; *Whoopee* 1983-85 (IPC)
When the school cruise ship S.S. *Blackboard* docked in the South Seas, everyone enjoyed a spot of shore-leave except the kids. The headmaster made them stay behind for a science lesson. While he was accidentally spilling the H2SO4 into the NACL 806 and TNT103, the ship drifted out to sea. The resulting 'Fizzz! Boom! Eeek!' wrecked the ship and the kids found themselves washed ashore on a desert island. Teacher soon got everybody busy building . . . a school, and their strip was soon promoted to the full-colour covers.

Shocker Jock
George Drysdale
Dandy 1954-55 (D. C. Thomson)
The boy from the future, the year 2250 to be precise, first came to Earth, Blackdean to be precise, on 12 May 1951 in No. 494 of *Dandy*, to be precise. At the time he was billed as 'The Boy from the Wonder World' (the United States of Europia) but he lost this tagline when he returned to Blackdean and *Dandy* on 31 July 1954. This time, instead of starring in a serial story, Jock starred in a picture strip, along with his old pals, Jim Blake and Coconut Jones.

The Shirkwork Brothers
Tom Radford
Merry & Bright 1910-26 (Amalgamated Press)
'Dear Readers and Brother Shirkworkers' was the way Bill and Joe addressed their readers from No. 1 of *Merry & Bright* (22 October 1910). This pair of manual labourers would do anything to get out of physical work, a task which exercised their brainboxes to a frazzle. Rather than walk to work, they sawed their coke-hammer in twain, hammered in their trowels, and made natty one-wheel bikes! By painting a milestone like an Egyptian mummy they got Prof. Noseall to dig it up for them. After a well-earned rest they returned as front-page stars (17 June 1922).

Shorty the Deputy Sheriff
Hugh McNeill
Comet 1949-53; *Valiant* 1962-63 (Amalgamated Press)
Decked out in a tall red ten-gallon hat and a wide white set of walrus-whiskers, Shorty the Deputy was given his first assignment by the Sheriff in No. 84 of *Comet* (3 December 1949). After a good deal of galloping all over the two-tone front page, sixteen pictures later Shorty found himself roped to his own hoss while Slippery Sam was a mere cloud of dust heh-heh-ing on the horizon. Despite promotion to full colour from 29 March 1952, Shorty continued to fail hilariously under new artist Reg Parlett (illustrated).

Sid's Snake
Mike Lacey
Whizzer & Chips 1969- (IPC)
Sid's snake's name is Slippy, and he was the front-page star of *Whizzer & Chips*, a two-in-one comic that began on 18 October 1969. Sid the kid did his best to control Slippy with a flute, but the comical constrictor found Sid's fluting toots anything but snake-charming: 'Wail!' 'Music, I hate it!' hissed Slippy as he skidded away. 'Oy, come back!' said Sid, 'You're my fearsome, frightening, man-eating snake and I'm the only one who can control you!' Interestingly, snakes were forbidden to be depicted in comics by editorial edict of the Amalgamated Press, predecessors of IPC.

Simon and Sally
Mike Noble
Robin 1953-69 (Hulton)
'Simon and Sally the Twins' lived in a little white house with their mother, father, and baby sister Sue, not to mention Tickles the pup and Topsy the cat. Their homely adventures started as a half page in *Robin* No. 1 (28 March 1953) with a pop to the shop. Imagine Mummy's surprise when they brought back soap flakes instead of corn flakes for breakfast! 'Oh you silly billies!' she cried. By 1957 they filled a full page, and by 1961 two. Then in 1965 the strip turned into an illustrated story series entitled 'The Twins: The Happy Adventures of Simon and Sally'.

The Sign of the Scarlet Ladybird
John Canning
Swift 1954-61 (Hulton); *TV Comic* 1956-62 (Beaverbrook)
Bill and Brenda were picnicking under a haystack on the full-colour back page of *Swift* No. 1 (20 March 1954) when a couple of crooks called Shorty and Slim grabbed for their Ladybird shirts. Fortunately for 'Fifties' propriety, Johnny the Jet Boy zoomed out of the sky and whooshed the baddies into the haystack. 'There's a ladybird painted on his plane!' noticed Bill. There was indeed, for the serial was sponsored by the well-known shirt company, and was full of sly messages, such as 'Everybody knows moths can't eat Ladybird sweaters!' In 1957 the title changed to 'The Secret Sign of the Ladybird Adventure Club'.

Simon the Simple Sleuth
Hugh McNeill
Knockout 1939-40; *Comet* 1949-50; *Sun* 1951-52 (Amalgamated Press)
'Simon the Simple Sleuth' got snooping in No. 1 of *Knockout* (4 March 1939), a comic contrast to 'Sexton Blake' who also opened up his detective business in the same issue. Simon, not wishing to be late at the Cop Shop on his first day, asked a passing thug the time. The chap smashed a window, grabbed a watch, and said 'Ten past nine!' 'Fancy going to all that trouble!' opined Simon, as the jeweller yelled for the police. 'Thieves? Where?', asked the Simple Sleuth.

The Silent Three
Evelyn Flinders
School Friend 1950-63 (Amalgamated Press)
'A Tyrannical Head Prefect! Fourth Formers unhappy under her harsh rule!' These were the sensational headlines that introduced the front-page serial on No. 1 of *School Friend* (20 May 1950), 'The Silent Three at St Kit's'. Joan Derwent and Peggy West, smarting under a hundred lines for making too much noise playing draughts, found a mysterious note in their study: 'If you would fight Cynthia Drew's tyranny, come secretly to the crypt at 6 o'clock!' Creeping into the crypt they were confronted by a masked, robed figure named No. 1. The three made a solemn vow – but Mildred Briggs, the form-sneak, was snooping in the shadows. . . .

Simple Spyman
Bill Ritchie
Cracker 1975-76 (D. C. Thomson)
'Meet the guy who's the World's Worst Spy!' Dressed totally in black – hat, coat, glasses, and beard – and known as S.S. for short, he signed on for the duration of *Cracker* from No. 1 (18 January 1975). But whatever his assignment, from eavesdropping on James Blonde's secret underwater cube, to finding out the secret recipe for Crunchi Choc Bars, the end result was always the same: total failure. The nearest S.S. came to success was when a gang gave him the third degree, and he got a nice sun-tan!

Sinbad Simms
Eric Roberts
Knockout 1957-60; *Big One* 1964-65 (Fleetway)
'Shark-Boy of the South Seas' was the subtitle for Sinbad Simms. His mother and father had been lost at sea in a shipwreck when Sinbad was but a baby. He was adopted by a brutal trader called Spike Marlin, who treated the lad like a slave. One day Sinbad swam ashore from Marlin's boat, *The Seadog*, and made his home on Effigy Island in the straits of Samoa. Here he chummed up with a young shark whom he named Jasper, and soon they were busy saving gullible natives from Spike and his crony, One-eye Bates.

Sindy
Pedigree Toys
June 1967-70 (IPC)
'The real-life adventures of that famous fashion doll, Sindy' were depicted in *June* as a serial strip entitled 'The Sindy Set', 'by arrangement with the manufacturers of Sindy dolls'. Featured were the Sindy series of dolls, including her kid sister, Patch, and her boy friend, Paul. Sindy was seen as running a boutique aboard a luxury liner bound for the Bahamas, and was soon entangled in a secret romance between Melanie Hessler, whose mother wanted to match her with the Vicomte du Chambrey, and Tony Everett, a young officer of the *Ocean Star*.

Singapore Jim and Billy
Jack Pamby
Tip Top 1937-39 (Amalgamated Press)
'Chums of the China Seas', Singapore Jim and Billy starred in an action-packed picture serial drawn in bold black-and-white. It all began when they were hired to navigate a Chinese junk called the *Shanghai Pearl*. They free Edda, a white girl, from the clutches of Gonzalez, 'a suspicious half-breed' in league with Ho Feng, a bandit chief. Cap'n Hawk, who helps them, turns out to be a traitor: 'Yes, it's a trap, Singapore Jim!', but he reforms when Ho Feng tries torture. 'This whip ees made of fine wires. Now ye shall taste its sting, white dog!'

Sing Hi and Sing Lo
Joe Hardman
Rainbow 1914-53 (Amalgamated Press)
These cheery little Chinese twins were great favourites of *Rainbow* readers from the first to nearly the last, a forty-year run for artist Joe Hardman. In their first adventure they had a weepy little brother, Sing Song:

> Cheeree uppee, poor little Sing Song!
> We wellee soon manage to help you along.
> We tie up our piggeetails, allee fine style,
> And stoppee you clying, and makee you smile!

Their later adventures involved tricks by Wo Ho the magician.

Sintek
Illustrator unknown
Tiger 1982-85 (IPC)
American motorcycle ace Bruce Tollman was almost dead on arrival when they brought his body into the local hospital. A pile-up at the Austrian Grand Prix in Salzburg had left him with severe brain damage, no sight, shattered legs, and severed arm tendons. Two hours later his body had gone: not to the mortuary, but stolen by Professor Sintek and his deformed assistant, Anton. In his secret laboratory Sintek rebuilt the dying man, kitting him out with powerful artificial eyes, heart, and arms. But when Anton kills Sintek, the rebuilt man wanders out into the world and meets ruthless sports promoter Hal Ford.

Sir Laughalot
Ken Hunter
Topper 1958-64 (D. C. Thomson)
Billed as 'Ye Good Knight', Sir Laughalot rode into *Topper* astride his noble donkey, Dandelion, and soon became popular enough to be promoted from a red-and-black inside page to the full-colour back. Here he hung up his shield-shaped shingle, proclaiming his services were available: Villains Vanquished, Dragons Destroyed, Fayre Maidens Rescued, Witches Hunted, Knaves Nabbed, and Giants, Ogres, Etc. The 'etc' covered a multitude of medieval myths, including a confusing encounter with a sinister centaur.

Sir Solomon Snoozer

Paddy Brennan

Dandy 1949-50 (D. C. Thomson)

Deep in a cave in the heart of England slept the Red Knight, Sir Solomon Snoozer, together with his horse, Ribshanks, and his page boy Robin O'Dare. Trapped by a landslide in the Middle Ages, they were awoken on 17 September 1949 (in No. 408 of *Dandy*) by a blast from some tunnel engineers. With a cry of 'Gadzooks!', Sir Solomon was soon charging a bobby on a bike. As the *Dandy* caption said: 'This Knight so Bold is Umpteen Hundreds of Years Old!'

Six Million Dollar Gran/Robot Granny/Gran's Gang

Ian Knox

Cheeky 1977-80; *Whoopee* 1980-85 (IPC)

Professor Peter Potts, expert in robot technology, unveiled his latest and most expensive ($6 000 000) invention on 22 October 1977. The place was the HQ of WASP (the World Authority for Scientific Powers), situated on page 9 of *Cheeky* No. 1. When sinister spies seek to snatch the robot in their burrowing 'Mole', the Prof. takes the mechanical man home with him, disguised as an old lady. For the rest of her run she acts as super-grandmother to the Potts kids, Pete and Pauline. Title changed to 'Robot Granny' (1981) and 'Gran's Gang' (1983).

Sitting Bull

Illustrator unknown

Sun 1949-52 (Amalgamated Press)

'Sitting Bull, Fighting Indian' went on the warpath on the two-tone front page of *Sun* No. 50 (1 October 1949). Originally a strip translated from the French, British artists took the saga over with a new serial, 'Sitting Bull and the Scarlet War-Bonnet, which started on 29 March 1952. This was the first of the new comic-book format series of *Sun* (No. 164), and the story concerned Sitting Bull's defence of the Sioux against Red Hawk, fierce leader of the Pawnees. Between the two warring factions were General Custer and the 7th US Cavalry.

The Skid Kids

Illustrator unknown

Buster 1966-68 (Fleetway)

High-speed thrills were promised when racing driver Simon Starr teamed up with Brainbox Cox. They were delivered in an unexpected way, for while the penniless pals roamed the world entering major races, their vehicles were always something of a surprise, especially to the other professional racers. Their clapped-out crock won the Grand Prix in Italy, thanks to Brainbox's hyped-up engine, and, on the Swiss Credor Run, their streamlined bob-sleigh, equipped with an all-round anti-crash bar adapted from a fairground bumper car, beat champion Dino Carletti.

S

Skid Solo
Illustrator unknown
Hurricane 1964-65; *Lion* 1965-81 (Fleetway)
Skid Solo told his story in the first person, starting in No. 1 of *Hurricane* (29 February 1964). 'In my daydreams it wasn't the rattle of the motor-mower I was hearing, but the roar of high performance racing cars!' Not long out of school, Skid used the money he made mowing his Aunty Mabel's lawn for lessons on the motor-racing circuit at Fernheath Racing Drivers School (ten bob a circuit). 'I gunned the engine and went off like a bomb!', passing Chaz Checker, three times runner-up for the world's championship, to break the lap record by one second. Then he inherited £1200 and was away!

Skit the Kat
Harry Banger
Topical Funnies 1940; *Slick Fun* 1940-46; *New Funnies 1941; Fresh Fun* 1941; *Thrill Comics* 1941; *War Comics* 1942 (Swan)
This famished feline was one of Harry Banger's finest creations, a skinny puss on the prowl who owed nothing to the fantastic qualities of Felix the Cat or the yet-to-come animated action of Tom and Jerry. Yet Skit strips were full of visual fun and fury as the Kat chased mice or was himself chased by bullish bulldogs. The early two-page epics were pure pantomime, but soon speech was added for the humans ('Scoff my breakfast, you thieving moggie!'), and eventually for Skit, although often confined to a final 'F'lup!'

Skinny and Scotty
Gerald Pain
Monster 1928-30 (Amalgamated Press)
'The Artful Antics of Skinny and Scotty, or All the Fun of the Pair!' was the full title of the front-page strip which signified the take-over of the independent *Monster Comic* by the mighty Amalgamated Press. By 1929 the full names of the long lad and his sawn-off sidekick were revealed in the new title of the strip, 'The Comical Capers of Skinny Skinner and Scotty Scrump'. Cast in the classical mould of comic double-acts, Skinny was the tall one in the big cap, while Scotty was described as 'our wee herb from the home of the haggis'.

Skippy
Robert MacGillivray
Zip 1958-59; *Swift* 1959-61 (Odhams)
'Skippy the Boy who Lives in a Barrel' was the full-colour front-page star of No. 1 of Zip (4 January 1958). The barrel he lived in was fitted into the branches of a tree, and was complete with a bell, a bucket of water labelled 'fire', and a special little doggie-door labelled 'Buster'. For cooking his kippers on a stick, Skippy had a battered brazier, and in the back pocket of his jeans was parked a catapult. When *Zip* merged with *Swift*, Skippy's strip turned educational: 'He is always learning about the exciting things around him', such as thatching.

Skit, Skat and the Captain
Basil Reynolds
Mickey Mouse Weekly 1936-40 (Odhams)
'Adventures of the World's Smallest Cabin Boy and his Skatty Cat' started in No. 1 of the *Mickey Mouse Weekly* (8 February 1936): one of the few characters not created by Walt Disney. Shipping aboard the S.S. *SOS*, Skit and Skat made life merry hell for poor old Cappy, although many a strip ended in rewards, such as the the time they accidentally hatched the eggs of the Extinct Lesser Jazzwoozle ('Auk!'), the sale of which enabled them to pay the last instalment on the lifebelts. Later they visited London Zoo to see the chimps, Booboo and Jubilee: 'would jubilee-ve it!' The mouse who lurked in corners was called Marmaduke.

Skookum Skool/Spookum Skool

Ken Harrison

Buzz 1973-75; *Cracker* 1975-76 (D. C. Thomson)

'Skookum Skool is never quiet – Every week's a proper riot!' The D. C. Thomson rhymester was right: from No. 1 of *Buzz* (20 January 1973) this bunch of juvenile delinquents declared war on their teachers in best Bash Street style. Their boots made so much noise that Teacher demonstrated how to tiptoe in stockinged feet. It was hardly anyone's fault that he promptly trod on Herbie the hedgehog. In 1974 *Buzz* readers discovered with a shock what went on at Skookum Skool when it was locked up for the night. It turned into Spookum Skool for a gang of ghosts! For more, see 'The Headhunters'.

Slade

Small

Hornet 1963-64 (D. C. Thomson)

J. A. Slade was the most feared gunman in the West. 'His gun was deadly. He'd as soon kill a man as look at him – and the man he was looking for was Wal Loader.' The feud between J. A. Slade and Wal Loader, ace rider for the Pony Express, had begun in *Wizard* in 1937. Then it was a serial story, but on 14 September 1963 the feud started all over again as a picture serial in No. 1 of *Hornet*. The original title, 'Pony Express', was now changed to 'Slade of the Pony Express', and the black-clad gunman found himself working alongside the man he had sworn to shoot.

The Sky Explorers

Reg Parlett

Comet 1952-53 (Amalgamated Press)

Professor Jolly and his niece Ann and nephew Peter originally appeared in a serial entitled 'Live Long Island'. Drawn by Geoff Campion, it told of the trio's adventures among a 200-year-old gang of pirates led by Black Bellamy the Scourge o' the Seas. It started in *Comet* No. 184 (26 January 1952). The title changed to 'Island of Secrets' from No. 193, and then they rocketed into space in 'Journey to Jupiter' (No. 202), drawn by Reg Heade. Reg Parlett took over the artwork from No. 206, the strip bursting into three pages of full colour as 'The Sky Explorers', moving on to the front page from No. 225 to No. 246.

Slaine

Mike McMahon

2000 AD 1983- (IPC)

'In the time before the flood, the saga is told of Slaine MacRoth of the Sessair – mercenary, cattle rustler and battle-smiter, who rose to become a legendary King of the Tribes of the Earth Goddess.' Slaine's story was narrated by Ukko, his faithful dwarf, from a script by Pat Mills. Book 1, 'The Beast in the Broch', was about a Nameless Horror lurking in a prison tower. Luckily Slaine had the help of Nudd, his subhuman assistant. Beasts continued to be a problem: Book 3, 'The Shoggey Beast', was about a man who could turn himself into a hairy fiend, by Lug!

Slicksure
Harry Banger
Fresh Fun 1940-45; *Thrill Comics* 1946-48; *Slick Fun* 1949 (Swan)
Slicksure 'the famous Secret Agent' was enjoying a pipeful of puff in No. 1 of *Fresh Fun* (April 1940) when the telephone summoned him to the War Dept. General Dogsbody had an assignment for him in Scotland: guard Professor Bigwit, and the plans of his new ray-pistol, from the enemy. Instantly unmasking Hermann from Hamburgh (*sic*) – 'Butlers don't wear moustaches, laddie!' – Slicksure thought he had the case solved, but he reckoned without Baron Von Splitz and – could it be the Loch Ness Monster? Continued next month!

The Sludgemouth Sloggers
Illustrator unknown
Jet 1971; *Buster* 1971-72 (IPC)
Just round the bend of the beach from the booming holiday resort of Brighthaven lay Sludgemouth, the loneliest seaside town in Britain. Thanks to a geographical freak, it was a permanent raintrap. Lady Bogmire, chairman of the council, despaired until entertainments secretary Ted Larkin came up with his 'What a Lark Contest', the Whacky World Cup. Long-legged Ted's team consisted of postman Knocker Smith (balancing), farmer Arfur Wurzel (skewer-the-swede), blacksmith Charlie Anvil (feats of strength) and Constable Flipper Finn (swimmer: his beat was underwater!).

The Slimms
Terry Bave
Cor 1972-74; *Whizzer & Chips* 1974-79 (IPC)
An amusing comment on the contemporary craze for dieting. Sammy Slimm was as his name suggests: the slim son of Mr and Mrs Slimm. His parents, however, were quite the opposite, horrendously overweight. Sammy saw it as his duty to help his folks conquer their craving for food, but their overpowering hunger pangs led to a perpetual feud over food. 'The Slimms will never tire – When getting food is their desire!' But sometimes the Slimms didn't win. When their boy dozed off, tired of guarding grub, they rushed drooling into the dining room and got jammed in the door. They had to lose weight to get loose.

Smarty Grandpa
Dudley Watkins
Dandy 1937-40 (D. C. Thomson)
With his walrus whiskers, grizzled chin-mat, baggy black suit, and floppy flat cap, Smarty Grandpa was the epitomy of the prewar pensioner. The old codger's cunning was reserved for helping his grandchildren, a scruffy couple of unnamed nippers who were doubtless dead-ringers for *Dandy* readers. Grandpa's tricks ranged from the simple (a brick down his back to cure a kicking bully) to the complex (writing '100' on the lenses of Grandma's specs when the kids came home with a bad school-report).

Slojak
Illustrator unknown
Cracker 1975-76 (D. C. Thomson)
This junior burlesque of the adult television series *Kojak* starred, instead of bald, lollipop-sucking Telly Savalas, a bald, lollipop-sucking boy. Billed as *Cracker*'s Top Tec, Slojak seemed keener on lolly-licking than crime crunching, although his obsession with confectionery occasionally came in handy: a sticky lolly pulled off a false beard to expose Baldy Briggs the Burglar to the law, aniseed balls tripped a purse-snatcher, and bursting bubble-gum scared a bank-robber. As Slojak was wont to say between slurps: 'Right on, baby!'

The Smasher
Hugh Morren
Dandy 1957- (D. C. Thomson)
'I'm not called The Smasher for nothing!' laughed the red-headed lad in the matching red-checked, zip-up windcheater. It was true, for wherever he turned, things smashed to pieces. Smasher is not just accident-prone, of course; much of the smashing that has been going on in his strip for a quarter of a century is cunningly planned, despite the inevitable climax of castor oil or dad's slipper. Nothing changes, except Smasher's hair, which has turned from red to black with the passage of time.

The Smasher/Crusher
James Walker
Dandy 1938; *Victor* 1962; *Bullet* 1976-78 (D. C. Thomson)
'From the Bubble comes a terrifying man-made metal monster' announced *Bullet* No. 1 (14 February 1976); quoth the robot, 'Smasher will destroy!' Then came the voice over the radio: 'This is Doctor Doom, master of the Smasher, calling the world. I intend to rule nations, govern the whole globe from pole to pole. Either obey me or face the onslaught of the Smasher!' But the world has heard this threat before. In No. 439 of the story-paper *Wizard* (2 May 1931); in *Dandy* No. 39 (27 August 1938); in *Victor* No. 58 (31 March 1962). But even when Red Raglan, explosives expert, destroyed the Smasher, Dr Doom came back with the Crusher!

Smiler
Nick Baker
Whoopee 1976-82 (IPC)
'Keep Smiling', the wartime motto, might have been coined for this curly topped kid. Smiler's battery of bright, white teeth would have put George Formby's famous grin into the shade. Nothing could wipe the smile off Smiler's face, although plenty of people (grown-ups, of course) have tried. Even his Uncle Egbert, a modern-day Scrooge, ended up cracking a grin. He tried to spoil Smiler's Christmas by snatching away a box of chox. 'Quite right, I might spoil my dinner!' smiled Smiler, giving the old goat a woolly scarf. It was enough to make Smiler's cat laugh.

Smiley
Harry Bishop
Swift 1958-60 (Hulton)
From out of Moore Raymond's novel, via the film of the same name, Smiley (the Boy from Down Under) came to the front page of *Swift* from 9 August 1958. The sunbaked setting was the bush settlement of Murrumbilla in the Australian outback, where Smiley lived with his pals, Jacky and Joey the Aborigine. It was the 'Abo' who started off the excitement with the discovery of a 'little fella roo' – a baby kangaroo orphaned when its mother was shot by neighbour O'Regan. Smiley adopts the orphan, calling it Firsty. But boundary rider Kafkey decides to shoot Firsty as revenge when Smiley reports him to Sergeant Flaxman.

Smiffy
Bill Ritchie
Beezer 1967- (D. C. Thomson)
Smiffy arrived in *Beezer* No. 577 (4 February 1967) and soon expanded from a half page to a full one. Smiffy was the scruffiest boy in his class, and in his school, for that matter. But he wasn't the scruffiest person at home: that dubious honour was reserved for his dad. Mr Smith, as scruffy haired as his son but with the added adult distinction of a highly unshaven chin, has the disreputable reputation of being the scruffiest parent in the history of British comics.

Smiler and Smudge
Bertie Brown
Butterfly 1926-40 (Amalgamated Press)
'The Comical Couple', Smiler, a white boy, and George Washington Septimus Smudge, a black boy (address; Number Nix, Nobody's Buildings), formed an unusual double-act for their prewar period. Although there was much conflict between the two (Smiler called Smudge 'Coalface'!), they remained the best of buddies for their fifteen-year run. From 1931 the strip sent its heroes to school as 'The Merry Antics of Smiler and Smudge, the Comical Couple of Carraway College', where they spent their remaining ten years terrorizing Dr Cake, Monsieur Mugwump the French master, and Peter Pumpkin the porter.

Smudge/Hy Jinks
Eric Roberts
Dandy 1947-49; 1955-57 (D. C. Thomson)
'Smudge is the girl – To keep things in a whirl – Fresh as a daisy – She drives her Dad crazy!' Thus the trailer for Eric Roberts' replacement for his successful prewar hero, Podge. This time, instead of an 'ordinary boy', he came up with an 'ordinary girl'. A bit of a tomboy, true, Smudge was designed to appeal to the boy and girl readers of *Dandy*, and was headlined in her first appearance (2 August 1947): 'Meet inside a tricky little gal – Make her your great new comic pal!' In 1955 Smudge reappeared in reprints, rechristened Hy Jinks.

The Smurfs
Peyo
Look-In 1978-81 (ITV)
The Anglicized version of a popular Belgian strip, *Les Schtroumpfs*. Created by Pierre Culliford under the pen-name Peyo, these little blue elves first appeared in the weekly comic *Spirou* (1960). They made their British comic debut in *Look-In* 1978), the Junior *TV Times*, under the title 'Meet the Smurfs!', but only in monochrome: black dot tint replaced their traditional blue. Their popularity in Britain relates to their American-made television cartoon series.

Snip and Snap
Michael Green
Sparky 1972-74 (D. C. Thomson)
Known as 'The Chewsome Twosome', these twin terrors were fierce little dogs with but one aim in life: sinking their sharp little fangs into the postman's leg. Snip and Snap were the beloved pets of a bespectacled spinster who lived at Number Three, where they lay in wait drooling their strange war-cry of 'rizzle!' Pity the poor postie; but once in a while he got his revenge, through such outlandish plots as a false leg filled with glue!

Snack-Man
David Mostyn
Whoopee 1982-85 (IPC)
Strip which reflected the contemporary craze for electronic arcade games. Billy Button was ace on the Snack-Man machine and on 23 October 1982, on the full-colour front of *Whoopee*, he hit the greatest score of all time. Snack-Man ate everything on the screen, then burst from its electronic confines to gobble up a girl's toffee apple! Then it ate all the sweets in the crane machine and started after Billy Button himself. From then on life was hard for Billy. The only time he was safe from the hungry ball was when there was a mock battle of Cavaliers and Roundheads: Snack-Man thought they were after him!

The Snobbs and the Slobbs
John Geering
Nutty 1980-85 (D. C. Thomson)
The game of not-so-happy families started in *Nutty* No. 35 (11 October 1980). The line-up was as follows: on the left, the Snobs (Mumsie, Daddy, and the twins, Percy and Charles); on the right, the Slobbs (Ma, Pa, and their kids, Hilda and skinhead Stan). Hostilities began when the neighbouring families tried to hang a picture on their adjoining wall: nails protruded, then punctured a water pipe, and war was declared! After some years of battle, they all got together to put on a pantomime in the 1983 Christmas number: 'I recognise that foot odour! This is your welly, Cinderella!'

Snowdrop's Zoo

Arnold Warden

Playbox 1938-55 (Amalgamated Press)

Snowdrop, a trim little miss in high-heeled boots and the 1938 version of the miniskirt, opened her Zoo in the pages of *Playbox*. Her right-hand man was Chic the Clown, ever on hand to fox the monkeys, a mischievous pair called Mig and Mog, lend a flipper to Percy Penguin and his well-dressed pals of the pool, or wreak a little mild revenge on the prankiest pets of the lot, Peter Panda and Piggy. Tee-hee, what larks!

Some Mummies Do 'Ave 'Em

Charles Sinclair

Sparky 1975-77 (D. C. Thomson)

Taking its title from the popular BBC television series, *Some Mothers Do 'Ave 'Em*, this strip translated it literally into a saga of a family of Egyptian mummies, bandaged beings who came to life by night much to the distress of the uniformed curator of a museum. There were four in the family: Daddymummy, Mummymummy, Babbymummy, and their pet Doggymummy, and they were given to uttering such ancient oaths as 'By the pharoah's fez!' Their full-colour adventures covered both front and back pages.

Snow White and Her Merry Friends

Walter Bell

Happy Days 1939;
Chicks Own 1939-57
(Amalgamated Press)

When Snow White moved into No. 23 of *Happy Days* (11 March 1939), she had quite a crowd of Merry Friends. There was naughty Tommy Tucker who blew Boy Blue's horn and scared Mary's Little Lamb. Then there was Little Miss Muffet and a whole classroom of nursery rhyme familiars crowding into Old Mother Hubbard's school. Soon they were all having full-colour fun on page one, a treat destined not to last. For *Happy Days* declined and combined with *Chicks Own*, and there was Snow White, reduced to a couple of bunnies called Bobtail and Flopears, and condemned to talk in hyphenated syllables for nineteen years!

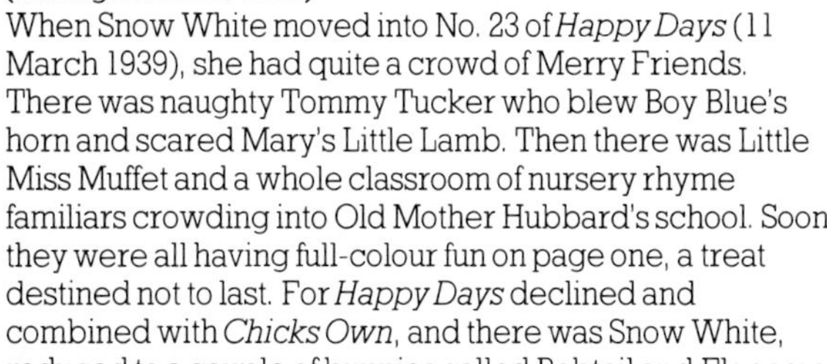

Sonny Bear and Micky

Freddie Crompton

Playbox 1935-55 (Amalgamated Press)

Sonny Bear and his little chum Micky the Monkey lived with jolly Mr Jolly on page one of *Playbox*. They sat on their own little bench for two in the front of Teacher Tippit's classroom, and nobody seemed to find it odd that these animals could talk, or wear clothes, even if Sonny never wore trousers and all Micky wore was a green school cap. Sonny was a brown bear until 1936, when he went white: perhaps he was a late-blooming polar? August 27, 1949 was a fateful day: they saved Twizzle, a long-eared creature that could change colour. What fun!

Softy Sir

Andy Robb

School Fun 1983-84 (IPC)

The first gay hero in British comics, Softy Sir pranced into *School Fun* No. 1 (15 October 1983) complete with long hair, bow tie, and spotty hanky in his top pocket. He came by bubble-car ('A motorised roller-skate!' hooted Butch) hoping for a ground-floor classroom as he couldn't stand heights. He called his class 'dear children' and flapped his hands at them rather limp-wristedly whenever he got cross. But now and then he showed a streak of sterner stuff, as, when on a museum visit, he locked his lot into torture instruments and made them a 'captive audience'.

Sonny Boy

James Malcolm

Buster 1962-65 (Fleetway)

'The bright little lad who makes trouble for his Dad – but makes you glad!' arrived in *Buster* on 5 May 1962. Sonny Boy's problem was his Dad, a well-meaning, well-whiskered, pipe-puffing parent. Each week he would do his best to improve the quality of his son's life, and each week he would end up the worse for wear. In trying to teach the boy to swim, Dad succeeded in draining the local pool and had to be hauled out of the plug-hole by the fire brigade. Sonny Boy decided he would stick to paddling.

Sonny Day
Reg Parlett
Wonder 1944-49 (Amalgamated Press)
'Meet Sonny Day and his boss Whiskers the Wizard in Magic While You Wait!' was the overlong title of this strip. Reversing the old tale of *The Sorceror's Apprentice*, Sonny Day, a buttoned-up pageboy, spent most of his time trying to clear up the consequences of his employer's magical mixtures, which invariably backfired. Creating a concentrated din-din pill for dogs, Whiskers fed it to their watch-pup who immediately grew so big he filled the whole house! Which made the pup a good house dog, of course: nobody else could get in!

Sonny and Sally
Hugh McNeill
Playhour 1957-85 (IPC)
'Sonny and Sally of Happy Valley' lived on a lovely farm called Cosy Corner, and everywhere that Sonny and Sally went, their lamb was sure to go. This was Pet, their pet, and she even hopped on to the bus one day. And where do you think Sonny and Sally found him? In the bus drivers' canteen gambolling to the piano! How they all laughed, and Pet helped the children tuck into tea – luckily for everyone it was Pancake Day! By 1959 Sonny and Sally were joint editors of *Playhour*, writing a weekly letter from Cosy Corner, Fleetway House, Farringdon Street.

Sooty Snowball/Sparky
Illustrator unknown
Magic 1939-40; *Sparky* 1965-69 (D. C. Thomson)
Race Relations Board please note: we quote the following introductory verse in the interests of history:

Here's Sooty Snowball, black as black
Sam Coot brought this cute little nigger back,
From Africa, far o'er the sea,
Where monkeys swing from tree to tree.

Monocled Sam Coot the explorer brought Sooty, his sister Topsy, and fat Cookie Ned to live in England, where civilization was a constant surprise to them all. Actually D. C. Thomson brought the strip back from Italy, where it had been popular for some years. The strip was Anglicized by Bob MacGillivray, and revived for *Sparky* by Ron Spence.

Sooty and Sweep
Harry Corbett
TV Comic 1954-56 (*News of the World*); *Playhour* 1960-64 (Fleetway); *Pippin* 1967; *Playland* 1968-75 (Polystyle); *Playgroup* 1984-86 (IPC)
'Izzy Wizzy, Let's get busy!' was the catchphrase of this little bear-cub as he waved his magic wand. Sooty was a glove puppet, first seen on BBC children's television in a 1952 slapstick series starring entertainer Harry Corbett. Sweep was Sooty's chum, a floppy dog. Interestingly, the Sooty strips in *TV Comic* were drawn by Tony Hart, who was to become a television star in his own right. The later strips for the front page of *Playland* were drawn by Fred Robinson.

S.O.S. Squad
Mike Lacey
Buster 1981-82 (IPC)
Gang of good-doers who zoomed to the rescue in their battered but jet-propelled pram. Roll-call: Biff Buggins; Zip Johnson, a black boy; Skypole Smith, the skinny beanpole in braces; Nosher Mulligan, the plump one; Effel Red, the girl in the gang; Baby Boffin; Bundle the dog; Cocky the cross-eyed cockatoo. Their boss was the mysterious Zed, a pair of eyes lurking in shadows of a half-opened soap-box. Their assignments included teaching little Maisie's pet, Cuddles, some tricks: it was a pet gorilla!

Space Ace
Illustrator unknown
Lone Star 1953-63; *Space Ace* 1960-63 (Atlas)
Originally billed as 'Ace Hart – Space Squadron Commander' in *Lone Star* No. 1, and as 'Space Ace' from No. 3, this former sheriff of Tarrant County, Texas, was knocked unconscious by a small meteorite which rendered him immune to all radioactivity. Professor McKay of the Gopher Gulch Anglo-American Interplanetary Research Station makes Ace commander of the spaceship *LS1*, and with Chief Pilot Bill Haines, Dr Wang Fu, physicist, Silas Granger, mining expert, Monty Milne, and Marmaduke, the monkey, they take off on 'Journey to Zimbolus'. Artists included Ron Turner (illustrated).

The Space Family Rollinson
Illustrator unknown
Knockout 1954-59 (Amalgamated Press)
The Rollinson Family – Dad, Mum, and their children, Betsy and Joey, the young ones, and Joy and Bob, the elder pair – journey through space in their Flying Sphere. The first of their many adventures took place on an unknown planet, millions of miles away from Earth. After being helped by the friendly Jelyonites, the girls are captured by Notoc and Titan and his mechanical minions, the Zektron-men. Then there are the Web-foot Men of Planet Aquarius to contend with, and a Jovian invasion of Earth to foil.

Souper Boy
John Dallas
Topper 1980-86 (D. C. Thomson)
'S.B.' are the bold black letters emblazoned on this small boy's tee-shirt. They stand for Sidney Braithwaite and Souper Boy, the mighty muscular marvel S.B. becomes as soon as he swallows a swig of Super Soup! Then with a 'ka-pow!' and a 'zap!', or sometimes with a 'Phap! Plang! Zoop!' just for a change, Souper Boy souper-swoops off to save the day, the hour, or even the minute. A similar strip, Souper Cat, ran in June 1971, starring a puny puss called Purrcy.

Space Cadet
Illustrator unknown
Ranger 1965-66 (Fleetway)
Jason January was the name of the hero of this science-fiction serial, a full-colour spread which started in No. 1 of *Ranger* (18 September 1965). He was Cadet Captain of the Rangers, the third-year students at the Royal Space Force Academy, which was founded in AD 2015. The day was a special one: King Charles the Fourteenth was to attend the ceremony by which Nelson's flagship *Victory* would be dedicated to the cause of Interstellar World Peace. But Hercules Canute had other plans: he and his space pirates intended to steal the historic ship.

The Space Girls
Keith Watson
Tina 1967; *Princess Tina* 1967-68 (Fleetway)
'Here Come the Space Girls' was the title of this two-page full-colour serial which took off in *Tina* No. 1 (25 February 1967). Billed as 'The Air Hostesses of the Future', Fran, Sally, and Kathy were smartly dressed space hostesses aboard the space liner *X-77*, bound for Venus via Moon City spaceport. The year was 2501 and Captain Pepper was commander of the ship. A Very Important Passenger with honey-coloured skin and raven black hair turned out to be Princess Fabia of Venus, who had a historic collection of Beatles records!

Space Jinx
Brian Lewis
Smash 1966 (Odhams)
'He's the reason why people in outer space want to come in!' explained the editor of *Smash* when Space Jinx blasted off across the full-colour centre spread of No. 1 (15 February 1966). The scene was Space City Zero where a rocketship captain was starting the countdown. Panicking at the sight of the Jinx – 'It's the boy who wrecked a hundred spaceships!' – he just fails to blast off before the boy is bunged aboard. Jinx did his best to console the captain by taking him a cup of tea, but he forgot they were in a gravity free zone – splosh! Escaping into what he thought was a cupboard, Jinx found himself adrift in space.

Spaceship Lollipop
Bob Dewar
Magic 1976-78 (D. C. Thomson)
Suzie and Steven Star lived in the wonderful world of Space. Their father, Doctor Star, was a famous space explorer. The family travelled in a super spaceship called Lollipop. 'Fasten your seat-belts!' said Dr Star in *Magic* No. 1 (31 January 1976), 'We are going to visit the Clockwork Planet!' The children walked to the Royal Palace: it was quicker than taking the train. Everything had run down because someone had stolen the king's key. Other planets visited in the full-colour centre spreads included the Pepper Planet, the Snowball Planet, and the Puppet Planet.

Space School
Mike Higgs
Whizzer & Chips 1969-70 (IPC)
'Two hundred years on from 1969, and earthmen have reached the planets. Our story is about a school for the sons of astronauts from different worlds. Klank the robot caretaker let the kids out for morning playtime.' And out rushed the oddest lot ever seen in a comic, let alone a school. There was two-headed Eddie from Uranus, Newto from Neptune with his space helmet full of water, bouncy Boing from Pluto, flying Dicky from Mercury, Oggie from Mars, legless Rollo from Jupiter, and the only normal boy (for a comic, that is), Tommy from Earth. The teacher, clad in trad mortarboard and kilt, was Mr McWhack.

Spadger
S. K. Perkins
Wizard 1925-56 (D. C. Thomson)
Spadger, a chirpy cockney sparrow of a kid, was captain of a backyard football team called 'Spadger's XI' who kicked off in the centre spread comic section of *Wizard* No. 126 on 14 February 1925. Running out of footer gags, Perkins handed over to Chick Gordon who sent the lads on a world tour. On 31 January 1931 Spadger and the rotund sailor, Skipper Sam, were wrecked on a desert island. With their page retitled 'Spadger Isle' the twosome set about Anglicizing the natives, a black race of cannibals whom they called 'Nigs' The strip shifted to the full-colour front on 28 October 1939, where it stayed to 12 August 1950.

Spare Part Kit
Vic Neill
Wow 1982-83; *Whoopee* 1983 (IPC)
Zoblobnians are the world's worst athletes, a fact which President Krunchski is forced to face up to when the '84 Olympics loom. Fortunately, Professor Tom Katz has perfected the manufacture of electronic spare parts, mighty arms and legs which can make even the puniest worker a mound of muscle. Not wanting his devices used to cheat in the Olympics, Tom and his son Kit Katz flee to England, where Kit wears them to foil the machinations of Fruitski and Nutski the superspies.

Speed Kings
Barrie Mitchell
Scoop 1978-81; *Victor* 1981
(D. C. Thomson)
'Crazy driver plus genius mechanic plus old banger equals Speed Kings': the formula for car-racing excitement that got off to a flying start in No. 1 of *Scoop* (21 January 1978). 'Speedy' Ron Hutton, lorry driver for King Transport, drove the boss, Colonel King, in a wild cross-country race against time to see a doctor. He used his pal 'Greasy' Tanner's souped-up banger and won for the pair of them a new job. Soon they were driving against Ace Hawkins of Gosforth Conversions – and winning. By the time *Scoop* closed (No. 194) they were in South America competing in the World Driver's Championships.

The Sparky People
Jim Petrie
Sparky 1969-77 (D. C. Thomson)
This unique strip set behind the scenes in a comic's editorial office, started off with an equally unique couplet, qualifying for the D. C. Thomson poet's worst yet:

Here's the story of us –
Blokes in the *Sparky* office!

Sparky was apparently edited by a Sir, seldom seen save for one well-aimed boot. The staff who suffered from its studded sole were Throgmorton, the subeditor, the walrus-whiskered printer, a bearded and bereted artist, the bespectacled Joke Man, Julie the typist, Dick the office boy, and a cat.

Speedboy
Illustrator unknown
Speed 1980 (IPC)
Schoolboy Timothy Barlow devoted his life to record-breaking. On the morning of 23 February 1980 (publication day of No. 1 of *Speed*) he made it from bed to breakfast-table in six minutes, beat his own five minutes best in the run to school, and was first to finish teacher's ten-question test – unfortunately he got every answer wrong! But he had better luck when his best pal 'Doc' Dawlish made a go-cart. After thirty-six fast-moving weeks, Tim's folks moved to Groundwood and he found himself a supporting player in 'Billy's Boots', in another comic!

The Spellbinder
Geoff Campion
Lion 1970-73 (IPC)
Young Tom Turville inherited ancient Turville Hall which stood in a remote spot in the lonely Suffolk countryside, its outward appearance sinister and forbidding, a place of legends and dark secrets. Tom found the Hall was inhabited by his ancestor, Sylvester Turville, an alchemist who had remained alive for four centuries, through the magic powers of the Turville Touchstone. This powerful charm was capable of curing a hurt paw of Merlin the black cat, or of glowing with a baleful green light when evil came nigh, as it often did.

The Spider
Reg Bunn
Lion 1965-67; *Vulcan* 1975-76 (IPC)
Roy Ordini was known as the Prince of Safe-breakers – neither locks, bars, nor burglar alarms could withstand his uncanny skill. Detective Lieutenant Bob Gilmore and Sgt Pete Trask were about to grab Ordini when he was snatched from a skyscraper by the black-clad Spider: 'I need you to help me build an Empire of Crime, crime on a scale of which no man ever dreamed. Serve me and I'll make you rich!' The Spider swung across New York's chasms via gossamer-like threads, stronger than nylon, and his lair was a castle moved from Scotland, stone by stone.

Spike and Dusty
John Chester
Tiger 1957-61 (Amalgamated Press)
'Frogman Spy-hunters' was the first serial to feature these two ex-navy frogmen, Spike North and Dusty Minton. They teamed up with their old wartime friend, Commander Blaine, to take underwater photographs of an amazing guided missile he had invented, but the Commander was kidnapped by spies. Another series, 'Destination Danger', revealed their wartime adventures in destroying the German battleship *Schneider* in its secret dry-dock. Later they teamed up with Captain Rex Royal, known as 'Commando One'.

© 1986 M.C.G.

Spider-Man
Steve Ditko
Pow 1967-68; *Smash* 1968-69 (Odhams); *TV 21* 1970 (City); *Marvel* 1972-73; *Spiderman* 1973-85; *Marvel Teamup* 1980-81; *Spiderman Pocketbook* 1980-82 (Marvel)
Credited with bringing about a renaissance in American comicbooks, Spider-Man, never seen without his 'Amazing', first slung a web in No. 15 of *Amazing Fantasy* (August 1952). This superhero's alter ego is Peter Parker, a shy teenager scorned as a bookworm. Bitten by a radio-active spider he found himself possessed of all that arachnid's peculiar powers: the ability to climb walls, dangle from ceilings, and spin webs. His British debut was in No. 1 of *Pow* (21 January 1967).

Splodge
Charles Grigg
Topper 1969-74 (D. C. Thomson)
'The Last of the Goblins' woke one morning (20 September 1969) to find himself on the back page of *Topper* No. 868. The birds were squabbling over seeds ('Sqwawk!'), the woodpeckers closing down branches everywhere ('Brrrrrm!'), and noisy chaos reigned in the forest. Splodge was no less rowdy, and was soon leaving his tree-home to wreak revenge on 'blooming humans' by organizing the Ant Army, or instituting National Yaargh Day. This consisted of seeing how many animals he could startle by shouting 'Yaargh!' in their unsuspecting ears.

Spider Wells
Rezzonico
Warlord 1975-77 (D. C. Thomson)
'It is 1916. World War One rages and for the first time in history aeroplanes play a major part in warfare. In the sky over the battlefields of France, pilots of the Royal Flying Corps clash with a German squadron.' Meanwhile in the fields outside an industrial town in the north of England, sixteen-year-old Johnny Wells, nicknamed 'Spider' because he is lean and lanky, flies his model Sopworth Pup. Accidentally killing his cruel stepfather for striking his little sister, Spider flees and enlists in the Royal Westland Fusiliers. Soon he is fighting in France: will he get his transfer to the RFC?

Spoofer McGraw
Gordon Bell
Sparky 1968-74 (D. C. Thomson)
'He Tells Tall Tales' was the billing for this scruffy headed schoolboy in the red cap. The victim of his weekly imaginings was a bulky boy named Bo, barely visible in his big black duffle-coat. After a year of Spoofer's inspired imagination, which included the ravenous Christmas Pudants who lived only for their one annual seasonal spree, ideas were solicited from *Sparky* readers at ten shillings a time. Michael Kelly of Macclesfield won for his explanation that one-storey houses got their name when a brick shortage caused builders to bung-a-low roof on them!

The Spooktacular Seven
Brian Walker
Whoopee 1977-78 (IPC)
One day, 8 October 1977 to be precise, the Innkeeper of the Scream Inn was watching *The Magnificent Seven* on his telly. Inspired, he organized his hitherto scary staff into a team of goody ghouls: Suffering Sam, Dennis the Devil, Bertie Bedsheet, Boneypart the skeleton, Cookie the witch, and Cyril the spider. Dottie the mad housekeeper opted to stay home and take messages. Their first mission was to stop bullying at Bungleton Apprehensive School. It was easy: Suffering Sam dressed as a schoolboy and when the bully threatened to knock his block off, Sam let him!

Sporty
Reg Wootton
Knockout 1949-63; *Valiant* 1963-65 (Fleetway)
The only strip in children's comics drawn by the brilliant newspaper artist, Reg Wootton, creator of 'Sporting Sam'. The theme was sport, of course, and Sporty was the shorty, Sydney the skinny, of this back-page double-act. (For a while in 1952 they moved to the full-colour cover.) Sporty, accompanied by a podgy little pup, was the one who knew best, while Sydney was the one who thought he knew best. They were based on W. Ridgewell's 'Percy and Steve', a 'Thirties strip in *Sports Budget* which had been reprinted on the early *Knockout*.

Sports Fan
George Martin
Nutty 1980-85 (D. C. Thomson)
'Sme!' was Sports Fan's proud announcement in her title panel. In her striped sweater and matching hair-ribbon, Fan was a true fanatic when it came to football. This generally unfeminine sport lost none of its traditional violence when Fan got weaving with her fancy footwork. Her poor parents and, of course, their windows, acted as unwilling goals for their tomboy offspring. But Fan's backside was seldom offside when it came to her dad's well-aimed slipper.

Spotsem and Getsem
Cyril Price
Butterfly 1939-40 (Amalgamated Press)
Named after the famous pair of broadcasting comedians, Flotsam and Jetsam, Spotsem was a bespectacled boy detective and Getsam his spotted sleuth-hound. Their first case was called 'The Jewelled Carrot', and the chase thereof formed a fast-paced comic serial with Spotsem and Getsem in pursuit of the Ivy Road Creepers. Chief Creeper was Jerry Jitter, and his masked minions included Alonzo Ardbake and Arthur Arfwit. Once the valuable vegetable was returned to Prof. Golightly, a weekly case ensued.

Spy School
Graham Allen
Whoopee 1974-75 (IPC)
It was on 9 March 1974, in No. 1 of *Whoopee*, that a spy sent his son to his old School for Spies. For a moment the lad thought it was his Auntie Florrie who sent him, but it was just his dad in spy's disguise. The boy arrived by good luck, having chewed up his secret instructions to stop them falling into the sinister hands of The Other Side. Luckily he was chewing some bubble gum at the time and the chomped instructions stuck to the stuff! The school itself was disguised as a haystack when it wasn't disguised as a lighthouse, which made the front step a little steep! Teacher was a schoolmaster of disguise, too.

Stage School
Robert Nixon
Cheeky 1979-80; *Whoopee* 1980-85 (IPC)
Stage School's first term opened on 7 July 1979 with a teacher determined to make his stage-struck pupils do mundane mathematics, while on their side the kids were equally determined to exercise their talents. The class included Olga the ballerina ('Don't dance into class, girl – walk!'), a juggler ('Oi! Stop eating my apples!'), a classical actor ('I cometh, sire!'), a ventriloquist and his dummy ('A gottle of geer!'), an escapologist stuck in his sack, a conjurer in a fez ('Don't bring that rabbit into my class!'); and a human cannonball complete with cannon ('Sorry, sir, my fuse was alight!').

Starhawk
Mones
The Crunch 1979-80; *Hotspur* 1980; *Spike* 1983 (D. C. Thomson)
Chaos reigned in the twenty-sixth century following the collapse of the mighty Terran Empire, and once again man's survival depended upon his skill with a weapon. Amid this chaos roamed law-bringer Sol Rynn, known as Starhawk, along with his robot companion, Droid. Man's greatest enemy was an alien race called the Krell. In deepest space, Krell battle-cruisers surrounded the Terran ship, *Calix*. But the commander had only to use Starhawk's communicator card to summon the Space Rider from the deepest void; and Droid came too.

Square Eyes
Malcolm Judge
Topper 1981- (D. C. Thomson)
Jack O'Nory is his real name (inspired by the BBC television series for young viewers, *Jackanory*), but this long-haired lad is known to one and all as 'Square Eyes – the TV Copy-cat!' He made his debut in *Topper* No. 1471 (11 April 1981) watching a police-car chase on his telly. Inspired to do better, Jack was off in his pedal-car at top speed, only to be slowed down by the wet cement in dad's new garden path! From 1982 his billing changed to 'The TV Fan'.

The Stainless Steel Rat
Harry Harrison
2000 AD 1979- (IPC)
'In the rich union of worlds that will be the Galactic Empire of the far future, crime will be virtually unknown. 99% of criminals will indulge in petty crime . . . There will, however, be that other 1%.' So began the saga of the Stainless Steel Rat, one James Bolivar diGriz, part of that 1% who turn to crime because they enjoy it: Slippery Jim! Happily heisting gold bars from a bullion lift, Jim threw gas capsules at pursuing monocycle cops – but then the Black Van was after him, manned by the sinister, secret Special Corps. Began *2000 AD* No. 140, illustrated by Carlos Esquerra.

Stark
Barrie Mitchell
Scoop 1978-81; *Victor* 1981-82 (D. C. Thomson)
'Matchwinner for Hire', that was the legend on Jon Stark's calling card. His terms: £1000 per match, plus £250 per goal; no payment for lost game. Stark, billed as 'The Footballer of the Future', made his debut in No. 1 of *Scoop*, a handsome sports comic dated 21 January 1978, coming to the rescue of Stone Orient in their Second Division match against Belmoor. Manager Drake didn't like it, but Stark scored a 2-0 win, and the crowd cried 'Superstark! King of the park!' Stark pocketed £1500.

Starr Tour
Illustrator unknown
Buster 1978-80 (IPC)
These adventures of Mr and Mrs Starr and their son Milo, plus Clumpy the Robot ('Gurrp!'), as they buzzed about outer space in their flying saucer, looking for a safe landing, were a comic combination of the successful TV series, *Star Trek* and *Lost in Space*. Each week from 27 May 1978 the Starrs touched down on a different planet. Pop mistook the bowings of some primitive planet-men as worship: they were actually ducking the low-flying turtles! Then the Starrs were captured as pets by a planet bossed by talking cats and dogs.

The Steel Claw
Jesus Blasco
Valiant 1962-68; *Vulcan* 1975-76 (IPC)
'In the hushed privacy of a science laboratory the brilliant Professor Barringer and his hard-faced young assistant, Louis Crandell, were experimenting with a new ray for medical purposes. The assistant's right hand was made of steel, replacing the real hand lost in a laboratory accident.' But the experiment goes awry: 'a crackling whiplash of ultra-high voltage smashed into Crandell's steel hand!' When the smoke clears, only the hand is left. But Crandall exists, made invisible by the electric shock. The Steel Claw has riches in its evil grasp. . . .

Star Wars
George Lucas
Star Wars Weekly 1978-80; *Empire Strikes Back* 1980-83; *Return of the Jedi* 1983-85 (Marvel)
The incredibly popular science-fiction film was adapted as a comic-strip serial by Roy Thomas (writer) and Howard Chaykin (artist), beginning in No. 1 of *Star Wars Weekly* (8 February 1978). Hero of the intergalactic epic was Luke Skywalker, 'an idealistic twenty-year old farmboy who longs to leave the remote, barren planet Tatooine'; villain was Darth Vader, 'dark Lord of Sith and personification of evil in the Galactic Empire'. Heroine was Princess Leia Organa of Alderaan; helpers were robots C3-PO and R2-D2. The sequel films were also adapted.

Steadfast McStaunch
Denis Gifford
Knockout 1950-51; *Tiger* 1965; *Whizzer & Chips* 1969-70 (IPC)
In the far-off days and the far-off land of Dogbod, more precisely No. 602 of *Knockout* (9 September 1950), the town crier cried forth a crowd of 'Hear-yes' and 'O-yezzes'. 'King Clueless the Umpteenth will give the hand of Princess Prettypuss to whosoever rids the realm of Wicked Witch Hazel!' Meanwhile one S. McStaunch, sole proprietor of the local odd-jobbery, bonked a bee with *Ye Olde Knockout* and proclaimed that he was not afeared of nothing, not nohow. He was promptly pushed into Puzzle Land where he duly did his dependable duty. Twenty years later he returned in human form as ye world's worst jester, doing ditto.

Steel Commando
Illustrator unknown
Thunder 1970-71; *Lion* 1971-74; *Valiant* 1974 (IPC)
The British Army's number one secret weapon went on parade in No. 1 of *Thunder* (17 October 1970). The place was a secret army base early in World War 2, where scientists were developing the Mark I Indestructible Robot. Unfortunately they could not control its actions and the metal man in the outsize uniform ran riot. Then, by chance, it was discovered that Private Ernie 'Excused Boots' Bates, the company potato-peeler, happened to have a voice that the robot responded to. Promoted to Lance Corporal (unpaid), Ernie was sent to France in charge of the robot.

Steve Larrabee
John Compari
Lone Star 1953-63 (DCMT)
'Lone Star high above the prairie . . . tall grass, rustlin' in the breezes . . .' This was the Song of the Lone Star Rider (words by Bob Mills, music by Eric Eastwell) as heard, not only in the pages of *Lone Star Magazine*, but over the air from Radio Luxembourg in his own programme. Steve Larrabee was a real personality who toured England, singing his Lone Star song, spinning his Lone Star Lariat, and generally demonstrating toy pistols and other stuff put out by Die Cast Metal Tools, publishers of his comic. His horse was called Smoky.

Steevie Star
Tom Williams
Nutty 1980-82 (D. C. Thomson)
Readers of *Nutty* No. 1 (16 February 1980) were invited to tune in every week to see Steevie Star starring in a batty burlesque of a famous film or television series. Steevie was such a success in *King Kong*, and as Captain Quirk in *Star Trick*, that his space was soon doubled to two pages. In this spread of screen-shaped frames, Steevie had scope to star in *The Lone Stranger* and appear as David Battyborough in *Strife on Earth*, David Spanner in *The Incredible Bulk*, and the chat-show host Michael Parkingzone.

Steve Samson
Nat Brand
Steve Samson 1953-56 (Sports Cartoons)
'Strong Man of the Circus', Steve Samson was the star of Major Lambert's international circus and his own monthly comicbook. 'Ladeez and gentlemen, meet Samson, the mighty man, the steel-muscled giant of the ring!' cries the ringmaster, but Steve finds himself doing more than merely lifting twelve men sitting on a plank. He catches the aerialist when his trapeze act is sabotaged by a rival showman, Green of the Motor Maniacs. The circus is set on fire, and King the killer lion is loosed, before the show can go on.

Stingray
Gerry Anderson
TV Century 21 1965-68 (City); *Countdown* 1971; *TV Action* 1972 (Polystyle)
'Stingray Lost! Titan Terror Fish Attacks W.A.S.P. Vessel!' Headlines that screamed across the front page of *TV Century 21* No. 1 (23 January 1965). The new comic with the cover made up to look like a full-colour newspaper of a hundred years hence was even dated 23 January 2065: future historians please note! Stingray was the name of the super-submarine, captained by Troy Tempest, and W.A.S.P. stood for World Aquanaut Security Patrol, headquarters Marineville, Commander Shore in charge. From the television series by Gerry and Sylvia Anderson.

Steve and Stumpy
Roy Wilson
Butterfly 1930-32 (Amalgamated Press)
'The World's Worst Cowboys' rode on to the green back page of *Butterfly* on 13 December 1930, signing on the payroll of Hiram Smart of the Bar Circle Ranch. Steve ('I'm the nice looking chap with the nicely-creased chaps!') described his pard as 'a podgy little four-by-two looking like a lump of lard with a hat on it!' Stumpy reckoned he could ride anything from a clothes-hoss to a bucking rhinopotamus, but was bested by a bronco called Earthquake. The form was a serial, and the pardners soon put paid to Pedro Pycrusto's plot to kidnap Dora of Peaceville Ranch, and were made deputy sheriffs.

Stonehenge Kit
Norman Ward
Knockout 1939-50; *Sun* 1958-59; *Big One* 1964-65 (Fleetway)
'Stonehenge Kit the Ancient Brit' was that rarity, a funny serial. Caveman Kit spent his weekly instalments doing his darnedest to save Glam his Gal Pal from the clutches of Whizzy the Wizard (real name G. Whizz) and his twin henchmen, Brit Basher No. 1 and Brit Basher No. 2. Old King Kongo (Kingy for short) was also ever being king-napped. Kit braved many prehistoric dangers, including the Buzzoffer, the Streamlined Ozzlebird, the Giant Cloudgobbler, and the Crocodilligator. For part of their time they all spoke in rhyme.

Stoogie
Harry Banger
Topical Funnies 1940-43; *Fresh Fun* 1940; *War Comics* 1942; *New Funnies* 1943; *Slick Fun* 1943-51 (Swan)
Stoogie, despite his simple nature, had the longest career of any of the many Harry Banger comic creations for the Gerald G. Swan comicbooks. With his big head, his bulging eyes, his bowler hat, and his almost non-existent mouth, Stoogie originally suffered through two-page spreads of slapstick at his expense. When *Slick Fun* became *Coloured Slick Fun*, he was promoted to the front page in a series of cover cartoons, and at the end of his career, as if to make up for all those bashings, he blossomed into a hero – Superstooge!

Storm Nelson
Richard Jennings
Eagle 1953-62 (Hulton)
Storm Nelson sailed into *Eagle* on 2 October 1953, scripted by Edward Trice. He soon proved worthy of his subtitle, 'Sea Adventurer', for he commanded his own private Silver Fleet. There was the two-man submarine, Silver Fish; the helicopter, Silver Hawk; the boat, Silver Spray. Manning the Silver Fleet was Storm's private navy: Bash the pilot, Spanner the mechanic, Jonah McCann the Scots engineer, and a young native lad called Happy Xmas, which came in handy once a year: 'Tuan Storm say he hope you all have Happy Xmas like me!'

Strang the Terrible
Dudley Watkins
Beano 1944-45 (D. C. Thomson)
'The Adventures of the Strongest Man in the World' began in *Beano* No. 240 (9 September 1944) with Strang, a dead deer slung over his shoulder, heading for home, a cave. 'Wearing only a leopard skin, with deerhide sandals on his feet, Strang's mighty limbs and powerful muscles showed that he possessed magnificent strength.' He needed it, for he lived in the Valley of the Giants, somewhere in South America, where 'roamed horrible monsters of a prehistoric age'. Another problem was 'the savage, hairy man-like apes who lived in holes', a menace since Strang's story began in *Adventure* back in 1931.

Store Wars
Jim Watson
Whizzer & Chips 1981- (IPC)
The title of this strip is a pun on the popular film *Star Wars*, but the plot is much more down to earth. It concerns two high street shops, one a vast superstore (run by Mr Superstore) and the other a little general store next door, Bloggs and Son (the son is young Ted). Every week Mr Superstore tries to force Bloggs and Son to close, but every week the homey little shop comes out on top. Perhaps it is Mr Bloggs' personal touch: 'Now, Mrs Evans, two bottles of ketchup and a musical sink-plunger?' When Bloggs wins customers by pulling down a shade against the rain, Superstore builds the biggest canopy in the country, but it pulls down the entire frontage.

Strange Hill
Martin Baxendale
Whizzer & Chips 1981-82 (IPC)
Inspired by the popular BBC television school series, *Grange Hill*, the pupils at Strange Hill School were literally little monsters! Mr Weeble was the nervous form-master of as odd a mob of monstrosities as ever escaped from a horror film. Never was a school badge more justified: a black skull and crossbones! Top of the class was a boy called Boss, who had horns on his head, a pointed tail, and spots. He may have been related to the boilerman in the basement, an overweight demon who stoked the heating system with a pronged fork! As to the head, he was literally that – a head!

Strawbelly
Ian Knox
Buster 1981-83 (IPC)
Inspired by the television series featuring the living scarecrow, *Wurzel Gummidge*, the star of this strip was Strawbelly, another living scarecrow who helped out on Trifle Acres, a farm owned by the unusually attractive (for a comic) Miss Sherry. Her deadly rival was the owner of Fyffe-Banana Towers, the lord who lived next door. He and his hulking henchman would stoop to any dastardly deed to starve out Miss Sherry, but Strawbelly was always ready to sacrifice all: including his stuffing to feed her horses, Telly, Jelly, and Nelly.

Strongbow the Mighty
Ron Embleton
Mickey Mouse Weekly 1954-57; *Zip* 1958-59 (Odhams)
Strongbow, blond and bearded, was known as the greatest archer in all Britain. What Robin Hood had to say about this claim goes unrecorded by the strip's scripter, Arthur Groom, but no doubt he would have been envious of the striking black-and-white artwork of illustrator Ron Embleton. Strongbow, accompanied on his quests by young Hal of Effingham or bulbous Bilbo, was aided by the Fraternity of Lost Men in his restoration of the Gold Plate of Brangwyn. However, no sooner was the Black Knight thwarted than it was away to the fortress of Clan MacDuff for the Lost Shield of the Hogarths.

Strongheart
G. W. Backhouse
Comic Life 1927; *My Favourite* 1928-34; *Sparkler* 1934-39; *Crackers* 1939-41; *Jingles* 1944-49 (Amalgamated Press)
'Strongheart the Magnificent' was his full title when he began his adventures on the back page of *Comic Life* No. 1524 (10 September 1927). Moving to *My Favourite* on 28 January 1928 he became 'Strongheart the Tracker', but retained his subtitle, 'The Wonder Dog of the Films'. By the time he jumped to *Sparkler* on 20 October 1934, the film connection was forgotten, and the great Alsatian remained faithful to his final strip in *Jingles*, 25 June 1949 as 'The Wonder Dog of the Woods'.

Strongbow the Mohawk
Geoff Campion
Comet 1953-57; *Knockout* 1961-63 (Amalgamated Press)
The saga of Strongbow began on 8 August 1953 in *Comet* No. 264. A white boy who fell off the back of a wagon train was found by Grey Cloud, Chief of the Mohawks, and raised as his own son. He called the boy Blue Eyes, initiated him as a fully fledged brave, tattooed a hawk on his chest, and when Howling Wolf and his Comanches despatched him to the Happy Hunting Ground, passed on to the lad the legendary sacred war bow. Renamed Strongbow he becomes brothers-in-arms with Hawkeye the Hunter; and together they swear to destroy the evil Rattlesnake, Chief of the Huron.

Strontium Dog
Carlos Ezquerra
Star Lord 1978; *2000 AD* 1978-85 (IPC)
'Time was when a man could commit various acts of evil and hide from justice for ever in an expanding galaxy! Times have changed! Today is the day of the Strontium Dog!' The day was 13 May 1978, the place No. 1 of *Star Lord*, although in the strip the day was *AD 2180*, the place Caytor, administration planet of the Dorian Nebula. Millions of light years from Earth, Johnny Alpha, mutated S.D. Agent licensed by the Galactic Crime Commission, and his partner Wulf ('A skull to crack mit der happy-stick und old Wulf is fine!') blast into action. S.D. stands for Search and Destroy: or, scornfully, Strontium Dog.

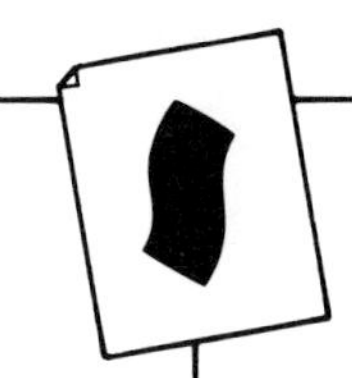

Stymie and his Magic Wishbone
Roy Wilson
Radio Fun 1938-47; *Jingles* 1948-49 (Amalgamated Press)
'The Dark Little Lad With Bright Ideas' was a surprising star for *Radio Fun* No. 1 (15 October 1938). He was modelled on Matthew Beard, 'Stymie' of Hal Roach's film comedy team, 'Our Gang'. 'Lawky! What am dat?' he queried, plucking something hard from his pie. 'Dat am a wishbone!' explained his Mammy, 'All yo' hab got to do is wish and de wish come true!' Stymie made it into a catapult and hit P.C. Breadbasket in the thatch-wrap. 'Golly, I wish he was only a quarter my size' stammered Stymie – and presto! The cop shrank. 'Buzz off, yo' little whippersnapper!' chuckled Stymie. 'Good ol' wishbone, yo' shuah am de cats whiskers!'

Sunnyside School
Roy Wilson
Tip Top 1949-54 (Amalgamated Press)
'Merry Days at Sunnyside School' began in *Tip Top* No. 557 with the arrival of new boy Dick: as the subtitle put it, 'Featuring our hero Dick Burton, Algy Lean and Tubby Trotter, with the head, Dr Dingle, and his daughter, Jill'. Dick arrived without the necessary top-hat. 'Pah!' sniffed Algy, 'A mere scholarship boy!' Tubby lent Dick his, but first coated the inside with glue, so the embarrassed newbug couldn't doff his topper to pretty Jill. But all came right in the end, as it would for the next seven years, with Dick taking tea with Dr D and Jill.

Sub-Mariner
Bill Everett
Terrific 1967-68 (Odhams)
One of the earliest American super-heroes, the Sub-Mariner, swam into No. 1 of *Marvel Comics* (November 1939), surfacing in Britain in No. 1 of *Terrific* (15 April 1967). Prince Namor the First of Atlantis, Emperor of the Deep, Lord of the Seven Seas, and Supreme Commander of the Undersea Legions, was the offspring of a union between Princess Fen of Atlantis and an American Naval officer, and as such was as much at home on land as on sea. His reprinted adventures began with his beloved Lady Dorma warning him of a rebellion engineered by warlord Krang.

Supercar
Gerry Anderson
TV Comic 1961-64 (TV); *TV Century 21* 1965-66 (City)
'It's Fantastic! It's Tremendous! It flashes across the sky! It zooms through water! It speeds over land! It's the Marvel of the Age!' It was, of course, *Supercar*, the first successful sci-fi TV series for children, created by producers Gerry and Sylvia Anderson (ATV 1961). Supercar zoomed on to the centre spread of *TV Comic* No. 483 (18 March 1961), with test pilot, Mike Mercury, at the controls. Going along for the ride were Jimmy Gibson and his pet monkey, Mitch. First artist to draw these puppets in strip form was T. Watts, followed by Bill Mevin (illustrated).

Sunbeam the Innocent
Percy Cocking
Chips 1903-31 (Amalgamated Press)
Sometimes billed as 'Our Innocent Little Imp', or 'The Mischievous Miss', Sunbeam was a chubby child with wide-open eyes of the kind once known as 'goo-goo'. Their long-lashed gaze covered a multitude of smileable sins in her twenty-nine-year career, such as the time she spoiled a bunch of her big sister's beaux by painting 'Gents Dressing Room' on the coal cellar door, or gave her maiden aunt a kiss from a cow: 'Tis Cousin George!' she cried in bliss. Some of Sunbeam's wheezes seemed unlikely: she fooled a pudding pincher with a spotted octopus! Bertie Brown took over from 1909 (illustrated).

Supercats
Badia
Spellbound 1976-78; *Debbie* 1978 (D. C. Thomson)
The sexiest strip in any British comic, the Supercats were the stars of *Spellbound* from its first issue (25 September 1976) to its last (14 January 1978), and must have come as a slight shock to the young readers of *Debbie* when they switched over to their comic. They were the all-girl crew of Spaceship Lynx of the Cat Patrol, operating out of Moonbase 4: Hercula the strong one, Electra who could generate electricity, Fauna who could alter her body like a chameleon, and the captain, Earth-girl Helen Millar.

S

Super Dad
Mike Brown
Whizzer & Chips 1970-75 (IPC)
The father-son relationship was probably never odder than the one illustrated in this strip, which started on 21 February 1970. Father was a doddering old dad, son was a bespectacled scruff-bag. To keep an eye on this horrible offspring and foil his constant lying and cheating, father had a secret system. Crying 'This looks like a job for Super Dad!' he would fling off his clothes and stand revealed in a super-suit – and bowler hat – ready to swing into action against his son! When the kid forged a sick note, asking to be struck by lightning if he was fibbing, Super Dad obliged with a bolt from the blue. 'Ooer!'

Supermum
Dicky Howett
Whoopee 1977-80 (IPC)
Terry's mum was a bit of a problem: she was Supermum. Not that she shouted secret keywords or popped into telephone booths to change into her super-uniform. In fact, her uniform remained boringly the same: a headscarf tied in a turban around her curlers, a flowered pinafore, and sagging stockings. Frankly, Terry found her a bit of an embarrassment. She used her strength in rather mundane ways: bringing in the firewood in bulk – one tree at a time. Once she super-sneezed down a coal hole and blew a burglar out of the bank across the street.

Supergirl
Giorgio Letteri
Judy 1983 (D. C. Thomson)
'The TV heroine with the Off-screen Secret' swooped into *Judy* No. 1217 (7 May 1983). Debbie Danger starred as the daredevil heroine of a popular television series, *Supergirl* (no relation to the American super girl of the same name!). Debbie shared a flat with her best friend, the bespectacled Jenny Brown. The two girls could not have been more different. Off screen, the blonde and beautiful Debbie was scared of mice, even clockwork ones, while plain, crop-haired Jenny was queen of her local karate club. So when Bimbo the bull escaped, it was Jenny who caught him and Debbie who got the reward.

The Super Seven
Mike Lacey
Knockout 1971-73; *Whizzer & Chips* 1973 (IPC)
'We, the Super Seven, pledge ourselves to the cause of justice for school kids everywhere. Let the word go out throughout the land that all in trouble may call on us!' With this awe-inspiring oath the Super Seven wound up their first front-to-back page adventure in *Knockout* No. 1 (12 June 1971). There was Dead Eye Dick, the Greatest Ink Pellet Twanger in the World; Windy who blew the Biggest Bubble Gum Bubbles Ever; Micky the Amazing Marble Player (his last name was Thunderball); Booter the Goal-getter; Stinker the Stink Bomb King; Whistler the World's Loudest; and Wanda Wheels who steered the Super Sevenmobile.

Superman
Jerry Siegel, Joe Shuster
Triumph 1939-40; *Radio Fun* 1959-61; *Buster* 1961 (Fleetway); *Super DC* 1969-70 (Top Sellers); *Super Heroes* 1980-82 (Egmont)
Superman, the character who changed the face of American comicbooks, was born in No. 1 of *Action Comics* (June 1938). As the sole survivor of the exploding planet Krypton, he rocketed to Earth and was raised by a country couple. Taking the name Clark Kent, he became a reporter on the *Daily Planet*, dropping his mild manners and donning his Superman costume whenever danger threatened the American way. The strip was reprinted in the British boys' weekly, *Triumph*, from No. 772 (1939), but his super-success seems not to travel.

Super Store
Bob Hill
Whizzer & Chips 1976-80 (IPC)
'You want it? We stock it!' was the motto of Super Store, an all-sorts emporium run by young Willoughby's rich Uncle Rich. This toff in topper and tails was bursting with bright ideas. When he installed check-out desks he found the staff too busy to cope with the adding machines. So he brought in an educated octopus to operate the lot. Customers were so impressed, Uncle Rich ran a sale of octopuses with the slogan: 'Many hands might like work!' When vandals spoiled the local park, Uncle sold the keeper a load of lions, complete with thrones to sit on (because they were kings of the jungle). Slogan: 'Take a Pride in your Park!'

SuperTed
Mike Young
Pippin 1983- (Polystyle)
'SuperTed is the world's most remarkable teddy bear. That is why you can see him flying through the sky like an aeroplane.' Zooming in from his BBC television series for young viewers, SuperTed became the front page star of *Pippin* from No. 890 (14 October 1983), flying over to the back page for the continuation of each adventure. SuperTed, the first superhero designed for the pre-Superman set, is accompanied on his travels by Spottyman, from Planet Spot, and his enemies are Texas Pete, Skeleton, and Bulk.

Surprise Corner
Illustrator unknown
Poppet 1963-64; *June* 1964-66 (Fleetway)
Chapter One: 'The Day It All Began' started on page 3 of No. 1 of *Poppet* (5 October 1963), and it was page 14 before schoolgirl Sally finished her first-person story of how the Starr family came to Surprise Corner: at twelve pages, the longest strip to feature in a weekly comic. Tom and Helen (Dad and Mum) Starr set up as antique dealers in their own shop, while Sally and her younger brother Bobby enrolled at a posh new school, Luke's Hall. Sally soon chummed up with Phillida Baker, and even big sister Marjorie mucked in.

Susie Sunshine
Austin Payne
Rainbow 1914-56 (Amalgamated Press)
'Susie Sunshine and her Pretty Pet Poms' were a popular feature of *Rainbow*, especially among its many girl readers. So popular, in fact, that Susie stayed a star of the comic throughout its forty-three-year run, although one of her Pretty Pet Poms disappeared somewhere along the way. The strip wound up as 'Susie and her Funny Pets'. There was Bouncer the dog, Ping-Pong the Siamese cat, Scotty the terrier, Pipsie, a tiny black puppy, and just one pomeranian called Pom. The artist was Anton Lock (illustrated).

Superwitch
David Gudgeon
Sparky 1974-77 (D. C. Thomson)
Old Gran looked like a harmless old biddy, but woe betide anyone who crossed her path, be it a shoplifter or her own ugly sister. With a faintly familiar cry – 'This looks like a job for Superwitch!' – Gran zapped into her other self, a classic crone with a pointed hat, pointed nose, and pointed chin. All she had to do was to mutter her magic word, 'Abraca!', and point her pointed fingers, for wonders to be worked. Then all would be well, with Gran getting the last laugh: 'Cackle!'

Susan of St Bride's
Peter Kay
Girl 1955-62 (Hulton)
'The Story of a Girl who wants to become a Nurse' was written by Ruth Adam, and became so popular with *Girl* readers that by 1958 it moved from the monochrome inside pages to the full-colour cover. Susan Marsh, daughter of Dr Marsh, soon chums up with student doctor Max Hunter, and enjoys working in the children's ward under Sister Martin. In the fullness of time she wins the Nurse of the Year Award, but is deprived of her medal due to the jealous machinations of Staff Nurse Freda Eastman.

Sweeny Toddler
Tom Paterson
Shiver & Shake 1974-85; *Whizzer & Chips* 1985- (IPC)
The original title for this strip was apt: 'Help! It's Sweeny Toddler!' It portrayed the bonneted brat sinking his fangs into Dad's leg: 'Chomp! Chew!' Sweeny may be a terror to his parents, but he is kind to animals. Hairy Henry the hound accompanies him on most of his adventures, as does a fat and grinning black cat. There are also little monsters who lurk between the pictures doing their worst: 'But Squiggly, you're supposed to kiss someone under the mistletoe not eat them!' Sweeny was promoted to the coloured cover in 1978, and took over the front of *Whizzer & Chips* in 1985.

Sweet-Tooth
Trevor Metcalfe
Whizzer & Chips 1972- (IPC)
Sweet-Tooth was a boy who certainly lived up to his nickname: his weekly strip revolved entirely around his lust for lollipops, desire for doughnuts, regard for rock, taste for toffee-apples, and mania for marzipan. This was all made physically visible by his one large tooth which protruded proudly at all times, even when licking his lips. Held in high regard by his local sweet-shop man, Sweet-Tooth had his opposition, not in the shape of his dentist, but of Greedy Greg. In 1980 Trebor marketed Sweet-Tooth sweets in rolls.

Swift Shaw
R. J. Macdonald
Sparkler 1938-39 (Amalgamated Press)
'The Lightning Detective' joined *Sparkler* on 26 February 1938 and was immediately plunged into a fifteen-pictures-a-week mystery, 'The Flying Pirates'. The 'tec was described thus: 'Young and famous, moving like lightning, that is Swift Shaw'. With the bullion robbers behind bars, there was 'The Mystery of the Bell Tower' to solve. In his next case Shaw was so helped by Newsboy Ned Nimble that the curly haired lad was signed on as his assistant to help 'Catch That Spy', one Julius Harker.

Swift Morgan
Denis McLoughlin
Swift Morgan 1948-53 (Boardman)
'Swift and Silver, aboard a new rocket air-ship, are in grave danger when out of control, their ship plunges towards a lake in unchartered (*sic*) territory at terrific speed.' Soon they were up to their necks in prehistoric monsters ('By the! A flesh eating tyrant dinosaur!'), a great beginning for a series of two-tone comicbooks that took Swift and Silver (identified in No. 2 as his fiancée) to Ancient Rome, Ancient Egypt, and up the Osumacinta River to a Lost City of the Incas.

The Swots and Blots
Leo Baxendale
Smash 1966-71 (Odhams); *Valiant* 1971-72 (IPC)
Warring factions at Riverside School, these rival gangs soon took over the front page of *Smash*, wherein they had made war since the first issue (5 February 1966). This ink-slinging saga opened on the school's annual prizegiving day, with their mortarboarded teacher (known as 'Teach' for short) awarding cups to Cyril Simper for neatness and Penelope Prigg for spelling. The decision swiftly aroused the scruffier schoolkids, and the scrimmage that ensued separated the pupils into Swots and Blots for all time.

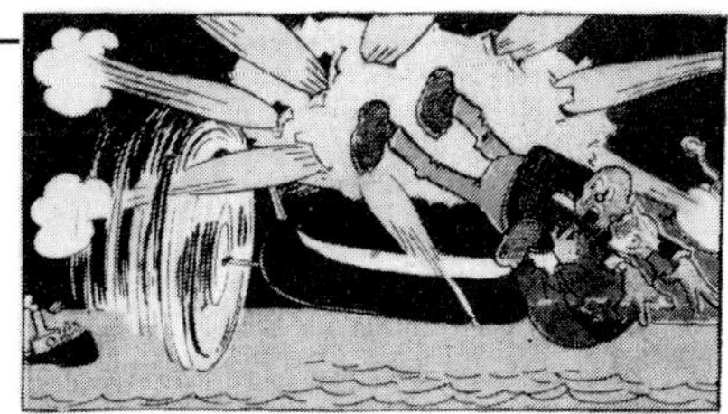

Tall Thomas and Butterball
H. O'Neill
Comic Life 1908-20 (Henderson)
Although based on the classic 'Weary Willie and Tired Tim' formula of tall and short, Tom and Butterball were both heavyweight enough to be billed as 'Our Fat Tramps'. They scrounged around *Comic Life*, finally bursting into colour in 1911. They were fond of dressing-up for their swindles, posing as the Giant Thick-legged Canary of Pangwungo and its Outsize Egg, or building fake inventions like their Shuttlecock Ship-Sheller with which they hoped to win World War 1. Their ignoble end was to stooge for two brats called Tot and Ted, who took over in 1918.

Tat the Cat
Bill Titcombe
Pippin 1981-83 (Polystyle)
Tat the Cat, who should really be christened Tat the Kitten, was created by the husband-and-wife team of Bill (artist) and Audrey (writer) Titcombe. Originally published as a series of small books for young readers, Tat was turned into a full-colour comic strip for Pippin, each story starting; 'Tat the Cat lives at Snuff Box Farm right in the heart of the countryside. His friends are Alexander, the big black cat with the large yellow eyes, Oscar the dog, and three posh ducks.' Other animals included Jones the Welsh Collie and Emmanuel the fox cub.

Tarna, Jungle Boy
Harry Bishop
Swift 1954-63 (Hulton)
Tarna, a juvenile variation on Tarzan, was the full-colour front-page star of the new comic, *Swift* (20 March 1954). A lad in a leopard skin, he was accompanied by Toto the chimp ('Yuk-yuk!'). All the African animals were his friends, and he understood their language. His adventures began with a bird saying 'Cheep-cheep!', which Tarna quickly translated as 'The winged one is telling us that hippo, the toothy one, is in trouble!' In a trice he was astride Tuski the elephant to save the hippo's calf from Carlo the hunter. When *Swift* upgraded its reader appeal, Tarna suddenly aged six years into 'a finely muscled figure of young manhood' (3 February 1962).

Teacher's Pet
Norman Mansbridge
Cor 1970-74 (IPC)
From the days of 'Keyhole Kate' and earlier, the token female characters in comics have tended towards the sneaks and the snitchers, thus guaranteeing a guffaw from the boy readers and a giggle from the girls. Teacher's Pet was no exception to this rule, as the new teacher found out when she arrived for her first day of school on the back page of No. 1 of *Cor* (6 June 1970). Patsy literally radiated unctuousness, with words like 'Smarmy' shining around her beribboned and becurled head.

Tarzan
Edgar Rice Burroughs
Pilot 1937-38 (Amalgamated Press); *Tarzan* 1951-59 (Westworld); *TV Tornado* 1967-68; *TV 21* 1968-70 (City); *TV Comic* 1971-76 (Polystyle)
The original white lord of the jungle, created in the novel *Tarzan of the Apes* by pulp writer Edgar Rice Burroughs, first appeared as an American newspaper strip on 7 January 1929. This was reprinted in Britain in the magazine *Tit-Bits*, and again in the boys' weekly, *Pilot*. His first coloured-comic appearance was in the English language version of a French weekly, *Tarzan the Grand Adventure Comic* (15 September 1951). British Tarzan artists included Don Lawrence (illustrated)in *TV Tornado*.

Teachers United
Jim Watson
School Fun 1983-84; *Buster* 1984-85 (IPC)
'One for All and All for One' is the motto of Teachers United. The boys wondered what they got up to when they went in the Staff Room. Little did they know that they went through a secret panel in the cupboard to their War Room, where the Headmaster, known as No. 1, outlined their battle plans. To suss out the mystery prankster playing japes on music master Eric Crotchet, a new teacher, Mr Jack, posed as a pupil, a whistle secreted in his mouth. Unfortunately he swallowed it and blew the whistle on the whole campaign: 'Pheep!' Next week: Round Two!

Team Mates
Tom Paterson
Wow 1982-83; *Whoopee* 1983-85 (IPC)
Glenn Doddle was kicked out of his street soccer team on 6 June 1982 (in No. 1 of *Wow*) and promptly started a team of his own. First to join was a black lad called Cyril Breeches: Glenn spotted him swerving a swipe from his dark Dad and gave him a signing-on fee of one mint humbug. Then Glenn spotted Clemence Ray saving a lady's dropped vase from certain smashery. He became goalie, while Kenny Dogleash, a great little header of falling apples, Dora Dribble, and the paper boy helped swell the team. Only one trouble: no ball!

The Teddies
Harry Neilson
Sunday Fairy 1919-21 (Amalgamated Press)
'The Holiday Adventures of the Teddies' was the front-page feature of *The Week Day Fairies' Pages*, which formed the central pull-out comic section to the semi-religious weekly comic, *The Sunday Fairy*. The four cubs of the Teddy family were Tim, Tom, Tilly, and Totty, the latter being the baby. The theory was that it was OK to show young animals up to mischief, but not children, lest young readers might attempt to emulate them. The artist went against all tradition: not only did he sign every strip, he signed every picture!

Teddy Bear
Illustrator unknown
Teddy Bear 1963-73; *Jack & Jill* 1973-85; *Teddy Bear's Playtime* 1981; *Playhour* 1985-86 (IPC)
Teddy Bear was not only the front-page star of his own comic, he edited it too, from Bear Green, Fleetway House, Farringdon Street! His strip, beautifully drawn (later in full colour in *Jack & Jill*) but never signed, introduced Teddy's furry family: Daddy and Mummy Bear, Bare Bear the baby, Grandma Bear, snivelling Grizzly Bear, ice-cream-cornet-loving Snowy Bear, bespectacled Bookworm Bear, tatty Fred Bear, guitar-twanging Hill Billy Bear, and Russian Ivan Bear.

Teddy and Cuddly
Hugh McNeill
Jack & Jill 1954-70; *Playhour* 1978-81 (IPC)
'The Happy Days of Teddy and Cuddly the Baby Bears' began in No. 1 of *Jack & Jill* (27 February 1954). 'Ha, ha, ha, it's a happy, happy day!' laughed the cubs, 'And so say all of us!', smiled Charlie Chipmunk. Then – whump – little Red-Ears the baby fox came rolling and bumping down the hill. Oh, I do feel dizzy!' said Red-Ears, 'And what's more, I'm lost, I am!' But Teddy and Cuddly soon saw him home to Mother Fox, who in turn gave the chubby cubs a ride home on her back in time for buns and honey! How lovely life was in those days, even among the animals.

Teddy and Greta
Vera Bowyer
Tiny Tots 1934-56 (Amalgamated Press)
'Teddy in Toyland' was the first title for this long-running serial. In 1939 it became 'Teddy in Noah's Ark Land', and in 1941 'The Tale of Teddy and Greta'. It was only fair that the teddy bear's wooden-dolly partner in adventure should share the title, too. According to the synopsis, 'Ted-dy and Gret-a are two jol-ly doll-ies who be-long to a lit-tle girl name-d Mar-jor-ie.' (*Tiny Tots* was a hyphenated comic for the young.) Mar-jor-ie and her Mum-my never knew that Ted-dy and Gret-a could come to life – but we knew!

Teddy Tail
Charles Folkard
Boys & Girls Daily Mail 1933-37 (Associated Newspapers)
'The mouse that will make your children laugh' was the first regular newspaper strip for children, beginning in the *Daily Mail* on 3 April 1915. And when that newspaper started a coloured comic supplement on 8 April 1933, Teddy Tail was the obvious star for the front page. Teddy, the mouse with a knot in his tail, went to Mrs Whisker's Boarding School with the rest of the Whisker Pets: Kitty Puss, Douglas Duck, and Piggy. Among several artists, the best was Herbert Foxwell (illustrated), who brought his Tiger Tim style to the strip.

T

Teddy and his Wonderful Toys
H. O'Neill
Sunbeam 1926-36 (Amalgamated Press)
What reader of *Sunbeam* didn't wish to be a boy like Teddy and own a shelf-full of living toys? There was Wallygog the clown, Gollywog the gollywog, and Dolly Dimple the dimpled doll, plus sundry teddy bears, toy soldiers, and the like as required by the plot. Teddy and his toys took turns in tricking one another. Teddy scared them by wearing a Guy mask, and they fooled him by sticking apple peel on a balloon so it burst when he bit it. 'Tee! Hee!' laughed Dolly Dimple. She didn't know the strip was based on 'Little Willie Winks' in *Butterfly*, 1908.

The Teeny Sweeney
J. Edward Oliver
Jackpot 1979-80 (IPC)
'Join our kid crime fighters on patrol – you'll cop it if you don't!' This was the editor's warning about Teeny Sweeney which went on the beat in No. 1 of *Jackpot* (5 May 1979). A junior variation of the Thames Television series *The Sweeney*, Georgie and Inspector Rogan zoomed into action in their Flying Squad-carts (soapboxes linked by two tins on a string) against Ronnie the Rotter, the bully who pinched Tich's comic. Despite Georgie's alarm – 'Peepaweepaw!' – Ronnie fought back with a castor-oil slick. However, an hour in the Interogashun Room with a feather on his bare feet soon reduced Ronnie to a wreck and restored the stolen comic.

The Teeny Toppers
Keith Reynolds
Topper 1983-85 (D. C. Thomson)
Terrible trio of triplets who terrorize their tired old dad in *Topper*. Lou, Hugh, and Sue are identifiable by their hairstyles: Lou sports the scruffy stubble, Hugh the tight crop of curls, and Sue the sawn-off ponytail. Otherwise they work in unison, racketting through their page or two of pictures trying to rouse poor pa from his well-earned slumbers. For a while during 1984 they were promoted to the colourful centre spread but have latterly returned to a single page. Dad remains stolidly asleep.

The Tellybugs
George Parlett
Smash 1966 (Odhams)
'No-one has ever seen a Tellybug, but we've all seen the effects on our screens when they're having fun!' Such was the nasty pattern that interrupted a pop song by the Earwigs when the Goggs family were watching their television set. Finding nothing in his television repair book about Tellybugs, Mr Gogg cured the complaint by chucking the book at his set. This put the picture right, but the upset Tellybugs got their own back. Sweeping up all the dust and fluff they could find, they whooshed it out during the weather forecast and filled the house with fog!

T

The Terrible Three
Martin Clifford
Sun 1956-58 (Amalgamated Press)
Created in the long-running series of stories by Martin Clifford (Charles Hamilton) in the boys' weekly *Gem* (1907-39), the Terrible Three started life anew as a picture serial in *Sun*, drawn by Reg Bunn. The Three were Tom Merry, Monty Lowther, and George Manners, schoolboys of the Lower Fourth form at St Jim's College. Mr Lathom, their master, falls foul of fat boy Baggy Trimble, and is replaced by James Silverson who falsely accuses Tom of striking him. Tom is expelled.

Terror T.V.
Barrie Appleby
Monster Fun 1976; *Buster* 1976-78 (IPC)
The Gogglers, Britain's champion family of telly-viewers, were bored to death with 'Smile bright, teeth white, with Gleamo!' Chucking a boot at the set, Dad chanced to hit the fatal fourth switch and: 'Hah-haarrgh! I, Magnus Murkysome welcome you to the Channel of Chills!' Fleeing into the night, the Gogglers were horrified to find the Terror TV Studio had been built next door, where producer Sir Dan Doom was preparing shuddery shows such as 'Supercronic', a pop show starring Ricky Rave and the Baytown Howlers, and 'Hag-Pie' with Susan Shrieks showing how to shrink heads.

The Terrors of Tornado Street
Rafart
Buster 1960-61 (Fleetway)
This wild bunch was let loose in *Buster* No. 1 (28 May 1960) and for a year or so roared through a regular page of pictures splattered with sound effects. 'Parp! Gneer!' went their old car; 'Whee-ee!' went their Zoomer Jets (given free with *Buster* No. 2!). Perhaps because their artist, a Spaniard, gave the local bobby such an un-British helmet, the Terrors switched style in '61 to become one outsize picture in the Casey Court tradition: same artist, too – Albert ('Charlie') Pease (illustrated).

Terry Brent
Illustrator unknown
School Friend 1950-59 (Amalgamated Press)
Terry Brent – detective – solved his first two-page crime 'The Case of the Ventriloquist's Dummy', in No. 1 of *School Friend* (20 May 1950). The only male hero in twenty pages of strips for and about girls, Terry hardly held that singular position for long. All too soon he was joined by a girl assistant, his niece Paddy McNaught. And as all Terry's clients were female, to boot, the wonder is that he held his masculine stronghold for as long as the decade which he did!

Terry and Trixie
Alexander Akerbladh
Crackers 1932-39 (Amalgamated Press)
'The Stars of the Circus' were Terry Wells and his chum, Trixie. They did a trapeze act in Bangler's Mammoth Circus, which performed on the three-colour back page of *Crackers*, running from No. 159 to No. 544. Their many adventures concerned saving a foreign Prince from a gang called the Daggers, saving Li Sing from Chinese pirates, saving Lord Summers' lost treasure from a villain called Waldo, saving old Carlo Corbetti, the Greatest Clown in the World, and Pepi, his pet bear, from the vengeance of the Barattis, and saving themselves from kidnap by circus rival Tobias Maggson.

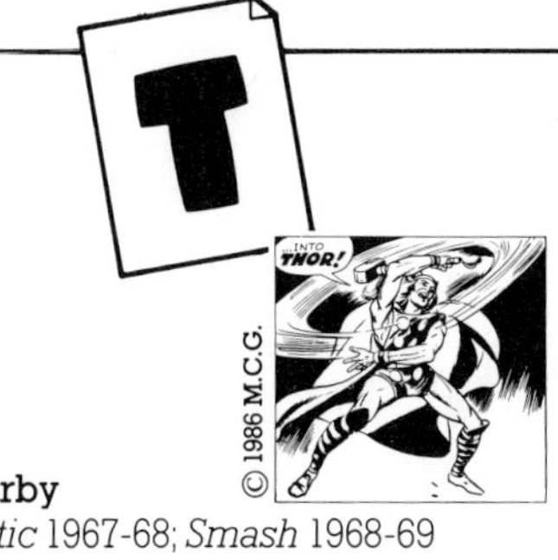

Thor
Jack Kirby
Fantastic 1967-68; *Smash* 1968-69 (Odhams); *Marvel* 1972; *Spiderman* 1973-79; *Valour* 1980; *Marvel Teamup* 1980-81; *Marvel Action* 1981; *Captain America* 1981-82; *Mighty Thor* 1983-84 (Marvel)
Created by Stan Lee, drawn by Jack Kirby, Thor the Mighty first appeared in the American *Journey into Mystery* No. 83 (August 1962) and was reprinted in No. 1 of *Fantastic* (18 February 1967). Dr Don Blake was on holiday in Norway when Stone Men from Saturn landed in their saucer. Fleeing, he falls into a dark cave. Striking a boulder with an ancient wooden cane, a flash of blinding light changes the stick into a weapon inscribed 'Whosoever holds this hammer, if he be worthy, shall possess the power of Thor' – and Dr Don into the God of Thunder.

The Three Bears
Leo Baxendale
Beano 1959-85 (D. C. Thomson)
'Once upon a time in the wildest days of the wild west, there lived the Three Bears, Pa Bear, Ma Bear, and Teddy Bear. Sometimes they were happy, sometimes they were sad, always they were hungry!' Baxendale's bears had long been popular supporting players in his Little Plum strip: now they branched out on their own in *Beano* No. 881 (6 June 1959), tummies a-rumbling, raiding the wagon trains of 'the dopey white-men'. Fortunately the bears were even dopier, lacing their stolen porridge with gunpowder instead of salt.

Thingummy Blob
Albert Holroyd
Sparky 1974-77; *Topper* 1977-79 (D. C. Thomson)
It was in the 500th issue of *Sparky* (17 August 1974) that Professor T. Pott made his greatest experiment – and his greatest mistake. With many a sound effect ('Glop! Frob! Ptsss!') he created a single drop of the Super Elixir of Life, but while dashing forth to tell the Royal Institute of Scientific Discoveries, and his old Mum, the Prof. tripped. The single drop plopped into a fire bucket and – 'Phwam! Phoom!' – out popped a beaming blob! Four years later Prof. Pott was still spending two pages a week trying to get rid of it.

Those Terrible Twins
Frank Holland
Halfpenny Comic 1898-1900 (Trapps Holmes)
Those Terrible Twins, who bore the rather embarrassing names of Willie and Wally Wanks, made their destructive debut in the Grand Easter Double Number of *The Halfpenny Comic*, dated 9 April 1898. When the comic was enlarged, the Twins were promoted to the full front page (23 July) where the fun grew even more ripping. Their grandpa took them to his office, where they made the clerks stick to their work by 'putting sealing-whacks on orl the stools'. The prank ended with more whacks! The year 1899 found them in the Transvaal blowing King Kruger off his soapbox throne.

The Three Beery Bounders
Illustrator unknown
Funny Cuts 1897-1900 (Trapps Holmes)
Their full names were Nosey Mosey, Flipper, and Felix, and they cut their capers on the front page of *Funny Cuts* where they went one better than the usual trampish twosomes. Some of their adventures were serialized, as when they took to the air in a balloon, upending bicyclists with the dangling anchor until shot down into a river. 'A watery grave arter all!' gurgles Flipper, but soon they were back on the job, whitewashing a wall – and a copper, too. 'Jee-wilikins!' cried the cook, 'Robert, why yer've broke hout all in a rash!' The peeler ended up head first in the whitewash bucket.

The Three Lodgers
Will Spurrier
Larks 1897-99 (Trapps Holmes)
Dickens buffs must have been baffled by this front-page strip in *Larks*: its three heroes were named Winkle, Tupman, and Snodgrass! They were a terrible trio forever up to some practical joke, such as passing themselves off as near-relations of Colonel Bombom for a Christmas box (they got one – the boot!), or as Indian potentates named Ram Chowdar, Sham Lowdar, and Ham Powdar to loot the Imperial Hotel (they hid the jools in their turbans). Betimes they sported with their pet baboon, Beelzebub.

The Three Pennys
Illustrator unknown
Twinkle 1968-76 (D. C. Thomson)
Little girls were, naturally, the heroines of *Twinkle*, a comic subtitled 'the New Picture Paper Specially for Little Girls.' But this strip really did the feminists proud by sporting no fewer than three. And they were all named Penny, which made for lots of laughs at Nursery School when kindly Mrs Martin, the teacher, made a little joke out of it. It was Penny Henry's first day (27 January 1968 to be precise, the day No. 1 of *Twinkle* was published), and she was a bit shy at first, but she soon chummed up with Penny Smith and Penny Wilson. But why didn't somebody think to call them 'threepence'?

Thunderbirds
Gerry Anderson
TV Century 21 1968-69; *Candy* 1967-68 (City); *Countdown* 1971; *TV Action* 1972 (Polystyle)
'Thunderbirds Are Go!' was the signal for action in the science-fiction puppet series made for television by Gerry and Sylvia Anderson, the most popular of the many they created. The Thunderbirds were the futuristic vessels operated by International Rescue from Tracy Island in the Pacific. The five Tracy sons each piloted a different Thunderbird: 1 (Scott) was the spaceship; 2 (Virgil) the super carcraft; 3 (Alan) the aircraft; 4 (Gordon) the super-submarine; and 5 (John) was the space satellite. On the ground, Brains the boffin. Artists included Frank Bellamy (illustrated).

Thunderbolt the Avenger
Illustrator unknown
Buster 1965-67 (Fleetway)
Police Constable Mick Riley was the laughing stock of the force. 'You're a shrimp!' mocked his Inspector, taking him off the beat. But the dying Professor Markham gives him his wristwatch – 'No ordinary watch. Inside it is a compartment containing thermo-clyodine-phostium. When the watch is set it passes a current into the wearer giving him super-human powers, untold strength, agility, power even to fly!' Abilities that came in handy for Riley. 'Suffering sputniks!' he said, 'I promise to fight the forces of evil, and they shall know me as Thunderbolt!'

T

Thunderbolt Jaxon
Hugh McNeill
Comet 1949; *Knockout* 1958 (Amalgamated Press)
On 13 August 1949, young Jack Jaxon, an orphan, strapped on a belt of ancient and curious design. It was the magic belt of Thor the Thunder God of the ancient Norsemen, and in a flash it changed Jack into a giant endowed with all the might and magic of Thor himself – Thunderbolt Jaxon! Jack's pal, Tubby the Tramp, was thunderstruck: 'Well, bless the bottoms of my boots!' he gasped. 'I'm off to look for Sheik Abdul Selim and to right the wrongs he has done!' cried Thunderbolt, leaping off to Wahzi to free Odette the desert flower.

The Tiddlers
Leo Baxendale
Wham 1964-68; *Pow* 1968 (Odhams)
The original billing in *Wham* No. 1 (20 June 1964) read: 'The Tiddlers, the Kids from Canal Road School co-starring Britain's most popular teacher, Super Sir!', but by 1965, promoted to the full-colour front page, they were just 'The Tiddlers'. Created in best 'Bash Street Kids' style, the rioting Tiddlers were soon tamed by their new teacher, the pipe-puffing sporty type they dubbed Super Sir. Despite his obligatory mortarboard, Super Sir won them over with his revolutionary method of having the class act out history: Caesar's invasion left the classroom in ruins.

Timothy Tester
Cliff Brown
Whizzer & Chips 1972-79 (IPC)
'Just testing!' was the motto of Timothy Tester, a bespectacled boy boffin with a determination to test everything in sight. With his war-cry of 'One-two-three-testing!' Timothy would sail into action, sometimes at the behest of readers of *Whizzer & Chips*, who would win a pound if their test was run. Stuart Bowdler of Cheadle wanted a mechanical toboggan tested, so Tim screwed Dad's lawn mower to his wooden sled and – 'Zooom! Brrrm!' Bang into the backside of Constable Flatfoot, of course: 'Eeowks!' Naturally the pompous policeman had to demonstrate his skill, whooshing into a snowman and rolling right into his own Cop Shop.

The Tickler Twins
Robert MacGillivray
Magic 1939-40 (D. C. Thomson)
Going one better than *Alice in Wonderland*, the Tickler Twins (Mick and Trixie) set out on their underground adventures on the highly coloured centre spread of *Magic* No. 1 (22 July 1939). 'To Wonderland, to Wonderland, the magic trip begins – Just come on down the rabbit hole with both the Tickler Twins!' After a quick swig of Shrinko, they follow a white rabbit to meet Humpty Dumpty, Wee Boy Blue, and the rest of the Wonderland crowd. Old King Boz is cold, so the Ticklers warm him up with the local dragon.

Tiger Tim
Julius Stafford Baker
Monthly Playbox 1904-13; *Rainbow* 1914-56; *Tiger Tim's Tales* 1919-20; *Tiger Tim's Weekly* 1920-40; *Tiny Tots* 1956-59; *Playhour* 1959-65; *Jack & Jill* 1966-85 (IPC)
Longest lived of all British comic-strip heroes, Tiger Tim emerged as the leading light of the assorted animals who originally attended Mrs Hippo's Kindergarten in the *Daily Mirror* on 16 April 1904. They became front-page stars of the full-colour *Rainbow* from No. 1 (14 February 1914), moving to Mrs Bruin's Boarding School, where they became known as the Bruin Boys: Jumbo Elephant, Georgie Giraffe, Willie Ostrich, Bobby Bruin, Jacko Monkey, Joey Parrot, Porkyboy Pig and Fido Pup. For their twin sisters see The Hippo Girls.

Tina
G. Higham
Sunny Stories 1958-71 (Newnes)
Tina was the Fairy Queen's favourite little fairy, and she made her first appearance in No. 1 of the new series of *Sunny Stories* (12 July 1958). After some weeks as the star of an illustrated story, Tina turned into a four-page strip. She was joined by her even tinier chums, Chubby and Moonbeam, but by 1962, changing times changed the title of her strip to 'Tina Through the T.V. Set'. She was now billed as 'a tiny girl, so small that she can step through the screen of a TV set and meet her puppet friends in TV Land'.

Tin Teacher
Peter Davidson
Buster 1965-70 (Fleetway)
'What we need is a strong man – of steel!' said the Head of Boot Hall as his last but one teacher left hurriedly – through the wall. 'Then I can help you!' cried an inventor, entering in ecstasy with his mechanical marvel. Swiftly slipping an everlasting battery into his backplate, popping a regulation mortarboard on to his head, and a regulation cane into his hand, the inventor sent T.T. (for Tin Teacher) into battle against the Boot Hall boys. Prefacing his every remark with a 'bleep!', T.T. was a burlesque of the D.C. Thomson hero, 'The Iron Teacher'.

Tiny Tim
James Clark
Topper 1953-59 (D. C. Thomson)
When Tiny Tim dozed off in *Topper* No. 1 (7 February 1953) he was not so tiny as he was when he woke up. 'Here's a most amazing thing – Tim's gone to sleep in a fairy ring – And he shrinks and shrinks like anything!' When he woke up in the morning, Tim was as small as a snail! 'He's less than one inch high – But he's a great wee guy!' Tim, a homeless orphan in our world, soon found a welcome in Insect Land, especially after he saved Liz Ladybird's children from fire with the aid of Sam Spider's web.

Tin Lizzie
Jack Prout
Dandy 1955-58 (D. C. Thomson)
Billed as 'the Mechanical Maid' and 'the Brassbound Butler', Tin Lizzie and her partner in fun, Brassribs, were the cast-iron couple created by the absent-minded inventor, Professor Puffin. The robots made their debut as short-story stars, but were turned into a picture strip in *Dandy* No. 721, on 17 September 1955. Prof. Puffin had given them the ability to think and talk like humans. Unfortunately they also behaved like humans, becoming deadly rivals, forever trying to outsmart one another. Lizzie's most endearing term for Brassribs was 'Old rusty rivets!'

Tiny
Carmichael
Topper 1968-81 (D. C. Thomson)
His billing was no exaggeration: Tiny was undoubtedly 'The World's Biggest Dog!' He lived in an extra-large red kennel to the left of his owner's house, where he lurked waiting the chance of walkies. Master was none too keen on taking Tiny for walks: the hound had a disconcerting habit of loping along on his hind legs, and thought nothing of following his man dressed in a bowler hat and carrying an umbrella in the hope he wouldn't notice. Tiny also had a tendency to join in the odd football match.

Tiny and Tot
Freddie Crompton
Tiny Tots 1927-59 (Amalgamated Press)
Ti-ny and Tot liv-ed on the col-our-ed front page of a love-ly com-ic call-ed *Ti-ny Tots*, aft-er them, of course. All the words in their fun-ny ad-ven-tures were bro-ken up in-to syll-a-bles so that lit-tle Child-ren could read them eas-i-ly. Ti-ny and Tot were bro-ther and sis-ter, and their pets were Tid-dles the kit-ten and Dum-py the pup-py, They spent most of their time in a room call-ed 'the nurse-ry' where they were look-ed aft-er by Nurs-ie. Mum-my and Dad-dy, being pre-war up-per mid-dle class, were much too bus-y to both-er with their child-ren.

T

The Tiny Toy Boys
Herbert Foxwell
Tiger Tim's Weekly 1920-39 (Amalgamated Press)
This mischievous gang of animated toys caused trouble for Tiger Tim and the Bruin Boys at the rate of one Bruin Boy a week, beginning with Jumbo. After ten years, they moved in with a real boy named Jackie, and played with him for another ten years as 'The Tiny Boys of Toy Town'. Ringleader of the Toy Boys was Jimmy Jingle, a clown with cymbals stuck to his hands. Then there was Baby Bunting with the big head and quiff, Tommy Atkins the toy soldier, Mr Top-Hat who bore a family likeness to Sunny Jim, and the inevitable Teddy Bear.

Tiny Wee
Mildred Entwistle
Chicks Own 1936-57 (Amalgamated Press)
'The Story of Tiny Wee', later changed to 'The Tale of Tiny Wee', was a particularly attractive strip for young readers, perhaps because drawn by a woman. Tiny Wee, a pretty little fairy, looked just like a nice girl with wings, while her perpetual playmate, Pipkin the Pixie, provided any necessary naughtiness. (Not that there was much of that, even if the two did live together.) By 1940 they had been joined in their adventures by Mrs Bunny's little ones, Billy and Bessie, and by 1950 Tiny Wee had won a magic wand.

Tiny Tycoon
Tom Williams
Whizzer & Chips 1974-78 (IPC)
The bright boy with the big specs and bigger head promised a wealth of laughs when he joined the *Whizzer & Chips* payroll on 5 January 1974. Tiny sported a flowing tie decorated with a '£' sign; his big pal Biff was content with a letter 'B'. Tiny's money-making wheezes were beezer: a job lot of bootlaces repaired Mrs Smith's broken washing line; the sweepings from Mr Barber's shop made a dainty doormat; a stack of discarded encyclopedias were just what his less-clever classmates wanted – for stuffing down the backs of their trousers! He even sold some hedgehogs to the zoo as elephant's nailbrushes!

Toby
Doris White
Toby 1976-78 (IPC); *Rupert* 1984; *Story Land* 1984 (Marvel)
Toby the Terrier lived with his Mummy and Daddy in a pretty thatched cottage on the front page of his very own comic, called, naturally enough, *Toby*. He bore no relation to the traditional Dog Toby, pet of Mr Punch, although close observers might find a relation to the traditional Rupert, pet of the *Daily Express*. Toby's adventures (the first was 'The Goose that Laid the Golden Eggs'), which began and ended in the safety of home, followed the famous fairytale format.

Toddles, Susie and Babs
G. M. Luckraft
Tiny Tots 1941-57 (Amalgamated Press)
This delightful family threesome, Toddles the boy, Susie the girl, and Babs their baby sister, brightened the rather traditional pages of *Tiny Tots* during the second half of its life. The drawings had a light, happy look that set them apart, although the balloons were saddled with the usual hyphenations: 'Oh, what is hap-pen-ing?' cried Babs. 'Well done, Tod-dles!' laugh-ed Mum-my. Their pup, by the way, was called Spot.

Tom Bowline
Arthur White
Chips 1909-25 (Amalgamated Press)
'Our Jolly Jack Tar' certainly sailed the seven seas and possibly more during his seventeen-year term of duty in *Chips*. One week he would be in Tibet, giving his llama the hump to smuggle ciggies past the Chinkee customs officer, the next shipwrecked with Seaweed Sam, or barging a bargee with his tight little tug, the *Speedy*. Never lost for a seaman's wheeze, Tom, when beached by smugglers, sawed slices out of the sides of his ship and opened up as seaside bathing huts. His mate was Sally, who remained true to the navy despite Toms busking of 'All the Nice Girls Love a Sailor'.

Tomboy
Brian Lewis
Cor 1970-74; *Buster* 1974-76 (IPC)
'Who kicked three goals and six opponents in a playtime football game? Who made the best go-kart in town and has the speeding tickets to prove it? Who has the biggest collection of frogs, white mice and creepy crawlies outside the zoo?' Yes, the answer to these questions posed in No. 1 of *Cor* was, of course, Tomboy ('She'd rather play with Doom Rays than dolls any day!'). When her mum and dad try to make her more feminine by buying her a 'mod' dress, she turns it into a teepee. 'That's our girl!' they cry.

The Toffs and the Toughs
Reg Parlett
Knockout 1971-73; *Whizzer & Chips* 1973-78 (IPC)
The Toffs were chauffeured into the full-colour centre spread of *Knockout* No. 1 (12 June 1971), installing themselves in their ancestral castle, Toff Towers. They were Montmorency Moneybags, Lancelot Lolly, and Milly O'Naire. 'And in case you're wondering what that bumper sized soggy matchbox is, it's the seedy hangout of the tattiest ten-year olds in these parts!' Namely Scruff, Ruff, and Fluff, alias the Toughs. When the Toffs mowed down their gang-hut with a cannonball and used the ruins for a barbecue, the Toughs still came out on top, thanks to left-over fireworks.

Tom, Dick and Sally
Keith Reynolds
Beano 1975-86 (D. C. Thomson)
This family trio turned up for the first time in *Beano* No. 1735, and ten years on they are still up to their tricks. Tom is the eldest, a long-haired lad in a red roll-neck pullover. Next comes Dick, in short-sleeved shirt and trousers to match. Last but never, as it happens, least, is Sally, who wears a pinafore dress over black jeans, perhaps to signify a tomboyish trait. It is Sally who always comes out on top at the end of every page, a refreshing change among the chauvinist characters who populate British comics.

Tom Horror's World
Ken Reid
Whoopee 1981-83 (IPC)
This bespectacled boy in a boilersuit is in the best tradition of schoolboy inventors. The strip takes its title from the BBC television series on science, *Tomorrow's World*, but Tom Horror's world of inventions is all his own. His proud but portly pa is invariably Tom's accidental victim, and wig-loss is a regular hazard. For instance, Tom's Instant Automatic Room-Tidier tidied everything away into a box, including dad, but that was nothing when compared to Tom's Christmas Card Printer. The rollers flattened father, but the greetings printed on him meant Tom had invented the walking Christmas card.

Tommy and his Trains
Charles Gill
Rainbow 1929-56 (Amalgamated Press)
Although seldom more than a three-picture strip running across the foot of page two of *Rainbow*, 'Tommy and his Trains' had a twenty-eight-year run, such was its appeal to young readers. Most boys of the period wanted to be a train-driver, and here was a mop-headed hero who had made that grade while still in short trousers. Tommy's were toy trains, of course, but sturdy enough to carry both him and his pet elephant, Tumpy, around the house, garden, down the street, and even to the seaside.

Tom and Jerry
William Hanna, Joseph Barbera
TV Comic 1969-84 (Polystyle); *Tom & Jerry Weekly* 1973-74 (Spotlight)
Tom Cat first chased Jerry Mouse in the 1939 animated cartoon, *Puss Gets the Boot* (MGM). It was the start of a thirty-year chase across the world's cinema screens, one which inevitably led to the full-colour front page of *TV Comic*. Here their slapstick action was excellently transferred to strip format by Bill Titcombe, who often included such subsidiary characters as Butch the Bulldog and the little mouse in nappies, Tuffy. Tom and Jerry also had their own weekly comic for a while, reprinting their American comicbook strips.

Tommy's Troubles
Illustrator unknown
Roy of the Rovers 1976- (IPC)
Tommy Barnes's troubles began in No. 1 of *Roy of the Rovers* (26 September 1976). The headmaster of St John's Road School banned him from playing football as he was so behind in his lessons, and at the same moment he was picked for the English Schoolboys Team. A compromise was reached, and his pal, Ginger Collins, offered to help him study in return for lessons in football. Later troubles included the pals moving to Crowhurst Road School where only rugby was played. They solve this problem by forming their own soccer team, Barnes United, funded by a jumble sale.

Tommy Walls
Frank Hampson
Eagle 1950-54 (Hulton)
'Tommy Walls the Wonder Boy' was the star of the first sponsored comic strip (as opposed to an advertising strip). His first full-page, full-colour adventure appeared in No. 1 of *Eagle* (14 April 1950), drawn by Dan-Dare artist, Frank Hampson, but the character was soon taken over by Richard Jennings. Tommy is watching a new jet liner making its first test flight when the 'plane's wing begins to break. Thinks Tommy: 'With the extra energy from that super delicious Wall's ice I had for lunch, and the magic 'W' sign, I should be able to save them!' He does, of course!

Tom Smith
Brian Delaney
Buddy 1981-82 (D. C. Thomson)
'Smith of the Lower Third' was originally a long-running schoolboy saga that started in the storypaper, *Wizard*, in 1947. Retitled 'Tom Smith's Schooldays' it began again as a picture serial in *Buddy* No. 15 (23 May 1981). Once again young Tom Smith, 'a rough diamond from the back streets of Ironborough, but a lad full of grit and determination' was awarded a scholarship to Lipstone Priors, 'one of the most select public schools in England'. Soon the new newt was having his cap swiped by townies, clocking in at Clay's House, and fisticuffing with Sprat Perkins, junior boxing champ and bully.

Tom Thumbscrew
Andrew Christine
Monster Fun 1975-76 (IPC)
'The Torturer's Apprentice' began operations in No. 1 of *Monster Fun* (14 June 1975) and kept it up until the final issue No. 73 (30 October 1976). 'You'll enjoy this rib-tickling torturer' wrote the editor, 'He's a great leg-puller!' And Tom was: he helped the King's team win a basketball game by stretching them on the rack! The next week he was shutting the King's knights in the iron maiden, not to torture them, but to puncture their tin suits thus providing them with air-conditioned armour! Tom's tortures were laughable, especially the time he used the Jester's bad jokes to make Baron Bigun pay his back taxes.

Tom Smart
Tom Wilkinson
Merry & Bright 1922-25 (Amalgamated Press)
'He doesn't look much, but he's got it where it's wanted!' was the bill-matter of Tom Smart the Schoolboy Inventor. Tom's first invention filled the back page of *Merry & Bright* No. 272 (17 June 1922), a steam-heated sleeping bag. Unfortunately when Tom's teacher tried it out on Mr Inspector Esq, it blew up like a balloon! Tom's later inventions were more ingenious, hence more disastrous. A device to demonstrate the formation of stalactites and stalagmites trapped teacher in a prison of plaster, and his hope to light the home with phosphorescent fish was foiled by the cat.

Tom Thumb
Dudley Watkins
Beano 1941-58; *Bimbo* 1961-69; *Little Star* 1973-75 (D. C. Thomson)
'Tom Thumb – The Brave Little One' made his bow in No. 1 of *Beano* (30 July 1938), but as a text story. Tom's illustrator, Dudley Watkins, later converted the six-inch-high hero into a two-page picture serial dealing with Tom's travels through medieval England mounted on his noble steed – Peterkin the cat! Tom's partner was Tinkel, a curly headed black boy who was also six inches tall. They shared both adventures and the cat. In 1961 Tom became the full-colour front-page star of the nursery comic *Bimbo*.

Tom the Ticket-of-Leave Man
Percy Cocking
Comic Cuts 1910-37 (Amalgamated Press)
'The Side Splitting Adventures of Tom the Ticket-of-Leave', as he was originally billed, began on page one of *Comic Cuts* on 15 October 1910. Inspired by the famous Victorian melodrama, *The Ticket-of-Leave Man*, Tom was an ex-con forever being persecuted out of a job by his arch enemy, P.C. Fairyfoot. In his first adventure, Tom is turfed out of a bank where he was polishing the quidlets, and would have been wiped out of window-cleanery had not his ladder trapped a motorized robber. On 20 January 1917 our hero reformed into 'Jolly Tom the Merry Menagerie Man', to be persecuted by Jackie and Sammy the Terrible Twins for twenty more years.

T

Tom Tip and Tim Top
Bert Hill
Target 1935-38 (Target)
'The Tricky Toddlers' were the front-page pair from No. 1 of *Target*, a green comic which came from Bath on 15 June 1935. Tom Tip was fat, Tim Top was thin, but they were a cut above the traditional tramps, despite being wanderers in search of work. Their methods were ingenious: they carved up a chunk of cheese by chucking it through some telegraph wires, and, when covered in assorted soot and flour, turned themselves into Black and White Minstrels and made some dough! Good-oh, lads!

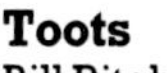

Toots
Bill Ritchie
Mandy 1958-86 (D. C. Thomson)
This little girl with the straight hair and spotted bow has been quietly clocking up a twenty-seven-year run in *Mandy*, ever since she filled a page in No. 1 (18 January 1958). She has changed little over the years, apart from losing the red-ink overprint on her page, thus causing her red spotted dress to change into a black one. Many of Toots' problems were caused by her little brother, such as the time she weighed herself and, not knowing Baby was on the scales behind her, went on a diet!

Tony Jackpot
John Dallas
Plug 1977-79 (D. C. Thomson)
The popularity of golf on television led to the creation of this boy golfer, named after the champion Tony Jacklin. His introduction in *Plug* No. 1 (24 September 1977) read: 'Tony Jackpot – under fourteen champion of Glenbeagles Golf Club – makes his own golf clubs – caddies for the golfing greats – pick up some handy hints and meet the champions!' The first champion Tony met was Arnold Barnpott, whose first stroke caused Tony to comment, 'Crumps! Thousands of innocent worms made homeless!' His clubs included a telescopic one for tree-top shots, and the flipper-flapper for splash shots.

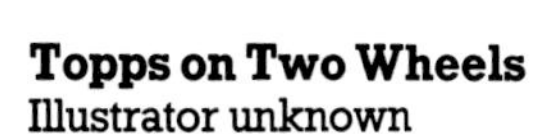

Topps on Two Wheels
Illustrator unknown
Speed 1980; *Tiger* 1980-84 (IPC)
Eddie Topps, the lad in the grease-stained jeans, worked as mechanic to Wendall Wonder, American motorcycle superstar and 'razamatazz stunt rider'. Eddie tried his hand at stunting using Wonder's costume and stunt bike, the Golden Streak. At the zenith of his leap into space, the engine failed. Eddie ditched into the river and 'fifty thousand bucks of the finest machine money can buy' was wrecked. Fired, Eddie buys the wreck of the Golden Streak, rebuilds it, paints it red, and astride The Beast, takes on the world of stunt riding as the Masked Mister Unknown.

Tony the Orphan Boy
Anton Lock
Bubbles 1921-41
(Amalgamated Press)
'A Lovely Movie-Picture Serial' was the subtitle to these heart-rending adventures. Each picture was framed like a cinema screen, but there the cinema connection ends. To quote the regular synopsis, 'Tony has no father or mother. His great friend is his dog Topsy, and they have many adventures together.' His early wanderings took place in Canada among the Indians, where he rode a horse with the odd name of Prairie Gwen. In 1934 the strip became 'Tony and his Garage', a mundane episode for a lad who had been to the North Pole in a land-sea-and-air vehicle.

Toppy/
Augustus Topping Esq
Roy Wilson
Merry & Bright 1932-35 (Amalgamated Press)
'The Travels of Toppy, a Cheerful Old Top, in Quest of a Living – Always on the Hop!' was the proper title of this strip, and the longest of the lot! Later they changed it to the more manageable 'Augustus Topping', and later still simply to 'Toppy'. After weekly workless wanderings on the front page of *Merry & Bright*, Toppy settled down at Miss Mee's School for Boys and Girls in the post of caretaker. Here he had to take care he didn't get japed by the prankish pupils, Cherry Pye, Parry Gorick, and Fat Tenham.

T

The Tornado
Bob Monkhouse
Oh Boy Comics 1948-51 (Paget)
Ace reporter on the *London Tribune*, Steve Storm was a man with a strange secret. Thirteenth member of the Storm family he escapes the fifteenth-century Curse of Grosta after 500 years. 'Like the bursting pressure of the Perra Volcano, the mighty force of the Storms thundered into the soul of Steve, that this powerful young hero might, at will, transform himself into the giant superman of justice, whirlwind prince of the Storms – Tornado!' His first job is to defeat 'a mass of stinking glutinous fungi and foul mud, the incredible horror from the half-world – the Growth!'

Tough Nutt and Softy Centre
Norman Mansbridge
Shiver & Shake 1973-74; *Whoopee* 1974-75 (IPC)
The difference between these nextdoor neighbours was soon shown in No. 1 of *Shiver & Shake* (10 March 1973). Tough Nutt stomped downstairs to his favourite breakfast, fried tree roots and nail sauce ('Nothing like grub you can get your teeth into!'), while Softy Centre, legs well talcked against the gentle breeze, was carried down by his Dad to his favourite breakfast, 'Nice soggy mushy cereal all mashed up so it doesn't hurt your delicate little gummy wummies!' Unfortunately for Softy, the milk was half a degree too hot! In the feud that followed the food, it was always Softy who came out on top.

Tornado Tom
Harry Banger
Fresh Fun 1940-45; *War Comics* 1941; *Slick Fun* 1945-50 (Swan)
'Blazing a trail through the Wild West comes Tornado Tom' and into *Fresh Fun* No. 4, carving T.T.'s into trees. Tough as they come, Swan comics' answer to Desperate Dan hugs a hungry grizzly and gives it a wasp-waist! Tom's four-page wanderings took him to Mexicana where Murky Miguel the Black-hearted Bandit did his worst, but Tom bested him: 'To a-da Coppa Shop! Big-a Rewards given for Bad Lads C.O.D.' Next month he was in the frozen snows of Eskimoland, then he was clouting crocs in India, thanks to a water-spout: a six-page epic, this. Finally he wound up as front-page star of *Coloured Slick Fun*.

Tough but Tender Tex
Norman Ward
Knockout 1944-46; *Comet* 1951-52; *Big One* 1964-65 (Fleetway)
Tough But Tender Tex had a curious career, even for a comic character. Starting as little more than a six-picture filler strip in which he appeared as a tough guy with a soft heart, Tex had a short run in 1944, returning in 1946 drawn by a different artist, Hugh McNeill. He suddenly reappeared in *Comet* No. 148 (19 May 1951) as simply Tough Tex. This time he was the strong-man star of a full-page picture serial, proving Otto Krook framed Joe Summers for stealing a circus payroll. Tex was drawn by Reg Parlett, and all the other characters by Reg Bunn! After which the strip turned funny again, as drawn by Wally Robertson (Illustrated).

Tough Tod and Happy Annie/Joe and Janie
Hugh McNeill
Knockout 1947-60; *Big One* 1964-65 (Fleetway)
'The Runaway Orphans' first ran away in No. 1 of *Knockout*, stars of a long-running serial story illustrated by Eric R. Parker. Their run grew even longer, for they returned to *Knockout* in 1947 as a picture serial in which they would be on the run for another fourteen years! Tod and Annie Gray were pursued through the pages by stingy old Silas Stiggins of the Sloansbury Orphanage, but Tod and Annie's motto was 'Keep smiling – never moan'. Modernized as Pam and Peter for *Princess* (1960).

Toy Boy
Terry Bave
Whoopee 1974-80 (IPC)
The big 'T' on his sweater stood for Toy Boy, a youngster utterly obsessed by his cupboard full of toys. He was so good at jigsaw puzzles that he could do them with his back turned. No wonder Toy Boy was the ideal chap to help a neighbour lay his crazy paving! His toys came in handy at times, water pistols to spray paint on Dad's garden shed, or his train set to chug round the table passing food at Mum's birthday party. Toy Boy began in No. 1 of *Whoopee* (9 March 1974) and was soon popular enough to be promoted to the coloured cover.

Tricky Dicky
Cyril Price
Cor 1970-73 (IPC)
'I can get out of anything!' was the proud motto of this tousel-headed lad with the sideways' schoolcap. It was his mop of hair that helped him dodge homework in *Cor* No. 1 (6 June 1970) as his mum discovered when she found the armchair contained nothing but a mop with a cap stuck on top. Dicky was hiding behind her clothes' drier watching telly! So mum locked him in his bedroom and took away his sheets so he couldn't tie them together and pop out of the window. That didn't stop Dicky: he dangled himself down on his braces ('Boing!'). Dad got the last laugh with a quick snip of his shears.

Tricky Dicky
John Dallas
Topper 1977- (D. C. Thomson)
This black-haired boy with the beetling brows could hardly have expected that he would one day be the front-page star of *Topper*. But, when that tabloid comic reduced in format (6 September 1980), it was Tricky Dicky who grabbed the full-colour front and back pages with his life-size inflatable elephant joke. Dicky's mum and dad were the water-soaked victims, of course. Dicky's Mad Mouse became the prize for the best 'Gag of the Week' contributed by a reader.

The Trigan Empire
Don Lawrence
Ranger 1965-66; *Look & Learn* 1966-82; *Vulcan* 1975-76 (IPC)
This was the most skilful and sumptuous science-fiction serial strip since Dan Dare, scripted by Mike Butterworth and hand-painted in full colour by Don Lawrence. The saga started in No. 1 of *Ranger* (18 September 1965), entitled 'The Rise and Fall of the Trigan Empire'. It was illustrated from the records recovered from a crashed cosmocraft as decoded by Richard Peter Haddon after a lifetime's work. Trigo, one of three brothers, founded the City of Trigan in the land of Vorg, on the continent of Victris, on the planet Elektron, which circled the star of Yarna, a billion miles from Earth.

Tri-Man
Illustrator unknown
Smash 1969-70 (IPC)
'Action! Action! Action!' was the headline for this complicated attempt at a British superhero. Professor Meek had invented a fantastic ray which gave teenager Johnny Small triple superpowers to fight crime in the guise of Tri-Man. With supersight, superspeed, and superstrength, Tri-Man still had his hands full trying to save the old Prof from the clutches of a mask-wearing master crook called Multiface, while, at school, Johnny Small had his troubles with bullying Tod Blacker.

T

Trixie's Treasure Chest
Robert MacGillivray
Debbie 1979-83 (D. C. Thomson)
There was an old chest full of mysterious and magical things in Trixie Robbins' attic. It had belonged to her seafaring grandfather who had gathered strange objects from all over the world. Trixie had a lot of fun with the things she found in the chest, despite the bane of her life, young Bobby Banks. There was the time when she found an old duster that made whatever she wiped invisible: very handy when she was stuck behind a pillar at a Rich Clifford pop concert! Other times, things backfired, like the snowball toy that caused a blizzard inside a bus!

T.V. Terrors
Illustrator unknown
TV Comic 1962-78 (Polystyle)
For an unbelievable seventeen years, week after week in *TV Comic*, Monica, Buttons, Cuthbert, and Spot, their pet pup, tried to sneak into the television studios without being spotted by Hoppit the doorman. Most times they succeeded, despite what Hoppit called his hobnailed kickers, big boots forever at the ready to eject unwanted, underaged interlopers. Many of their early episodes feature bright burlesques of current TV series, such as *Juke Box Jury* ('Pick Your Pop') and *Do It Yourself* with Barry Bucknall (Larry Buckhall).

The Trolls
Hugh McNeill
Tina 1967; *Princess Tina* 1967-73 (Fleetway)
'You've seen them in all the shops – now meet them in person. Start laughing now!' The Trolls were a funny little family of long-haired pixies from Norse mythology, or 'supernatural pigmy cave-dwellers' as one dictionary has it. Troll dolls were something of a rage in the 'Sixties, so perhaps it was no surprise to find them turning up in *Tina* No. 1 (25 February 1967), playing their pixie pranks on a farmer and his gormless son in a double-page adventure.

Tuffy and His Magic Tail
Arnold Warden
Playbox 1939-55 (Amalgamated Press)
Originally billed as 'Tuff the Pup', this endearing little hound had only to wag his long tail to cause all sorts of magical mischief, although to be fair most of the time he was trying to be helpful as befitted a star of a nice comic like *Playbox*. Tuffy was the pet of Topsy and Skippy, who was the boy with the regular catchphrase: 'Look, Tuffy's magic tail is wagging!' One famous tailwag turned Duke Doolittle's crown into a delishus jelly!

12½p. Buytonic Boy/Super Steve
Robert Nixon
Krazy 1976-78; *Whizzer & Chips* 1978- (IPC)
This is a broad, boyhood burlesque of the American television series, *The Bionic Man*, starring in an explosive full-colour spread in No. 1 of *Krazy* (16 October 1976). Steve Ford crashes his soapbox car and buys a bottle of Vitamin Tonic from Professor Nutz, Inventor, for 12½ new pence: 'That's just half a dollar, sonny!' A swift gulp and Steve leaps into action saving some suitably labelled Secret Plans from suitably sinister spies. 'Zoooom! Kapow!!' From 1983, the title of the strip was changed to 'Super Steve'.

The Twickenham Twins

W. F. Coles

Funny Cuts 1903-05 (Trapps Holmes)

Bobbie and Billy Cheerychub, known as the Twickenham Twins, were the cover stars of *Funny Cuts*. They were in the curious care of a one-legged old seadog called Tom Towline, who was given to much crying of 'Belay there, ye swabs!' and other naughty nauticalities. Tom's old shipmate, Bill Hawser, once gave the boys a monkey called Jacko. The animal poured beer all over the bald dome of Spuds the gardener, much to the twins' mirth. It made a change from horseshoes in boxing-gloves.

The Twitz of The Ritz

Bill Ritchie

Buzz 1973-75 (D. C. Thomson)

'The staff of The Ritz – Will keep you in fitz!' was the promise of the D. C. Thomson rhymester in No. 1 of *Buzz* (20 January 1973), and they certainly did their best in the full-colour centre spread of this tabloid comic. Mr Grumpp was the chap in charge, an officious official in his blue uniform: 'You 'orrible, ignorant, insolent, impudent, overfed, underworked lot!' The hotel staff was led by Billy Buttons, the pill-boxed pageboy but, such were Billy's bright ideas, that when Mr Balderdosh from the Hotel Safety Organisation asked for safety suggestions, Grumpp said 'Sack the Twitz!'

Twiddle and Nobb

Roy Wilson

Jolly 1935 (Amalgamated Press)

'Always On The Mike!' was the original, and apt, title of this radio-based strip which took the air in No. 1 of *Jolly*, 19 January 1935. Mister Twiddle ('the boob behind the boiled shirt') was the commentator and Master Nobb his oscillating assistant for the outside broadcasting unit of the JBC (the Jolly Broadcasting Company) bossed by Sir Hector O'Dine. Their first OB, broadcasting the bray of a laughing donkey at a circus, caused chaos when the moke kicked them on to the joy-wheel, setting a pattern of disaster for many more to follow. From No. 24, they were promoted to page one as 'The Jolly Broadcasting Boys'.

The Two Pickles

H. O'Neill

Rainbow 1914-56 (Amalgamated Press)

'Dear Readers, Everyone calls us the Two Pickles. I don't know why, unless it is because we are always getting into a pickle!' Thus, did Peter and Pauline address their young readers in No. 1 of *Rainbow*, 14 February 1914; little did artist, H. O'Neill, reckon that he would still be drawing their pranks in the last number of *Rainbow*, 1898 issues later! Peter and Pauline were the innocent-eyed offspring of an upper-middleclass Ma and Pa, looked after by Mary the maid, and accompanied by a talking dog called Fluff.

Twisty

Barrie Mitchell

Bullet 1976-77 (D. C. Thomson)

'Criminal in the making, or soccer star of tomorrow?' was the question posed about Twisty Lunnon, a youth of the Sleethorpe slums. Twisty had been left with a slightly deformed left leg after a car crash, but this did not stop him running rings around Badger Smith's back-alley football team: 'Sheesh! That cripple's as slippery as an eel!' Barney Hollis, the manager of United's Youth Team, was impressed, too, and soon the lad had left the cruel guardianship of his Uncle Charlie for the football field.

Typhoon Tracy

Illustrator unknown

Hurricane 1964-65; *Lion* 1965-69 (Fleetway)

'Roar into Action with Typhoon Tracy, Trouble-Shooter!' was the front-page splash on *Hurricane* No. 1 (29 February 1964), the Paper with Punch! Five pages of punch-packed pictures followed, introduced thus: 'Trouble was his trade and battle his business. Six feet six inches of globe-trotting, mighty-muscled fighting man, the toughest soldier of fortune who ever fought on the side of right against wrong. The bigger the odds he faced, the wider his smile. The more furious the fight, the greater his joy, and when he burst into battle-loving laughter, anything could happen!' Added Typhoon: 'Ho! Ho! Ho!'

Uncle Oojah
Flo Lancaster
Oojah Sketch 1921-29 (*Daily Sketch*); *Jack & Jill* 1954-58 (Amalgamated Press)
Uncle Oojah the elephant in striped pyjamas and King of Oojahland, was created as the children's corner of the *Daily Sketch* by Flo Lancaster. Her stories, illustrated by Thomas Maybank, developed into a strip and soon filled the front page of a weekly comic supplement, *Oojah Sketch*. After a long run of annuals, Oojah returned to comics in No. 1 of *Jack & Jill* (27 February 1954) drawn by H. M. Talintyre (illustrated), in the serial, 'The Wonderful Adventures of Jerry, Don and Snooker'.

Union Jack Jackson
Gordon
Hotspur 1962; *Warlord* 1974-84; *Victor* 1982 (D. C. Thomson)
'Somewhere in the Pacific in 1943 the British warship *Attacker* slips to its watery grave, the victim of a Japanese air attack. As Japanese aircraft strafed the boats leaving the sinking ship, a Royal Marine, Jack Jackson, leaped from one of the boats, still carrying his rifle. Three days later, on a remote island where some American Marines were based, a raft drifted into shore.' After a bit of a dust-up ('A Royal Marine doesn't crawl for anyone!' 'Don't make me laugh, Limey!'), Jackson pals up with tough-guy O'Bannion and, with a Union Jack on his helmet, attaches himself to the U.S. Marines.

Uncle Squibs and his Naughty Nibs
Bill Radford
Jester 1928-32 (Amalgamated Press)
No reader of the penny *Jester* ever paused to wonder why it was that the Naughty Nibs, Nicky and Sis by name, lived out their lives with their Uncle Squibs. Was there the shadow of an orphanage in the background? Or was the explanation simply that their artist dreamed up the catchy title and took it from there? Alas, we shall never know. So let us laugh at the slapstick havoc the Naughty Nibs wreaked around poor old Squibs, and echo their cheery cry of 'Good old Uncle!.

Valda
Dudley Wynn
Mandy 1969-82 (D. C. Thomson)
The Amazing Valda, Girl of Mystery, was found by Dorcas the Gypsy over 200 years ago, and named after the dust which spelled Valda on the surface of a pool. Valda grew to learn the secrets of the herbs and the language of the animals. After Dorcas died, Valda journeyed underground to the Emerald Grotto of Ice and Fire. Here, the cold flames gave Valda the secret of eternal youth. Then, in 1969, the earth split open and an old woman came out to bathe herself in the Fire of Life. Young again, Valda had returned!

Val's Vanishing Cream
Mike Lacey
Cor 1973-74; *Buster* 1974-76 (IPC)
The postwar successor to 'Margie the Invisible Mender' was Val, who used a jar of magic vanishing cream to make herself disappear. A freckle-faced redhead in sweater and jeans, Val lacked the inborn honesty of her predecessor. She was not opposed to rubbing the cream over herself to get into a funfair without paying, or smothering her overdue library books with the stuff to escape the fine. She also got her dad to carry the pile down for her by cunningly leaving the bottom book visible.

Victor Drago
Mike Dorey
Tornado 1979 (IPC)
'Victor Drago – a name that struck terror into the most hardened of evil-doers, from the slums of London's East End to the teeming waterfront of Shanghai. Drago was the private detective who never gave up a case, often succeeding where the toughest policeman failed.' Set in the snowswept London of 1929, assisted by the teenage Spencer and his faithful bloodhound Brutus, it didn't take much detective work to unmask this pipe-smoking sleuth as a disguised Sexton Blake, with Tinker and Pedro.

Von Hoffman
Illustrator unknown
Jet 1971; *Buster* 1971-72 (IPC)
'Von Hoffman's Invasion' was the title of this serial which took top place in No. 1 of *Jet* (1 May 1971). 'The crazy inventor who planned to destroy Britain' was Doktor Von Hoffman who, in the Germany of April 1945, unveiled 'The mightiest weapon of war ever devised by man – my new armoured rocket-firing, flame-throwing centipede!' 'Zum teufel!', gasped a general, and the machine said 'Glinkle! Gloinkle! Glinkle!' The Doktor explained, 'Thanks to an ingenious system of interlocking plates the centipede can slither across any known obstacle!' The RAF bombed it, so he created a giant eel with enlarging gas: 'Buu-awww!'

Vanessa from Venus
Illustrator unknown
June 1961-67 (Fleetway)
'The Most Amazing Friend an Earth Girl ever had' arrived in a Flying Saucer in *June* on 16 March 1963. Sally Prentice lived with her relatives, Mrs Gribble and Alison, who treated her like a servant. Her only escape was into her favourite science-fiction stories, but they got so much on her mind that she mistook Elsie the home-help for the Plutonian Pragglesnap! On her way home from the shops, Sally had a strange encounter – with the glamorous Vanessa from the planet Venus, a girl with mysterious powers. Later Vanessa left Sally and wandered the world on her own.

V for Vendetta
David Lloyd
Warrior 1982-85 (Quality)
'Good evening, London. It's nine o'clock and this is the voice of Fate, broadcasting on 275 and 285 on the medium wave.' It is the fifth of November, 1997, sixteen-year-old Queen Zara is on the throne, and British comic readers are about to encounter, for the first time, child prostitution, police gang-bangs, bad language ('Oh, God! . . . 'You bastard!' . . . 'Holy Christ!') and a classically quoting hero: 'Fortune, on his damned quarrel, smiling showed like a rebel's whore!' Costumed like Guy Fawkes, he also acts like him: he blows up the Houses of Parliament!

The Wacks
Leo Baxendale
Wham 1964-68 (Odhams)
Wack and Wack were two young wackers of Liverpool who brought a comic version of the popular Mersey Beat to No. 1 of *Wham* (20 June 1964). Inspired to do better than an old busker with a fiddle, they twanged their guitar in the gutter singing 'Woo! Woo! Wow! Ah'm a real gone cat! Yeah! Yeah!' They got what most gone cats get: a well-flung boot! It gave the bigger Wack such a bump that he couldn't get his comb through his Beatle-cut. Then they tried a sad ballad: 'Lizzie had a lollipop, each time she tried to suck it, the clouds above opened up, and rain came down in buckets!' Cue for a pail of water.

Wear 'Em Out Wilf
Mike Lacey
Whizzer & Chips 1969-76 (IPC)
'Meet Wilf: He wears out everything except a welcome!' Wilf started wearing things out in No. 1 of *Whizzer & Chips* (18 October 1969): he wore a hole in his trousers on the park slide. His mum promptly knitted him a new pair – with steel wool! The ensuing itch made Wilf wear his way through Miss Goldpurse's old chair revealing her granddad's hidden savings! When Wilf polished the floor, he wore it so thin his mum fell into the cellar. Wilf wheeled her round to the doctor, a short-sighted gent mistook her for a guy (Fawkes!), and Wilf was quids in!

Wacky
Mike Attwell
Nutty 1980-82 (D. C. Thomson)
Wacky, a boy with a nose like an upturned sausage, was billed as 'The Crackpot Inventor'. Most of his inventions were designed to help his distraught old dad. These included an alarm-clock that crowed dad awake, a pop-up bed that tipped him out, and an express skateboard that whizzed him to the bus with a speedy slice of breakfast stuck to his face. Everything worked to get dad to his office on time, except that it was Saturday! Wacky's mum got her share of help with his pedal-powered dish-dryer, but the neighbours thought the flying saucers were here!

Waddles the Waiter
Alexander Akerbladh
Comic Cuts 1912-25; 1938-47 (Amalgamated Press)
'Our Whimsical Waiter' worked in a posh café, but it is doubtful that his salary, quoted at five bob a week, ever increased during his lengthy employment. Once he embossed the menu on his celluloid shirt-front: 'Fag-paper Soup, Jugged Sole, Filleted Hen, Hair Soup, Filtered Plaice and Novau (*sic*) Jelly' – plush stuff, but this was 1913. His rival was a French waiter called Alphonse, who served 'Ze rost biff, of old England, ze pudding de Yorkshire, and ze college of Oxford' for afters. After thirteen years' retirement, Terry Wakefield revived him for another ten years' hard slog.

Walter Hottle Bottle
Illustrator unknown
Jack & Jill 1963-77 (IPC)
'Charles Millington Montmorency Brown was warm and cosy in bed. He had fallen asleep with his toes on his hot-water bottle. But suddenly there was a wriggle underneath the bedclothes, and out popped the hot water bottle!' It was 9 March 1963, and Walter, having introduced himself, explained: 'I can come to life only in your dreams! Would you like to meet the Maker of Dreams?' Of course, Charles said he would, so up a moonbeam they went and into the Moon to meet the Maker and his men. They made Charles a dream about the seaside, the first of hundreds to come.

We Are United
Peter Foster
Champ 1984-85; *Victor* 1985- (D. C. Thomson)
'We are the greatest!' is the proud boast of the United Football Club, who kicked off in *Champ* No. 1 (25 February 1984). Club captain and long-serving right back is Joe Pearson ('You give us support, son, and we'll give it everything on the pitch!'), and the manager is John Bland, the one with the dark glasses and the big cigar ('Remember, anyone who doesn't perform is out!'). A complete history of the team was published in episode one: founded 1885; ground The Mill; capacity 62 000; club colours red and yellow with black trim; First Division champions 1899; Football Association Cup winners 1903; and more.

Wee Davie
Ken Hunter
Beano 1952-57 (D. C. Thomson)
'Who can save Pomegrania from Hunk the Terrible Giant?', asked the editor. 'A knight on a white charger? No – a wee boy on a dusty donkey!' *Beano* readers were invited to meet the World's Oddest Giant-killer in 'Wee Davie and the Great Big Giant' starting in No. 513 (17 May 1952). Davie and Duncan the donkey, with considerable help from Snort the fire-breathing dragon, and Zok the alchemist, set himself up as the Royal Dragon Tamer in Chief, much to the delight of gouty King Willie.

Weary Willie and Tired Tim
Tom Browne
Chips 1896-53 (Amalgamated Press)
'The World Famous Tramps' made their casual debut on page one of *Chips* No. 298 dated 16 May 1896, in a six-picture strip entitled 'Innocents on the River'. Recognizing something worth repeating in his classic fat-thin combination, owing much to his admiration for Don Quixote and Sancho Panza, artist Tom Browne brought his heroes, Weary Waddles and Tired Timmy, back for a replay five weeks later. From No. 310, they filled the front page every week, right to the final issue of *Chips*, No. 2997, dated 12 September 1953, under their revised names of Weary Willie and Tired Tim. Percy Cocking took over from 1909, drawing the characters for forty-four years.

Wee Peem
James Jewell
Beano 1938-40; 1951-52 (D. C. Thomson)
Saddled with the silliest name in comics, this little boy with the big head seems to have been christened purely for the sake of the rhyme: 'Wee Peem – He's a Proper Scream!' Big head apart, Wee Peem was a pretty typical 'bad boy', hiding a cat up his striped jumper so that its howls would get him rejected from the school choir. Peem was reborn on 10 November 1951, this time with a jar of Magic B-Pills: 'B-Quick', 'B-Heavy', 'B-Elastic', and so on.

Webster
Terry Bave
Shiver & Shake 1973-74 (IPC)
'The Spider whose Webs have Everyone in a Spin' spun into No. 1 of *Shiver* (10 March 1973), the creepy comic that formed the front half of *Shiver & Shake*. Webster ('scuttle! scuttle!') was the first eight-legged creepy-crawlie strip star since Septimus Spider threatened Freddy the Fearless Fly back in the prewar *Dandy*. 'Aaaagh! Wassat 'orrible web doing in yer sentry box you 'orrible soldier!' screamed a sergeant, ordering the luckless sentry to fix feather-duster and charge. But Webster's webs were made of tougher stuff, and the superstrong strands even sealed up a circus cannon to the wrath of a big shot.

Wee Sporty
Bill Mevin
Express 1956-61 (Beaverbrook)
Wee Sporty, 'the outdoor type who's game for anything', had the longest run of any character, comic or otherwise, in *Express Weekly*. He made his debut in the first issue of the new full-colour format, No. 74 (18 February 1956) as a simple, single-line strip: in three panels Sporty tried to put the shot but the shot put him! By the end of the year, the wee one was filling a full tabloid page as a member of Britain's Olympic team and, by Christmas 1959, he was the full-colour, front-page star! But, by the end of the comic's run, he was back again as a single strip. As Sporty would have said: 'Crivvens!'

Wee Sue
Illustrator unknown
Sandie 1972-73; *Tammy* 1973-81 (IPC)
Although many strips had starred short characters in a comic capacity, this was the first to show how an unnaturally short person might survive the cruel taunts of those of superior height. Sue Strong also had another burden to bear: besides being a titch, she was also the only scholarship girl at an upper-crust public school. Backhurst School for Girls, famous for its sporting activities, was on the decline when Wee Sue arrived in *Sandie* No. 1 (12 February 1972), but she showed them that height was not everything.

Wells Fargo
Don Lawrence
Zip 1958-59; *Swift* 1959-61 (Odhams)
Jim Hardie (played by Dale Robertson) was the hero of the American television series, *Tales of Wells Fargo*, from which this serial strip took its inspiration. Jim was a special agent for the famous overland express stagecoach system, Wells Fargo & Co. He posed as a passenger to foil the series of hold-ups on the Denver to Julesburg line staged by a mysterious gang known as the Faceless Men: they wore flour bags over their heads. Jim's later adventures included getting an ammunition coach through to Pueblo, a garrison besieged by Indians.

Wee Willie Haggis
Illustrator unknown
Pow 1967-68 (Odhams)
Adapting his name from the eccentric pop singer, Wee Willie Harris, this sawn-off Scot was billed as 'The Spy from Skye'. Wearing the standard issue turned-up raincoat over his kilt, he was called in to recover Cleopatra's Needle on 21 January 1967, in No. 1 of *Pow*. Suspecting that Archibald Krook the arch-crook was behind the snatch, and pausing only to dust his sporran with a wee smattering of dandruff remover, Wee Willie hopped aboard his hover-haggis and was hot on the trail. His self-inflating tam-o-shanter proved handy when Krook's mob closed in.

Wendy
Sidney Pride
Playbox 1935-55 (Amalgamated Press)
'Tales of her Wonderful Adventures' illustrated this helpful heroine's wanderings in a fairyland of fabulous but familiar folk: Sindbad the Sailor, Tom the Piper's Son, Jack the Giant Killer. In her serial, she was supported by her own magic carpet: it flew whenever she brushed it and, in twenty years, never let her down. In her final adventure, Wendy saved Cinderella's slipper and arrived at the ball on time.

Wendy and Jinx

Ray Bailey

Girl 1952-64 (Hulton)

Wendy and Jinx, inseparable chums of the Fourth Form, were in School House of Manor School. They were the new heroines of the full-colour front page of *Girl*, 'Sister Paper to Eagle', who replaced the original stars, Kitty Hawke and her All Girl Air Crew who proved unpopular with readers. Whereas Kitty and Co lasted less than a year, Wendy and Jinx ran for the rest of the comic's life although, from 1958, they moved to the monochrome interior. Their form mistress was Miss Brumble, known as Bumble-bee, and chums included Nasrullah, known as Dusky.

What Price Glory

Harry Banger

Fresh Fun 1940; *Extra Fun* 1940; *Thrill Comics* 1940; *War Comics* 1940; *Slick Fun* 1945; *Cute Fun* 1948 (Swan)

The title of a famous comedy film set in World War 1 formed a fine pun for the title of this strip. Glory was a skinny spinster ever out to catch a man, a slightly sophisticated theme for a British comicbook of the 'Forties, and the only gesture publisher Gerald G. Swan made towards female readership. Always failing to win her man despite overdoses of beauty treatment, Glory had equally poor luck in her patriotic attempts to join the Roof Spotters (she wound up on a barrage balloon) or the Land Army.

The Whizzers from Ozz

Paddy Brennan

Topper 1966-80 (D. C. Thomson)

Young Willie Walker was camping close to his home town of Workchester when his potato peeling was more than slightly disturbed by the sudden arrival of a space car! The occupants were Krik and Krok, twin brothers from the country of Whizz on the planet of Ozz. Pausing only to save Willie from an upset bull with their handy ray-gun ('Slamph!'), Krik and Krok enlisted him in their space geography quest to find a list of Earth items: number one – a Union Jack!

We Three

Illustrator unknown

Tip Top 1949-54 (Amalgamated Press)

The title should really have been 'We Four', for the Clarke children were quite inseparable from their donkey, Ned. Nobby, Nan, and Little Joe were orphans left to fend for themselves. Nan worked as a maidservant in London, while Nobby worked on a farm. Joe stayed home minding the donkey. For a while, their adventures were pretty predictable, Nan's problems with nasty Mrs Grime, Nobby's with bully Briggs the greengrocer, but 1950 found them shipping to the United States to live on a ranch with jolly Pierre and rascally redskins.

Whistler and his Dog

Illustrator unknown

Topper 1983-86 (D. C. Thomson)

Taking their title from a popular prewar tune often heard in BBC *Children's Hour*, Whistler and his Dog are, in fact, an up-to-date variation on another prewar comic pair, Professor Switch and his Wireless Watchdog, Zipp. Confirming the trend away from adult heroes to kids, Whistler is a boy whose best pal is his mechanical dog, Bonzo (another prewar name!). A command blown on Whistler's whistle ('Toot! Toot!') brings an instant reaction from Bonzo: his legs extend, he grows wings, and flies, and generally comes in useful.

Whoopee Hank

Roland Davies

Beano 1938-39 (D. C. Thomson)

'Whoopee Hank – the Slap-dash Sheriff' shot his way into *Beano* No. 1 (30 July 1938) as a kind of law-enforcing equivalent of *Dandy*'s Desperate Dan. As the editorial poet put it:

> Star on his Shirt – Slugs in his Gun,
> Laugh at the Sheriff – He's chock full of Fun!

Big-Shot Smith the bank robber laughed on the other side of his ugly mug when Hank got cracking with a Civil War cannon:

> Pop! Bang! Boom! and Whizz! Bang! Slap!
> Big-Shot's caught in Whoopee's trap!

Why, Dad, Why?

Manny Curtis

Whizzer & Chips 1970–72; *Cheeky* 1979-80 (IPC)

The traditional father-son relationship got severely strained in this series. While Dad and Son were basically the best of pals, certainly they seemed inseparable and Mum was seldom seen, their continuing conversation was like a one-way quiz contest. Whatever they saw, did, or happened to them, Son wanted to know why, so that, by the end of their page, poor Dad was driven to distraction in his desperate attempts to explain. 'Why are you going back into the maze, Dad? Won't you get lost?' 'I hope so!'

Wild Boy of the Woods

Toby Baines

Beano 1939-42; 1947-49 (D. C. Thomson)

'Here is a picture story of a young Tarzan' was the honest introduction to this serial which started in *Beano* No. 1, 30 July 1938. Derek, 'the brown-faced boy in the strange clothes made of rabbit skin', lived in a secret cave, entered through a hollow tree, with an old hermit whom he called Grandfather. The woods were near the town of Barchester, but Derek was soon forced to move to Scotland because of his penchant for saving foxes from huntsmen. With the war, Derek became 'the deadliest foe Germany ever had', using the hermit's Gyro-Flyer to save Africa from a black dictator!

Wild Bill Hickock

Derek Eyles

Sun 1955-56; *Radio Fun and Adventures* 1959-61 (Amalgamated Press)

'The buckskin-clad scout sent a hail of hot lead into the frenzied redskins, wreaking havoc amid their vast ranks! Together, man and horse blazed a trail of adventure across the West. The gallant mare was called Gypsy, the man was named Wild Bill Hickock!' The editorial introduction to the new front-page star of the revamped *Radio Fun and Adventures* (22 August 1959): although Wild Bill had no radio connections, it was hoped the television craze for cowboys might save the flagging comic: it didn't, despite top artwork.

The Wild Bunch

Illustrator unknown

Giggle 1967-68; *Buster* 1968 (Fleetway)

Taking their name from the popular western film, the Wild Bunch ganged up in No. 1 of *Giggle* (29 April 1967). The roll call ran: Dodger (black cap and specs), Joker (duffle coat and catapult), Twister (curly mop and striped sweater), Debbie (long lank hair and black stockings), and Little Pet (a big-eyed baby blonde). Their main opposition came from Beefy Burgess the bully. The Bunch built a Special Agents (soapbox) Car and the bully bashed it in. So they rebuilt it with improvements: a super-sprung ejector seat that smothered Beefy with tomatoes, and a marble-blasting machine-gun.

Wildfire the War Horse
Jack Glass
Dandy 1940-41 (Thomson)
An unusual story of World War 1 to find in World War 2, and an unusual hero, an artillery horse. Wildfire 'was a magnificent black and white stallion whose proudly-arched neck and clean-cut legs and hoofs stamped him as a king amongst horses.' Set in shell-torn Flanders, Wildfire was separated from his beloved master, Tim Holt, in episode one (*Dandy*, 7 September 1940) and spent the rest of his serial strip searching for him. His quest was a success, of course.

Willie Bunk
Frank McDiarmid
Whizzer & Chips 1969-70 (IPC)
'The Spectacular Adventures of Willie Bunk' started in *Whizzer & Chips* No. 1 (18 October 1969) with the bespectacled boy bunking from a bunch of bullies determined to pinch his buns. Ducking down an old alley, he fell into the cellar of an aged optician who gave him an odd pair of square specs. 'Just give the lenses a rub if you're in trouble, and for ten minutes you'll see quite a change in yourself!' The bullies pounced, Willie rubbed, and 'Wow!' – Willie saw himself as a noble knight routing his foe on his trusty steed. Actually he was on his bike, but thanks to the magic specs (which turned the pictures red!), Willie found courage.

The Wild Rovers
Ken Harrison
Nutty 1980-85 (D. C. Thomson)
This bunch of hungry hounds, inspired by, but both hungrier and tougher, than *Beano*'s Pup Parade, was first let loose across the full-colour centre spread of *Nutty* No. 1 (16 February 1980). The gang of nine were named as Hunk, the ginger giant in the deerstalker hat; Magnus Peek, the bespectacled brainbox; Singh Songh, a brown hound in a turban; Patch, the pink'un with one eye; Lady, the bitch in the blue collar; Silly Villy, the one with spots; Dogsbody, the mixed-up mongrel; Taff, the Welsh terrier; and Haggis the dotty Scottie. Their eternal enemy was Basil Crumb the Dog-catcher.

The Wild Wonders
Illustrator unknown
Valiant 1964-73 (Fleetway)
Because of the arduous life they had led on bleak Worrag Island in the Hebrides, the brothers Rick and Charlie Wild had developed into super athletes, and the strongest boys in the world. Their rich Aunt Amelia placed them under the guardianship of Mike Flynn, the Olympic swimmer, and they went to live at Mike's garage in the outskirts of London. But the boys were endless trouble, preferring to say 'Sliggle oinx ngu!' to the English he tried to teach them. So they were sent to school at Highgate Hall, with Mike as sports master.

Will Hay
Bertie Brown
Jolly 1936-39; *Comic Cuts* 1939-40 (Amalgamated Press)
'The Master of Mirth' from stage, screen, and radio, brought his Boys of St Michael's to the front page of *Jolly* on 24 October 1936: term lasted four years. Will introduced his pupils: 'The head, or fathead, boy is Jimmy Harbottle. He might be described as the perfect schoolboy howler! He has grown whiskers in the service of the school and now pays his fees out of his old age pension! Another prominent pupil is Tommy Watt. When there's a spanking due he usually "books" his seat. I had to wallop my way through the Hundred Years War before I could make him feel a tickle!'

W

Willie and Wally
Bertie Brown
Funny Wonder 1914-17 (Amalgamated Press)
'The Wonderful Wonder Boys', Willie and Wally, were the fiendish front-page stars of *Funny Wonder*, later moving to the centre spread to be drawn by Bertie Livett (illustrated). The ticklish twins were yet another pair of pranksters modelled on 'The Katzenjammer Kids', Willie being the fair-haired fellow and Wally the one with the black bush. Although they lived with Ma, the chief butt of their japes was Uncle Jeff, a bearded old boy reminiscent of the Katzies' 'der Inspector'.

Willie Woodpecker
John Mason
Dandy 1942-44 (D. C. Thomson)
This bright and busy little bird flew into *Dandy* during the war and pecked his way into the hearts of young readers. Willie, unlike his probable American inspiration, Woody Woodpecker, was no mere feathered friend: he wore snappy little shorts suspended by a single brace. Vengeance was Willie's main concern, wreaking beaky havoc on those who crossed his path. But revenge was not always sweet: when he pecked through a bullying carpenter's chair-leg, Willie got tipped into a pot of glue and had to walk home to his tree!

Willie Wart and Wally Warble
Bert Hill
Rattler 1936-39 (Target)
'How d'ye do, readers!' wrote the editor of *Rattler* on the front page of No. 147 (13 June 1936), 'Today we meet a couple of new fun makers. Have you all got clean collars on?' The latest in a long line of comic-strip double acts was Willie Wart, the rotund half in the check waistcoat, and Wally Warble, tall, thin, and topped off with a bowler hat: 'As fine a brace of funsters as ever filled the front page of any fun paper!' Their debut doings took place at Seabreeze-on-the-Whiskers, a seaside resort between Southgate and Tooting, and ended with the bagging of a burglar.

Wilson
Ripoll
Hornet 1964-76; *Hotspur* 1976-80 (D. C. Thomson)
'The Greatest Boy's Story Ever Written!' was the front-page headline on *Hornet* No. 53 (12 September 1964). 'That's what they said in the newspapers, on the radio, and on television about this story. Now for the first time ever it is told in exciting picture-story form.' The title was 'The Truth About Wilson' and it had first appeared on 24 July 1943 in No. 1069 of the story paper, *Wizard*. W. S. K. Webb, a young sports reporter, was on the scene when William Wilson, running barefoot in his black one-piece, came out of the Yorkshire moors to break the barrier of the four-minute mile: he did it in 3 minutes 48 seconds'!

W

Winker Watson
Eric Roberts
Dandy 1961-86 (D. C. Thomson)
When Winker Watson arrived for the new term at Greytowers School in 1961, he could hardly have dreamed it would be for the term of his natural life: twenty-five years so far and still no sign of promotion from the Third Form, or escape from Mr Creep his master! This, despite Winker's well-known billing as 'the world's champion schoolboy wangler'. Winker's wangles always included his best pal, Tim Trott, and are often angled against his kid brother, Wallie Watson, no mean wangler himself.

The Winners
Mike Lacey
Jackpot 1980-82; *Buster* 1982- (IPC)
Sporting foursome – mum, dad, and the kids – with a mania for entering every event in sight, and a determination to win at all costs. Nature often conspired to assist: When Mr Winner went in for a golf tournament he got a birdie by hitting his ball into a nearby nest. The affronted sparrow kicked it out, straight into the hole! A fierce bull came in handy during a cross-country race. And, while sawing wood for a garden shed, Dad produced 14961 slivers, the exact number of 'Duck Vista' matches that fit into a 20-cm square box. He won – another garden shed!

Winkle and Binkle Minor
Entwistle
Lot-O-Fun 1908-20 (Henderson)
'The Adventures of Winkle and Binkle Minor' was a long-running schoolboy strip which, for a while, expanded to the coloured cover of *Lot-O-Fun*. It retailed the mischievous pranks of Willy Winkle and Billie Binkle, naughtiest of the Eton-collared scholars at Dr Swisham's boarding school. Butt of many japes was Billy Bungle the fat boy: 'Oh, my little Mary! You'll give me indigestion under the wishbone! Oh-o-o-o!' and Froggy the French master was no better served: 'Ah! Dees is vat ze Eengleeshe call ze disappearing trick! Ah!'

Winnie-the-Pooh
A. A. Milne
Playhour 1955-57; *Candy* 1967-68 (City); *Disneyland* 1972-76 (IPC)
Winnie-the-Pooh, Christopher Robin's pet name for Edward Bear, first appeared in *Punch* in 1924, and was gathered into his first book in 1926. The inseparable illustrations to A. A. Milne's stories were by E. H. Shepherd, and these had little influence on Peter Woolcock's comic-strip adaptation for *Playhour*. 'Winnie-the-Pooh and the Happy Adventures of Christopher Robin' began in No. 32 (21 May 1955), announced as 'Here for the first time ever in pictures!' The Disneyland version of Pooh was drawn by Roland Davies.

Wireless Willie and Bertie Broadcast
Reg Carter

Monster 1922-28 (United)

'Dear Listeners-in! Hallo! Hallo! It's Bertie Broadcast calling!' was the introductory caption to this ultramodern strip on the front page of No. 1 of *The Monster Penny Comic* (23 September 1922). And the sign-off to the strip was equally topical: 'Good-bye. I'm closing down now until next week! Good-bye!' Actually, this comic couple were regulation double actors, fat and thin, but their hats were decorated with an aerial (Willie the thin) and a loudspeaker (Bertie the fat). Fascinatingly, this strip predates the BBC by two months.

Wizard Prang and Demon Druid
Mike Brown

Smash 1968-69 (Odhams)

Wizard Prang ('Something unforeseen is always happening when he's around!') and Demon Druid ('He spells trouble for just about everyone!') costarred in a strip which also bore the title 'Wiz War!'. It was war of the wizards, with W. Prang, the one in the white robes and whiskers to match, forever at magical loggerheads with D. Druid, the spotty fat one in black. Old Prang usually came out the victor of the week with occasional thanks to his pet eagle, or possibly vulture, Englebert: 'Aaawrk!'

Witch Winkle
Tom Kerr

Twinkle 1974-80 (D. C. Thomson)

Wendy Wilson moved into a new home called Tudor Cottage on 21 September 1974, in No. 348 of *Twinkle*. The cottage was hundreds of years old and, while Wendy was putting her toys in the cupboard, out jumped a black cat! Pulling away the torn wallpaper, Wendy uncovered a flight of steps leading to a dusty little attic. Inside she found a strange old woman. Wendy scoffed when she announced herself as Witch Winkle, but soon regretted it when the old witch chanted: 'This naughty child will laugh no more – make her a frog upon the floor!' There was a flash and Wendy turned into a frog. 'Fancy having a witch in my toy cupboard!', she gasped.

Wizzo Ranch
Albert Pease

Comic Cuts 1951-53 (Amalgamated Press)

This 'Gurgle-making Gang of Japers in the Wild and Woolly West' cantered into *Comic Cuts* No. 2917 (10 February 1951) and took over the red-and-black front page. Tommy Trigger was the handsome cowboy hero, whose optic was on Pretty Poppy the Pride of the Prairie, much to the ire of Pauncho the Menace from Mexico. This bad bandit was in league with Big Chief Giggling Goat, but the real stars were the chums, Nibbo the cowboy kidlet and Chickweed the Injun papoose, who often saved Gran'pappy from eviction.

The Wizard of Football
Eric Bradbury

Buster 1969-72 (Fleetway)

Cyril Clarkson of the Duffield Rovers dreamed of becoming a soccer star, but had little success until he encountered a strange old ex-actor called Nathan Flintlock. A fantastic figure in wide-brimmed hat and black, flowing cloak, Nathan's overblown mannerisms and flowery language so inspired Cyril that his play improved, he was bought by Western United, and Nathan became that First-Division team's chief coach. Nathan's main problem was to hide from Cyril the fact that he was really a broken down bluffer on the breadline.

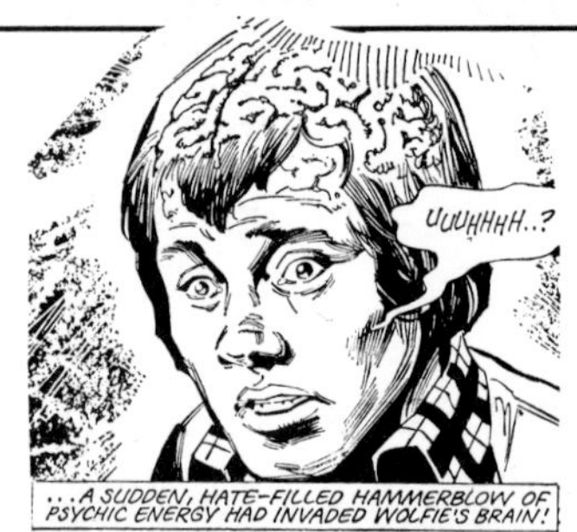

Wolfie Smith
Vanyo

Tornado 1979; *2000 AD* 1979 (IPC)

By the time he was nine years old, Ernest Patrick Smith of No. 11 Mason Street, Humberton, could make a pepper pot move, just by thinking about it! Small wonder his mother cried 'Oooops!', his father cried 'Wuuaaargh!', and Ernie cried 'Aaaowwgh!' as his ear was thoroughly boxed. And small wonder his serial was entitled 'The Mind of Wolfie Smith', especially as his nervous schoolmates noted that 'he prowls around like a ruddy wolf, he does!' Born with ESP, Wolfie learned he could do anything – if he put his mind to it.

The Wolf of Kabul
Higson

Hotspur 1961-75; *Buddy* 1981 (D. C. Thomson)

This classic hero of the prewar story paper *Wizard* is also a perrenial picture-serial favourite. As the preamble in *Buddy* No. 1 (14 February 1981) explained: 'It is 1930. High in the hills of the North West Frontier of British-ruled India a man dressed in native clothes watches. He is actually a British agent in disguise. His name is Bill Sampson, better known along the North West Frontier as the Wolf of Kabul!' The Wolf's faithful servant is Chung whose weapon is a blood-stained cricket bat, 'Clicky-ba'. The Wolf's boyhood was illustrated in *Warlord* (1974) as 'Young Wolf'.

Wonderman
Mick Anglo

Wonderman 1948-51 (Paget)

'John Justice, son of the world renowned scientist, the late Edward Justice, is a scientific product of his father's genius. Under the name of Captain Justice, John is known as an easy-going, wealthy good-for-nothing, but secretly, in the guise of Wonderman, he uses his amazing strength, invulnerability, and superhuman atomic powers to fight evil.' Thus, the permanent prelude to the red-and-blue adventures of 'the Atomic Marvel', who wore a big 'W' on his chest to prove he wasn't Superman.

Wonder-Car
Ron Turner

Whizzer & Chips 1970-77 (IPC)

'The Go-Anywhere Do-Anything Man-Made Masterpiece' was a fantastic vehicle invented by crippled Alistair Hardy. He was Uncle Alistair to his crew, three children called Patti Morgan, Colin Miller, and Porky Bates. They manned the big blue land/sea/aircraft for him, while he sat in his control room issuing orders. Their first rescue job turned sour when the shipwrecked sailor turned out to be villainous Captain Volney after treasure hidden in the Taoli Mountain in the Sahara. But that was just the start of their adventures.

Wonder Man/Wonder Mann
Tony Harding

Victor 1961-62; *Bullet* 1976 (D. C. Thomson)

H. K. Rodd was raised by Professor William Graves and Dr Erasmus Codrington, to be physically and mentally perfect, a superman of sport. Dubbed 'The Wonder Man', Rodd's story was told in text under this title in *Rover*, beginning No. 1132 (30 March 1946). Turned into a serial strip, 'The Wonder Man' ran again in *Victor* from 1961. Fifteen years later, *Bullet* No. 2 (21 February 1976) introduced 'Wonder Mann', the story of H. E. Mann who was raised by Professor Wilkie and Tom Brace to be physically and mentally perfect, a superman of sport.

Wonder Wellies
Andrew Christine

Cracker 1975-76 (D. C. Thomson)
Jim Kellie was a long-haired lad who wore a pair of extraordinary wellington boots. These Wonder Wellies acted as a telephone to keep Jim in touch with a mysterious Boss who sent him on secret missions: a wellyphone call! Sticking one of his wellies on his head, Jim could fly to the scene of the crime, thanks to his wellycopter! Then, from on high, he could spot trouble through his other boot: his wellyscope! In fact, Jim's picture strip might be described as wellyvision.

Wonder Worm
Illustrator unknown

Buster 1966-69; *Cor* 1973-74 (IPC)
Unlikeliest candidate in the superhero stakes was Wonder Worm. Apparently harmless, definitely armless, this humble hero found his lack of limbs no handicap. (A handy cap, incidentally, was his only gesture towards a superuniform.) Wonder Worm's nether end worked like a whip, gripping a snow-shoe and flipping Slippery Sam McGrew into a Mountie's clutches. No crime was too big or small for Wonder Worm, bagging a bag-snatcher or clobbering Count Von Turpentine's mechanical monster. Artists included Reg Parlett (illustrated).

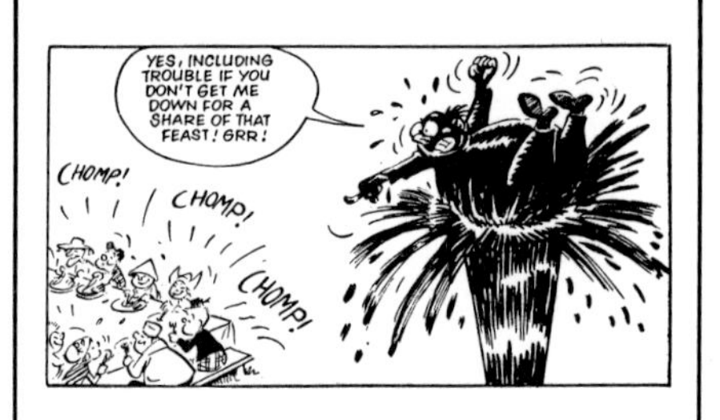

Worldwide School
Reg Parlett

Whizzer & Chips 1983-85 (IPC)
Diplomats from all over the world arrived at the United Nations Building for the start of a new session. On the same day, 12 February 1983, their children arrived for the start of their first term at Worldwide School, down the road. 'Good luck to their teacher!' said the Russian delegate, 'At lessons my Ivan is terrible!' The boy from Britain wondered what the teacher would be like. A stout gent in check trousers rolled in. 'No wonder they call it Worldwide School – teacher's the same shape as the world!' National characteristics came in handy. The Indian boy did the rope trick to repair the ceiling.

Wonder Wellies
Dave Follows

Buster 1983-85 (IPC)
Willy got his Wonder Wellies, not from the D. C. Thomson reject shop, but from Professor Krankpot. He borrowed them to use as test-tubes in an experiment for turning apples into solid gold but, when it didn't work, returned them to Willy. The wellies were never the same again. They took on a life of their own, not merely walking but, when commanded by Willy, leaping him over ponds, walking him up the sides of trees, and floating him gently down to the ground. They also had a mind of their own, shooting Willy out when his socks got too smelly!

Woppit
Illustrator unknown

Robin 1953-67 (Hulton)
'The Story of Woppit' started with him falling out of a pram in the middle of a dusty road, in No. 1 of *Robin* (28 March 1953). Woppit, a somewhat misshapen teddy-bear, or possibly pig, wearing a short-sleeved cardigan, felt very sad and lonely until a shaggy little donkey called Mokey came along. 'Let us be friends and have adventures together!', said Woppit, 'I always wanted a Mokey!' So off they set on their fifteen years of fun in the countryside, chumming up with Tiptop the Scarecrow, living with dear old Mrs Bumble and, by 1961, expanding to two pages drawn by Roland Davies (illustrated).

Worzel Gummidge
Barbara Euphan Todd

Look-In 1980-82 (ITV); *Worzel Gummidge* 1981-83; *Rupert* 1983 (Marvel)
Worzel Gummidge, the humanized scarecrow of Scatterbrook, first came alive to young Susan and John in Barbara Euphan Todd's book (1936). A popular radio series in *Children's Hour*, it was adapted for television by Willis Hall and turned to a series by Southern TV (1980). Worzel then came into comics in a strip drawn by Mike Noble for *Look-In, The Junior TV Times*. Soon he was promoted into his own comic monthly (October 1981), then weekly (9 March 1983), by the English end of Marvel Comics.

Wrath of the Gods
Don Lawrence
Boys World 1963-64; *Eagle* 1964 (Odhams)

'From the ancient, crumbling ruins of the once mighty Greek Empire there still lives a strange, time-worn legend. It deals with a proud mortal who dared to challenge Fate and defy the most powerful Greek God of all, Zeus. The mortal's name was Arion, and his story began 3,000 years ago.' Or on 26 January 1963 across the cinematic centre spread of *Boys World* No. 1, in blazing, hand-painted colours. Returning from the Trojan wars to Delos, Arion mistakenly slays his best friend, Patreios. Zeus promises to restore him to life if Arion recovers the stolen Bow of Delos within six months.

Wurzel Farm
Bert Hill
Sparkler 1931-32 (Provincial)

'Breezy Moments on Wurzel Farm' was the full title of this front-page series which ran from No. 1 of *Sparkler* (10 September 1931), the pink penny Provincial Comic published in Bath. 'Here's a new lot of pals for you' wrote editor Jack Long, 'Look at Jarge the farmer's boy, pursuing his ambitions with Maisie the milkmaid. But the boss, Farmer Spudato, is in the offing. Look out, Jarge!' Jarge, who called the farmer a respectable 'zur', was less respected by the farmer: 'You double-breasted consuptive earwig!' and 'You clumsy underdone turnip!' were milder samples.

Wyatt Earp
Harry Bishop
Junior Express 1955-56 (Beaverbrook); *Sun* 1956-57 (Amalgamated Press); *Swift* 1957-58 (Hulton); *T. V. Heroes* 1958-60 (Miller)

The popularity of the American television series starring Hugh O'Brian as the legendary western marshal ('Wyatt Earp, Wyatt Earp, Brave, courageous and bold . . .') prompted several comics to feature his adventures: Earp himself was, of course, well out of copyright! In *Sun* he appeared as 'Wyatt Earp, Fighting Marshal of Tombstone City', while in *Swift* he was 'Wyatt Earp, Frontier Marshal'. In *T. V. Heroes*, which was careful to disavow any direct connection with television, Wyatt was drawn by Colin Andrew and Don Lawrence.

Wulf the Briton
Ron Embleton
Express 1956-61 (Beaverbrook); *Forces in Combat* 1980 (Marvel)

'Out of the Desperate Days of Ancient Rome leaps Wulf the Briton!' Originally the hero of a full-colour serial called 'Freedom Is the Prize', Wulf the Briton's name became the title when the strip was promoted to the front page of *Express* in 1957. So popular (and so brilliantly drawn) was J. M. Butterworth's story, that it soon expanded to two pages, moving in 1959 to fill the entire centre spread. Wulf, British slave to the Roman Lucellus, had to survive seven trials to win his freedom. After adventures in Egypt, he eventually reaches home and leads the fight against Agricola's Roman armies.

Wuzzy Wiz
Bill Holroyd
Dandy 1949-55 (D. C. Thomson)

'Wuzzy Wiz – Magic Is His Biz' was the couplet that introduced this medieval magician in *Dandy* No. 369 (21 May 1949). His first trick was to satisfy the Inspector of Magic that he knew his job. Conjuring up a couple of spotted monstrosities failed to convince the uncivil servant, so Wuzzy waved his wand and away flew the inspector's report book! On 11 September 1954, Wuzzy expanded his strip from six panels to half a page, but one year later did the vanishing trick, permanently.

X-Men
Jack Kirby
Fantastic 1967-68; *Marvel Superheroes* 1975; *Spiderman* 1976; *Marvel* 1979; *X-Men Pocketbook* 1981-82; *Original X-Men* 1983; *Mighty Thor* 1983 (Marvel)
Created by writer-editor Stan Lee, X-Men first appeared in No. 1 of their own American comicbook (September 1963) and, in Britain, in No. 1 of *Fantastic* (18 February 1967). In an exclusive private school, crippled Professor Xavier summoned his superhero students: Hank McCoy (The Beast), Bobby Drake (Iceman), Slim Summers (Cyclops), and Warren Worthington the Third (Angel). Here they met the newest member of the team, Jean Grey, about to become Marvel Girl – mutants all.

Yogi Bear
William Hanna, Joseph Barbera
TV Land 1960-61; *TV Express* 1960 (TV); *Huckleberry Hound* 1961-67; *Yogi Bear's Own* 1962-64 (City); *Yogi and his Toy* 1972; *Fun Time* 1972-73 (Williams); *Top Cat* 1984 (Marvel)
'Smarter than the average bear', Yogi Bear (pun-named for the American sports star, Yogi Berra) lived in Jellystone Park with his small-sized buddy, Boo-Boo. Their insatiable appetites made life hectic for Mr Ranger and the picnickers. Yogi made his American comicbook debut in 1959, graduating from the *Huckleberry Hound* television series, and first appeared in the British *T. V. Land* in 1960, drawn by Chick Henderson. On 27 October 1962, he was able to shout, 'Ya, hey, hey! It's here at last!' from the cover of his own comic, *Yogi Bear's Own Weekly*.

X-Ray Specs
Mike Lacey
Monster Fun 1975-76; *Buster* 1976- (IPC)
'No-one pulls a fast one on Ray – he can see through anything!' Young Ray was passing by the shop of Mr I. Squint, Optician, on 14 June 1975 (in No. 1 of *Monster Fun*) when out popped the optician. 'Hey, son, try these!', he said, proffering a pair of square spectacles. Ray did, and was surprised to discover they were X-Ray Specs. 'Crikey! I can see through things! This should be fun!' And it was. He spotted his school report before Dad opened the envelope, and a bucket of whitewash perched over the classroom door. Thus, Ray avoided it; more than his teacher could! 'Gloop!'

Young Arfur
Pete Dredge
School Fun 1983-84; *Buster* 1984- (IPC)
Arthur Dally, known as Young Arfur, is the coolest cockney kid in his class. Smiling behind his sunglasses, he made his entry in No. 1 of *School Fun*, 15 October 1985. While ordinary schoolkids have to walk, bike it, or go by bus if they're lucky, not our Arfur. Spotting his schoolteacher, 'ol' skeleton', he asks him for a five-letter word meaning Government charges, then asks 'ol' skeleton' to speak up as he is a bit Mutt-and-Jeff (deaf). 'Taxes!' yells teacher, up screeches a taxi, and Arfur's getting a lift to school before 'ol' skeleton' knows what's hit him. Inspired by Arthur Daley in the Thames TV series, *Minder*.

Young Foo
Brian Platt
Cracker 1975-76 (D. C. Thomson)
'Honourable Fun with Number One Son!' was promised when Young Foo, billed as 'The Kung Fu Kid', arrived at Gorsdale School in No. 1 of *Cracker* (18 January 1975). 'Hey, look at that new boy with no hair and no shoes!, laughed Basher McConkey the school bully, with many a 'Har-har-har!' He was soon laughing on the other side of his hon. face, however, once Young Foo got busy with his fists and feet: 'Aieeee!' – 'Varoom!' – 'Woomph!' This two-page set-to wound up with a suitable joke: 'What go in bath black and come out yellow? Chinese coalman!'

Young Robin Crusoe
Jack Prout
Bimbo 1962-70 (D. C. Thomson)
Taking its inspiration from the classic story of *Robinson Crusoe* by Daniel Defoe, this modernized serial for nursery readers told the adventures that befell the Crusoe family after their yacht sank in the Indian Ocean. Young Robin and his sister Sally helped Mum and Dad Crusoe build a tree-house, and a basket-lift to lower their pet dog Kim to the ground. Soon the children had other pets, a baby elephant they named Jumbo, and a couple of naughty young chimps, one of whom was called Charlie.

Young Joey
Hugh McNeill
Sun 1949-51 (Amalgamated Press)
'Always Late for School' was the subtitle for Young Joey who first set out to be on time on the front page of *Sun* No. 54 (26 November 1949). 'Sorry I'm late, sir, but I've got an excuse!' became Joey's catchphrase as he finally arrived, after a page full of crazy adventures, in the last picture. Reworked by Hugh McNeill from his early *Knockout* strip, 'Our Ernie', Joey visited such unlikely places as Jumbletown, where babies pushed granddads in prams, and the cheese quarries on the Moon.

Young Marvelman
George Parlett
Young Marvelman 1954-63 (Miller)
'The Mightiest Boy in the Universe' took over from Captain Marvel Junior when that American reprint comicbook had to be discontinued. Thus, *Young Marvelman* No. 1 is numbered 25 (3 February 1954). The youthful superhero's origin was simply explained: 'Marvelman has given orphan Dicky Dauntless, whose hero he is, the power to assume the form of Young Marvelman, by shouting the name "Marvelman"!' Dicky, who worked for the Transatlantic Messenger Service, ran into bank robbers, shouted his keyword and, with a familiar 'Woof!' atomic strength crashed down: 'Taste some of this knuckle, pal!' 'Whop!'

Young Sid
George Martin
Beezer 1964- (D. C. Thomson)
'Young Sid – the Copper's Kid' went on patrol in No. 457 of *Beezer* (17 October 1964), one of the new characters introduced in the first sixteen-page edition. Young Sid's headline was 'Fun non-stop – with the son of a cop!', as he emulated his dad's search for a cat burglar. Causing some Grievous Bodily Harm while seeking the school milk thief, Sid found the culprit was indeed a cat burglar – the school pussy! Sid's pet pup, the lolloping Fido, wasn't much better in his role as a would-be police dog, either.

Z

Zip Nolan
Joe Colquhoun
Lion 1963-74; *Valiant* 1974-76 (IPC)
Zip Nolan of the Highway Patrol, 'handling his zooming bike with the iron-nerved skill of a stunt rider', roared into *Lion* on 19 January 1963. His first case looked like being a dead loss, as the crooks he catches appear to be innocent of a smash-and-grab raid. Captain Brinker of the Pensburgh police tells Zip it's men like him who get the cops a bad name. But Zip plays a hunch, sets a trap, and gets his men. From 1964, readers were invited to 'Spot the Clue with Zip Nolan'.

Z.9./S.A.S.
Illustrator unknown
TV Fun 1954-59 (Amalgamated Press)
'Calling Z.9.' was the title of this serial strip which started in *TV Fun* No. 38 (5 June 1955). Subtitled 'High Speed Thrills with Alan Brady, Secret Service Agent' it told how this former Army motorcycle despatch rider returned from Korea, Malaya, and the Middle East to live with his Auntie at Rose Cottage. Planning to become a speedway rider, he is summoned to Room 37, Astral House where a mysterious voice enlists him in the Secret Service, giving him the number Z.9., and a new motorbike. Driving home, the radio buzzes and Z.9. is off on his first assignment, a parachutist sighted at North Bridge Mill. From 1958, Brady transferred to the S.A.S., giving the strip a new title.

INDEX

This index is to comics and to creators
Entries in *italics* are comics or other publications

INDEX

INDEX

INDEX

INDEX